D1566124

Fighting for General Lee

*General Rufus Barringer
and the North Carolina Cavalry Brigade*

Sheridan R. Barringer

SB

Savas Beatie
California

First Edition, second printing

Library of Congress Cataloging-in-Publication Data

Barringer, Sheridan Reid, 1943- author.
Fighting for General Lee : General Rufus Barringer and the North Carolina Cavalry Brigade / Sheridan R. Barringer.—First Edition.
pages cm
Includes bibliographical references and index.
ISBN 978-1-61121-262-4 (alk. paper)—ISBN 978-1-61121-263-1 (ebk.)
1. Barringer, Rufus, 1821-1895. 2. Generals—Confederate States of America—Biography. 3. North Carolina—History—Civil War, 1861-1865—Biography. 4. United States—History—Civil War, 1861-1865—Biography. 5. United States—History—Civil War, 1861-1865—Cavalry operations. 6. United States—History—Civil War, 1861-1865— Campaigns. 7. Cabarrus County (N.C.)—Biography. 8. Charlotte (N.C.)—Biography. I. Title.
E467.1.B27B37 2015
973.7'45672092—dc23
[B]
2015029288

SB

Published by
Savas Beatie LLC
989 Governor Drive, Suite 102
El Dorado Hills, CA 95762

Phone: 916-941-6896 / (web) www.savasbeatie.com / (E-mail) sales@savasbeatie.com

Savas Beatie titles are available at special discounts for bulk purchases in the United States by corporations, institutions, and other organizations. For more details, please contact Savas Beatie, P.O. Box 4527, El Dorado Hills, CA 95762, or you may e-mail us at sales@savasbeatie.com, or visit our website at www.savasbeatie.com for additional information.

Proudly published, printed, and warehoused in the United States of America.

For Shannon and Michael

Table of Contents

Table of Contents (continued)

Preface

Almost twenty years ago, I had the good fortune to meet Gen. Rufus Barringer's grandson, Rufus Barringer (since deceased) of Rocky Mount, North Carolina. It was Rufus who helped inspire me to write this book about his grandfather. For some time I had been doing genealogical research on my ancestors. While researching the Barringer lines of North Carolina, I continued to come across all sorts of interesting information about Brig. Gen. Rufus Barringer (1821-1895). My interest increased when I discovered he was my first cousin (five times removed), and my great-grandfather was probably named after him. Grandson Rufus was interested in having someone write the story of his grandfather's life. He knew I had self-published a biography of General Barringer's grandfather, John Paul Barringer, who was also my direct ancestor. I was interested in the challenge of writing a more comprehensive book that would build upon the learning experience of the first one. Between grandson Rufus's interest and my desire to write another book, I embraced the task. Rufus was my constant advisor and friend throughout the process. After several years of researching and writing, I completed the initial manuscript. Dr. James M. Morris, a history professor (now retired) at Christopher Newport University in Newport News, Virginia, agreed to review my manuscript, and a partnership was born.

While conducting research, I learned an interesting origin for my first name, Sheridan. I am often asked where I got the name. It is "different"—rare in fact, for a first name. I was named after my father. But where did my father get his name? My parents are deceased, but my mother had always told me when

I was growing up that my father, Sheridan Kutter Barringer, was named after a Civil War general. Of course, I discovered that there was no Confederate general named Sheridan. The only general named Sheridan was the famous Union cavalry commander Philip Sheridan. How could it be that my father, being from a pro-Confederate North Carolina Barringer family, was named after a Union general?

It turns out that my great-grandfather, Rufus Osborn Barringer, was probably named after his first cousin, the Confederate Gen. Rufus Barringer, who commanded a cavalry brigade in the Army of Northern Virginia. General Barringer was a successful lawyer before the war, while my great-grandfather was a poor farmer. My grandfather, Jason Alexander Barringer, named his son (my father) Sheridan Kutter Barringer. Near the end of the war, Union Gen. Philip Sheridan defeated Rufus Barringer's cavalry brigade and captured Rufus. My grandmother's family included Unionists from Illinois, and I believe that my father's parents named their son Sheridan after the Union cavalry commander. Did my grandmother's family so despise General Barringer, or were they such Union sympathizers that they named their only child after the very Union general who captured Rufus? I have no idea, but it makes for a good story.

Sheridan R. Barringer
Newport News, Virginia

Acknowledgments

I wish to express my sincere thanks to the following individuals and institutions for their contributions to this book:

Horace Mewborn, who twice reviewed the war chapters of the manuscript. Horace's tireless efforts made the manuscript a much better product. He finally convinced me to slow down, and get back to primary sources in my research.

Dr. James M. Morris of Christopher Newport University. Jim became my partner during the early stages of this project, and made many invaluable suggestions and contributions to the quality of this book. He also taught me that history is more than just a collection of facts; it is the telling of a story around those facts. Jim has been my friend, collaborator, and mentor.

Edward G. Longacre, Staff Historian, Headquarters Air Combat Command, Langley Air Force Base in Hampton, Virginia, for his review of the entire manuscript and his most helpful comments and suggestions.

Steve Meserve (deceased) for his review, suggestions, and editorial comments.

Rufus Barringer (since deceased) of Rocky Mount, North Carolina, grandson of General Barringer. Rufus was my cousin, friend, and a motivating force behind the creation of this book.   Thanks to Rufus's lovely wife, Nanette, for her hospitality and friendship over these past years.

My wife Pam, and to my children, Shannon and Michael, for their encouragement and for putting up with all the time I was away from them, while doing research or at the computer updating the manuscript.

C. Minor Barringer (deceased) of Chadds Ford, Pennslvania, and to Rufus Barringer (now deceased) of Lyme, Connecticut, brothers and grandsons of General Barringer, who offered much valuable information and encouragement.

Thanks to my friend, Nancy Shields of Poquoson, Virginia, for her editing help, ideas, and encouragement. Thanks to my cousin, Larry Welch, for his interest, research, and support.

Thanks to Civil War historians and authors Bob Krick, retired Chief Historian at the Fredericksburg and Spotsylvania National Battlefield; Chris Calkins, Manager of Sailor's Creek Battlefield State Park, Dr. Louis H. Manarin of the Virginia State Archives; William C. Davis, noted historian and author; Clark B. Hall, expert on the Battle of Brandy Station; and James I. Robertson, of Virginia Tech.

Thanks to Chris Hartley for his wise counsel and encouragement. Chris reviewed the entire text and some of the war chapters twice. His suggestions considerably improved the manuscript. Thanks to my friend, Tonia J. Smith, of Pinehurst for her interest, review, research, help, and support in rewriting parts of some of the war chapters. Thanks to Bryce Suderow and Robert Trout for their review and comments. Thanks to historian and author Thomas D. Perry for writing the Foreword to this book.

Thanks to my publisher Savas Beatie and its director, Theodore P. Savas, for his belief in the project and for mentoring me in achieving my goal of producing a quality book. Thanks also to editor, Mark A. Moore for all his guidance and observations, and to production manager Lee Merideth for including me in the entire process.

Thanks also are due to the staffs at Grissom Public Library and Christopher Newport University in Newport News, Virginia, who helped me with untold numbers of inter-library loan requests. Thanks to cousins Syd Barringer, Larry Welch, and to many who must remain unnamed due to the fact that I must stop listing names at some point.

Thanks to the staffs at the following institutions: State Archives of North Carolina; State Library of North Carolina; Virginia State Library; Perkins Library at Duke University; the Southern Historical Collection at the University of North Carolina; the Reynolds Library at Wake Forest University; the Alderman and Small Libraries at the University of Virginia; George Grugg, Curator of the University Libraries Department of Special Collections at the University of Notre Dame; the National Archives; the Sargeant Room at Kirn Library in Norfolk, Virginia; the Carolina Room at the Charlotte Public Library; the Local History Room at the Cannon Memorial Library in Concord, North Carolina; the Virginiana Room at Charles Taylor Library in Hampton, Virginia; and the Genealogy Room at the Salisbury Public Library in Salisbury, North Carolina.

Foreword

Thomas D. Perry, author and historian

"**I**f anyone speaks to you of subjugation, tell them it shows a total ignorance of what constitutes *our armies*. Long after the inhabitants crouch to the conqueror our armies will tread with the triumph of victorious freemen over the dead bodies of the vainglorious foes. North Carolina has done *nobly in this army*. Never allow her troops to be abused in your presence."[1]

General J. E. B. Stuart wrote these words to his wife Flora Cooke Stuart on February 8, 1864, two days after his 31st (and final) birthday. By this time, the famous Confederate cavalry commander knew the value of his North Carolina troopers, and used them as "shock troops" on many occasions before his death on May 12, 1864.

Stuart knew much about the Old North State, having been born and raised in Patrick County, Virginia, just over the state line from Mount Airy, North Carolina. His family traveled across the border to attend church, shop, and pick up their mail. The Stuarts lived in the area at the same time the famous Siamese Twins, Eng and Chang Bunker, lived in the town that later became synonymous with Mayberry on *The Andy Griffith Show*.

With the deaths of Stuart and Gen. James B. Gordon in May 1864, Gen. Rufus Barringer assumed command of the North Carolina Cavalry Brigade in the Army of Northern Virginia. Rufus was promoted to brigadier over several senior colonels who outranked him. General Wade Hampton replaced Stuart and took command of the cavalry corps in August 1864.

---

1   J. E. B. Stuart to Flora Cooke Stuart, February 8, 1864. J. E. B. Stuart Papers, Virginia Historical Society.

Barringer's war ended on April 3, 1865, at Namozine Church in Amelia County, Virginia, when he was captured by Philip Sheridan's cavalry. Barringer was escorted to City Point, Virginia, and then sent to the prison camp at Fort Delaware near Philadelphia, Pennsylvania.

When Barringer's brother Moreau served in the U. S. House of Representatives, he had shared a desk with an Illinois congressman named Abraham Lincoln. Showing the magnanimous spirit for which he was known, President Lincoln gave prisoner Rufus Barringer a letter of introduction to Secretary of War Edwin M. Stanton. After meeting with the cabinet official, Barringer was given his choice of prisons, which led him to Fort Delaware.

It is easy to view historical figures through a modern lens. Presentism is not something I agree with as a rule, but in the case of Rufus Barringer, I see a man with vision. If more of his contemporaries had agreed with him, the United States of America would surely have made faster progress on the racial front—and with less conflict and loss of lives over the next century.

In a time when many Southerners wanted to keep the newly freed African Americans from having the rights granted by the 13th, 14th, and 15th Amendments to the United States Constitution, Barringer saw it differently. Before and after the war, he supported public works such as railroads, voting rights, and dabbled with reforming the judiciary. He showed a pattern for not running with the popular crowd, and opposed secession as war loomed.

Ulysses S. Grant wrote that the Southern cause "was, I believe, one of the worst for which a people ever fought, and one for which there was the least excuse. I do not question, however, the sincerity of the great mass of those who were opposed to us."[2]

Barringer, unlike many of his fellow Southerners, changed his views on African Americans after the Civil War. With slavery eradicated, he believed that accepting former slaves and free blacks as citizens was the best approach for restoring the Union and moving the country forward.

Barringer switched political parties multiple times in his life and became a Republican—a rare act of courage in the postwar South. Clinging to "Lost Cause" ideology, former Confederate Gen. D. H. Hill (Barringer's former brother-in-law) was outraged. Hill called Rufus and James Longstreet "lepers in

---

2 Ulysses S. Grant, *Personal Memoirs of U. S. Grant*, 2 vols. (New York, NY, 1885), vol. 2, 489-490.

their own community." Like Barringer, Longstreet (a former Confederate general) had also switched to the Republican Party after the war.

Politics, then and now, makes strange bedfellows. Hill, a Presbyterian church elder, refused to serve Barringer communion, saying, "Republicans were not fit to sit at the Lord's Table." Today, some might say the same of the opposing party. History can repeat itself in the strangest of ways.

The fact that Rufus had illegitimate children with a former mulatto slave may have influenced Barringer's political views, as his children would suffer under the oppression of restored Southern hierarchy after Reconstruction. His personal interests led him to support voting rights for African Americans, and a failed run for lieutenant governor in 1880 was his ultimate attempt to shape the future of his beloved North Carolina. However, he did not support social equality for blacks. Barringer left politics and lived another 15 years—long enough to see the political forces he opposed enact Jim Crow laws to suppress African American rights. It was the same mindset that had led the South to secede from the Union and fight a war to preserve slavery.

Having previously supported Grant's presidency, Barringer became disillusioned with the national Republican Party. He supported Democrat Grover Cleveland for president in 1888. Barringer's subsequent switch to the Democratic Party restored his standing somewhat in the eyes of his former compatriots.

Nevertheless, Rufus Barringer left a legacy far different from most Confederate generals. His biracial sons left an indelible mark on the Tar Heel State. One of them, Warren Clay Coleman, became one of the richest African Americans in North Carolina, owning and operating a textile mill in Concord.

Another interesting legacy of Rufus Barringer is his son Paul Brandon Barringer, who became the sixth president of my and the author's alma mater—The Virginia Agricultural and Mechanical College (now Virginia Tech). Paul Barringer, whose uncles included D. H. Hill and Thomas J. "Stonewall" Jackson, served in Blacksburg from September 1, 1907, until 1913. J. E. B. Stuart's brother, William Alexander Stuart, had served on the Board of Visitors at VMAC in the 1870s. Indeed, a number of Stuart's former subordinates attended or worked at the university.

What lessons can we learn from the life of Gen. Rufus Barringer? Today, it is easy is to dismiss a man who fought in a war on the side whose cause was the preservation of slavery—but that misses the point. Barringer was not a stereotypical Southerner for his era. He was progressive, a man with vision who changed his thinking and fought for positive change in North Carolina. If more

Southerners had followed his lead, the racial strife of the twentieth century might have been less severe.

That this book illuminates one of the lesser known brigadier generals in the Army of Northern Virginia would no doubt please J. E. B. Stuart. Like many from the Tar Heel State, Rufus Barringer fought nobly for Stuart.

*   *   *

Author's note: Thomas Perry started the J. E. B. Stuart Birthplace Preservation Trust, Inc. in 1990. The non-profit organization has preserved 75 acres of the Stuart property, including the site of the house where Stuart was born on February 6, 1833.

Introduction

Rufus Barringer was a North Carolina lawyer, legislator, and war hero who took up the cause of Reconstruction after the war. He was a Republican in a state dominated by Democrats. He was one of a handful of former Confederate commanders, including James Longstreet, Williams C. Wickham, and John S. Mosby who became progressive Republicans.

Barringer was descended from two generations of Southern aristocracy, and continued in the family's tradition of public service to his state. A lawyer by profession, he became interested in politics at an early age. He was scholarly, disciplined, and thorough in preparation, whether for the law or other areas in life. He was a cultured man, fond of literature, history, and political science. He served in the North Carolina legislature prior to the war, and was instrumental in the development of the North Carolina railroad system. He supported other progressive endeavors in education, agriculture, and civil rights.

Rufus married three times: first to Eugenia Morrison in 1853, second to Rosalie Chunn in 1861, and third to Margaret Long in 1870. Through his first marriage, Rufus acquired two future Confederate generals as brothers-in-law: Thomas J. "Stonewall" Jackson and Daniel Harvey Hill. Barringer had a close relationship with Jackson, and got along well with Hill during the war. However, after the war Hill and Barringer became estranged over Reconstruction politics.

Barringer opposed secession until March 1861, just before the Civil War broke out. When armed conflict became inevitable, he volunteered for service, raised a company of cavalry, and was elected its captain. He had no formal military training, but served with distinction in more than 76 engagements. He rose to the rank of brigadier general in command of the North Carolina Cavalry Brigade in the Army of Northern Virginia. He was aggressive and dependable in combat, and distinguished himself for bravery in many battles, including Brandy Station, where he was seriously wounded. He convalesced for five months before returning to action during the Bristoe campaign. He was captured by Maj. Gen. Philip Sheridan's Union cavalry at Namozine Church in Amelia County, Virginia, on April 3, 1865. A prisoner of war, Rufus was sent to City Point, Virginia, where he met with President Abraham Lincoln. He was sent to the old Capitol Prison in Washington, and then to the dreaded Fort Delaware prison camp, where he remained until July 1865. While in prison, Rufus got to know and appreciate the attitudes of the people and leaders in the North.

After his release from prison, Barringer returned home a war hero, convinced that the societal wounds of war should be quickly healed. He called on North Carolinians to accept Reconstruction. As a "Radical" Republican, he continued to support liberal causes, including black suffrage, education, and participation of blacks in governing. His bold letters to the public in1867 and 1868 stamped him as a man of great political sagacity, vision, and foresight—a true statesman. In 1875, he was elected to the State Constitutional Convention from his strongly Democratic district. As a Republican, he attracted Civil War veterans, blacks, and progressives as voters.

Throughout his life, Rufus Barringer was generous to those less fortunate than himself. He was a devout Christian, and was active in the Presbyterian Church. He labored hard for many reforms, especially judicial, educational, and agricultural improvements. He ran unsuccessfully for lieutenant governor in 1880. His political beliefs made him a traitor to the South in the eyes of many, especially the Democratic press. However, he remained true to his principles and to the common people throughout his life.

The initial impression of anyone meeting Rufus Barringer was that he was scholarly, amiable, and a refined gentleman. He was normally congenial in his dealings with others. Just below the surface, however, was a temper that flared when others attacked his "code of honor," which included his military service, political values, and the honor of North Carolina soldiers. His pugnacious nature manifested in stinging, well-crafted written or verbal attacks on political opponents who dared question his military service, or his progressive stand on the issues of the day. His combativeness was effective because he was logical, scholarly, and masterful in the use of language. His confrontational persona nearly landed him in duel with a political foe. Through the press, he engaged in numerous back-and-forth caustic arguments with opponents, including Jubal Early, newspaper editors, "un-Reconstructed" politicians, and his brother-in-law D. H. Hill.

Aside from arguing with political foes, Barringer listened to the opinions and views of others, especially those of the people he met while in the North. He took action and promoted values that he believed would make Reconstruction easier on the people of the South. However, "un-Reconstructed" politicians and most white Southerners rejected his advice, which frustrated him and brought out his combativeness.

Rufus Barringer switched to the Democratic Party in 1888, supporting Grover Cleveland for president. The dominant Democratic press, which had hounded him since the days of Reconstruction, all of a sudden recognized him as a true hero and admired of him for the rest of his life. He remained active in civic affairs as long as his health permitted. In 1894, he became seriously ill and died of stomach cancer in February 1895.

Though a Southern aristocrat with wealth and power, Barringer boldly championed the poor, political rights for blacks, and the masses—a truly progressive Southern gentleman. He was clearly ahead of his time and made a difference in the lives of North Carolina's citizens.

Chapter 1

"An important period is drawn to a close! This day brings an end to my boyhood. . . .
But farewell—forever—farewell to childhood dreams. Alas! I'm now a man."
— *Rufus Barringer's Journal, December 1, 1842.*

The Young
North Carolina Lawyer

Rufus Barringer descended from two generations of Southern aristocracy. His grandfather, Johann Paulus Beringer, was one of the early German Lutheran settlers to migrate to western North Carolina, where he became a leading civilian in the area. His father, Paul Barringer, was a wealthy farmer, civic leader, business man, and politician of Cabarrus County.

These men had an enormous influence on the young man who would mature into a lawyer, a Confederate general and war hero, and Tar Heel politician of influence.

Johann Paulus Barringer (1721-1807)

Johann Paulus Beringer (anglicized to John Paul Barringer) was one of the early pioneers who settled near Mount Pleasant, North Carolina, 28 miles northeast of Charlotte. Johann was born in June 1721 and baptized a few months later on September 25 in Schwaigern in the southern German Duchy of Wurttemberg (near the present town of Heilbronn). Johann grew into a strapping young man and left home at the age of 22, like so many young men do, in search of adventure and the desire to own his own land. He sailed from

Rotterdam for America aboard the American ship *Phoenix* and landed at Philadelphia on September 30, 1743.[1]

Unlike many emigrants from Germany who were able to pay for their trip to America, John Paul paid for his passage by becoming an indentured servant to his future father-in-law. He completed his service in one year and in 1744 married Ann Eliza Eisman, a young woman who had come to America at the age of nine. The couple settled near the present town of North Bethel in Bucks County, Pennsylvania.[2]

About 1750, the tide of German Lutheran emigration turned from previous movement to the western counties of Pennsylvania southward toward western North Carolina. German Lutherans by the hundreds departed their Pennsylvania homes and moved southward to the Piedmont region for a variety of reasons. Some sought more abundant hunting grounds as skin and fur trading remained profitable. Others desired good, fertile, and inexpensive farmland. Others felt the call to greater religious freedom and a chance for expanded missionary activity. The Carolinas afforded all of these opportunities and more.

John Paul, Ann Eliza and their daughter Catherine, born November 24, 1750, left for North Carolina about 1751. The couple's son John was born on November 26, 1752, after the Barringers reached their new home at Dutch Buffalo Creek, two and one-half miles northeast of Mount Pleasant in Anson County (now Cabarrus County).[3]

Barringer, as one of the early settlers in the fertile lands of the piedmont section of North Carolina, became a successful farmer. He also prospered through commerce by sending corn, wheat, barley, rye, and indigo to Charleston, South Carolina, via the well-traveled wagon road from Salisbury, North Carolina. In addition to farming, he operated a saw mill and also accumulated considerable property. What began with his original homestead of 300 acres would grow to more than 2,500 acres of prime farmland. Perhaps because of his success, he made it a point to help others arriving from

---

1   Church Records, Evangelical Lutheran City Church, Schwaigern, Germany; I. Daniel Rupp, *Thirty Thousand Names of German, Swiss and Dutch Immigrants in Pennsylvania from 1727to 1776* (Baltimore, MD, 1965), 163-164.

2   Samuel A. Ashe, *Biographical History of North Carolina From Colonial Times To Present*, 8 vols. (Greensboro, NC, 1905), vol. 1, 89; Deed record, Land Office of the Historical and Museum Commission, Harrisburg, PA, Book A, vol. 62, 166.

3   Ibid.

Pennsylvania to settle in their new homes, and became increasingly influential among the German settlers.[4]

In 1768, Royal Governor William Tryon, in an effort to conciliate the people of restive western North Carolina, made a visit to Mecklenburg County. Governor Tryon wanted to assure the people that measures were being taken to curb recent abuses of power by county officials. In this way, he hoped to diffuse the "Regulators," a group of citizens who were taking steps to oppose increased taxation and other moves by the Crown. Among others, Tryon visited John Paul, who by this time was a militia captain. In the governor's journal is recorded the following: "Wednesday, August 31, 1768. The Governor waited on Captain Barringer; a beautiful plantation and skillfully managed, particularly the meadow land, which produced excellent hay." Governor Tryon left believing he had no "stauncher friend for the Crown than the 'Gallant Dutchman' [Barringer] in all the county." In this, however, Tryon would be disappointed. Seven short years later, Barringer's loyalties rested with the colonists during the American Revolution.[5]

John Paul was a man of deep religious convictions and was generous to his church. At his suggestion circa 1771, members of the Lutheran Church separated themselves from their German Reformed brethren and built their own church on the site of the upper portion of the old graveyard. St. John's Lutheran Church was built chiefly at Barringer's expense, and out of gratitude the congregation erected a raised and enclosed pew for the special use of his family.[6]

John Paul and Ann Eliza Barringer spent 25 laborious, productive, and happy years together, although they had no children other than Catherine and John. Sadly, Ann died just before the Revolutionary War broke out in 1775.[7]

John Paul had been appointed a magistrate for the Crown on December 31, 1762, and served in that capacity until the Revolution. One month after the

---

4 Sheridan R. Barringer, *John Paul Barringer of Mecklenburg and Cabarrus Counties,* North Carolina (Newport News, VA, 1990), H-19.

5 William L. Saunders, ed., *North Carolina Colonial Records,* 10 vols. (Raleigh, NC, 1890), vol. 7, 825; Ashe, *Biographical History of North Carolina,* vol. 1, 92-93; Gotthardt Dellmann Berheim, *History of the German Settlement and the Lutheran Church in the Carolinas* (Bowie, MD, 1990), 761.

6 Ibid., 249; Saunders, *North Carolina Colonial Records,* vol. 8, 761; Ashe, *Biographical History of North Carolina,* vol.1, 93.

7 Ibid., 91.

historic passage of the Declaration of Independence at Philadelphia, the Hillsboro Provisional Congress of August 1776 set up a provisional North Carolina government and began preparations for war. On November 12, a constitutional convention at Halifax established a state constitution and bill of rights. Under the provisions of the new constitution, on December 23, 1776, John Paul was appointed a justice of the peace. Thereafter, advocates for breaking all political ties with the mother country used his home as a rallying place.[8]

When armed conflict between Great Britain and her colonies broke out, Royal Governor Josiah Martin offered John Paul a military command in an effort to secure his allegiance to the Crown. The Dutch plantation owner, however, refused. He was already a member of the Mecklenburg County "Committee of Safety," a group of "selectmen" formed to organize, drill and equip troops. They also managed the county government, which included the collection of taxes and expenditure of funds, in support of the rebellion. In 1778, the Committee of Safety appointed John Paul as road overseer, and in 1779 as overseer of the poor and tax assessor. Recent research indicates that though he was 55 years old in 1776, he and his eldest son (John Barringer Sr.) both served as captains in the Mecklenburg Militia. John Paul's younger brother Mathias, also a captain, was killed with five others in a Cherokee Indian ambush near present-day Newton, North Carolina. (A monument erected in their memory at the courthouse square still stands today.) In mid-1779, while still a member of the Committee of Safety, John Paul was captured by Tories. Along with other prominent citizens, he was taken to Camden, South Carolina, and not released until after the battle of Camden on August 16, 1780. His war service, however, was over.[9]

There was more on John Paul's mind during this period than defeating the Crown. In 1777, two years before his capture, the 56-year-old Barringer married 22-year-old Catherine Blackwelder. Catherine hailed from a prominent Mecklenburg County family. She was younger than John Paul's grown children and shared a name with his own daughter. The couple moved to the opposite

---

8   Saunders, *North Carolina Colonial Records*, vol. 6, 799.

9   John E. Misenheimer Jr., "Captain John Paul Barringer: A Commander of German Patriot Militia From Mecklenburg, North Carolina, During the American Revolution," in *The Cabarrus Golden Nugget* (Winter 2007), vol. 15, No. 4, 108-122; Saunders, *North Carolina Colonial Records*, vol. 10, 441-442; Ashe, *Biographical History of North Carolina*, vol. 1, 93; Smith Barrier, "Deutschland in Piedmont North Carolina," in *Uplift*, Part 3, January 23, 1937, 17.

side of Dutch Buffalo Creek and built "Poplar Grove," a home described as "half residence, half castle." The marriage proved fruitful and 10 children were born to the couple. One was a son named Paul, who would become a general in the War of 1812 and Rufus Barringer's father.[10]

John Paul continued to be a prominent and influential figure in western Carolina after the Revolutionary War. He was appointed a member of the legislature in 1793 to represent the newly formed Cabarrus County, perhaps because the previous year he had been a driving force in bringing about the separation of that land from Mecklenburg County. Tradition has it that this division was driven by John Paul's frustration and even anger at the people of Charlotte for making fun of the fact that he gave his militia commands in German.[11]

John Paul Barringer died at age 86 on January 1, 1807, and was buried in St. John's Lutheran churchyard in Concord. At one time, John Paul had owned 13 slaves. He willed one to his son, Paul, leaving the others to work the plantation where his wife, Catherine, would continue to reside. Catherine lived until the age of 94 and died in 1848, having had the privilege of seeing both a son (Daniel Laurens Barringer) and a grandson (Daniel Moreau Barringer) elected to the United States Congress. She was buried alongside her son, General Paul Barringer.[12]

Paul Barringer (1778-1844)

Rufus's father Paul was born on September 26, 1778, at Poplar Grove. Paul was the first child born to John Paul and his second wife Catherine. Paul's early education was chiefly in the German language, but at the age of 18 he was sent off to an English-language classical school. He remained there for three years and learned to speak and write both German and English fluently. This bilingual education would prove useful when he later became involved in various mercantile enterprises. In 1799, Paul settled in Concord, North

---

10 Anna Barringer, *The Natural Bent: Memoirs of Dr. Paul Brandon Barringer* (Chapel Hill, NC, 1949), 146; Ashe, *Biographical History of North Carolina*, vol. 1, 91-92.

11 Ibid., 92.

12 Barrier, "Deutschland in Piedmont North Carolina," Part 2, January 16, 1937, 20. Revolutionary War Pension files, File #R564, Microfilm No. M-804, Roll 158, 0804-0810, National Archives. Document transcribed by Sheridan R. Barringer.

Carolina, and with the aid of his father, began his career as a planter and merchant.[13]

On February 21, 1805, the 27-year-old Paul married Elizabeth Brandon, the 22-year-old daughter of Matthew Brandon of nearby Rowan County. The young couple settled in Concord, where they remained until 1811, when they moved to Poplar Grove (where Paul's mother still lived). They raised 11 children, including Daniel Moreau, Margaret, William, Rufus, and Victor.[14]

Like many other Southerners, Paul viewed the War of 1812 as a Northern war disadvantageous to the South. When North Carolina Governor William Hawkins made a hurried call for volunteers, however, Paul responded. Because of his considerable influence throughout western North Carolina, he was commissioned a brigadier general of the Eleventh Brigade of North Carolina Militia Troops on December 23, 1812.[15]

Paul Barringer was "in stature near six feet tall, a little stooped, bald head, dark curly hair, blue eyes, fair complexion, high forehead and small hands and feet." He was a "fine looking man, of large sturdy frame, intelligent, quick in thought and speech, and independent in action." These qualities were evident in his growing economic success and the high esteem in which others held him. Paul served as a representative from Cabarrus County in the North Carolina House of Commons (1806-1815), and in the state Senate in 1822. In 1823, he refused to seek re-election because his business interests demanded more of his time.[16]

In 1838, Paul's multiple interests—three plantations, two stores, a tannery, and a cotton mill—forced him to leave Poplar Grove and move closer to the center of his activities. He built a new home, "Bellevue," two and one-half miles west of Concord.[17]

Paul was not only economically successful, but a man of generosity and progressive public spirit. In 1838, for example, he subscribed $2,000 for the construction of the Raleigh & Gaston Railroad, and the following year invested

13 Ashe, *Biographical History of North Carolina*, vol. 1, 95.

14 Ibid., 95-96.

15 Ibid., 98; *Raleigh Star*, December 25, 1812. Though Paul was militia officer, he was 55 years old and probably never saw combat. His duties may have been limited to the Committee of Safety.

16 Ashe, *Biographical History of North Carolina*, vol. 1, 97.

17 Ibid., 97-98.

General Paul Barringer (1778-1844), Rufus Barringer's father. *North Carolina Division of Archives and History.*

$5,000 in stock in the Concord Cotton Mill, one of the pioneer mills in that part of the country.[18]

Paul owned as many as 15 slaves, but eventually reached the point where he was no longer in favor of the institution of slavery. He eventually gave his slaves to his son Paul Brandon to take to Mississippi, stating he did not believe the practice was morally or economically sound and that he no longer wished to own them.[19]

Like his father, Paul was raised Lutheran and remained active in the church throughout his life. These qualities would be reflected in the principled life of Rufus.

Rufus, Moreau, and Victor Barringer

Rufus Barringer was born December 2, 1821, at Poplar Grove. Rufus's oldest brother Daniel Moreau (who was known simply as "Moreau"), his younger brother Victor, and his sister Margaret were his favorite siblings. Moreau, Rufus, and Victor became lawyers and served their state as elected politicians.

Moreau won election to the House of Commons in 1829 and was reelected for six successive sessions. He served as chairman of the Committee on the Judiciary and on other important committees. When he fell ill in 1835, he

18 R. D. W. Conner, *History of North Carolina* (London, 2013), 74; "First Cotton Mill," in Dr. James Edward Smoot Papers, North Carolina Division of Archives and History; Ashe, *Biographical History of North Carolina*, vol. 1, 98.

19 William S. Powell, ed., *Dictionary of North Carolina Biography*, 6 vols. (Chapel Hill, NC, 1979), vol. 1, 98.

traveled to Philadelphia for medical treatment but his slow recovery forced him to refrain from public activity for several years.[20]

Victor Barringer, Rufus's younger brother, was born on March 29, 1827. The teenager was enamored with Kentuckian Henry Clay, a powerful orator and leader of the Whig Party. Clay had also been one of the "War Hawks," a strong supporter of the War of 1812. Impressed by the older man's eloquence and public spirit, qualities greatly admired in democratic, western frontier America, Victor adopted the politician's last name as his middle name, and used it for the rest of his life.[21]

Victor entered the University of North Carolina at the age of 15, where during his sophomore year an altercation with a French professor resulted in a year-long suspension. Unwilling to miss so much school, he finished his sophomore year at Gettysburg College in Pennsylvania and returned to UNC in 1845, where he graduated in 1848.[22]

Rufus entered UNC in 1838 at 16, after attending preparatory school at Sugar Creek Academy in Concord. His college class consisted of 34 students, and he was the only one from Cabarrus County. His friends nicknamed him "Motz" in his freshman days at Chapel Hill after old John Motz of Lincolnton, a well-known part-owner of High Shoals Iron Works. A friend claimed that Rufus walked like one of his legs was shorter than the other. One student remembered that he "walked like old 'Motz'. . . lame in one of his short legs."[23]

College students in those days were not unlike students of other times. Many drank too much, and more than a few visited prostitutes or lower class

---

20 Ibid., vol. 1, 99; Ashe, *Biographical History of North Carolina*, vol. 1, 102.

21 Victor Barringer to Rufus Barringer, October 30, 1841, in Rufus Barringer Papers, University of Virginia.

22 Ashe, *Biographical History of North Carolina*, vol. 1, 125.

23 University of North Carolina Alumni Association, *A Record of the Proceedings of the Alumni Association of the University of North Carolina at the Centennial Celebration of the Act of Incorporation, Being an Account of the Alumni Banquet and Alumni Class Reunions, June 5, 1889* (Raleigh, NC, 1889), 173-174; Kemp P. Battle, *History of the University of North Carolina*, 2 vols. (Raleigh, NC, 1912), vol. 1, 408-409. In a letter from Barringer at Fort Delaware prison to Maj. Gen. Francis P. Blair in Washington, dated June 3, 1865, Rufus recalled that as a young man he was "universally known as 'Motz.'" Rufus Barringer's account books for Sugar Creek Academy and the University of North Carolina indicate that, as early as 1837, he used the middle initial "M." He signed his personal journal "R. M. Barringer" on August 17, August 28, October 22, November 15, and November 30, 1842. He signed his name "R. Motz Barringer" on November 3, 1842. Rufus's middle name has been erroneously reported by some as "Clay." He was short in stature at five feet, six inches tall.

women to whom etiquette meant little. Three of the places for illicit sex visited by UNC students included "the Depot," "the Fishery," and "the Kingdom." The young men practiced a kind of "apprentice courtship," in preparation for more serious lasting relationships later in life. It was not merely sex with random nameless women. Rather, they cultivated relationships that provided the young men with practice in sexual intimacy before marriage without violating, at least in their minds, more elite and gentlemanly sexual mores.[24]

James Lawrence Dusenbery was one of Rufus's friends in the UNC class of 1842. Both were members of the Dialectic Society, and both would serve in the Civil War—Dusenbery as a surgeon. According to Dusenbery, he, Rufus (whom he dubbed "the mighty songster"), and someone identified as only "Gabriel" visited the nearby house of a man named Edward to meet three girls. One, Edward's daughter, was supposedly "in love" with Dusenbery, who stayed with her all night. Rufus attempted to take up with another girl in the same house, but when she proved sick he ended up spending the night with another woman. He "prevailed with her & solaced himself in her arms all night long. She was into him as the loving hind & the pleasing roe; her breasts did satisfy him at all times, and he was ravished always with her love."[25]

Dusenbery, ever the gossipy scribe, recounted in his diary another event involving himself and Rufus. The pair sneaked off campus at nightfall to visit a place called "Ned's" to meet some girls. To do so, they "borrowed" a horse from William K. Woods, a nearby resident who boarded about 25 college students. Together, Dusenbery and Rufus rode the horse slowly along paths through the woods until they reached the open road leading to Ned's, at which point they galloped at "headlong speed" to their destination. "While there we met with all the success we could have anticipated & about midnight we roused our steed most unceremoniously from his slumbers and returned," Dusenbery recorded. "My companion [Rufus] expressed himself as 'having been in clover,' while I was perfectly disgusted, & fully resolved in my own mind, never to repeat the visit."[26]

Rufus frequented Ned's on several occasions, as well as a place called "old Bartimeus's," where he stored an old black trunk. Dusenbery bragged in the

---

24 Roger L. Geiger, ed., *Curriculum, Accreditation, and Coming of Age in Higher Education: Perspectives on the History of Higher Education* (Brunswick, NJ, 2009), vol. 27, 16.

25 James Lawrence Dusenbery, journal, September 12, 1841, Southern Historical Collection.

26 Ibid., September 36, 1841.

third person about Rufus, a student from Burke County, and himself when he wrote, "these three men and the acts they did & how they sung, behold are they not written in the Chronicles of the mighty men of the West [West Building, where they lived on campus]." Evidently, Rufus and Dusenbery had a falling out and by graduation were no longer on speaking terms. Dusenbery specifically mentioned in his diary that he did not ask Rufus to sign his Dialectic Society Diploma—an honored custom that Society classmates had long performed.[27]

At UNC, Rufus was deeply interested in the Dialectic Society—what would later be called a debating club. The rival Dialectic and Philanthropic Societies, both founded soon after the university opened in 1795, dominated student life outside the classroom. Each society maintained lavish quarters filled with fine furniture, portraits of distinguished alumni, and extensive collections of newspapers, journals, and books addressing the leading issues of the day. These societies operated as self-governing bodies, granting their own diplomas and enforcing rigorous codes of conduct through secret trials. "Fear of incurring their censure," one alumnus recalled, "was far greater than that of offending the Faculty"[28]

Rufus was a primary leader of the opposition to "secret fraternities," a new movement at UNC during his college days. The push for secret fraternities was hard-fought, and Rufus and others opposing such organizations succeeded in having them prohibited. In future years, however, such fraternities were established as class sizes increased and outlets other than the Dialectic and Philanthropic Societies were needed by students. Rufus's primary objection was the secretive nature and cruel hazing that accompanied these organizations. "I can now look back on the warm and generous rivalries of those days as a source of real benefit to me all through a long, active and varied life," he explained many years later. "There is nothing like self-reliance, honest conviction, and the early struggle of mind with mind," he continued. "Without this, we never know ourselves. I soon came to know, too, that there was far less harm than I supposed in the fraternities. To my relief and surprise, I found them in several

---

27 Ibid., September 5, 1841, and April 30, 1842. Dusenbery often concealed the identities of his companions by referring to them by the counties from which these North Carolina students came. Thus, Rufus was sometimes identified as "Cabarrus" and at other times by his nickname, "Motz." Occasionally, he was acknowledged by his real name. The author has been unable to determine whether Rufus and Dusenberry ever reconciled.

28 Battle, *History of the University of North Carolina*, vol. 1, 72-85, 565-569.

of my warmest friends. But the struggle fixed the faith and practice of my life: ever open to the new, but clinging unswervingly to the old—the church, the State, and the home—as the only divine institutions for reforming and saving the world."[29]

The Young Law Student

Rufus was not one of the top students in his class, but he was respected and in demand as an orator, mostly on topics dealing with history. He graduated from the University of North Carolina on June 2, 1842, and spoke at Commencement on "Principles of the Old Federal Party." The class of 1842 was the first where each graduate was presented with a Bible. Once he had his degree in hand, Rufus began reading law with his brother Moreau (a law partner of Richmond M. Pearson, who would become North Carolina's Supreme Court Chief Justice in 1858). Rufus was appointed deputy clerk of the County Court for the July term. In this position, he prepared the courtroom for the day, observed the proceedings, and counted the cash receipts before retiring to his living quarters—a room in the southwest corner of the Concord courthouse.[30]

Concord in the early 1840s was a small town of about 700 people, 20 miles northeast from Charlotte. Its leading citizens were a hearty stock and included Rufus's father Paul and his oldest brother, Moreau. Concord's economic prosperity was hampered by the limited number of railroads (and accompanying industrial and agricultural growth) in the South. The nearest railroad was at Danville, Virginia, 110 miles distant.

Lacking railroads, trade in Concord in the early 1840s was conducted almost entirely by wagon. Goods were usually brought in from Charleston or Georgetown, South Carolina, or from Petersburg, Virginia. The town's lawyers, doctors, and preachers quietly controlled most public affairs. Despite their economic importance, the farmers' influence over public authority concerning trade had diminished during the late 1830s and did not return until years later.

On February 16, 1839, an organizational meeting was held by subscribers to the first cotton mill to be built in Concord. Paul Barringer was elected president. The directors also welcomed investments in the name of Victor C.

29 Ibid.

30 Rufus Barringer, journal, July 21, 1842, Southern Historical Collection.

Barringer and Rufus Barringer. The meeting helped raise $24,000 to build the Concord Manufacturing Company. By 1842, the mill was in full operation. Rufus's involvement in the cotton mill enterprise, which was likely more difficult than he ever imagined, taught him valuable lessons he carried forward into his career as a lawyer.[31]

Meanwhile, Rufus continued reading law with Moreau. While he studied hard to master the legal profession, he also took time to socialize. Shortly after the close of the July 1842 court term, the busy young law student spent five days of what he described as "frolic." He attended the graduation examination at William J. Bingham girls' school in Charlotte, where the schoolmaster questioned students in a public ceremony. On another evening, he enjoyed the "Great Fair" in the same city. There, he met two young ladies and ended up spending the considerable sum of $6.00 in one evening. The next day, Rufus traveled with his nieces Susan Boyd and Mary Grier to visit Davidson College, 20 miles north of Charlotte, to attend its graduation exercises. He had a "bustling time" going from a cousin's house (where they stayed) to and from the college at night. After the graduation ceremonies, a grand party was held at the neighboring home of Maj. Rufus Reich. "[We] never had a more pleasant time," professed the young law student, who danced until the early morning hours.[32]

During the years of Rufus's legal apprenticeship, fevers in general, and typhoid in particular, swept the region. When disease took the life of a close friend, he wrote in his journal, "I must confess, to see and hear of so much sickness in the country fills me (and particularly at this time of continued preaching) with glorious thoughts of the future of man. Oh! How glorious is the thought of a conscious immortality beyond this "veil of tears' and yet horrid the thought of tasting, of losing that immortality! But I am not a religious man and cannot profess Religion."[33]

---

31 "First Cotton Mill," in James Edward Smoot Papers. For the next two years the enterprise flourished, but hard times began in 1844. The visionary but inexperienced businessmen struggled to keep their dream afloat. In 1849, the mill was leased to Caleb Phifer, but hard times continued. The mill was finally sold in 1856 to John McDonald. It passed through many hands and was largely destroyed by fire in 1908. However, it was rebuilt and eventually became part of the extensive Cannon Mills.

32 Barringer, journal, July 29, 1842. Margaret Barringer's first husband was Andrew Grier, and her second husband was John Boyd.

33 Ibid., July 21, 1842.

Though raised a Lutheran, Rufus was nominally a Presbyterian during this period, a time when religious revivals swept across the state. Rufus's brother William, who would later become a prominent Methodist minister, experienced a religious conversion during this time. Unlike his brother, however, Rufus was not caught up in the religious fervor and would not "convert" until about a decade later when he formally joined the Presbyterian Church.[34]

Whatever his religious convictions, Rufus enjoyed socializing (as surely evidenced by his college escapades), and this included Whist, a card game with simple rules laced with scientific complexity. Although he did not gamble, he did play the game as often as he could get a good set of players together. While playing cards (without the gambling aspect) was one of his light vices, drinking was not. "I have never been fond of liquor and have never followed a very foolish habit among young men—drinking for politeness," he wrote in his journal. "I therefore, [have] ever been a temperate man—at Chapel Hill, I joined a Temperance Society."[35]

Rufus's healthy dose of religious skepticism, coupled with a temperate lifestyle, was balanced by his eye for the ladies. In addition to his college adventures at Ned's and elsewhere, Rufus made a trip to a Presbyterian synod while studying the law in late October 1842. "I saw and gallanted several of my best female acquaintances, Misses Mebane, Brown, Morrison, Brevard, etc.," he boasted. "Went with the three first to Ed Harris's and passed the times most agreeably."[36]

Ties to family remained important to the young Barringer, a character trait that instilled a sense of duty extending beyond him. In November 1842, the young lawyer-to-be paid a visit to his mother and father. They seemed anxious to be at peace after spending a lifetime of hard labor to raise their children in comfortable circumstances. "I know no man, considering his own opportunities, who has done more for his family than my father," confessed Rufus. "He has given all his daughters a good education and such of his sons as would accept it."[37]

34 Ibid., July 30, 1842.

35 Ibid., August 21, 1842.

36 Ibid., October 31, 1842. Miss Morrison was apparently one of the older Morrison sisters—not Eugenia, Rufus's future wife, as she would have been only nine years old at this time.

37 Ibid., November 10, 1842.

On the day before his 21st birthday, Rufus took some time to reflect upon his life thus far. "An important period is drawn to a close!" he wrote. "This day brings an end to my boyhood. . . . On this day . . . I receive for the last time, as a duty, the kind advice and careful watchings of my earthly father. I only wish my heart was in a condition to permit and enable me, with effect, to call upon my father in heaven. But I have never yet experienced a change of heart in regard to Religion. . . . But farewell—*forever*—farewell to childhood dreams. Alas! I'm now a man."[38]

Rufus ended his 1842 journal with a description of what he viewed as a momentous event—the day his father paid him a visit to give him the "free portion" with which to start his adulthood: "Today he came in my room here and told me that as I would not have as good an opportunity of making money (in the store, etc.) as the others had, he would give me a little more and also a little sooner," explained the younger Barringer. "He drew forth a bundle of notes and counted me out about four thousand dollars with interest from date for me to collect to hold as mine forever. And then too he counted out about five hundred dollars for my Education."[39]

Rufus and his brother William were both then boarding with their brother-in-law, William C. Means. Upon completion of the July court term of 1843, Rufus left Concord to spend the summer in Mocksville, about 50 miles north of Charlotte. He reported in his journal that, deep down, he had been unhappy in Concord. He was too distracted to concentrate on reading law while there and also wished for a better intellectual and social climate. He missed more challenging philosophical and political discussions. He also liked courting the ladies and saw greater opportunities away from home.[40]

On June 13, 1843, Barringer obtained his license to practice law. To become licensed, he had taken a nine-hour written and oral examination administered by Supreme Court judges in Raleigh, North Carolina. He passed on the first try. Then, in August, whatever his previous feelings about the town, he moved back home to Concord from Mocksville. After a few days in Concord, he left on a planned trip to the mountains and visited Morgantown, Mocksville, Asheville, and Sulphur Springs. He remained at Sulphur Springs

---

38 Ibid., December 1, 1842.

39 Ibid., December 7, 1842. The sum of $4,000 in 1842 equates to about $100,000 in modern currency.

40 Ibid., January 1, 1843.

and Pleasant Gardens several days each, partying much. He particularly enjoyed dancing every night. One night he spent some time with two "Misses Scott" from Georgia, who "weighed over 500 pounds between them." Barringer, weighing no more than 140 pounds, reported that he consumed a good portion of the evening dancing with one of them. He continued his vacation, returning to Concord on September 27. These distractions behind him, Barringer was not happy to be back in Concord: "I am in this little 'hog-hole.' A year since I expected to be far-far away from it. But so the Fates ordain and here I am."[41]

Barringer was now boarding at the Harris Hotel in Concord. In January 1844, he moved into Moreau's office and continued tending to his brother's and his own business, working hard on Moreau's case load. In 1843, Moreau had been elected to the United States Congress. At the same time, Rufus steadily built a clientele of his own.[42]

In February 1844, the young attorney, having been admitted to the bar a year earlier, attended a party at former United States Congressman Green W. Caldwell's house. Caldwell was at that time the superintendent of the Branch Mint in Charlotte. It was not a pleasant affair, or at least Rufus did not think so. There were too many older and married people in attendance and not enough young and single people his age. By this time, the 23-year-old bachelor was beginning to take seriously the thought of finding a wife and settling down. "Colonel [W. J.] Alexander has the most amiable, beautiful, intelligent and accomplished daughters," Barringer wrote in his journal. Alas, he would not find a wife for another decade.[43]

Rufus also became active in local Whig politics during the 1840s. In May 1844, he was appointed to a committee to draft resolutions at a Whig convention in Charlotte. Selected as the committee chairman, he addressed the convention and was warmly received. After the close of the convention, Rufus attended a ball at the Charlotte Hotel. "We danced 'till 3 o'clock and had lots of fun," he recalled, "but I never saw so large a number of persons in a ball room with so few good looking ones, gentlemen or ladies." Whatever the occasion, he still enjoyed a vigorous social life and the company of young ladies.[44]

41 Ibid., December 1, 1843.

42 Ashe, *Biographical History of North Carolina*, vol. 1, 103.

43 Barringer, journal, March 1, 1844.

44 Ibid., May 22, 1844.

While Rufus's political career was in its early ascendancy, his father, who had been ill for some time, traveled on June 2, 1844, to Wilson's Springs hoping the water there would help his condition. He felt better and began his journey home but took ill along the way. Rufus went to see him at Burton's Hotel in Lincolnton, where the elder Barringer slipped into a coma and died about 4:30 p.m. on June 23. "Nearly all the family gathered at 'Bellevue' and the largest concourse of people, up to that time, ever seen in Concord, attended the funeral," noted the *Raleigh Register*. "In the family group was a striking figure, his aged mother, then eighty-nine years old."[45]

The death of his father—the first death he had personally witnessed—struck Rufus hard. "Oh God the trial it was to me! I was all alone. I never had stood over a death bed and here I was weeping over the corpse of my father!" he scribbled in his journal. "I had never before attended a relative to the grave and never saw a 'human soul take wing.' And hard, hard indeed it was that my first great trial should be the death of my dear father. My best friend and protector." After the funeral, Rufus vowed to "plant cedars over his grave and water them with my tears."[46]

---

45 Wilson's Springs is now Cleveland Sulfur Springs near Shelby, North Carolina. *Raleigh Register*, July 2, 1844; *The Lutheran Observer*, July 19, 1844, reported the date of death as July 20. The exact nature of Paul's illness is not known.

46 Barringer, journal, June 23, 1844.

Chapter 2

"It is verily true that 'sorrow comes not single file, but in battalions.'"

— *Rufus Barringer after the death of his mother and other family members.*

Politics, Tragic Love, and Secession

Like his earlier years, the 1840s and 1850s continued to help mold Rufus's character. He would become involved in politics, continue to build his law practice and expand his professional relationships, suffer the loss of his loving parents, survive an attempted murder by a political nemesis, marry, and lose his beloved first wife to typhoid fever. Before his first marriage, he would become involved in an illicit liaison with a neighbor's slave, producing two sons, one of whom would become one of the South's wealthiest and most influential African Americans. All of these experiences would help shape Barringer's progressive values, including black suffrage, internal improvements, and measures to aid the ordinary lives of fellow North Carolina citizens.

On October 22, 1844, Barringer was elected solicitor for Cabarrus County. Though he had been active in local politics for a few years, energetically supporting other Whig Party candidates for local offices, this was his first public office, and he looked forward to serving.[1]

During that same October of good fortune for Rufus, his mother Elizabeth became ill and was confined to bed. Her children feared death was near, but held out hope that she would somehow recover. In late November, after a long

---

1 Barringer, journal, October 26, 1844.

struggle, she died. Ten days later, Barringer described the events leading to her passing:

> It was feared from her first sickness that her feeble and aged construction would hardly stand the violence of a salvation; which, though slight at first, being produced by Blue pill, seemed to pervade her whole system. Its effects were terrible. Her physicians found it necessary to extract nearly all her teeth and operate on the jaw bone. She bore the effort with all the patience characteristic of her whole life. . . . For several weeks she ate nor drank nothing and was sustained merely on quinine. For nearly three weeks death was hourly expected from exhaustion. Slowly, but gradually and certainly the hour approached. . . . On her bed recline eight weeping children. She talks of life and death; bids each one to prepare for her final home; converses freely of the things of this world and of that which is to come; says that she is ready and willing to die. . . . But the hour is not yet come! She sleeps and awakens and still lingers: as calm as the slumber of a new born infant. . . . At last the eternal spirit leaves its earthly tenure and wings its way to its home in Heaven. On Friday the 22nd of November about the hour of three in the morning came the awful moment. . . . Oh Dear Mother! How much happier were thy dying moments than those of my beloved father. Around his bed stood one child: around thine many children.[2]

Before the next year had passed, Rufus lost another half-dozen near and dear relatives. "It is verily true that 'sorrow comes not single file, but in battalions,'" he wrote.[3]

With Elizabeth buried next to his recently deceased father in St. John's Lutheran churchyard in downtown Concord, Rufus spent most of the following year settling his father's considerable estate. He also continued to take over more of Moreau's business, as his brother became increasingly active in state and national politics.

Despite these obligations, Rufus found time to travel north for five weeks during May and June of 1846. He visited Boston, Saratoga Springs in New

---

2 Ibid., December 1, 1844. The "Blue Pill" was a mercury compound, perhaps calomel, used as a cathartic and for several ailments at the time, including "bilious attacks" and typhoid fever. Gum problems and loose teeth were typical side effects of mercury poisoning. Newspaper and family accounts attribute Eugenia Barringer's later death to typhoid fever, but it is possible that she, too, was a victim of mercury poisoning. Ailing people were often literally poisoned to death by their doctors' treatments in the mid-nineteenth century.

3 Ibid., December 1, 1845.

Daniel Moreau Barringer (1806-1873). The brother of Rufus Barringer shared a desk with Abraham Lincoln in the U.S. Congress. Moreau served a pair of terms in the House of Representatives, and also served as America's ambassador to Spain under Presidents Zachary Taylor and Millard Fillmore. *North Carolina Division of Archives and History.*

York, and Washington. Big city life and social elegance agreed with him, and he thoroughly enjoyed the sojourn.[4]

During this period of rising prospects, the young North Carolina lawyer reflected on his life—and his status as a bachelor, in particular. He confessed in his journal that he had thoughts of "changing my condition in life but have not yet seen the one on whom I could lavish 'my all'. . . . There are several young ladies on whom I have my eyes, and if my better feelings grow on me I should not be surprised, the other party willing, if I am a married man twelve months hence."[5]

While he may have contemplated marriage in his hours of introspection, Rufus's major concern was handling more of Moreau's business. His older brother was re-elected to Congress in 1845, and again in 1847. Younger brother Victor graduated from the University of North Carolina in 1848 and went to Washington to study law with Moreau. On August 15, 1848, at the age of 42, Moreau married Elizabeth Wethered. The 26-year-old Elizabeth was the daughter of Lewin Wethered, a prominent Baltimore merchant. Moreau did not run for re-election to Congress in 1849, preferring instead to seek a diplomatic appointment. Later that year, President Zachary Taylor appointed Moreau as Minister to Spain. In 1851, he was reappointed to the same position by President Millard Fillmore. Victor Barringer served as Secretary of Legation to his brother in Spain until they both came back to North Carolina in 1853. Moreau had taken his slave, Jerry, to Spain during his service there, and

4   Ibid., December 1, 1846.

5   Ibid.

described him as "a universal favorite." Upon Moreau's return to North Carolina in 1854, he served a term in the House of Commons, where he introduced an emancipation bill for Jerry, stating that he was remarkable for his "honesty, humility, and was one of the best colored men living." With Moreau's support, the bill passed the House of Commons by a vote of 94 to 17, and shortly thereafter became law.[6]

Waking Up "Old Rip Van Winkle"

In the 1840s, when Rufus first became involved in politics, the sectional feuding between the eastern and western parts of North Carolina was intense—and had been for decades. The financial condition of the state was deplorable, with economic fortunes showing steady decline, year after year. Rufus saw railroad reform as a solution that would turn around the faltering Tar Heel economy, particularly in the western part of the state, where his interests lay. The eastern Carolinians, however, enjoyed a power advantage over the westerners in the state legislature. In 1847, a group of Virginia and South Carolina capitalists proposed to build a railroad from Charlotte to Danville, Virginia. The project did not require any financial support from the State of North Carolina, and the people of the areas affected warmly endorsed the proposal because it would increase commerce. As a leading figure in western North Carolina, Rufus zealously advocated for this railroad measure. In 1848, he was elected to the House of Commons, where he urged support for its construction.[7]

Like his father, Rufus was a Whig in politics. He called himself "a born Whig reformer." He deplored what he termed the "Old Rip Van Winkleism," the exceedingly slow pace of change that delayed the reforms he deemed necessary. Rufus also advocated a progressive system of internal improvements, including a statewide railroad system. The Whigs supported such improvements, but the Democrats generally opposed appropriating state funds for such purposes. However, on the question of the proposed Charlotte-to-Danville rail line, the eastern Whigs opposed it. They had a lock on

6 Powell, *Dictionary of North Carolina Biography*, vol. 1, 99; *Greensborough Patriot*, December 23, 1854; John Hope Franklin, *Reconstruction After The Civil War* (Chicago, IL, 1961), 32.

7 Rufus Barringer, "History of the North Carolina Railroad," May 10, 1894, in Rufus Barringer Papers, University of Virginia.

the North Carolina railroads, with no lines west of Raleigh. They did not want to pay for any improvements or lose their monopoly on rail transportation within the state. Thus, early in the 1848 session, the outlook for passage of the railroad bill seemed hopeless.[8]

Samuel A. Ashe, a Democratic senator from New Hanover County (on the eastern seaboard encompassing Wilmington), was another strong advocate for internal improvements. He proposed an alternate bill that would incorporate a regional North Carolina railroad system to run between Greensboro and Charlotte. The bill provided for an appropriation of two million dollars in public funds, and called for another one million in public stock subscriptions. When the "Charlotte and Danville" bill came before the House of Commons, the eastern delegates who controlled the railroads opposed the measure. When Barringer urged its passage, Edward Stanly interrupted with a charge of "selling out" to Virginia and South Carolina. Rufus resented this, and defied Stanly "to make us an offer of any bill providing for a general North Carolina system, likely to pass, and with sufficient state aid to secure its completion, and I for one, would vote for it." Finally, on January 18, 1849, the "Ashe bill" passed by a majority of eight votes. Barringer, pledging the support of the western delegates, was instrumental in getting the bill passed in the House of Commons, after the "Charlotte and Danville" bill had been tabled. Barringer recalled that "the chances in the Senate were in doubt. . . . The roll call began . . . the clerk announced 22 'yeas' and 22 'nays.'" Speaker Calvin Graves cast the deciding vote in the affirmative, and the bill was passed. This "Ashe bill" formally incorporated The North Carolina Railroad Company, which subsequently constructed the state railroad system, including the Greensboro-to-Charlotte line (which included a station at Barringer's home town of Concord). This event signaled the awakening of the "Rip Van Winkle" state.[9]

After the railroad bill passed, Barringer and other dignitaries crisscrossed the state addressing crowds in search of public support and subscriptions. The state pledged to fund two-thirds of the cost of the new railroad, and public subscriptions were needed to cover the remaining one-third. It would be

8   Ibid.; Joseph Gregoire de Roluhac Hamilton, *Party Politics in North Carolina, 1835-1860* (Durham, NC, 1916), 132-134.

9   Rufus Barringer, "History of the North Carolina Railroad," May 10, 1894, in *Papers of the North Carolina Historical Society at the University of North Carolina* (Raleigh, NC, n.d.); William K. Boyd, *History of North Carolina* (New York, NY, 1919), vol. 2, 233-234; Hamilton, *Party Politics in North Carolina*, 133-134.

September 1854 before regular train service began on the western end of the line. The counties north of Charlotte and west of Raleigh were enthralled by the new rail service, and towns held celebrations upon arrival of the first trains. On January 4, 1854, Rufus Barringer served as grand marshal of a large celebration of the opening of the Concord-to-Salisbury stretch of track. He led a procession from the courthouse to the depot. Brass bands played, and the first locomotive arrived at 11:00 a.m. The *Raleigh Register* reported: "In all, 24 hogs, 16 sheep, and assorted other animals were served with 1400 pounds of bread and a ball was held at Murphy's Hall. The huge turnout, at up to 15,000 people, exceeded the barbecue and the sleeping accommodations available." Rufus remained interested in railroad improvements throughout his life, as a lawyer for the North Carolina Railroad system and a member of various state and county railroad committees. He would later call the granting of the railroad charter "the basis and the beginning of our entire present system of internal improvement, now reaching every part of the state."[10]

In 1849 and 1850, Rufus helped pass many other progressive and reform measures, including railroad authorizations, funding of asylums and other public charities, systems for education, and other plans for improvement of the state's people. He advocated a thorough reform of the judiciary system, including more North Carolina Supreme Court justices and an appeals court system which, if adopted, would have helped spare North Carolina the deluge of crowded dockets and delayed justice that followed.[11]

In the Assembly session of 1850-1851, Rufus voted with the Democrats for free (equal) suffrage and various changes in the road law. Up until that time, all white male taxpayers could vote for governor and members of the House of Commons. Free blacks were not allowed to vote under any circumstances, having lost that right in the state constitutional convention of 1835. To vote for state senators, a man also had to own at least 50 acres of property. This gave eastern North Carolina more power, with larger landowners there than in the western portion of the state. Free suffrage would eliminate the requirement of owning 50 acres of property before one could vote for state senators. Delegate

---

10 Allen W. Trelease, *The North Carolina Railroad, 1849-1871, and the Modernization of North Carolina* (Chapel Hill, NC, 1991), 36-37; *Raleigh Register,* January 10, 1855; Edward Mims and William G. Glasson, eds., *The South Atlantic Quarterly,* vol. 5 (Durham, NC, 1906), 42.

11 *Charlotte Journal,* April 13, 1849; *Charlotte Daily Observer,* August 19, 1875; *Raleigh Signal,* August, 12 1880. This was an account of Barringer's July 31, 1880, campaign speech at Morganton during the 1880 gubernatorial election.

Barringer also favored working the public roads by contract—a combination of public labor and taxation—instead of by the public labor laws alone. The Democrats in 1848 advocated free suffrage. The Whigs were undecided on the issue, which almost cost them the election of 1848. The Democrats would stand on this matter in future elections and thereby gain control of the legislature in 1850.[12]

Rufus Barringer was clearly a progressive. He sided with the masses, and his forward thinking on the issues of his day helped wake the "Old Rip Van Winkle" state from its deep slumber. Rufus firmly believed that the only way to preserve an institution was to reform it. He believed that "if a system goes on a long time while unreformed, it is not then reformed but destroyed."[13]

"An Invitation To The Field"

All of Rufus's political activities during these years were conducted in an atmosphere of high decorum. However, from August through October 1849, he and Democratic political rival Green Washington Caldwell (1806-1864) engaged in a vigorous "letters to the editor" campaign against each other in area newspapers. The hostilities began during the 1849 election campaign, with Barringer questioning Caldwell's integrity.[14]

Caldwell was a well-known political figure in Mecklenburg County. He had been trained as a physician, but had become dissatisfied with medicine and had taken up study of the law. He had subsequently been admitted to the bar, establishing his practice in Charlotte. Caldwell had been elected to the House of Commons in 1836 and was re-elected three times thereafter. In 1841, he had been elected to the United States House of Representatives, defeating Rufus's older brother Moreau. Caldwell had declined re-election in 1843 and returned to Charlotte, where in 1844 he secured an appointment as superintendent of the United States Mint. He was the choice of the Democratic Party for governor in 1846, but declined the nomination because of ill health.[15]

---

12 *Charlotte Journal*, January 26, 1849; *Raleigh Signal*, August 12, 1880.

13 Ibid.

14 *Carolina Watchman*, September 27, 1849; *Raleigh Carolina Star*, October 3, 1849.

15 Powell, *Dictionary of North Carolina Biography*, vol. 1, 303; J. B. Alexander, *The History of Mecklenburg County From 1740 to 1900* (Charlotte, NC, 1902), 99.

Caldwell had volunteered for duty during the Mexican War and was made a captain of the Third Regiment of Dragoons in 1847. This unit had been formed by Congress for a one-year period. When the brief war ended, a public celebration was held in Charlotte on September 11, 1848, to welcome home the returning volunteers, including Caldwell. Dignitaries were present and many toasts were offered. A similar ceremony was held in Concord for the Cabarrus County volunteers. Among the Cabarrus celebrants was Rufus Barringer, who toasted, "[To] Women—Conservators in peace—arbiters in war—our chief blessing all the time." Rufus had not served in the Mexican War. He had supported the Whig position that it was a "foreign war" and unnecessary.[16]

In November 1848, Green W. Caldwell had announced as an "independent" candidate for the United States Congress. The Whigs ran ex-Congressman Edmund Deberry against him. Caldwell had attempted to convince Whig voters that he was no longer interested in the principles of the Democrats, and was truly an independent with many interests of the Whigs at heart. The Whigs did not buy the pitch, and Caldwell was defeated in the election on August 2, 1849. During the heated campaign, Rufus supported Deberry by writing two anonymous letters to the editor of the *Charlotte Journal.*[17]

The text of the first letter, which appeared in the *Carolina Watchman*, stated in part: "A man never looks so ridiculous as, when he is attempting to prove himself to be, what his whole life proves him not to be—judge then, how Capt. Caldwell looks while trying to make out that he is a very decent sort of something in the shape of a Whig! . . . He wants Whig votes. He cares not the value of a penny for Whig principles."[18]

Rufus wrote a second anonymous letter, which appeared in the same issue of the *Carolina Watchman*. This time he accused Caldwell of chicanery. He stated that in 1841, when Caldwell was in Congress, President John Tyler used the enormous patronage of the government to attempt to buy votes for a shady fiscal scheme. Barringer declared: "A certain measure known as his 'fiscal

---

16 *Charlotte Journal*, September 13, 1848.

17 Ibid.

18 *Carolina Watchman*, September 27, 1849; *Raleigh Carolina Star*, October 3, 1849; *Hornet's Nest*, September 15, 1849; *Charlotte Journal*, July 27, 1849, September 21, 1849. Victor Barringer actually wrote this letter and Rufus edited it (*Carolina Watchman*, December 9, 1850). The Barringers withheld this information for two years, perhaps in an attempt to protect young Victor from the possible danger of a duel challenge.

Agent' scheme for collecting and disbursing the Public revenue was employed as a feeler in the House of Representatives. This absurd financial project received only some twelve or fifteen votes in the House. That number consisted of . . . Green W. Caldwell and others. It is known, sir, that nearly every member who voted for that abominable measure received from John Tyler a lucrative appointment. Mr. G. W. Caldwell received the best office in North Carolina . . . Does Mr. C. think the people have forgotten these things?"[19]

Caldwell was furious when he learned that Rufus authored the two letters. He responded to Barringer in a letter dated August 17: "Now, sir, both of those communications (especially the latter) I consider a gross and unprovoked attack upon my character, for which I demand of you satisfaction."[20]

Rufus considered the letter a direct "invitation to the field." He consulted four friends, including Dr. Alexander M. Henderson. All concluded that Caldwell's letter was indeed a challenge to a duel. Rufus made preparations and went to Catawba Springs, about 35 miles north of Charlotte, where a meeting would take place between the designated seconds to make preliminary arrangements for the contest. While there on August 27, 1849, Rufus wrote to Caldwell attempting to clarify the intent of his letter. Was Caldwell's letter in fact a challenge to armed confrontation?[21]

Rufus recalled that his uncle, Daniel L. Barringer, had challenged political opponent Willie P. Magnum to a duel during an 1823 campaign for the United States House of Representatives. Barringer and Magnum had both sworn a public oath not to campaign for votes, which at that time in Cabarrus County was considered beneath a gentleman's dignity. Daniel had been accused of violating the pledge and became furious and embarrassed. He challenged Magnum to a duel, but friends intervened successfully to prevent it.[22]

---

19 Ibid. John Tyler was the first vice president to assume the nation's highest office upon the death of a sitting president. He succeeded William Henry Harrison, who died a month after taking office. Tyler, a Southern former Democrat, split with his party to run with Harrison on the Whig Party ticket. However, as president, Tyler found that many Whig programs clashed with his beliefs. He vetoed almost every important bill. Angry Whigs tried to impeach him, the first such move against a president. They failed, but the Whig program was virtually destroyed.

20 *Carolina Watchman*, September 27, 1849; *Raleigh Carolina Star*, October 3, 1849; *Hornet's Nest*, September 15, 1849; *Charlotte Journal*, July 27, 1849, September 21, 1849.

21 Ibid.

22 Henry T. Shanks, ed., *The Papers of Willie P. Magnum*, 5 vols. (Raleigh, NC, 1950-1956), Vol. 1, 51-52, 61, 65, 70-79; Bertram Wyatt-Brown, *Southern Honor, Ethics and Behavior in the Old South*

In a continuing effort to determine if Caldwell truly meant his letter as a challenge to a duel, Rufus and Caldwell traded letters through their respective friends, Dr. Henderson and Edward C. Davidson. Caldwell replied from nearby Lincoln County on the same day, August 27, and stated that he had not meant his letter to be "an invitation to the field," but as a demand for satisfaction, necessitating an apology.[23]

Rufus responded from Catawba Springs and backed off from his charges of outright corruption. Although the situation was delicate, the dispute seemed resolved to Caldwell's satisfaction. Rumors, however, abounded over the matter. In Charlotte, gossip circulated that Barringer had backed down from Caldwell's challenge. Dr. Henderson learned of the rumors and notified Rufus about them. As a result, Rufus published the entire written record in the newspapers, to let the public know the facts of the situation.[24]

Caldwell considered this a reopening of the insult and again took offense. He wrote a letter to the editor of the *Carolina Watchman* demanding satisfaction from Barringer, and implying that Barringer had backed down from a fight. Rufus, now clearly agitated, responded in a public letter, again raising the specter of corruption and denying Caldwell's allegation that he had backed down.[25]

Caldwell once again "demanded satisfaction" in a letter to Rufus, who responded:

> I received another cartel from the Hon. Gentleman, in which he demands personal satisfaction "for the general bearing and tone of my last communication . . . and its reiteration of the charge of corruption against him. . . . Why all your parade, precaution and preparation? . . . Why carry with you "the instruments [pistols]?" Why your daily practice? . . . I was there ready . . . "to deliver an acceptance and arrange the

---

(New York, NY, 1982), 57. Daniel L. Barringer lost the election to Magnum, but in 1826 was chosen to fill the seat left vacant by Magnum's resignation. Barringer would go on to serve four successive terms in the House of Representatives.

23 *Carolina Watchman*, September 27, 1849; *Raleigh Carolina Star*, October 3, 1849; *Hornet's Nest*, September 15, 1849; *Charlotte Journal*, July 27, 1849, and September 21, 1849. Edward C. Davidson had served under Caldwell in the Mexican War.

24 Ibid.

25 *Carolina Watchman*, October 4, 1849; *Raleigh Carolina Star*, October 10, 1849; *Charlotte Journal*, October 5, 1849.

preliminaries for an immediate meeting in the field,"—you sit down and say under your hand, "It was not intended as an invitation to the field."[26]

Yes sir! You have done all this! I forced you to "withdraw" or "fight." You chose the former . . . it was a deliberate, cowardly backout in every shape and form. . . . Yes, sir, you showed the white feather and vamoosed! . . . I am now done with you, I am a man of Peace, but I warn you not to try my "science of self-defense."[27]

Rufus was as able with a pen as any cavalryman with a sword during the forthcoming Civil War, but Green Caldwell could stand no more. Barringer was in Charlotte on Monday night, October 27. Lewis S. Williams, a mutual friend of the two men, informed Barringer that Caldwell would not attack him. Rufus naively believed his friend. After 10:00 p.m., Barringer and three friends from Concord stood under the piazza in front of Sadler's Hotel. The lighting was either dim or out, making face recognition difficult. A crowd had gathered.

Rufus and a friend puffed on cigars, as all three talked, laughed, and enjoyed themselves. Caldwell's brother walked by, but Caldwell and his friends—Joseph Davidson and Charles Tittermary—stopped at the piazza. Caldwell felt insulted and sure that Rufus and his friends were laughing at him. In the dim light, Caldwell stepped up to Rufus and asked, "Who is this?" Taken by surprise, Rufus answered, "Barringer," and was immediately attacked. The two men grappled at close quarters and Caldwell fired a shot from his pistol. A second shot followed, and after some shoving by both men, a third shot was fired. Both men fell down, and a fourth shot went off. Rufus had been fortunate to grip Caldwell's right hand and alter the bullets' trajectories. Three of the shots missed, but a fourth wounded Rufus in the fleshy part of the leg, just below the knee. The three other shots passed through his long coat. William F. Taylor finally intervened after a lighted candle helped illuminate the scene. The two men were separated, and Caldwell's pistol was taken from him.[28]

The *Charlotte Journal* reported that "Caldwell had loaded his pistol with fresh charges the night before the attack. Though Caldwell was clearly the aggressor and had nearly killed Barringer, both men were arrested and appeared before the Superior Court of Charlotte to face charges for the fight. Caldwell was a

---

26 *Carolina Watchman*, October 18, 1849.

27 Ibid.

28 *Carolina Watchman*, December 9, 1850.

favorite politician in town, as Charlotte was in his senatorial district." On November 17, 1849, both men were bound over for trial and released with the condition that they appear during the next court term. They were ordered to "keep the peace towards all the Citizens of North Carolina & especially towards each other."[29]

Their court cases were continued several times. Rufus initially pled innocent, but changed his plea during an appearance in the fall term of the Superior Court of nearby Iredell County the next year. He was fined $50. Caldwell's case was resolved on November 12, 1850. He pled guilty and was sentenced to 20 days in jail.[30]

The *Carolina Watchman* reported that influential friends and an angry crowd of hundreds demonstrated for Caldwell and were determined to get him released. After a day or two, the judge yielded to the pressure and freed him.[31]

Barringer and Caldwell both served in the North Carolina legislature that year as state senators. Apparently, there was no further trouble between them. Caldwell remained in the Senate in 1850, but was unsuccessful in a bid against Whig candidate Alfred Dockery for the United States Congress in 1851. During the 1851 election, in the wake of the Compromise of 1850, Caldwell defended the South's right to withdraw from the Union. Dockery declared that if South Carolina or even North Carolina should attempt secession, he would vote for an appropriation to keep the offending State within the Union. Caldwell returned as superintendent of the United States Mint, and died in Charlotte on July 10, 1864.[32]

While Rufus was generally even-tempered and respectful, the conflict with Caldwell demonstrated that once Barringer's temper was aroused, he became aggressive and intransigent. Rufus's "hot button" issues were politics and the questioning of his honor. His anger would surface again after the Civil War, in the wake of Reconstruction politics. As a Radical Republican after the war, he was politically fearless and inflexible, and reacted angrily to Democrats who

---

29 *Charlotte Journal*, November 14, 1850; Mecklenburg County, Charlotte Superior Court Minutes, November 17, 1849, North Carolina Division of Archives and History.

30 Ibid., November 12, 1850; Iredell County Superior Court Minutes, Fall Term, 1850, North Carolina Division of Archives and History.

31 *Carolina Watchman*, November 28, 1849; *Republican Compiler*, December 2, 1850.

32 *Raleigh Standard*, June 28 and July 5, 1851; William K. Boyd, *North Carolina on the Eve of Secession* (Washington, DC, 1912), 171; Powell, *Dictionary of North Carolina Biography*, vol. 1, 303.

challenged him. His political principles and angry responses would bring scrapes with his brother-in-law, D. H. Hill, and Jubal Early—both of whom were uncompromising war veterans.

Storm Clouds of Secession

Even before the Caldwell affair, Rufus had become weary of political life in the House of Commons. In a January 1849 letter to his brother Moreau, he described his desire to return to private practice in Concord: "I am pretty well tired of legislating for North Carolina. I had no idea I would become so much wearied with it. I am extremely anxious to leave and return home to business."[33]

Nevertheless, Rufus went on to serve in the state Senate in 1850. He displayed unusual ability in that body, too, in supporting judicial, educational, and county government reform measures. Free suffrage had become an issue in the 1848 gubernatorial campaign, but did not become law until 1857. The Whigs, concerned about the land interests of the powerful eastern Whigs, were against free suffrage and stalled its passage for nearly a decade. The Whigs were out of step with the people of North Carolina on this issue, and their position against free suffrage resulted in the decline of the Whig Party. Rufus, by supporting many reform and improvement measures, established himself as a progressive long before the Civil War. His advanced beliefs would be reinforced and expanded by his experiences during the conflict.[34]

Despite his duties in the state legislature, Rufus enjoyed the social climate in Raleigh and dated frequently. In a June 1849 letter from Victor Barringer to his brother Moreau, the younger sibling revealed that part of Rufus' social life involved his ongoing search for a suitable bride: "He seems to be determined to carry out your advice about getting married—but when? or where? He is a wily old coon in such matters."[35]

During this time, people throughout the country were concerned over the expansion of slavery into the Territories west of the Mississippi River. Rufus

33 Rufus Barringer to Daniel Moreau Barringer, January 10, 1849, in Moreau Barringer Papers, Southern Historical Collection.

34 William James Cooper, *The South and the Politics of Slavery, 1828-56* (Baton Rouge, LA, 1978), 311.

35 Victor Clay Barringer to Moreau Barringer, June 5, 1849, in Moreau Barringer Papers, Southern Historical Collection.

Purported photograph of Roxanna Coleman Young (1829-1904). Rufus Barringer and slave Roxanna Coleman had two illegitimate children, Thomas Clay Coleman in 1846 and Warren Clay Coleman in 1849. Roxanna married John F. Young in 1852. *From the Estate Papers of historian Marvin Krieger of North Carolina. Photo Courtesy of Rex Butler, Cornelius, North Carolina.*

Barringer completed his term in the North Carolina Senate as the slavery issue came to a head with the Compromise of 1850, which threatened to split the country apart. Strangely, he was not excited enough about these issues to seek reelection.

Affair with Roxanna Coleman
and the Birth of Warren C. Coleman and Thomas C. Coleman

Despite national turmoil over the institution of slavery, Rufus Barringer abstained from politics and focused on his professional career and personal matters. He did not marry until 1854. However, there is substantial circumstantial evidence that Rufus and Roxanna Coleman, a mulatto slave owned by his neighbor, Daniel Coleman, engaged in a long affair. The illicit union resulted in the births of two illegitimate sons, Thomas Clay Coleman and Warren Clay Coleman. Thomas was born on June 2, 1845, when Roxanna was 16 and Rufus was 24. Warren was born on March 25, 1849, during Rufus's

Warren Clay Coleman (1849-1904). Coleman, purported black son of Rufus Barringer, became one of the South's wealthiest black men. He organized and built the Coleman Manufacturing Company, one of the first black owned and operated textile mills in the United States. *North Carolina Division of Archives and History.*

tenure in the House of Commons in Raleigh. Rufus's relationship with the light-skinned Roxanna lasted four years.[36]

Roxanna had a third illegitimate son, Joseph Smith, after Rufus and Roxanna broke off their relationship. She subsequently married John F. Young in 1852 and died in Concord on April 24, 1904.[37]

Although there is no direct documentation that proves Rufus was the father of the two boys, it was a matter of general knowledge in the Concord area. Moreover, the boys shared the middle name Clay, the adopted middle name of Rufus's brother Victor. Some have erroneously reported that Clay was also Rufus's middle name.[38]

After emancipation, Warren Coleman worked as an apprentice to William M. Coleman. In 1869, before his 21st birthday, Warren paid $600 for a half-acre business lot in Concord. He would have required financial assistance to buy this

36 Powell, *Dictionary Of North Carolina Biography*, vol. 1, 401-402; Marvin Krieger, "Warren Clay Coleman, Promoter of the Black Cotton Mill: An Analysis of an Early Effort to Develop Black Economic Power" (M. A. Thesis, Wake Forest University, 1969), 25; Noel Yancey, "The Cause of Righteousness," *Spectator Newspaper*, May 11, 1989.

37 Powell, *Dictionary of North Carolina Biography*, vol. 1, 401.

38 Krieger, "Warren Clay Coleman," 16. Krieger's thesis provides considerable circumstantial evidence that Barringer was the father of Warren Coleman. Warren's marriage license does not list his parents' names. Thomas Coleman's marriage license lists John and Roxanna Young as his parents. However, John F. Young could not have been the father, since he would have been only 10 years old at the time of Thomas's birth (in 1835 per the 1870 Census for Cabarrus County, N.C.) Roxanna was born in 1829. It is likely that Barringer was also the father of Thomas Clay Coleman.

property, which he probably received from Rufus or William M. Coleman. Rufus is not mentioned in any documentation on Warren, nor is Coleman mentioned in any Barringer documentation, such as Rufus's will. In order to keep his relationship to Warren secret, Rufus would have had to provide any support through William M. Coleman.[39]

The connection between Rufus and Roxanna, however, was supported by Holland Thompson, who knew Rufus Barringer and served as superintendent of Concord's public schools during the 1890s. Thompson authored a book titled *From the Cotton Field to the Cotton Mill*, which hinted at the identity of Warren Clay Coleman's father. According to Thompson, "The moving spirit [behind the formation of the black-owned and black-operated cotton mill] was a mulatto, Warren Coleman, who had an unusual career. He was born a slave and his reputed father was a white man, afterward distinguished by military and financial ability, who is said to have assisted the boy."[40]

The Southern and Western Textile Excelsior, a respected trade journal published in Charlotte from 1893 to 1923, stated in an 1897 feature editorial: "the colored man in Concord, North Carolina [Warren Coleman], who has shown so much enterprise in getting up a cotton mill for the colored people, is reported to be the son of a very distinguished white Confederate General, and could not help inheriting some of the distinguished character traits of the late Gen. B[arringer]."[41]

Religious Conversion

Whatever Rufus's relationship with Roxanna Coleman and her sons, at the end of his term in the North Carolina Senate Rufus essentially withdrew from politics and devoted himself to growing his law practice. In 1851, he was urged by prominent citizens to run for the United States Congress, and flatly refused. Rufus would not run for public office again until he was elected as a delegate to

---

39 Deed Book 22, Register of Deeds Office, Concord, NC, 585; Krieger, "Warren Clay Coleman," 19.

40 Holland Thompson, *From the Cotton Field to the Cotton Mill* (New York, NY, 1906), 253; Krieger, "Warren Clay Coleman," 12.

41 Ibid., 18; *Southern and Western Textile Excelsior*, October 2, 1897. The number of blank letters in the last name, beginning with the letter "B" in the quoted paragraph, matches the number of letters in "Barringer."

the state constitutional convention in 1875, a full quarter of a century later and a decade after the end of the Civil War.[42]

Throughout this period, Rufus and Victor Barringer remained close. Victor was hot-tempered and impetuous, while Rufus was farsighted and realistic in his thinking. Although there was great dissimilarity between them, the two brothers shared a profound affection for each other. Both were successful lawyers and bachelors. However, on May 27, 1852, Victor married Maria Amanda Massey of Morganton, the only daughter of Maj. George Valentine Massey and Adeline McKesson Massey.[43]

Insight into Rufus's life and values during this time is revealed by his "Commonplace Book," a journal he kept during these years. He recorded treasured extracts of his readings and his thoughts on the issues of the day. Rufus's book reveals his developing character between 1853 and 1858. Apparently, significant events in his life had occurred during the period immediately preceding his first entries.[44]

At some time prior to July 1853, Rufus fell in love with a young lady who did not return the sentiment. This experience of unrequited love had a tremendous effect on him. The pain of rejection is evident in his journal: "I was in love with Miss [Fanny?] B—; she who seemed dearer to me than all the earth & heaven besides. But I was doomed to a disappointment in her. I then tried to be gay—to forget her, who had slighted my love. . . . Whatever may have been my affection for the young lady, I came to the conclusion that she gave no indication of reciprocating to such an extent & in such a way as to lead me to believe a union with her, in my recently changed feelings, would be judicious. Indeed I do not feel sure I could have won her at all.[45]

---

42 William S. Powell, ed., *Dictionary of North Carolina Biography* (Chapel Hill, NC, 1979), 1: 99-100.

43 Anna Barringer, ed., "The First American Judge in Egypt," vol. 1, 179-180, in Rufus Barringer Papers, University of Virginia. Obituary for Maria Massey Barringer, as published in "The Churchman," December 7, 1901, 762.

44 Rufus Barringer, "Commonplace Book," in Rufus Barringer Papers, University of Virginia.

45 Ibid. The name of the young woman Rufus was in love with was erased from the Commonplace Book. A name was partially re-entered at a later date, in a different handwriting. This was probably done by Dr. Paul Brandon Barringer or his daughter, Anna Barringer. Extensive efforts have been made to determine if a young woman named Frances (Fanny) Barrier might have existed and might have been the woman whose name was partially written in Rufus's journal. Census data, marriage registers, and other documents have yielded no clues.

Rufus underwent a religious conversion following his rejection by the young woman. He states in his journal that he had always been religiously inclined (he was raised a Lutheran), but in his own eyes had fallen short of the life the Lord would have him live. His journal describes the particulars of his pursuit of material things since reaching manhood: "I set out upon my new career with the fixed & firm resolution to make a fortune. I now deeply regret that I had no higher motive. . . . I came to reflect every day that wealth did not & never could give the bliss, for which we seek. At all periods in my life . . . unrepented sins of a wicked past would intrude themselves upon my peace. I even felt & acknowledged the authenticity of the scriptures, & the consoling power of the Christian religion. I looked round & almost envied the quiet, cheerful happiness it confirmed upon all the true followers. But alas! for me: now this, & again that object of worldly pleasure, pride or ambition would lead me off, & onward in the way of sin." Barringer also wrote that "I have committed all the sins peculiar to every hardy man." He obviously experienced guilt over his past "wicked ways" and sought to repent.[46]

Rufus attended a revival in Charlotte, and the preaching of Reverend Daniel Baker of Texas greatly moved him. "He affected me deeply," wrote Barringer. "I would weep in the church, but would laugh it away when I went out. Love then troubled me more than religion." Rufus left but returned again seeking God, stating he "did not believe in revivals and instantaneous conversions." He again left—affected but not "converted." Back in Concord, he read a letter from his brother William urging him to think of religion. The letter deeply touched Rufus. He spent several hours in his room reading and reflecting on his life. He "offered up my first prayer to the Throne of Grace." For the next four days he attended preaching and inquiry meetings held by Reverend Baker at Davidson College. Rufus recorded that he "found new light bursting upon me both from the will of God and the preaching of the Gospel. I found I had never properly comprehended the wondrous atonement of Christ." He continued to struggle with temptations and "thoughts wandering from God," but set his mind "to pursue and lead a Christian life."[47]

46 Ibid.

47 Ibid.

Eugenia Morrison

Shortly after Rufus's rejection by the unnamed woman and his religious conversion, he began courting Eugenia Erixene Morrison. They met at a church service, and in January 1854 became engaged to be married. The young lawyer wrote in his journal that Eugenia was "a young lady whose piety, accomplishments, character, and beauty fill up and absorb my soul."[48]

In all likelihood, Rufus would not have been allowed to court Eugenia had her father known of Rufus's fatherhood of two illegitimate mulatto sons. These circumstances would become known over time by folks in Concord and Charlotte, but when Rufus met Eugenia, they were still secret—especially as far away as the Morrison home in Lincoln County. Rufus's illicit fatherhood remained a secret outside of Concord until after his death in 1895. Somehow, his political adversaries and the press never learned of the relationships until just after his passing.

Eugenia was born on February 5, 1833, in Concord. She was the fifth child of the Reverend Robert Hall Morrison (1798-1889), a prominent Presbyterian minister, and Mary Graham Morrison (1801-1864). Mary was the daughter of Gen. Joseph Graham of Revolutionary War fame. She was also the sister of William A. Graham (1804-1875), who would become governor of North Carolina, a United States Senator, and Secretary of the Navy under President Millard Fillmore.[49]

Reverend Morrison was an educator and the first president of Davidson College, a Presbyterian school for men located 35 miles northwest of Charlotte. He was the driving force behind raising the funds to buy the land and construct the buildings, and became known as the "Father of Davidson College." Morrison served as the school's president from 1837 until 1840, when illness forced him to retire.[50]

Morrison then constructed a large, old-fashioned three-story house called "Cottage Home." It was surrounded by an extensive grove of trees on a 200-acre tract in Lincoln County that Mary inherited from her father. Reverend

---

48 Ibid.

49 Laura Morrison Brown, "Historical Sketch of the Morrison Family" (Charlotte, NC, 1919), 7.

50 Ibid., 11.

Morrison seldom left his new home except to preach at the local Unity, Castamea, or Machpelah Presbyterian churches.[51]

Long before his and Eugenia's engagement, Rufus attended church where Dr. Morrison ministered. Morrison enjoyed a reputation as a fine orator and theologian. It is apparent, however, that Rufus did not enjoy the reverend's discourse. "I went to church and heard a bad sermon from Morrison," Rufus recorded in his journal. On another occasion, he wrote: "I went to the Presbyterian Church, and heard Dr. Morrison preach a long, tautological sermon."[52]

Some of the Morrison children became well known due to varied accomplishments, while others became known as a result of their marriages to prominent Civil War figures. All 12 of the Morrison children received unusually rigorous educations for their times, first at home and then in schools of higher learning. For example, the four older sisters—Harriet Abigail, Mary Anna, Isabella, and Eugenia—were educated at the Salem Female Academy at Salem, North Carolina.[53]

Harriet Abigail Morrison married James Patton Irwin, a prominent planter and merchant. Although she had no formal architectural training, she became well known for designing a hexagonal (or six-sided) house. On July 16, 1857, Mary Anna Morrison (called Anna) married Thomas Jonathan "Stonewall" Jackson, the famous future Civil War general. After the war, she authored a biography of her husband. Isabella Morrison married Daniel Harvey Hill, another future Civil War general. Thus, when Eugenia married Rufus Barringer, he became a brother-in-law to Jackson and Hill. Rufus enjoyed a close relationship with Stonewall Jackson. Rufus and Harvey Hill, however, grew to detest each other after the war, due primarily to Reconstruction politics.[54]

Daniel Harvey Hill was born in 1821 in York District, South Carolina, the youngest of 11 children of Solomon and Nancy Cabeen Hill. Hill's father died when he was only four years old, an event that plunged the family into financial crisis and his mother into despondency. In later years, Hill would hold his

51 Record of Deeds, Lincoln County, North Carolina, vol. 39.

52 Barringer, journal, August 14, 1842, and November 27, 1842.

53 Beverly Heisner, "Harriet Morrison Irwin's Hexagonal House: An Invention to Improve Domestic Dwellings," in *The North Carolina Historical Review* (April 2, 1981), vol. 58, No. 2, 106; Barringer, *The Natural Bent*, 74.

54 Heisner, "Harriet Morrison Irwin's Hexagonal House," 106.

mother's moods responsible for the dark traits he recognized within himself. "I have always had a strong perception of right and wrong," he declared, "and when corrected from petulance or passion, I brooded over it, did not forget it, and I'm afraid did not forgive it."[55]

Almost everything was "black or white" with Daniel H. Hill; there simply was no gray area in between anything. He was brilliant, a courageous soldier, and an overly pious Presbyterian—a complicated man whose relationship with Isabella, essentially an ongoing battle of wills, was at times strained during the war.[56]

In the beginning, Hill's relations with Stonewall Jackson and Rufus Barringer were cordial. By 1862, however, Hill's relationship with Stonewall and Anna Jackson changed. When Isabella suggested that he could be warmer toward the Jacksons, Hill responded: "God forgive me for all the wrong I have done. You are now distressed about my coldness to Anna and the General. Do you really think I ought to seek a social correspondence with those, who entertain so contemptible opinion of me?"[57]

Isabella or Hill—or perhaps both of them—believed Stonewall was cold and rather aloof toward them after his promotion to major general; Hill had not yet risen to that esteemed rank. However, relations seemed to return to normal once Hill made major general. Hill greatly admired Jackson's military prowess, and would in 1863 lament Jackson's death as a tragic and irreplaceable loss to the Southern Confederacy.[58]

Eugenia Morrison was described by her sister Laura as "a woman of rare beauty, and of great gentleness and purity of character." According to Laura, Eugenia was the most beautiful lady in the area. Her portrait presents a delicate oval face framed with huge black curls and large, dark eyes. She was soft spoken, shy, and humble, yet charming and feminine. She and Anna, who was two years older, became like twins. They were so devoted to one another as to be almost inseparable. Laura was a gifted artist, painting a portrait of her father

---

55 Harvey Hill to Isabella, January 26, 1862, in Hal Bridges, *Lee's Maverick General* (Lincoln, NE, 1991), 16-17.

56 Ibid.

57 Ibid., February 21, 1862, 33; Kathy Neill Herran, *They Married Confederate Officers* (Davidson, NC, 1997), 66-67.

58 Bridges, *Lee's Maverick General*, 33.

for Davidson College and a postwar portrait of Gen. Rufus Barringer in full Confederate uniform.[59]

Rufus and Eugenia were married on May 23, 1854, by Rev. P. T. Penick in the parlor of spacious "Cottage Home." The nuptials were conducted in the cool of early evening, and continued in the Morrison tradition of candlelight weddings. They were not married by Eugenia's father because he was far too emotional to conduct the service for any of his daughters. Eugenia chose her sister Anna as her maid of honor, and her younger sisters as bridesmaids. Again, continuing a family custom, Eugenia's trousseau was imported from New York, as were delectable fruits such as pineapples and bananas.[60]

"Our wedding was small," explained Rufus. "A few days afterward, we went North on a Bridal tour. At Niagara Falls, my dear wife took cholera & came near dying. The trial was a sad one but the Lord was merciful. We returned & spent the balance of the summer in the mountains of this state."[61]

In October, the couple returned to Salisbury, North Carolina, with the expectation of settling there. However, after spending just three months in town, they abandoned the idea and returned to Concord. After boarding for a year, they purchased a large lot adjacent to Victor's home and built a white clapboard house there. Rufus and Victor also built a small, three-room office building between the two houses, where they maintained their law offices.[62]

Rufus was interested in public education and institutions of higher learning, as well as industrial education. He was elected a Trustee of Davidson College in 1853, probably running for the office at the urging of Eugenia's father. Rufus served in that capacity until 1872. He was also appointed to the first Board of Trustees for the North Carolina College of Architecture and Agricultural Arts, which became North Carolina State University.[63]

Rufus and Eugenia's first child, Anna Morrison Barringer, was born in 1855, and Paul Brandon Barringer was born two years later. Family tradition

59 Laura Morrison Brown, "Historical Sketch of the Morrison Family", 27.

60 Mary Anna Jackson, *Life and Letters of "Stonewall Jackson"* (Harrisonburg, VA, 1995), 103; Herran, *They Married Confederate Officers*, 25; Barringer, *The Natural Bent*, 17; Clem D. Fishburne to Paul Brandon Barringer, April 8, 1903, Southern Historical Collection.

61 Barringer, "Commonplace Book."

62 Ibid.

63 W. A. Withers, ed., *Semi-Centennial Catalogue of Davidson College, Davidson, N.C., 1837-1887* (Raleigh, NC, 1891), 5.

Eugenia Erixene Morrison Barringer (1833-1858). Eugenia was the first wife of Rufus Barringer. She was one of three Morrison sisters to marry soon-to-be Confederate generals. *Albert and Shirley Special Collections Library, University of Virginia, Charlottesville, Virginia.*

states that Barringer was so excited about the birth of his first son that he sent a trusted servant, Bill York, on the 35-mile journey to carry the good news to the Morrisons during a record 30-inch snowfall. Both children were delivered at home with the aid of a midwife, and were later cared for by their mother and several female slaves.[64]

Rufus, who had shunned running for state or national office, was elected mayor of Concord on January 31, 1857, and re-elected on January 25, 1858. He resigned on May 1, 1858, but withdrew his resignation on the same day when his elected replacement, C. R. Cook, declined the office. Rufus served a third year until January 31, 1859, when his neighbor, Daniel Coleman, was elected. Rufus also served as County Attorney in 1860.[65]

Rufus and Eugenia spent their brief four years of their marriage happily raising their young children. Tragedy struck in June 1858, when Eugenia became ill with typhoid fever. Her mother and younger sister Laura rushed to Concord to help care for Rufus's stricken wife. He described her final days in his Commonplace Book:

> On the 9th of June, my poor wife was attacked with a slight fever. The physician . . . treated it as bilious. Other physicians were called in & it was pronounced a very slight attack of Typhoid Fever. But there was no alarm, & we were assured . . . that she would soon recover. Things then continued until Friday morning the 25th of June, when

64 Barringer, *The Natural Bent*, 3-4.

65 Eugenia Lore Files, Local History and Genealogy Room, Cannon Memorial Library.

unexpectedly to us all, she had a convulsion. We were shocked & then for the first time saw & felt her terrible condition. During the day she was quiet, but at night she had an ecstatic dream, during which she seemed to see the savior & bid her children, friends & all farewell, & added her dying benediction. During the night I asked to be left alone with her & then leaning over her bosom, I told her she would probably die. She expressed no surprise or alarm, but rather sought to comfort & quiet myself. I then asked if she felt entirely resigned & confident in the promises of Jesus. She replied with indescribable sureness, "Oh Yes!" I then inquired if she did not feel great anxiety in leaving our dear little children? She calmly replied, "Not at all—I have long since entrusted them to my savior—I know & feel that He will take care of them." This was spoken with a simplicity & faith that melted me in tears.

After some further talk, I expressed the hope & prayed the Lord might yet spare her, but asked that if He should will otherwise, I desired then to seek His parting blessing, & that if I had ever in act of will manifested to her the least unkindness, I sought her forgiveness. She embraced me with the tenderest emotion & assured me that I had "ever been to her the kindest of husbands." She then implored me to love the savior & to join her in Heaven. . . . Toward day her delirium began to return & continued until the afternoon. She then became unusually calm & ever bright & cheerful...During the night she again began to wander in the mind. . . . She then lingered until next day—Sunday the 27th of June, when her darling children were laid upon her bosom, & they & I kissed her for the last time in life; & so at 7 1/2 o'clock p.m., her spirit took its flight to the realm of bliss.[66]

Eugenia Morrison Barringer was only 25 years old when she died on June 27, 1858. She was buried in the First Presbyterian Church cemetery in Concord. After their mother's death, Paul and Anna Barringer spent most of their time at their Uncle Victor's and Aunt Maria's house in Concord. They spent holidays and summers at the Morrisons' home in Lincolnton. They also spent time with their Aunt Harriet Irwin Hill in Charlotte.[67]

In 1860, Barringer's property—including a 79-acre farm in Concord—was valued at $1,000. His total real estate holdings amounted to $8,000, and his personal estate $60,000. His total estate of $69,000 would be in excess of $1,750,000 in modern currency. He owned 13 slaves, ranging in age from 3

66 Barringer, "Commonplace Book."

67 Barringer, *The Natural Bent*, 5.

months to 44 years. All or most these slaves were given to Rufus and Eugenia by his late wife's parents.[68]

In March 1859, just 14 months after Eugenia's death, Rufus was introduced to Rosalie Augusta Chunn of Asheville. They met in a local store when as she shopped for material for a new dress. Born October 29, 1841, Rosalie was Maria Barringer's cousin and the daughter of Alfred B. and Sarah M. Chunn. Mr. Chunn was a farmer and represented Buncombe County in the House of Commons from 1846 to 1848. Rufus and Rosalie married on January 9, 1861, on the eve of the Civil War. Facing an uncertain future, many new couples wed during this period, as armed conflict loomed. Officiating in Asheville was Rev. Robert Hall Morrison, father of Rufus's deceased first wife.[69]

A week earlier, while returning to Concord from Raleigh, Rufus had been involved in a railroad accident. A train from Charlotte bound for Raleigh passed two miles beyond Queries Turn Out station, because the engineer could not get the steam turned off. A westbound train carrying Barringer collided with the cars bound for Raleigh. There were fatalities, but most passengers escaped without serious injury. Though not seriously hurt, Barringer was bruised when thrown against a door during the collision.[70]

In early1861, Rufus opposed the South's secession from the Union until President Abraham Lincoln issued a call for 75,000 volunteers to help put down the rebellion—including troops from North Carolina. Barringer soon raised a company that would join one of the finest cavalry regiments of the Confederacy.

---

68 United States Population Schedule, *1860 Census for Cabarrus County, North Carolina; Slave Schedule for 1860, Cabarrus County, North Carolina; 1860 Agricultural Schedule for Cabarrus County, North Carolina,* (Raleigh, NC, North Carolina Division of Archives and History).

69 Barringer, *The Natural Bent*, 33.

70 *Charleston Courier*, January 7, 1861.

Chapter 3

"If war came, Rufus argued, it would prove to be the 'fiercest and bloodiest of modern times' and would involve not only the continuance of slavery but also 'the entire structure of Southern society.'"

— *Rufus Barringer in early 1861*

Sectional Crisis, Slavery, and Secession: Prelude to War

With Rufus minding his brother Moreau's law practice, Victor took up the mantle of political service, assuming a leadership role in the state Senate as the storm clouds of war gathered. Rufus and William A. Graham, a former governor and 1852 Whig vice presidential candidate, were Unionists who opposed secession of the Southern states. The Barringer family served in positions of influence and helped shape North Carolina's prewar stance as the secession debate commenced. The breakup of the Union was averted until President Lincoln's call for Southern troops to help put down the rebellion. This experience helped Rufus mature into a man seasoned in the knowledge of politics and prepared him for a command role in the forthcoming war.

A New State Constitution

After North Carolina's prolonged period of "Rip-Van-Winkleism," demand for constitutional reform threatened to split the state's counties into eastern and western factions. In 1834, a group of diverse factions—all opposed to President Andrew Jackson's policies—had formed the Whig Party. Lacking unity except for common antagonism toward Jackson, the new party comprised proponents and opponents of protective tariffs, federal aid to state projects, the right of states to nullify unpopular federal laws, and national banks. The following year, the Whig Party was established in North Carolina and elected seven of the state's 13 congressmen. It also won a fairly large minority in the General Assembly. The formation of the North Carolina Whigs hampered the eastern conservative elite plantation holders' ability to dominate the state's role in local and national politics.[1]

Until 1835 the counties east of Raleigh, by virtue of their number, held the balance of power in the legislature, while those to the west had greater resources and grew more rapidly in population. The western counties, under the leadership of Governor David Lowry Swain and Senator Willie P. Mangum, put the issue of reform to the people in a referendum. In accordance with an 1834 popular sectional vote, a constitutional convention met at Raleigh in 1835. Governor Swain, from western Buncombe County, chaired the convention. Moreau Barringer was a delegate from Cabarrus County. Through a series of amendments, representation in the House of Commons was apportioned among counties according to their population (meaning the white population plus three-fifths of the slave population) and in the Senate according to the amount of taxes the districts paid. The General Assembly lost much of its power by establishing biennial instead of annual sessions and by granting election of the governor to the people.[2]

After vigorous debate, the North Carolina convention narrowly approved a constitutional provision (67 to 42) denying all African Americans the right to vote. The provision was decided strongly along sectional lines. Seventeen of the 25 counties whose delegates voted against disfranchisement of blacks lay in the piedmont and mountain regions of the state, while 19 of the 26 counties whose delegates voted entirely in favor of disfranchisement lay in the heavily slaveholding eastern region. Therefore, in 1835 the last vestiges of political rights for African Americans disappeared from all parts of the future Confederacy.[3]

1 Boyd, *North Carolina on the Eve of Secession*, 169; Fred J. Vatter, "Whigs Restored Two Party Rule to Chatham and North Carolina," in *Chatham County Line* (Fall 2004).

2 Boyd, *North Carolina on the Eve of Secession*, 167.

3 Ford, Lacy K. Jr., "Making the 'White Man's Country' White: Race, Slavery, and State-Building in the Jacksonian South," in *Journal of the Early Republic* (Winter 1999), vol. 19, Issue 4, 734.

These constitutional reforms were ratified by a sectional vote, with all western counties giving a majority for the revised constitution and the eastern counties (except Granville) voting against it. Long after these reforms in representation were made, the sectional feuding continued and remained a potent influence in politics.[4]

Unlike the Deep South, the slave system never developed extensively in North Carolina, except in a group of middle and eastern counties. In1860, less than 28 percent of North Carolina families owned slaves, and the average number of slaves held per household was 9.6. In strong contrast to the planter class were the non-slaveholders. Aside from yeoman farmers, their industries included two classes of manufacturing—factories in which North Carolina ranked next to Virginia and Georgia, and domestic arts and hand trades such as blacksmithing, tannery, shopkeepers, and other artisans. The latter industries were important because they afforded each plantation or community a large degree of economic self-sufficiency.[5]

Economically, western North Carolinians were far removed from the planter class of the coastal plain. The loamy soil and terrain in the west prohibited them from concentrating on single-crop production ("King Cotton"). The once dominant staple of tobacco, whose success had sustained demand for slave labor, fell into comparative decline. Alternative cash crops emerged, including grains such as wheat and oats, which required substantially less labor than tobacco (except during harvest). With sharp peaks and valleys in the demand for labor, grain cultivation rendered slavery—with its high fixed costs for labor—inefficient and financially prohibitive. Thus, while some areas within the Upper South remained heavily dependent on the institution, the future prospects for the region's slave-labor economy appeared to be declining.[6]

In contrast to the Southern cotton states, the "Whig Party of North Carolina was most popular in the counties where slavery and its industries did not predominate; these included the western part of the State, a portion of the central region, and the marshy swamp country along the coast." The reason for

4   Hamilton, *Party Politics in North Carolina*, 14.

5   Boyd, *North Carolina on the Eve of Secession*, 168.

6   Ibid., 717; Boyd, *North Carolina on the Eve of Secession*, 167-168; Ford, "Making the 'White Man's Country' White," 717.

this popularity was the "Whig program of progress; these sections needed internal improvements which could only be accomplished through State aid."[7]

Whig Ascendency to Power

The 15 years between 1835 and 1850 marked the period of Whig ascendency to power. In national politics, able leaders like William A. Graham, Willie P. Mangum, and George E. Badger kept North Carolina loyal to the party. While their efforts brought to the state a sentiment which later opposed secession, the party's true power came from its identification with the cause of domestic progress. Three notable achievements were made under Whig leadership in the areas of education, internal improvements, and humanitarian efforts. Chief among these was the inauguration of a public school system.[8]

Public Education

In 1825, the General Assembly provided a literary fund for educational purposes. By 1838, this amounted to $1,732,485. After a few appropriations had been made, a revised school law was enacted in 1840 that distributed income among the counties according to Federal census population, and empowered the county courts to supplement it with a local tax. There were many difficulties. The county taxes were not mandatory and many failed to give local support. Schools were not established in all counties until 1846, and there was no attempt at organized educational administration until 1852, when Calvin H. Wiley was appointed Superintendent of Common Schools. In 1860, on the eve of the Civil War, more than $255,000 was spent for public education. Schools were kept open throughout the war and the literary fund was kept a sacred trust. However, with the failure of banks and financial collapse after the war, the literary fund was lost. Between 1840 and 1860, the number of male colleges increased from three to six. Foremost among them—aside from the long-established University of North Carolina—were Davidson, Wake Forest, and Trinity. The number of female colleges also increased from one to 13.[9]

7   Boyd, *North Carolina on the Eve of Secession*, 170.

8   R. D. W. Connor, *Ante-Bellum Builders of North Carolina* (Greensboro, NC, 1914), 122-136.

9   Julian Alvin Carrol Chandler, *The South in the Building of the Nation: The History of the Southern States*, 12 vols. (Richmond, VA, 1909), vol. 6, 476.

Internal Improvements

Whig leaders adopted a more liberal policy toward internal improvements. Better transportation infrastructure was necessary, but the failure of earlier corporations and the state's investment in them aroused opposition to further state aid. A new period opened with the completion of the Wilmington & Weldon and Raleigh & Gaston Railroads in 1840, both lines benefitting from liberal state aid. The western counties were unsupplied. In 1845, a crop failure created famine while corn rotted in the fields of eastern counties. Whig leaders, principally William A. Graham, John M. Morehead and William S. Ashe, urged the building of a road from the coast to the mountains. However, Democrats and the eastern counties resisted.[10]

Meanwhile, on October 16, 1859, religious zealot John Brown and 18 of his followers attempted to seize the federal arsenal at Harpers Ferry, Virginia, in hopes of instigating a slave revolt. The enterprise failed, but the Northern press's reaction to the stated goal of the raid, and the subsequent martyrdom of Brown following his execution on December 2, led many Southerners to believe the federal government might not protect them in the event of a slave rebellion. Terrified by such a prospect, many Southern states increased their militias the following year.[11]

The rising tide of secession and proslavery sentiment met strong opposition. In 1858, John W. Ellis, a "states' rights" Democrat, received his party's nomination for governor. In the contest for the nomination, Ellis defeated William Woods Holden, a man of the people who had little in common with the more aristocratic leaders of his party. In the general election, Ellis was opposed by Duncan K. McRae, an independent who sought to turn the people's minds from slavery to economic development and education. Though Ellis was victorious, McRae received a large number of votes. Holden, disappointed by Ellis's nomination and his own subsequent defeat for reelection to the United States Senate, drifted from the radicals to conservatism.[12]

---

10 Ibid.

11 Rev. Samuel Vanderlip Leech, *The Raid of John Brown at Harper's Ferry as I Saw It* (Washington, DC, 1909), 4, 17.

12 William C. Harris, *William Woods Holden: Firebrand of North Carolina Politics* (Baton Rouge, LA, 1987), 68-81.

By 1860, opposition to slavery and secession was even stronger. The Whig Party, temporarily revived, nominated John Pool for governor. At its convention, the party ridiculed secession and advocated an *ad valorem* slave tax on merchandise imported from the non-slaveholding states to offset agitation over the Fugitive Slave Act (which resulted from the Compromise of 1850). The Whigs hoped this would divert attention from slavery questions during the election. The Democrats re-nominated Ellis and incorporated a strong "states' rights" clause in their platform. During the campaign, Ellis—himself a member of the planter class—tried in vain to arouse the people on the national question of slavery. He resisted the *ad valorem* tax and narrowly won reelection. However, the Democratic majority was reduced to 10,000 less than it held in 1858, though the vote was the largest ever polled in the state. Clearly, conservative North Carolinians hesitated to endorse radical views regarding slavery and secession.[13]

While the "fire-eaters" of South Carolina and other Deep South states led the secession movement of 1860-1861, North Carolinians, for the most part, still favored remaining in the Union. North Carolina soil was not as conducive to growing cotton and there were fewer large slaveholding plantations. In 1860, about one-third of North Carolina's population of 992,622 were enslaved African Americans, a smaller proportion than many Southern states. Moreover, the state had more than 30,000 free blacks. Citizens of the mountain region of western North Carolina, East Tennessee, eastern Kentucky, western South Carolina, and western Virginia were predominately non-slaveholders and saw no reason to support an institution in which they had little interest. Statewide, 77 percent of North Carolina's slaveholding families had fewer than 10 slaves in 1860, and 72 percent of North Carolina's families had no slaves at all. Among members of the power-wielding General Assembly, however, 85 percent were slaveholders.[14]

In the decades preceding the Civil War, anti-slavery sentiment and societies originated in the mountainous regions of Appalachia among the Germans, Scotch-Irish, and Quakers. From these, three groups of anti-slavery advocates emerged. The American Colonization Society wanted to rid America of blacks and send them back to Africa or to a Caribbean colony. The emancipationists

---

13 Ibid., 480; Boyd, *North Carolina on the Eve of Secession*, 165-177.

14 John Hope Franklin, *The Free Negro in the Economic Life of Antebellum North Carolina* (Chapel Hill, NC, 1995), 359; Paul D. Escort, *Many Excellent People: Power and Privilege in North Carolina, 1850-1900* (Chapel Hill, NC,1985), 15.

wanted the gradual elimination of slavery, while the abolitionists wanted an immediate end to the institution. Thus, sentiment for supporting any secessionist movement was far from unanimous in these border regions. Influential non-slaveholding white citizens had strong Unionist sentiments, and would have to be grudgingly convinced for any secessionist movement within the state to succeed.[15]

The 1860 Election

During the 1860 presidential campaign, William Woods Holden, editor of the *Raleigh Standard* and future governor of the state, editorialized for Unionism and a "wait and see" attitude. He was particularly wary of Governor Ellis, whom he saw as a political enemy. Stricken with a serious bout of neuralgia in the summer of 1860, Holden asked Rufus Barringer's older brother and prominent Democrat, Moreau, to write an editorial about the political situation. Moreau was a former North Carolina legislator and former United States Congressman. He had served as Ambassador to Spain from 1850 to 1853, and upon returning to North Carolina in 1854 had served one term in the House of Delegates before declining to seek reelection. Why Holden chose Barringer, an intimate confidant of Ellis, is unclear. Perhaps it was because Moreau was an influential Democrat who, at that time, still hoped secession could be avoided. Regardless of the reason, Moreau accepted the task and his editorial, "The Crisis," appeared in the September 12 issue of the *Standard*. Barringer went much further in supporting Southern "states' rights" than Holden would have preferred. Barringer even suggested that if Abraham Lincoln was elected president, separation from the Union was inevitable. Holden was stunned by Moreau's editorial. When he returned to Raleigh, Holden tried hard to undo the damage to the Unionists' position and to stem the rising tide of secession.[16]

The presidential election of 1860 set the stage for the Civil War. The nation had been divided throughout most of the 1850s on questions of states' rights and slavery. In 1860, these issues finally came to a head, fracturing the formerly dominant Democratic Party into Southern and Northern factions. Abraham

---

15 John C. Inscoe, *Appalachians and Race: The Mountain South from Slavery to Segregation* (Lexington, KY, 2005), 21; Guion G. Johnson, *Ante-Bellum North Carolina*, (Chapel Hill, NC, 1937), 469.

16 *Southern Historical Society Papers*, vol. 24, 6; *Raleigh Standard*, March 20, 1861.

Lincoln and the new anti-slavery Republican Party rose to power without support from a single Southern state.[17]

Lincoln's election gave new life to the secession movement. Public meetings were held throughout the state to discuss the question of separating from the Union. When the General Assembly met in November 1860, resolutions asserting and denying the right of secession were introduced, but neither was adopted. The secessionists demanded the call of a state convention to consider federal relations. The people's conservatism, however, was greater than their leaders', and the call for such a convention went unheeded. The secessionists' efforts did not abate, however, and the trend of events would soon favor them.[18]

During the heated campaign of 1860, Rufus Barringer was a presidential elector who made an earnest canvass on behalf of the two Constitutional Union Party candidates—John T. Bell of Tennessee for president and Edward Everett of Massachusetts for vice president. Bell and Everett were supported by the old line Whigs, whose party was disintegrating. The question of secession soon became the paramount issue of the campaign. There were violent disagreements throughout North Carolina and among members of the General Assembly in Raleigh. North Carolina would be the next to last state to enter the Confederacy, due largely to the views of its leaders and influential public figures such as William A. Graham and Rufus Barringer. The old line Whigs opposed the war, while Democrats like Moreau Barringer, along with his brother Victor, a Whig, supported secession.[19]

States in the Deep South, particularly South Carolina, had already begun talk of secession if the country elected Abraham Lincoln—the "Black Republican." On November 6, 1860, telegraphs and newspapers around the country quickly spread word that Lincoln had indeed been elected President of the United States. This news frightened almost everyone in the South, and many North Carolinians became concerned, alarmed, and dismayed. Some leading newspapers in the Tar Heel State were more optimistic, urging calm and time to give the new president a chance. Lincoln's election was enough to trigger

17 J. G. De Roulhac Hamilton, *Reconstruction in North Carolina* (Gloucester, MA, 1964), 95.

18 Escott, *Many Excellent People*, 34; John G. Barrett, *The Civil War in North Carolina* (Chapel Hill, NC, 1963), 4.

19 Samuel A. Ashe, *Cyclopedia of Eminent and Representative Men of the Carolinas of the Nineteenth Century*, 2 vols. (Madison, WI, 1892), vol. 2, 624.

secession of the Deep South states, but North Carolinians, in general, did not believe this single event was sufficient grounds for breaking up the Union. Elder statesmen, including former Governor William A. Graham, urged moderation and a "wait and see" attitude. These leaders and many citizens, especially those of the western mountain counties, wanted to see what course of action Lincoln would take. However, many North Carolinians would flock to the cause of secession if Lincoln tried to coerce the Southern states.[20]

After Lincoln's election Graham, who was approached unofficially about a post in the new cabinet, counseled patience. He urged North Carolinians to rely on the Constitution as a sufficient guarantor of their rights, advising that there would be time enough to seek proper remedies after any overt, illegal action by the national government.

North Carolina Governor John W. Ellis was not surprised by the cautious approach to secession. When the General Assembly met in Raleigh on November 19, 1860, Ellis's address to the legislature was anxiously awaited, as it would outline the state's policies during the crisis.[21]

Rufus Barringer's younger brother Victor was a leading member of the State Senate in 1860, having lost election as President of the Senate to Henry T. Clark of Edgecombe County (by a vote of 28 to 16). Though a Whig, Victor was a strong secessionist. Rufus, in the meantime, was in Concord serving as mayor, attending to his and Victor's law practices, and searching for a wife to help raise his two small children. Opposing the views of his two closest brothers, Rufus was a strong Unionist.[22]

Governor Ellis's address to the General Assembly favored the radical secessionists who desired immediate action by North Carolina. Those who opposed Ellis were called "conservatives" or "Unionists." Ellis did not openly advocate secession, but wanted to call a conference with "those states identified with us in interest and in the wrongs we have suffered; and especially those lying immediately adjacent to us." Following the conference, Ellis recommended a convention of the state be called and the militia thoroughly reorganized.[23]

20 David M. Potter, *The Impending Crisis, 1848-1861* (New York, 1976), 488-489.

21 Barrett, *The Civil War in North Carolina*, 4.

22 John Wheeler Moore, *History of North Carolina From Earliest Discoveries to the Present*, 2 vols. (Raleigh, NC, 1880), vol. 2, 143.

23 Speech of Hon. John W. Ellis, Delivered before the Democratic State Convention, Raleigh, NC, March 9, 1860.

Ellis's message was welcomed enthusiastically by radicals and condemned by Unionists, but both sides agreed on the principle of military preparedness. The General Assembly passed a $300,000 appropriation for the purchase of arms and ammunition, and a military commission was established to help the governor administer the funds. Debate heated up throughout the state on the heels of the legislative session. Secessionist sentiment grew rapidly, and secession meetings had already been held in Cleveland County and in Wilmington.

Radical speakers flocked to all parts of the state, urging a convention to consider secession. Meanwhile, South Carolina withdrew from the Union on December 20, 1860. South Carolina's action was received with joy by the radicals and condemned by conservatives, especially those from the mountainous western counties. Most North Carolinians were still of the "wait and see" attitude.[24]

Most North Carolinians did not support secession simply because of Lincoln's election, but were united in opposing the use of force to compel any seceded state back into the Union. One contemporary expressed the feeling of many when he wrote: "I am a Union man but when they send men South it will change my notions. I can do nothing against my own people." This stance would be prevail throughout the border states, and only Lincoln's call for Southern troops to put down the rebellion in April 1861 would tip the scales in favor of immediate secession.[25]

At the time Rufus Barringer married Rosalie Chunn in Asheville, the legislature returned on January 7. By January 19, 1861, four more states had seceded from the Union. These developments put intense pressure on the General Assembly to call a convention.[26]

On January 30, 1861, through the strenuous efforts of Judge S. J. Person, W. W. Avery, Victor C. Barringer, and others the General Assembly, passed an act to call a convention to consider the issue of secession. An election to determine whether North Carolina's citizens approved of the proposed

24 Hamilton, *Party Politics in North Carolina*, 17.

25 Barrett, *The Civil War in North Carolina*, 6; R. G. Gurthy to Z. B. Vance, January 16, 1861, Zebulon B. Vance Papers, North Carolina Office of Archives and History.

26 Barrett, *The Civil War in North Carolina*, 8-9.

convention was to be held on February 28. Delegates for the proposed convention, if it was held, would also be chosen via the election.[27]

The March 20 issue of Holden's *Standard* reported the official vote as 467 delegates against a convention. With the addition of 194 votes from Davie County, which arrived too late to be included in the official returns, there was a majority of 661 votes against a convention. Holden also estimated that 93,000 popular votes were cast, 60,000 of which were pro-Union.[28]

In February 1861, with the Confederacy a reality, William A. Graham led Union men in defeating a statewide referendum to call a convention to consider disunion. However, after the firing on Fort Sumter and Lincoln's call for troops, Graham accepted the inevitable, declaring that "blood was thicker than water." Although he abhorred secession, he was overwhelmingly elected to represent Orange County in the Constitutional Convention of May 1861. In opposition to the original secessionists, now in the ascendancy, Graham stood unsuccessfully for the convention presidency and supported an abortive resolution upholding the right of revolution as the appropriate response to perceived tyranny. Only when there seemed no honorable alternative did Graham cast his vote for secession.[29]

Having done his best to prevent the breakup, Graham supported the Confederate cause to the extent his principles allowed. With others, he negotiated the terms by which North Carolina would enter the Confederate States of America, and remained an active participant in the deliberations of the convention. The war troubled Graham and many other Southern Unionists. On the one hand, five of his sons served as Confederate officers, and innumerable relatives and friends were involved militarily. Three of his Morrison nieces were married to future Confederate generals, including Rufus Barringer. Their commitments had to be adequately sustained by his political and economic efforts. On the other hand, the rights of the states and citizens had to be protected against the encroachments of a government at war. Herein lay the conundrum: how could a new nation predicated on state sovereignty command the unity necessary to win the war? Graham became a champion of personal

---

27 Hamilton, *Reconstruction in North Carolina*, 16-17; *Southern Historical Society Papers*, vol. 24, 6.

28 *Southern Historical Society Papers*, vol. 24, 6; *Raleigh Standard*, March 20, 1861.

29 William A. Graham, convention speech on the Ordinance concerning Test Oaths and Sedition, Raleigh, N.C., December 7, 1861 (Raleigh, NC, 1862); Hamilton, *Reconstruction in North Carolina*, 30.

liberties, constitutional government, and states' rights. As such, he was a frequent critic of Confederate President Jefferson Davis's administration. Graham sometimes found himself in strange company. He was allied with old line Whigs, American Party members, former "states' rights" Southern Democrats, and perhaps most surprisingly with erstwhile adversary William W. Holden.[30]

Meanwhile, in December 1860, the final session of the 36th Congress of the United States had met. In the House of Representatives, the "Committee of Thirty-Three," composed of one member from each state led by Ohio Republican Thomas Corwin, was formed to reach a compromise to preserve the Union. In the Senate, former Kentucky Whig John J. Crittenden, elected as a Unionist candidate, submitted six proposed constitutional amendments that he hoped would address all outstanding issues. Hopes were high, especially in the Border States, that the lame-duck Congress could reach a successful resolution before the new Republican administration took office.[31]

A fourth avenue toward compromise came from the state of Virginia. Former president John Tyler—now a private citizen but still interested in the fate of the nation—had been appointed as a special Virginia envoy to President James Buchanan. Tyler urged Buchanan to maintain the status quo in regard to the seceded states. Later, Tyler was an elected delegate to the Virginia convention called to consider whether to follow the Deep South states out of the Union. Tyler believed that one final collective effort should be made to preserve the Union. In a document published on January 17, 1861, he called for a convention of six free and six slave states to resolve the sectional split. Governor John Letcher of Virginia had already made a similar request to the state legislature, which acted by agreeing to sponsor the convention while expanding the list of attendees to all of the states. Thomas Corwin agreed to hold off any final vote on his House plan pending the final actions of the Peace Conference.[32]

The Peace Conference convened on February 4, 1861, at the Willard Hotel in Washington. Meanwhile, the seven Deep South states that had already passed ordinances of secession prepared to form a new government in Montgomery,

30 Powell, *Dictionary of North Carolina Biography*, vol. 2, 169-171.

31 Potter, *The Impending Crisis, 1848-1861*, 530-533.

32 Ibid., 545-546.

Alabama. As John Tyler, selected to head the Peace Convention, made his opening remarks in Washington, his granddaughter ceremonially hoisted the flag for the convention in Montgomery. Fourteen free and seven slave states attended the conference. However, the Deep South states were not represented, nor were Arkansas, Michigan, Wisconsin, Minnesota, California, and Oregon. North Carolina's representatives were Moreau Barringer, George Davis, Thomas Ruffin, and John M. Morehead. Many of the delegates attended in the honest belief that they could be successful. Many others, from both sides of the spectrum, showed up to act as "watchdogs" for their sectional interests. The 131 delegates included six former Federal cabinet members, 19 former governors, 14 former senators, 50 former representatives, 12 state Supreme Court justices, and one former president. Many delegates qualified as "senior statesmen," and the meeting was derisively referred to as the "Old Gentleman's Convention."[33]

On February 6, 1861, a separate subcommittee was formed to draft a proposal for the entire convention to consider. Headed by James Guthrie, the committee consisted of one representative from each state. The entire convention met for three weeks, and its final product was a proposed seven-point constitutional amendment that differed little from the Crittenden Compromise. The key issue, expansion of slavery into the Territories, was addressed simply by extending the Missouri Compromise line to the Pacific Coast, with no provision for newly acquired territory. This section narrowly passed by a vote of 9 to 8.[34]

The proposed constitutional amendment also required that the acquisition of all future territories had to be approved by a majority of both free and slave states. Other features included prohibiting Congress from passing any legislation that would affect the status of slavery where it currently existed, prohibiting state legislatures from passing laws that would restrict the ability of officials to apprehend and return fugitive slaves, a permanent prohibition on the foreign slave trade, and 100 percent compensation to any slave owner whose fugitive slave was freed by illegal mob action or because of intimidation of officials required to administer the Fugitive Slave Act. Key sections of this

---

33 Ibid., 546; Robert Gray Gunderson, *Old Gentlemen's Convention: The Washington Peace Conference of 1861* (Madison, OH, 1961), 547.

34 Potter, *The Impending Crisis*, 547.

amendment could be further amended only with the concurrence of all of the states.[35]

In failing to limit the expansion of slavery into all new Territories, the compromise failed to satisfy hardline Republicans. In failing to protect slavery up to the point where a Territory drafted a state constitution for the approval of Congress, the compromise failed to address the issue that had divided the Democratic Party into Northern and Southern factions in the 1860 presidential election. The convention's work was completed with only a few days left in the final session of Congress. The proposal was rejected in the Senate by a vote of 28 to 7, and never came to a vote in the House. A less all-encompassing constitutional amendment submitted by the Committee of Thirty-Three was passed by Congress, but it simply provided protection for slavery where it currently existed—something that Lincoln and most members of both parties already believed was a state right protected by the existing Constitution.[36]

With the adjournment of Congress and the inauguration of Lincoln as president, the only avenue for compromise involved informal negotiations between Unionist Southerners and representatives of the incoming Republican government. Congress was no longer a factor. A final convention of strictly slave states still in the Union scheduled for June 1861 never occurred because of the events at Fort Sumter. With the failure of the Washington Peace Conference, the secessionist movement gained momentum, and many feared war was inevitable.

Secession

Rufus Barringer's growing law practice had claimed his undivided attention until the campaign of 1860 drew him once again into active politics. The Dred Scott decision, bloody fighting between sectional partisans in Kansas, and John Brown's raid on Harpers Ferry had greatly widened the gulf between the free and slave states. Rufus clearly saw the consequences of the secession movement in which the Southern states were engaged. He took a strong stand against leaving the Union, urging that secession would surely be accompanied by war. If war came, he argued, it would prove to be the "fiercest and bloodiest of

---

35 Hamilton, *Reconstruction in North Carolina*, 18-19.

36 Potter, *The Impending Crisis*, 550-51.

modern times" and would involve not only the question of continued slavery but also "the entire structure of Southern society."[37]

Before North Carolina's secession ordinance was passed, Rufus advocated immediate preparation for a war he had come to see as inevitable. After Lincoln's call for troops, the contending pro-and anti-secessionist factions in North Carolina realized the state would be dragged into the fight. Lincoln's call for North Carolinians to help put down the rebellion resulted in differences converging into almost unanimous support on the side of the Confederacy. Before hostilities erupted at Fort Sumter, Rufus had urged the legislature to arm the state and had warned the people that they must prepare to fight. He believed the only hope of success lay in aggressive action and that delay meant destruction. He did not want war, but once he realized it was coming and that North Carolina was going to secede from the Union, he came down on the side of his state.[38]

Although a call for a convention to consider secession had been rejected by North Carolina voters in February, events occurred rapidly to cause all to reconsider the question. The failure of the Peace Convention was followed in rapid succession by the firing on Fort Sumter, the call of President Lincoln for troops, and the secession of Virginia. The issue was not whether the state would secede, but whether the people would fight on the side of their neighbors and kindred of the South. On that issue, there would be no division or hesitation.[39]

The legislature, called to a special session by Governor Ellis, met on May 1. In just two hours after assembling, it ordered another referendum for May 13 on the question of calling a convention to assemble, if approved, on May 20. The convention was voted and passed by a large majority. The convention delegates unanimously voted to repeal the act of November 1789 by which North Carolina had acceded to the federal Union, and declared the state to be no longer one of the United States. A subsequent resolution declared the accession of the state to the Confederacy, by whose congress it was accepted as a member one week later on May 27. The state did not vote to join the

---

37 Rufus Barringer, "To the People Of Mecklenburg County," July 24, 1872, Broadsides Collection, Duke University, Durham, NC. Broadsides were political or business announcements, printed on one side, and circulated by the author. Newspapers would sometimes republish them; *Richmond Dispatch*, Friday, May 10, 1861.

38 Ibid.

39 Charles C. Bolton, *Poor Whites of the Antebellum South: Tenants and Laborers in Central North Carolina and Northeast Mississippi* (Durham, NC, 2003), 143-144.

Confederacy until President Lincoln called on it to invade its sister state, South Carolina. Even before the final act of secession was passed, North Carolinians had begun volunteering for military service. Rufus Barringer was among them, organizing a cavalry company from Cabarrus County.[40]

At the convention which assembled at Raleigh on May 20, there were two distinct factions—one dominated by the principles of the old Whig party, and the other representing the opinions of the Democrats. In the preliminary test of strength the latter element proved supreme, with Weldon N. Edwards being chosen president over William A. Graham. Two sets of resolutions concerning the method by which North Carolina would withdraw from the Union were then offered. George E. Badger recommended separation by means of revolution, without mentioning secession in its applied meaning. The other resolution, framed by Judah P. Benjamin and introduced by Burton Craige, based on the idea of constitutional secession, abrogated and rescinded the ordinance of the convention by which North Carolina had ratified the constitution of the United States in 1789. Badger's resolutions were rejected, and after a test vote those of Mr. Craige were unanimously adopted. The Whigs and Conservatives sacrificed their political convictions in the interest of a greater cause. Thus on May 20, 1861, North Carolina left the Union.[41]

Preparing for War

Even before the convention met, the state began preparing for a war that had become inevitable. On April 15, Governor Ellis had replied to the call of United States authorities for two regiments: "You can get no troops from North Carolina." While he waited for the legislature to convene in Raleigh on May 1, Ellis ordered state troops to seize the coastal forts, the United States arsenal at Fayetteville, and the Federal Mint at Charlotte on April 16. He also called for volunteers and formed a camp of instruction at Raleigh under Rufus's brother-in-law, Col. D. H. Hill, to train new troops.[42]

The legislature, without waiting for the assembling of the convention, directed the governor to enroll 20,000 volunteers for 12 months and 10,000

---

40 Barrett, *The Civil War in North Carolina*, 14-16; *Carolina Flag*, June 11, 18, 1861.

41 Hamilton, *Reconstruction in North Carolina*, 26-32.

42 Barrett, *The Civil War in North Carolina*, 10; *OR*, vol. 1, 486.

state troops for the war, the former to elect their own officers. The officers of the state troops were appointed by the governor. The legislature also allocated $5,000,000 for the public defense and authorized the governor to send troops to Virginia to aid in the defense of that state. The 1st North Carolina, later known as the "Bethel Regiment," speedily organized with Hill as its colonel and proceeded to Virginia. Three companies arrived at Richmond on May 18, followed by the remaining seven companies on May 21. On June 10, the regiment participated in the war's first battle at Bethel, Virginia. As Virginia did not secede until May 17, and her troops were not turned over to the Confederacy until June 7, the North Carolina soldiers were initially in Virginia simply as allies.[43]

James G. Martin, an old army officer who had served in Mexico and lost an arm at Cherubusco, was appointed adjutant-general by the state. He pressed the organization of the troops and the collection of arms and war materiel with zeal and intelligence. In seven months, the state raised and equipped 40,000 troops and turned over their control to the Confederacy. By May 1862, the state had nearly 60,000 men under arms. North Carolina would ultimately field some 125,000 troops for the war effort, the largest number furnished by any single state in the entire Confederacy. Of these, more than 33,000 would be killed or die of disease.[44]

The most serious difficulty at first was the want of arms and materiel. When it seized the United States arsenal at Fayetteville, the state found 30,000 muskets, most of them in poor condition, and a large proportion flint and steel. These were converted into percussion muskets as rapidly as the scarcity of workmen permitted. Also found in the arsenal were six cannons and a large quantity of gunpowder. Four more cannons came from the military schools of Col. Charles C. Tew at Hillsboro and D. H. Hill at Charlotte. With such antiquated equipment North Carolina entered into one of the greatest wars in history. As fast as workmen could be found or educated, factories were established for the manufacture of swords, bayonets, muskets, percussion caps, gunpowder, cartridges and cartridge boxes, belts, clothing, caps and shoes, and other supplies for the army. With such a large number of volunteers, some regiments were sent to Virginia partly armed with shotguns and "buck and ball"

---

43 Barrett, *The Civil War in North Carolina*, 15, 22, 30.

44 Walter Clark, ed. *Histories of the Several Regiments and Battalions from North Carolina in the Great War, 1861-1865*, 5 vols. (Goldsboro, NC, 1901), vol. 5, xii.

ammunition—and some were unarmed altogether. Artillery companies were hurried to the front without cannons or horses. The deficiency was soon relieved by battlefield captures at Manassas and other victories, supplemented by arms and ammunition made in the state and Confederate armories. Much needed imports also arrived through the port of Wilmington.[45]

A clothing factory for the troops was established at Raleigh, and all the cloth product of the state's cotton mills was appropriated. Many blankets, quilts, comforters, and carpets were contributed by patriotic women. The carpets, cut up and lined, served fairly well for blankets. Additional captures from enemy stores were indispensable in making up deficiencies in clothing, arms, and equipment.[46]

The quartermaster and commissary departments were organized efficiently and well officered. The state bought the steamer *Ad-Vance*, which under Capt. Thomas M. Crossen ran the Union blockade 12 times. Such vessels brought in goods, arms, and ammunition from overseas through neutral ports in Bermuda, the Bahamas, and Canada. North Carolina troops were not only the best clothed and equipped, but the state often contributed to the Confederacy from its eventual surplus of arms and stores. The state bought up 100,000 barrels of resin and 11,000 bales of cotton, which it shipped out to be exchanged for whatever it most needed. Among the stores brought in by the *Ad-Vance* and other blockade-runners were 250,000 pairs of shoes, 250,000 uniforms, 50,000 blankets, 12,000 overcoats, 60,000 pairs of cotton cards, 5,000 sacks of coffee for the hospitals, medicines, machinery, arms, ammunition, and other supplies. Up to March 1864, North Carolina had received $6,000,000 from the Confederacy for the supply of such articles, in excess of its own needs, which it had turned over, besides stores of great value furnished to the Confederate government without charge.

Aside from clothing its own troops, North Carolina, in the winter after the September 1863 battle of Chickamauga, sent 14,000 uniforms to Lt. Gen. James Longstreet's corps then serving in the Western army. Dr. Thomas D. Hogg, head of the state commissary department, reported to Governor Zebulon B. Vance during the last months of the war that he had fed half of Gen. Robert E.

---

45 Walter E. Clark, "North Carolina in the Confederacy," in *The Southern States of America* (Richmond, VA, 1909), vol. 1, Chapter 4, 2-3.

46 Barrett, *The Civil War in North Carolina*, 28.

Lee's army, doing so in part with provisions brought through the blockade, especially bacon.[47]

Even after secession, some North Carolinians still refused to support the Confederacy. This was particularly true of non-slave-owning farmers in the state's mountains and western piedmont region. Some of these farmers remained neutral during the war, while some covertly supported the Union cause. Approximately 2,000 North Carolinians enlisted in the Union army and fought for the North during the war. Two regiments of mounted infantry served the Union in the western part of the state and in East Tennessee. Two additional Union regiments were raised in coastal areas of the state that were occupied by Union forces in 1862 and 1863. Black North Carolinians served the Union in three infantry regiments and one artillery regiment (which also fought outside its borders) raised in the state. Confederate troops from all parts of North Carolina served in virtually every major battle of the Army of Northern Virginia, the Confederacy's most famous fighting force.[48]

47 Zebulon B. Vance, "North Carolina's Record, 1861-1865," White Sulphur Springs, Va., Aug. 18, 1875, in Clark, *Histories*, vol. 4, 463-481.

48 John C. Inscoe, *Mountain Masters: Slavery and the Sectional Crisis in Western North Carolina* (Knoxville, TN, 1989), 228-235.

Chapter 4

"If the North ventures to invade our soil, it will be with an army of five hundred thousand men. If they come at all, they will come to exterminate. We must prepare to meet them on the threshold!"

— *Captain Rufus Barringer at Concord ceremony honoring Company F, "Cabarrus Rangers."*

Rufus Barringer: North Carolina Cavalry Officer

Rufus Barringer's wide and varied life experiences helped prepare him for the long and bloody civil war that was no upon the nation. His natural horsemanship, organizational skills, and the logical thinking of a trained lawyer aided him in raising a company and serving as its captain as part of one the finest cavalry regiments of the war—the 1st North Carolina Cavalry. Although he had no formal military training, he would serve under stern West Pointer Col. Robert Ransom, learning discipline and cavalry tactics that would help prepare him to lead men in battle. These organizational and tactical skills, along with bravery and discipline, would in due course lead to regimental and brigade command.

In the wake of North Carolina's secession from the Union on May 20, 1861, thousands of Tar Heels rushed to join the Provisional Army of the Confederate States of America. By August 1862, 64,636 volunteers from the state had enlisted in the cause of Southern independence. Within two years, an additional 21,608 men would join their ranks. These men, along with 21,343 conscripts after the passage of the Conscript Act of April 1862, were assigned to 80 regiments, 20 battalions, and 15 independent companies that were formed in North Carolina. About one-sixth of all the troops who fought for the Confederacy hailed from the state.[1]

Formation of the North Carolina Cavalry Units

As each North Carolina infantry, cavalry, and artillery regiment formed it was numbered in the approximate order in which it was raised. Cavalry and artillery regiments were also numbered by branch of service. Following these numerical designations, each cavalry regiment was given a second designation by order of activation by branch of service. The first cavalry unit formed was authorized under the 1861 "Act to Raise Ten Thousand State Troops," which specified that one of the 10 regiments raised for the duration of the war would be a cavalry regiment. This first cavalry unit was designated the 1st North Carolina Cavalry. However, since it was the ninth regiment of army troops, it was known within the state as the 9th Regiment of state troops.[2]

Initially, units were automatically transferred to the Confederate armies. However, with more of the state coming under Union control in 1864 and the menace of Gen. William T. Sherman's army advancing toward the Carolinas from Georgia in 1865, Governor Zebulon Vance determined to bolster the state's defenses by keeping the 69th North Carolina and the 15th Battalion North Carolina Cavalry within state borders.[3]

In all, five North Carolina cavalry regiments and one battalion served with the Army of Northern Virginia during all or part of the war. These were the 9th Regiment (1st North Carolina Cavalry), 19th Regiment (2nd North Carolina Cavalry), 41st Regiment (3rd North Carolina Cavalry), 59th Regiment (4th North Carolina Cavalry), 63rd Regiment (5th North Carolina Cavalry), and the 16th Battalion North Carolina Cavalry.[4]

Three cavalry brigades composed entirely of North Carolinians served with the Army of Northern Virginia at various periods during the war. These were

---

1 Hamilton, *Reconstruction in North Carolina*, 34.

2 *Public Laws of the State of North Carolina Passed by the General Assembly at Its First Extra Session of 1861*, c. 6, ss. 1-15; Greg Mast, *State Troops and Volunteers: A Photographic Record of North Carolina's Civil War Soldiers* (Raleigh, NC, 1995), 119.

3 Louis H. Manarin, ed. *North Carolina Troops; 1861-1865, A Roster*, 19 vols. (Raleigh, NC, 1968-2013), vol. 2, xi.

4 Ibid.

Captain Rufus Barringer, 1861. Rufus, at age 39, and brother Victor volunteered for service in the cavalry. *Albert and Shirley Special Collections Library, University of Virginia, Charlottesville, Virginia*

Beverly H. Robertson's brigade (1863); Laurence S. Baker's, then James B. Gordon's, then Rufus Barringer's brigade (1863-1865); and William P. Roberts's brigade (1865). Robertson's brigade included two regiments,

Barringer's brigade four regiments, and Roberts's brigade one regiment and one battalion.[5]

The method of appointing officers and supplying units varied according to the law under which the unit was organized and the authority under which it served. Two regiments, the 1st and 2nd North Carolina Cavalry, were to be mounted and equipped by the state. All field officers were supposed to be appointed by the respective colonels. In the case of the 1st North Carolina Cavalry, however, the governor took an active part in selecting the field officers. The men of the regiments elected the company officers (captain and below).[6]

All other North Carolina units that were transferred to the Confederate armies were either mounted by the Confederate government or the men were reimbursed by the government for the use of their own horses. As with the 1st and 2nd regiments, the men elected their company officers. Field officers (the ranks above captain) were voted on by their peers and then recommended to Confederate authorities in Richmond for official appointment. A cavalry company usually contained from 64 to 100 men when first organized. A regiment usually consisted of 10 companies.[7]

Captain Rufus Barringer, Company F, 1st North Carolina Cavalry

After the failure of the Peace Conference of February 4-27, 1861, Rufus began to see the inevitability of war. His older brother, Moreau, served as a North Carolina representative to the Peace Conference and kept Rufus informed of the failed talks. Rufus declared in a March 6 speech that the Lincoln Administration sought to place the border states "between the upper and nether millstone, and grind us to an impalpable powder," and that he now wished for the speedy withdrawal of North Carolina from the Union.[8]

---

5   Ibid., xii. Under the cavalry reorganization of September 9, 1863, Baker was assigned to command the North Carolina cavalry brigade. Having been wounded, however, Baker never actually assumed field command of the brigade and was assigned to special duty. On September 28, 1863, Gordon was promoted to brigadier general and took command of the brigade.

6   Ibid.

7   *Public Laws of the State of North Carolina Passed by the General Assembly at Its First Extra Session of 1861*, c. 6, ss. 1-15; Manarin, *North Carolina Troops*, vol. 2, xiii.

8   *State Journal*, March 20, 1861; Joseph Carlyle Sitterson, *The Secession Movement in North Carolina* (Chapel Hill, NC, 1939), 232-233.

This is the Battle Flag of Company F, the "Cabarrus Rangers," of the 1st North Carolina Cavalry Regiment. This flag was presented to Captain Rufus Barringer by the ladies of Concord on June 29, 1861. The colors are: Field: blue; Top Stripe: red; Middle Stripe: White; Bottom Stripe: red; Block Letters: gold; and Stars: white. The flag is trimmed in gold fringe. This flag is now housed in the Old Courthouse Building in downtown Concord, North Carolina. *Concord Museum, Concord, North Carolina*

Weeks before North Carolina's official secession, Governor John W. Ellis began planning for the eventual need to raise troops, which would include cavalry. Among the first men to offer their services to the state were Rufus and his younger brother, Victor. Both brothers were practicing attorneys in Concord, the seat of Cabarrus County, when they volunteered on April 19, 1861. Their older brother, Moreau, prior to serving as the United States minister to Spain during Zachary Taylor's administration, had represented North Carolina in the United States Congress, sharing his desk with a representative from Illinois named Abraham Lincoln. This relationship would prove fateful to Rufus before the war ended.[9]

9 J. B. Alexander, *History of Mecklenburg County From 1740 to 1900* (Charlotte, NC, 1902), 203.

At age 39, Rufus was five feet six and one-half inches tall, and weighed about 140 pounds. He had hazel eyes, auburn hair, and a florid complexion. He also had the typical Barringer physical characteristic of a large head with a high forehead, balding on top. Rufus was a superb rider and decided to join the cavalry. He organized Company F, known as the "Cabarrus Rangers," in Cabarrus County and on May 16 the men elected him captain. Victor Barringer and James B. Gordon were appointed regimental majors. Colonel Robert Ransom, having recently resigned from the U.S. Army, became the first commander of the 1st North Carolina Cavalry. The state's ordinance of secession passed on May 20, 1861. By June 8, 62 men had enlisted in Barringer's Company F, and by June 15 more than 100 men had volunteered.[10]

After the company elected officers, a tender of service was made to Governor Ellis, who assigned Captain Barringer's unit to Colonel Ransom's regiment. The men immediately went to work securing small arms, uniforms, and equipment—all at their own expense. They met once a week to drill.[11]

Captain Barringer's first responsibility was to equip and train his men. Initially, the training exercises were more like social gatherings than serious business. Private J. C. Neel recorded, "They met in Concord once a week and galloped around and had a big time. . . . Patriotic ladies joined in the fun serving the men fine dinners." Neel remembered: "On the 22nd of June, 1861, we passed our medical examination and were sworn into service for a term of two years. This was unusual since most soldiers were 90-day volunteers." As the new recruits were sworn in, they were ordered to proceed to Asheville for training.[12]

On June 29, 1861, a ceremony was held in Concord to honor the Cabarrus Rangers. The ladies of Concord and Cabarrus County presented a beautiful handmade flag, inscribed "Cabarrus Rangers," to the troopers of Company F. Prominent attorney William M. Coleman, who would become the state's attorney general in 1868, gave a speech in which he told the assembled men of Company F "of the responsibility resting upon them in sustaining that flag." He

---

10 *Carolina Flag,* June 11 and June 18, 1861; Compiled Service Records for Confederate Generals and Staff Officers, and Non-Regimental Enlisted Men, National Archives, M-331, Roll 17, July 24, 1865.

11 *Carolina Flag,* June 11, 1861.

12 J. C. Neel, "War Reminiscences," Civil War Collection, State Archives of North Carolina, Raleigh, NC; Ibid.

hoped that it would "serve as a declaration of the high appreciation the ladies have of the noble and manly efforts that [they] are now making to disperse the dark clouds now hovering over our beloved country."[13]

The speeches were filled with patriotic zeal. Victor Barringer, who had been strongly pro-secessionist from the beginning, assured his audience that the war would last only three months. Rufus had argued against secession until March, and at the ceremony spoke of President Lincoln's call for 500,000 men to put down the rebellion. He asserted that a large Federal army would cross the Potomac River and would have to be met by a large Southern army. Disagreeing with his brother, he warned that the war would be long and hard fought. Regarding the nature of the upcoming struggle, he had stated publicly more than two months earlier: "If the North ventures to invade our soil, it will be with an army of five hundred thousand men. If they come at all, they will come to exterminate. We must prepare to meet them on the threshold!"[14]

The stirring speeches met with great enthusiasm. A determined Capt. Rufus Barringer told a friend that "North Carolina was going to hell, but he was going with her." Victor's and Rufus's older sister, Margaret Grier, who had been steadfast in her opposition to secession, had a foreboding of things to come. She would lose three of five sons to the war, and would often chastise Victor afterward over his enthusiasm for secession.[15]

Rufus's cavalry company, 100 men strong, left on July 3 to rendezvous at Asheville with the five western companies of the regiment for drill and discipline. The men were transported by rail to a point three miles beyond Hickory—the end of the railroad line at that time. Not yet equipped with horses, the newly formed cavalry marched the remaining distance to Asheville. Crossing the Blue Ridge Mountains at Swannanoa Gap, they followed the Swannanoa Rive to their final destination and camped two miles north of the

13 *Carolina Flag*, July 2, 1861.

14 Barringer, "To The People Of Mecklenburg County," July 24, 1872; *Richmond Dispatch*, May 10, 1861.

15 Anna Barringer, "The First American Judge in Egypt," 153, Rufus Barringer Papers, University of Virginia; Compiled Service Records for three sons (John Laban Grier, Paul Barringer Grier, and Robert Hall Grier) who died in the war and two sons (Samuel A. Grier and William M. Grier) who served and survived the war; Manarin, *North Carolina Troops*, vol. 2, 53; D. A. Thompkins, *History of Mecklenburg County and City of Charlotte From 1740 to 1903* (Charlotte, N. C., 1904), 172, 177. Paul Brandon Barringer (son of Rufus Barringer) mistakenly recalled in *The Natural Bent* (page 45) that five of Margaret Grier's sons died in the war.

city. The trip took about two-and-a-half days. Undeterred by their horseless status, the men drilled on foot daily. During their time at Asheville, the companies procured arms and horses. The troopers were mounted on horses furnished by the state. Those who owned horses were required to take them before a board of evaluation to have them appraised before selling them to the state. No soldier was allowed to take a private horse into the service.[16]

When Captain Barringer's company was assigned to Asheville, his wife and children accompanied him. Many of the young men of Company F had never been away from home. This was a great adventure, and initially they seemed to enjoy themselves. Private Neel remembered that "we had a good time sight-seeing and swimming in the French Broad River." Another trooper remembered that "no liquor is allowed in camp, and the consequence is I have seen no drunken man since we have been here"[17]

While Company F and four other western companies drilled at Asheville, the first battle of Manassas took place in Virginia on July 21, 1861. In this, the first major engagement of the war, the Union army was vanquished. The Confederacy's successful use of interior lines and railroads, and Union Gen. Robert Patterson's failure to prevent Confederate Gen. Joseph E. Johnston from leaving the Shenandoah Valley and joining Gen. P. G. T. Beauregard southwest of Washington, greatly contributed to the Federal defeat. The stunning Confederate victory dashed Union hopes for a quick end to the war.[18]

In August, the 1st North Carolina Cavalry was ordered to rendezvous at Camp Beauregard near Warrenton, 60 miles north of Raleigh. The camp had been named in honor of the flamboyant hero of the recent Confederate victory at Manassas. Accordingly, on August 11, the five western companies broke camp and began the march to Warren County. On August 15, the gray-clad troopers boarded railroad cars at Salisbury, 125 miles east of Asheville. They arrived at Raleigh about daylight the following morning. On August 17, the troopers moved by train to Ridgeway, 60 miles north of Raleigh. Camp Beauregard was located about three-fourths of a mile from the railroad, on

---

16 Beverly Barrier Troxler and Billy Dawn Barrier Auciello, *Dear Father: Confederate Letters Never Before Published* (North Billerica, MA, 1989), 81; William A. Curtis diary, in Stephen D. Pool, ed., *Our Living and Our Dead*, vol. 2, 41.

17 Neel, "War Reminiscences," 1; William L. Barrier to father, July 9, 1861, in Troxler and Auciello, *Dear Father*, 81.

18 Ibid.

roughly one square mile of rolling terrain crossed by two branches of Rocky Creek.[19]

At Camp Beauregard, the regiment was formally organized with 10 companies. The field and staff officers were Col. Robert Ransom (commander), Lt. Col. Laurence S. Baker, Maj. James B. Gordon, Maj. Victor C. Barringer, Adjutant James L. Henry, Sgt. Maj. Richard T. Fulghum, Surgeon William L. Hilliard, Asst. Surgeon Charles J. O'Hagan, and a chaplain. The regiment numbered 881 enlisted men, 43 officers, and two doctors.[20]

While Ransom was a gallant officer with experience in leading and training cavalry, he was not overly popular with his men. He was considered too much of a "regular," a West Pointer with a bias against volunteers that many U.S. Military Academy graduates in both armies exhibited. One of his veterans would later say of Ransom, "If he had understood volunteer soldiers, and [had] realized that four-fifths of the men in the ranks were as careful of their personal honor as he, he would have been one of the greatest generals in Lee's army." Still, he would prove to be cool under fire and of sound judgment, never hesitating in giving orders or deciding tactics. In the heat of battle, his men ceased to grumble about his discipline and eventually agreed that they would rather have Robert Ransom commanding them than any other man. He knew how to move them swiftly with minimal losses.[21]

Indeed, under Ransom the regiment would earn an enviable reputation for discipline and courage. Before many more months passed, its men held a maxim: a commission in the 1st North Carolina Cavalry meant "a hole in your hide." Eventually, every field officer of the regiment would be killed or wounded with the exception of Ransom.[22]

Shortly after their arrival at Camp Beauregard, the 10 companies of the regiment were mounted and began drilling. They underwent hard cavalry training for more than two months. Conditions were tough and the enlisted

19 *Carolina Flag*, August 16, 1861; Frances B. Dedmond, "The Civil War Diary of Harvey Davis," *Appalachian Journal* (Summer 1986), vol. 13, No. 4, 382-383. Davis reported that the troopers of the western companies arrived at Camp Beauregard on August 17. Perhaps some of the other four western companies (including Davis's) did arrive on August 17, but Company F arrived on August 10.

20 Ibid., 383. The name of the chaplain is not known.

21 Clark, *Histories*, vol. 2, 295-296; Douglas Southall Freeman, *Lee's Lieutenants*, 3 vols. (New York, NY, 1942-1944), vol. 2, 327-328.

22 Clark, *Histories*, vol. 1, 484.

men felt as if "all liberties had been taken from them." Here, there was no swimming or sight-seeing. The officers, in dress parade, would charge the men with sabers drawn, threatening to "split their heads" open if they were even a little out of line. The men remained in camp under strict military discipline and drilled hard every day, sometimes on foot and other times mounted. Under the stern, watchful eyes of former West Point officers, boys were turned into men, and the men into soldiers. Barringer noted, "No troops ever went through a severer ordeal. At times and on occasions there were loud complaints against Colonel Ransom for the rigid rules and harsh measures adopted."[23]

During August, Victor's wife Maria visited Raleigh and stayed until September 23, and had visits to and from Victor at Camp Beauregard as often as possible. She lamented in her diary on August 30, "I spent an almost sleepless night thinking on my dear Victor's entrance into the service for which he is so illy prepared by physical strength."[24]

On September 26, Maria arrived at Camp Beauregard and found "Rosalie [Rufus's wife] very comfortably fixed with two tents—one for eating in and the other for sleeping in." Rufus's children, Paul and Anna, were also at the camp. On October 4, Maria took over care of Rufus's children and returned with them to Raleigh and then to her home in Concord, where they stayed often during the war. Having no children of their own, Maria and Victor (who had resigned from the service on September 30 after a 90-day enlistment) treated the kids as their own and called them, "our children." Rosalie would stay at the camp until October 11 or 12.[25]

The neophyte horsemen of the 1st North Carolina Cavalry were well equipped, with the exception of inferior rifles and pistols. They had good uniforms and their state-furnished horses were in good condition. At this early stage, thanks to Ransom and his company officers, these troopers were some of the best trained cavalry in the Confederacy. On October 11, the privates were paid $44.00 each, their first wages as soldiers.[26]

23 Neel, "War Reminiscences," 2; Rufus Barringer, *The First North Carolina: A Famous Cavalry Regiment*, n.d., n.p. (Bethesda, MD, 1990).

24 Maria Barringer, diary, August 30. 1862.

25 Ibid., October 4, 1862.

26 Dedmond, "The Civil War Diary of Harvey Davis," 383; *Raleigh Register*, November 6, 1861.

On to Virginia

Two days later, on Sunday, October 13, 1861, the regiment broke camp and headed for Richmond. On October 16, they crossed the Roanoke River and reached the Virginia state line about noon, camping that night at Belfield in Sussex County. On the 17th, the regiment arrived at Stony Creek and the next day entered Petersburg, 20 miles south of Richmond. Citizens of Petersburg greeted them warmly and set out a large public table for both breakfast and supper.[27]

The regiment continued on to the Confederate capital on October 19, camping on Reservoir Hill. The *Richmond Examiner* reported: "The sight presented by this magnificent body of horsemen, as their long line wound its way up Main Street, from Mayo's bridge, was one well calculated to inspire emotions of pride in the spirit and determined resistance to tyranny."[28]

Three days later, the officers and men were reviewed by President Jefferson Davis and Gen. Robert E. Lee, who at that time was an aide to Davis and head of the Virginia state military establishment. Davis was "highly pleased with the efficiency and exceptional appearance of the command." The *Richmond Dispatch* reported, "To North Carolina belongs the honor of sending forth the finest body of cavalry now in the service of the country."[29]

Within a week of their arrival, the regiment left Richmond for Manassas Junction, about 100 miles to the north. Six days later, having followed the Telegraph Road, the 1st North Carolina Cavalry passed through Ashland, Massaponax Church, Fredericksburg, and Dumfries before moving to the northwest to camp on the field where the recent battle of Manassas had taken place. According to the *Fredericksburg Reporter*, the regiment "was the best looking set of men and horses that we have ever witnessed. . . . Their presence brought out an immense concourse of people to see them, and the ladies seemed to be 'perfectly carried away' with the regiment."[30]

Shortly after reaching Manassas, Rufus wrote his children a letter from that famous crossroads battlefield, describing what he witnessed there. He also

---

27 Dedmond, "The Civil War Diary of Harvey Davis," 383.

28 *Raleigh Register*, October 23, 1861; *Richmond Enquirer*, October 23, 1861.

29 *Raleigh Register*, October 30, 1861.

30 Dedmond, "The Civil War Diary of Harvey Davis," 382-383; *Fredericksburg Reporter*, as quoted in *Raleigh Register*, November 6, 1861.

mentioned that their uncle, Thomas J. Jackson, was on the same field. "Papa is at last where the War is," he began. "Tonight we camp on a battle field where a great battle was fought—when the Yankees came to kill our people & our people killed them. . . . There are so many people here [that] came to the war (like Papa did) to fight the Yankees if they come back . . . but Papa hopes the Yankees will never come back any more, and he can soon return home to see his dear little Rats & Mamma & Aunt Ria & Uncle Victor & all the friends. . . . Uncle [Stonewall] Jackson is here. Uncle Jackson asked so many questions about the children."[31]

The regiment then moved out and passed Centreville, five miles northeast of Manassas and 35 miles west of Washington on November 1. It stopped at "Camp Johnston" for three or four days. On November 5, they moved about four miles to "Camp Ashe," located one and one-half miles outside of Centreville. Here they were assigned picket duty.[32]

Sometime during these movements in northern Virginia, Rufus experienced an interesting incident involving Colonel Ransom, which resulted in the loss of Barringer's prized silk umbrella. Ransom was a stickler for discipline. On one occasion, while breaking camp (probably during the march to Manassas) Captain Barringer's body servant neglected to pack his handsome silk umbrella with the baggage. The servant was a 14-year-old Barringer family slave named Alfred, who would serve with Barringer for two years. After Alfred and the baggage train had been sent ahead, Barringer discovered the overlooked umbrella and, unwilling to leave it behind, strapped it to his saddle.[33]

As the regiment passed out of camp, Colonel Ransom and his staff sat on their horses and reviewed the marching column. When Barringer rode by at the head of his company, Ransom called out in loud and peremptory tones, "Captain Barringer, what in hell is that you have on your saddle?" "A silk umbrella," replied Barringer. "A silk umbrella!" shouted the colonel. "A silk umbrella! Throw it away, Sir! Who ever heard of going to war with a silk

31 Barringer, *The Natural Bent*, 38-39. Letter dated October 30, 1861.

32 Dedmond, "The Civil War Diary of Harvey Davis," 383.

33 Soldier's Application for Pension, July 11, 1927, State Archives of North Carolina. This application was witnessed and signed by General Barringer's son, Osmond Barringer; Joseph Blount Cheshire, *Nonnulla* (Chapel Hill, NC, 1930), 153.

umbrella? Throw it away, Sir," continued Ransom, adding a string of profane expletives. Thus Rufus lost the use of a camp comfort.[34]

On November 26, 1861, the 1st North Carolina Cavalry began a scout and had its first real fight just west of Vienna, 10 miles northwest of Alexandria. Colonel Ransom, with 125 men from Companies B, D, E, G, H, and K, and about 20 men coming off picket duty near Hawkhurst's Mill, surprised an equal number of Union troopers belonging to a scouting party from the 3rd Pennsylvania Cavalry. In the ensuing melee, the Confederates scattered the Yankees, killing one, wounding six, and taking 26 prisoners while suffering no enemy-inflicted losses. The Tar Heel troopers also took 17 horses, 26 sabers, 25 side arms, 15 Sharps carbines, and other equipment as prizes of war. Barringer's company and that of Captain T. N. Crumpler were held in reserve, but joined in the pursuit once the rout of the hapless Federals began. One trooper described the pursuit of the Union horsemen as "something like a fox chase." This first victory was a source of great pride among the regiment and folks back home. Colonel W. W. Averill of the 3rd Pennsylvania Cavalry later berated members of his command in front of the remainder of the regiment. One Union horse soldier recalled: "This recollection of the 1st North Carolina cavalry hung over us like a dark curtain over all, especially those who were participants in the unfortunate stampede."[35]

For the remainder of the winter, the regiment remained in camp near Centreville, serving on picket and scouting duty. All of the cavalry units assembled near Manassas were without brigade organization until December 1861, when Brig. Gen. J. E. B. Stuart formed the First Cavalry Brigade. It was composed of the 1st, 2nd, 4th, and 6th Virginia Cavalry, the 1st North Carolina Cavalry, and the Jeff Davis Legion.[36]

On December 20, General Stuart led a 1,600-man expeditionary force consisting of four infantry regiments, 150 troopers, and four guns to protect a

---

34 Ibid., 154.

35 Clark, *Histories*, vol. 1: 419; *Raleigh Register*, December 11, 1861; *The War of the Rebellion: A Compilation of the Official Records of the Union and Confederate Armies*, 128 vols. (Washington, DC, 1880-1901), Series 1, vol. 5, 444-447. Hereafter cited as *OR*. All references are to Series 1 unless otherwise noted. Ransom's report says he had about 145 men, while Clark's *Histories* states that Ransom had 200 men and was opposed by about the same number; *Richmond Dispatch*, December 6, 1861, also stated that Ransom had 200 men; Troxler and Auciello, *Dear Father*, 86; *Philadelphia Weekly Times*, January 20, 1883.

36 Clark, *Histories*, vol. 1, 419.

large number of wagons gathering valuable forage in the area between Leesburg and Alexandria, on the Alexandria and Leesburg Turnpike. Stuart's horsemen, scouting ahead of the infantry, included portions of Ransom's 1st North Carolina Cavalry (under Maj. James B. Gordon) and the 2nd Virginia Cavalry. Stuart planned to set up protection for his wagons just west of Dranesville, Virginia. However, when he reached Dranesville, Stuart found that Union Gen. Edward O. C. Ord's forces had arrived shortly before them. Upon surveying the situation, Stuart feared for the safety of his wagons. He moved to attack the enemy's rear and left flank and sent for his infantry. While attacking, he sent the Virginia horsemen to secure the road to Leesburg and start the wagons back toward camp. The North Carolina cavalrymen were held in reserve, as a two-hour artillery duel ensued with neither side gaining an advantage.[37]

Believing his wagons had escaped, Stuart began withdrawing his forces. Gordon's North Carolinians served as a rear guard for the retreating Virginians. Stuart's men had saved the army's wagons, but suffered heavy losses of 43 killed and 143 wounded.[38]

An amusing incident concerning wagon master Jacob Dove resulted from the near disaster at Dranesville. When Colonel Ransom heard of the disastrous fight with Ord, he asked about the safety of the wagons. One of his troopers replied: "Yes, Jacob Dove not only brought out his teams, but brought them loaded, and even made them jump fences."[39]

These preliminary engagements honed the 1st North Carolina Cavalry into an effective fighting unit. This seasoning would prove invaluable during the hard battles yet to come in the Peninsula and Antietam campaigns of 1862. The record showed they fought hard and well. In the actions that followed these initial engagements, whether through necessity or by confidence in the 1st North Carolina Cavalry, General Stuart would increasingly call on this Tar Heel regiment to lead charges against enemy horsemen.

In the coming months, Captain Barringer would mature as a cavalry officer and gain the respect of his men and superiors. The normally taciturn T. J.

---

37 H. B. McClellan, *The Life and Campaigns of Major-General J. E. B. Stuart* (Edison, NJ, 1993), 43-45; *OR*, vol. 5, 490-494; Edward G. Longacre, *Lee's Cavalrymen* (Mechanicsburg, PA, 2002), 60-61.

38 McClellan, *The Life and Campaigns of Major General J.E.B. Stuart*, 45; *OR* 5, 494.

39 Clark, *Histories*, vol. 1, 419-420; Rufus Barringer to Victor Barringer, January 27, 1866, Southern Historical Collection.

Jackson, Barringer's brother-in-law, would feel confident enough with him to share his plan for a controversial "black flag" campaign, i.e., Jackson didn't want to take Union prisoners. The coming days would also witness the onset of serious illness regarding his second wife, Rosalie Chunn Barringer.

Chapter 5

"I only succeeded in getting the dispatch safely through by sending reliable couriers on fleet horses over different routes. But in a very few days the shout of victory was hushed and stilled in the universal wail for our fallen chieftain [Stonewall Jackson]."

— Captain Rufus Barringer at Hanover Junction,
upon hearing of the mortal wound of Stonewall Jackson.

The Campaigns of 1862 and Early 1863

W ith a mere 100 miles separating the opposing capitals and their armies, Virginia was fated to become a major theater of the war. The ground between Washington and Richmond—particularly between the Rappahannock and James Rivers—was low, swampy, and covered with woods and underbrush. The roads were deep in mud throughout the winter and much of the spring, and many were impassible.

Following a relatively quiet winter, the spring of 1862 brought a renewed determination to take the Rebel capital. A Union offensive against Richmond presented formidable difficulties. There were two primary approaches to the city. The first was a direct southern approach by land through Manassas and Fredericksburg and down the Richmond, Fredericksburg & Potomac Railroad. The second was an approach by sea to Fortress Monroe at the tip of the Virginia peninsula formed by the James and York rivers. Once ashore, the army would march up the narrow neck of land to Richmond.[1]

---

1 David G. Martin, *The Peninsula Campaign* (Conshohocken, PA, 1992), 55.

The overland approach to take Richmond had failed at the battle of First Manassas, when Confederate forces under Gens. P. G. T. Beauregard and Joseph E. Johnston routed those of Brig. Gen. Irvin McDowell. On July 27, 1861, due to his defeat at Manassas, Lincoln replaced McDowell with 34-year-old Maj. Gen. George B. McClellan. Already popular with his men, McClellan's recent victories in Western Virginia placed him in high regard with the Northern people, but more importantly with the President, his cabinet, and the Northern press.[2]

McClellan's first order of business after taking over from McDowell was to restore the army's faith in itself. McClellan's organizational ability was unmatched. Within weeks, he had the disrupted army that had raced to the safety of Washington's defenses from the plains of Manassas organized and ready once more for battle. Next, he turned his sights on restoring discipline to Washington. On November 1, McClellan succeeded Gen. Winfield Scott as commander of the entire army.[3]

The Union army, twice the strength of General Johnston's Confederates, looked better than it ever had. However, McClellan was still reluctant to take the offensive. While everyone clamored for action, he stayed near Washington. Desperate to get his commander moving, Lincoln issued President's General Orders No. 1 and 2, specifically ordering McClellan to move on Manassas Junction by February 22, 1862.[4]

Instead of preparing to move his army as instructed, McClellan wrote a multi-page letter to Secretary of War Edwin Stanton advising against another move on Manassas. McClellan offered instead his "Urbanna Plan," designed to shift his army down the Chesapeake Bay to Urbanna, Virginia, on the south bank of the Rappahannock, just 50 miles from Richmond. However, he was forced to abandon his Urbanna Plan when General Johnston, on March 11, preempted him by crossing to the south side of the Rappahannock River first.[5]

2   Ibid., 11-12.

3   Steven W. Sears, *George B. McClellan: The Young Napoleon* (New York, NY. 1988), 97, 100, 125.

4   Ethan S. Rafuse, *McClellan's War: The Failure of Moderation in the Struggle for the Union*, (Bloomington, IN, 2005), 177.

5   George McClellan to Edwin Stanton, January 31, 1862, in Stephen Sears, ed., *The Civil War Papers of George B. McClellan: Selected Correspondence 1860-1865* (New York, NY, 1992), 169.

Meanwhile, Union Brig. Gen. Ambrose E. Burnside enjoyed considerable success along the coast and eastern part of North Carolina. On February 8, 1862, Roanoke Island fell to the invading Federals, quickly followed by New Bern on the 14th, Fort Macon on March 20, and Beaufort on the 24th. For his efforts, Burnside was promoted to major general. This Union thrust in rear of General Lee's army by a mobile force that could be reinforced quickly by water was a menace to Lee's operations in Virginia.[6]

Fearful that Burnside's success would be followed by deeper Union penetration into eastern North Carolina, Confederate Secretary of War Judah P. Benjamin, on instructions from President Jefferson Davis, dispatched troops from the Army of Northern Virginia to support Gen. Theophilus H. Holmes. The Confederates were concerned that the vital Wilmington & Weldon Railroad, the main supply line from North Carolina to Petersburg and Richmond, would be attacked. On March 22, the 1st North Carolina Cavalry, including Capt. Rufus Barringer's Company F, was one of three regiments ordered back to North Carolina from northern Virginia to help protect the rail line. The regiment moved through Richmond and Weldon and arrived at Kinston, 65 miles southeast of Raleigh, where the troopers bivouacked at "Camp Ransom" (named by the men for their commander, Robert Ransom).[7]

While Barringer was stationed in eastern North Carolina, his wife Rosalie gave birth to a son, Rufus Chunn Barringer. "Rosie" continued in delicate health after the birth. She suffered anxiety due to the war and the pressures of managing the family in Concord without her husband. Rufus must have been anxious to go home to visit her. However, Kinston and Concord were approximately 200 miles apart, and because of the seriousness of the military situation in the Kinston area at that time, he could not go to his wife's side.[8]

In Virginia, with his Urbanna Plan now useless, McClellan fell back on the less desirable alternative of approaching Richmond from the Peninsula. On March 17, he began moving his men to Fortress Monroe. McClellan concentrated his troops, numbering about 122,000 men, at the Union fort and

6 Barrett, *The Civil War in North Carolina, 104-105*, 109, 114; Ezra J. Warner, *Generals in Blue: Lives of the Union Commanders* (Baton Rouge, LA, 1995), 57.

7 *OR* 51, pt. 2, 512, 542.

8 J. K. Rouse, *Historical Shadows of Cabarrus County North Carolina* (Charlotte, NC, 1970), 20.

nearby Hampton and Newport News, in preparation for the Peninsula campaign.[9]

The only obstacle between McClellan and a clear road to Richmond was the 11,000 Confederates posted at Yorktown under Maj. Gen. John B. Magruder. Despite the overwhelming numbers heading his way, Magruder stood his ground and bought precious time by implementing an audacious ruse. "Prince John" created the illusion that his force was formidable by splitting his command, sending half of it racing through the woods with orders to show themselves often enough that the enemy would take note. As soon as one half made the route, he sent in the other. Round and round they went for hours, long enough to bring McClellan's advance to a standstill. By the time the commander of the Army of the Potomac realized he had been fooled by clever subterfuge, substantial reinforcements arrived from Richmond.[10]

Meanwhile, on March 1, 1862, Robert Ransom was promoted to brigadier general and assigned to command an infantry brigade. Ransom transferred to the infantry because there were not any brigadier slots in the cavalry at the time, and leaders in North Carolina wanted more of her sons holding the rank of general. It did not hurt that General Beauregard supported Ransom for promotion. Unfortunately, Ransom suffered from frequent illness, and sick leave was necessary. On April 2, the 1st North Carolina Cavalry, now under Lt. Col. Laurence S. Baker, arrived by rail in Kinston, North Carolina, and temporarily reported to Ransom's infantry brigade.[11]

On April 3, a detail of the regiment was observed in Halifax County near Scotland Neck, bringing horses and baggage wagons from the railroad station at Weldon, where the main body of horsemen had boarded a train to Kinston. Catherine Ann Edmondston, wife of a Halifax County planter, witnessed the cavalry passing: "such a set . . . [of horses] I never before saw, galled, sore backed, poor, lame—some of them with scarcely a hair upon them. . . . I did not think 280 such jades could be found." A trooper of the 1st North Carolina

9 Steven W. Sears, *To the Gates of Richmond* (New York, NY, 1992), 24.

10 Paul D. Casdorph, *Prince John Magruder: His Life and Campaigns* (New York, NY, 1996), 143-145; Sears, *To the Gates of Richmond*, 36-39.

11 Warner, *Generals in Blue*, 253-254; John N. Opie, *A Rebel Cavalry Man with Lee, Stuart and Jackson*, (Chicago, IL, 1899), 238. Opie suggests that Robert Ransom suffered from chronic heart problems.

Cavalry wrote: "I long for a good horse. . . . I will pay from my own pocket. . . . [A] man's life is often dependent upon it."[12]

Laurence Baker, new commander of the 1st North Carolina Cavalry, was born to Dr. John Burgess Baker and Mary Wynn Baker Burgess at Coles Hill in Gates County, North Carolina, on May 15, 1830. In 1847, he received an appointment to U.S. Military Academy where he graduated dead last (he was too fond of drinking and partying) in his class in 1851. Baker resigned his commission on May 10, 1861. Less than a week later, on May 16, he was appointed lieutenant colonel of the 1st North Carolina Cavalry and would rise to the rank of brigadier general. Always one of Gen. Wade Hampton's favorite commanders, Baker enjoyed a similar position with J. E. B. Stuart until the cavalry commander learned that Baker had a drinking problem. Rather than bring him up on charges, Stuart—himself a total abstainer—had Baker sign a pledge that he would not drink again for the duration of the war. While Stuart continued to recommend Baker for promotion, he felt the Tar Heel commander was not "as 'dashing' as he had been before."[13]

In the early spring, while at Kinston, General Ransom organized his infantry brigade. Among his staff, serving as assistant adjutant and inspector general, was Maj. Victor Barringer, Rufus's younger brother. Victor had received orders on March 17 to report to Ransom. On April 16, 1862, the Confederate Congress had passed the Conscription Act, which provided for the drafting of all white males between the ages of 18 and 35. Later, this would be extended to include the ages of 17 and 50. Victor had resigned from earlier service on September 30, 1861. In September and October 1861, he had been encouraged to run for the Confederate Congress, but declined. However, he had been elected to a state convention in September. Victor, now 35, had sought a commission to either avoid being drafted or to choose where he

---

12 Beth Gilbert Crabtree and James W. Patton. eds., *Journal of a Secesh Lady: The Diary of Catherine Ann Devereux Edmondston, 1860-1866*, (Raleigh, NC, 1995), 144; W. L. Barrier to his father, April 1862, in Troxler and Auciello, *Dear Father*, 91; ibid., 92. Indeed, Barrier would purchase a horse from home for $175 in May.

13 Lt. (Ret.) Charles Braden, "Necrology of Laurence Simmons Baker," in *Thirty-Ninth Annual Reunion of the Association of Graduates of the United States Military Academy at West Point, June 12, 1908* (Saginaw, MI, 1908), 83; Powell, *Dictionary of North Carolina Biography*, vol. 1, 132; Emory M. Thomas, *Bold Dragoon: The Life of J. E. B. Stuart*, (Norman, OK, 1986), 202; J. E. B. Stuart to Samuel Cooper, January 6, 1863, Virginia Historical Society.

wanted to serve. Effective April 5, 1862, he was appointed assistant adjutant general to Ransom.[14]

In Virginia, on May 4, McClellan began his slow movement up the Lower Peninsula. By the end of the month, he had finally worked his way to within about nine miles of Richmond. When he became entangled in the swamplands of the Chickahominy River, Gen. Joseph E. Johnston's Confederate forces moved out to meet him. The resulting battle of Seven Pines, or Fair Oaks (May 31-June 1) was indecisive and badly fought on both sides. Johnston was severely wounded and Confederate President Jefferson Davis assigned Gen. Robert E. Lee to replace him in command.[15]

Back in North Carolina, despite Confederate Gen. Lawrence O'Bryan Branch's substantial entrenchments, the Confederates continuously fled as Burnside's Union forces advanced. Burnside, however, was effectively contained at New Bern. The Confederates west of New Bern could quickly send reinforcements by railroad if they were attacked. However, if the Federals were attacked, any reinforcements would have to traverse the shallow waters east of New Bern by boat.[16]

As it turned out, there was not much fighting involving the 1st North Carolina Cavalry. They primarily rested, patrolled, and picketed. In early May, Rufus was allowed a short furlough and visited Rosalie and the children for six days, leaving her on May 15.[17]

On May 27, Companies E, G, and K of the 1st North Carolina Cavalry, under Lt. Col. James B. Gordon, left for Richmond and arrived on June 15. On May 30, the remainder of the regiment, Companies C, D, F, H, and I (minus A and B) left for Richmond under Col. Laurence Baker. The Carolinians had been ordered back to Richmond to participate in the expected battles developing there, as the Federals ominously approached the Confederate capital from the southwest.[18]

---

14 *Journal of the Congress of the Confederate States of America, 1861-1865* (Washington, DC, 1904), April 19, 1861, vol. 2, 208; *Carolina Watchman*, September 30, 1861, and October 14, 1861. The reason for Victor's resignation was probably the completion of a 90-day enlistment.

15 Sears, *To the Gates of Richmond*, 70, 138, 140, 145.

16 Ibid., 114.

17 Maria Barringer, diary, May 15, 1862.

18 Manarin, *North Carolina Troops*, vol. 1, 1.

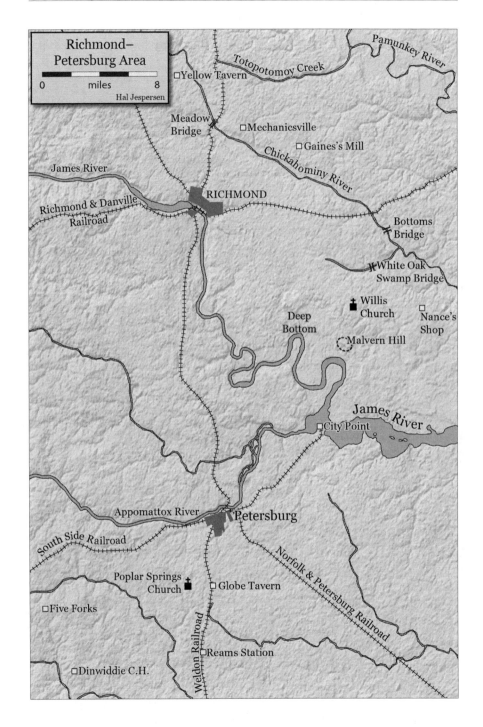

Richmond–
Petersburg Area

0   miles   8
Hal Jespersen

Yellow Tavern

Totopotomoy Creek

Pamunkey River

Meadow
Bridge

Mechanicsville

Gaines's Mill

Chickahominy River

James River

Richmond & Danville
Railroad

RICHMOND

Bottoms
Bridge

White Oak
Swamp Bridge

Willis
Church

Nance's
Shop

Deep
Bottom

Malvern Hill

James River

City Point

Appomattox River

Petersburg

South Side Railroad

Norfolk & Petersburg Railroad

Poplar Springs
Church

Globe Tavern

Five Forks

Weldon Railroad

Reams Station

Dinwiddie C.H.

On May 25, Companies A and B, under General Ransom, were ordered to the Roanoke River to defend against expected enemy attacks on the railroad bridges at Weldon. Companies C, D, F, H, and I finally reached Richmond on June 28, after several countermarches between Halifax, Scotland Neck, and Tarboro to confuse the Federals.[19]

During a June 7 march through Scotland Neck in a hard driving rain, Catherine Ann Edmondston sheltered some of the 1st North Carolina troopers. She recalled in her diary:

"Rain again yesterday & the day before. During the hardest of it came a squad of the 1st Cavalry on foot seeking shelter, very miserable, cold & wet did they look. Had a fire kindled in the Work Room for them & set hands to work to get them some dinner. Gave them all what I am sure the poor fellows had not had for some time—a good hot & strong cup of coffee. I dare say they would have preferred whiskey, but they were not asked! All day they straggled past in two's and three's & although it was rainy and cold, they were uncommonly thirsty."[20]

Gordon's horsemen of Companies A and B finally left for Richmond on May 30, and arrived there on June 28, 1862. It was during this time that a curious and unexplained event happened to Victor Barringer. On June 24, Maria Barringer recorded in her diary: "Telegram from Victor. He was in an action yesterday afternoon—He & Gen. Ransom have parted company. How thankful I am!" On June 26, Gen. Robert Ransom placed Victor under arrest, stating only that his assistant adjutant general was "guilty of highly disrespectful and insubordinate conduct." He further reported that Victor was "now under arrest and the service will be benefited by his leaving it. He can no longer serve on my staff." The exact offense and Victor's response to the charges are unknown. However, Victor tendered his resignation on July 5, 1862, and it was accepted on July 11.[21]

19 Dedmond, "The Civil War Diary of Harvey Davis," 387; OR 11, pt. 2, 525.

20 Crabtree, Journal of a Secesh Lady, 189.

21 Maria Barringer, diary, June 24, 1862; Compiled Service Records of Confederate Generals and Staff Officers and Non-Regimental Enlisted Men, NARS, M331, Roll 17. The exact offense committed by Victor Barringer cannot be determined. Both he and Ransom had "hot tempers." Perhaps it dealt with the failed prisoner exchange episode described in the Official Records (Series II, vol. 3, 655). On July 5, 1862, Barringer wrote a resignation letter stating that he had been sick and that another position awaited him. Victor had served an earlier enlistment in Ransom's 1st North Carolina Cavalry from April to September 30, 1861. Family tradition has it

Colonel Robert Ransom (1828-1881). Ransom was the first commander of the 1st North Carolina Cavalry Regiment. Ransom, a West Point graduate and strict disciplinarian, would prove to be cool under fire and of sound judgment. He never hesitated giving orders or deciding tactics. *North Carolina Division of Archives and History*

Back on the Peninsula, Robert E. Lee had assumed command of the army, after General Johnston was wounded, on June 1. On the 25th, McClellan launched an attack at Oak Grove in a failed attempt to get his siege guns within striking distance of Richmond. This attack opened what became known as the Seven Days' battles.[22]

Lee sought to mitigate the disparity in numbers by building a series of fortifications that would require fewer defenders. His goal was to drive McClellan off the Peninsula, thus relieving the pressure on the Confederate capital. Lee was aided in his quest by information gleaned from General Stuart's famous reconnaissance ride of June 12-15 around McClellan's army, which showed that the Union commander's right flank was "in the air" and thus vulnerable to attack. In addition to reinforcements from Georgia and the Carolinas, Lee called Gen. Thomas J. Jackson from the Shenandoah Valley. Despite Jackson's late arrival, Lee launched his first attack of the Seven Days' on June 26 at Mechanicsville. Darkness and Jackson's failure to arrive greatly contributed to Lee's loss of the battle. Following the attack at Mechanicsville,

that Victor was seriously wounded at First Manassas, returned home a war hero, and was confined to a wheelchair for several years. However, Victor's regiment was not at First Manassas and thus he could not have been wounded there. In fact, his regiment had not seen any fighting by the time of First Manassas or his resignation on September 30, 1861. Being forced to resign by Ransom did not have a negative effect on Victor's postwar career. He did suffer from knee inflammation pain and traveled by horse drawn carriage after the war. He probably suffered from rheumatoid arthritis.

22 Sears, *To the Gates of Richmond*, 183-184.

Colonel Laurence S. Baker. Baker was the second commander of the 1st North Carolina Cavalry Regiment. Baker was seriously wounded on August 1, 1863, and forced to resign from the cavalry service, after having been promoted to brigadier general. *North Carolina Division of Archives and History*

Lee struck the Federals at Gaines's Mill. Although McClellan's forces greatly outnumbered Lee's, the Virginian maneuvered and threw 57,000 troops against about half as many Federals under Brig. Gen. Fitz John Porter. The Union V Corps had become isolated on the north side of the Chickahominy River. Porter's forces fought valiantly, but by sundown of June 27 the Federals had no choice but to retreat across the Chickahominy.[23]

By mid-June McClellan had shifted his supply base from White House Landing on the Pamunkey River to Harrison's Landing on the James, 12 miles southeast of Richmond. Lee learned that McClellan moved his troops to the James and tried unsuccessfully to turn the Union retreat into a rout. He attacked the Federals at Savage's Station and Frayser's Farm on June 29-30, but the attacks were uncoordinated and failed. During the night of the 29th, McClellan retreated across White Oak Swamp, a shallow tributary of the Chickahominy. Generals James Longstreet and A. P. Hill attacked him on the 30th and the Federals escaped to higher ground at Malvern Hill.[24]

On June 29, 1862, five companies of the 1st North Carolina Cavalry (C, D, F, H and I) and the 3rd Virginia Cavalry—all under Lt. Col. Laurence Baker—reconnoitered McClellan's army. They proceeded down the New Market and Charles City Roads to the vicinity of Willis's Methodist Church on the Quaker Road, about 10 miles southeast of Richmond. The North Carolinians were in

23 Ibid., 174, 211-212, 249-250.

24 Ibid., 307-308.

front and charged Federal pickets near Willis's Church. Lieutenant William E. Miller, with a portion of Company H, 3rd Pennsylvania Cavalry, made a brief stand and then fell back on their reserves. The Federals then retreated farther to their infantry and two pieces of artillery.[25]

The Confederate column, led by Maj. Thomas N. Crumpler of the 1st North Carolina Cavalry, pursued the retreating pickets. When the Confederates reached a point about 50 yards from the two guns, Union artillery and infantry fire ripped into them. The Rebel troopers had ridden into an ambush. Hiding in the woods with the 3rd Pennsylvania Cavalry were the 2nd Rhode Island, 7th Massachusetts, and Battery C, 1st Pennsylvania Light Artillery. The startled Confederates discovered that maneuver and communications were impossible. Rufus later recalled: "In an instant the artillery and infantry of the enemy opened upon our devoted heads, all huddled up in the lane, where orders and maneuvers were alike impossible . . . and the whole command was forced to retire in utter confusion." Private John M. Monie remembered that he escaped by jumping a fence near a wheat field, but his lost his rifle, which was slung across his back and shoulder. "[W]hen his horse cleared the fence, the strap had broken and the gun had dropped in the wheat field near the fence."[26]

Elisha Hunt Rhodes of the 2nd Rhode Island recorded in his diary: "With the help of 2 guns with us, we about ruined this cavalry regiment [1st North Carolina Cavalry] . . . as we were concealed in the woods and the enemy rode right up to us and did not hit even 1 of our men."[27]

There were 63 Confederates killed, wounded, or captured at Willis's Church, including 48 prisoners taken. Major Crumpler was mortally wounded. As the Confederates began to retreat, Company F was in the center of the regiment's column. Rufus apparently did not hear the order to retreat and commanded his men to stand firm, which they did under intense artillery fire. When notified of the order to fall back, he commanded an orderly withdrawal. Captain Barringer's conduct during this action greatly strengthened the confidence of his men. Rufus later stated that "this disaster served as a

25 William Brook Rawle, William E. Miller, James W. McCorkell, Andrew J. Speese, and John C. Hunterson, *History of the Third Pennsylvania Cavalry (Sixtieth Regiment Pennsylvania Volunteers) in the American Civil War, 1861-1865* (Philadelphia, PA, 1905), 85-87; *OR* 11, pt. 2, 235, 525.

26 Ibid.; Clark, *Histories*, 1; John M. Monie, "Reminiscences," 16, State Archives of North Carolina.

27 Sears, *To the Gates of Richmond*, 265; Robert Hunt Rhodes, ed., *All For the Union: The Civil War Diary and Letters of Elisha Hunt Rhodes* (New York, NY, 1992), 72.

Victor Barringer was the younger brother of Rufus Barringer. Victor resigned under adverse circumstances from General Robert Ransom's staff on July 5, 1862. In April 1865, Confederate President Jefferson Davis stayed at Victor's home in Concord, as he fled southward from Richmond. After the war, Victor served his state and the United States Government with distinction. He served as an International Admiralty Court Judge in Egypt for 20 years. *North Carolina Division of Archives and History*

wholesome lesson in making mounted charges." It was later rumored that Baker had ordered the charge under the influence of "too much whiskey." The 3rd Pennsylvania Cavalry considered the victory at Willis's Church sweet revenge for a similar ambush they had suffered at the hands of the 1st North Carolina Cavalry at Vienna on November 26, 1861.[28]

The final attack of the Seven Days' battles occurred on July 1 at Malvern Hill. The 1st North Carolina Cavalry was present, but not actively engaged. General Lee was determined to destroy the retreating Federals before they reached the James River and safety, but the ensuing battle proved to be a Confederate disaster from start to finish. A lack of coordination and communication among Rebel commanders allowed the Union artillery to take advantage of its superiority in numbers. Enemy gunners punished the Confederates, effectively destroying the Rebel batteries one by one as they came on the field. The infantry was cut also to pieces as they charged up the long slope toward the entrenched Federals.[29]

Confederate casualties during the Seven Days' battles were nearly two to one, compared to those of the Federals. However, General McClellan ceded the field to the Confederates, adhering to his earlier decision to set up a new base on the James at Harrison's Landing. This relieved the pressure on Richmond. It would be another two years before the Confederate capital would again come under Union attack. McClellan continued his retreat before reports of the successful battle at Malvern Hill reached him, and against the protests of his subordinates. Generals Phil Kearney and Fitz John Porter believed that they could hold the ground and then attack Lee, forcing him back to Richmond.[30]

On General Lee's orders, J. E. B. Stuart's cavalry relentlessly pursued the retreating Federals, while providing a steady flow of information on the enemy's movements to the Confederate commander. On July 3, Stuart discovered that Evelington Heights, an area towering 60 feet above Herring Creek that separated Harrison's Landing from the mainland, was but lightly defended. Possession of the heights would afford Lee an excellent position from which to launch an attack that could conceivably trap McClellan's army

---

28 Clark, *Histories*, vol. 1, 420; Rawle, *History of the Third Pennsylvania Cavalry*, 85-87; Dedmond, "The Civil War Diary of Harvey Davis," 387; *Philadelphia Weekly Times*, January 20, 1883.

29 Sears, *To the Gates of Richmond*, 316-318, 322, 329, 332, 335.

30 Joseph P. Cullen, *The Peninsula Campaign, 1862* (Harrisburg, PA, 1973), 20-21, 168-169; Martin, *The Peninsula Campaign*, 229-230.

against the river. Stuart lost no time in relaying this valuable piece of intelligence to Lee, who immediately ordered Generals Longstreet and Jackson to ready their troops for a march to meet Stuart.

Perhaps out of pique as a result of Jackson's slothful performance during the bulk of the Seven Days' battles, Lee decided to put Longstreet's troops ahead of Jackson's for the march to the heights. This decision caused a needless delay while the two large bodies of troops traded positions for the march. Meanwhile, Stuart prematurely ordered his favorite artillerist, the young and rather dashing Capt. John Pelham, to open fire with a single howitzer on the small Union force that was then holding Evelington Heights. Stuart obtained the desired effect of driving those troops from the high ground, but the action alerted McClellan to his vulnerability from that direction. The Union commander immediately dispatched nearly half his army to Evelington and the surrounding area. Stuart's poor decision to open fire, coupled with Lee's decision to swap the marching order of Jackson and Longstreet, effectively ended the Confederates' last chance to trap or seriously harm McClellan's army on the banks of the James River.[31]

With the successful containment of McClellan's army at Harrison's Landing, the Rebels withdrew to a more favorable defensive position closer to Richmond. The Southern cavalry was charged with the task of observing McClellan's army and spent July and August on picket and scouting duty. During this period, the 1st North Carolina Cavalry fought minor engagements at Philips's Farm, Riddle's Shop (where they took about 20 prisoners), and Turkey Creek.[32]

The "Black Flag" Policy of General Stonewall Jackson

McClellan's failure in the Peninsula campaign led to changes in the Union army. On June 27, Maj. Gen. John Pope, who had achieved a measure of success in the Western Theater, assumed command of the three Valley armies now designated the Army of Virginia. Boastful and arrogant, Pope was a physically imposing man with a talent for telling clever stories. He desired to

---

31 OR 11 pt. 2, 519-520; Douglas Southall Freeman, R. E. Lee, 4 vols. (New York, NY, 1934-1935), vol. 2, 225; Brian K. Burton, Extraordinary Circumstances: The Seven Days Battles, (Bloomington, IN, 2001), 380-384.

32 Rufus Barringer to Victor Barringer, January 27, 1866, Southern Historical Collection.

step up the assault and announced his intention to make short work of the Confederates.[33]

Pope, barely two weeks into his command tenure, issued a series of general orders that provoked bitter resentment in the South and shocked his more conservative fellow officers. However, the orders met with little opposition among the enlisted men and lower grade officers, for they encouraged Union troops to seize food and supplies from Virginia farmers. Moreover, they threatened to hang, without trial, anyone suspected of aiding the Confederates. General Lee would later call the blusterous Pope "a miscreant" who should be "suppressed."[34]

General Stonewall Jackson, Barringer's brother-in-law, decided that the best way to deal with John Pope was to fight fire with fire. Jackson devised a plan of "no quarter," which he hoped might shorten the war and cause fewer casualties. The plan was based Jackson's belief that Southern soldiers had more will to fight than their Northern adversaries. Thus, if the full horrors of war were unleashed upon them, their will might fail and the war would end. Jackson's "black flag" campaign was not put into action, but the situation with Pope caused Jackson to renew his call for such a plan as retaliation against the Union commander. By definition, fighting under a "black flag" meant that quarter was neither asked nor given. The policy was hardly a new one, except in America. European armies had practiced it for centuries. Neither was it the first time that Jackson had entertained the notion. He recalled that he had discussed a variation of his plan with his brother-in-law over dinner in Lexington, as early as 1860.[35]

Virginia Governor John Letcher revealed in an address at Danville that "'Stonewall' Jackson was in favor of conducting the war under the 'black flag,' and so expressed his sentiments to him seven days after the secession of Virginia, proposing to set the example himself by first carrying that flag in the face of the enemy."[36]

---

33 John J. Hennessy, *Return to Bull Run: The Campaign and Battle of Second Manassas* (Norman, OK, 1993), 3-6; Peter Cozzens and Robert I. Girardi, eds., *The Military Memoirs of General John Pope* (Chapel Hill, NC, 1998), 129.

34 Peter Cozzens, *General John Pope: A Life for the Nation* (Chicago, IL, 2000), 86-87, 89.

35 Jackson, *Life and Letters*, 309.

36 *Raleigh Daily Progress*, February 2, 1864.

General P. G. T. Beauregard recalled that in 1875 he had written Tennessee governor James D. Porter: "After the battle of the First Manassas, when it was reported that the Federal Government refused to recognize Confederate prisoners as 'prisoners of war' . . . Gen. Thomas J. Jackson and myself advocated that the Confederate Government should then proclaim a 'war to the knife' neither asking nor granting quarter. We moreover thought that the war would thereby come sooner to an end, with less destruction, finally, of life and property." Jackson's campaign would carry the war to the North and would be fought in a manner as harsh as the methods threatened by Pope.[37]

On July 14, 1862, while Rufus was picketing along the Chickahominy and James Rivers with a squadron of men from Companies C and F, he received a note from Col. L. S. Baker. The note originated from Jackson through General Stuart, and asked that Barringer be sent to see Jackson immediately. Jackson was preparing to leave Richmond, after the Peninsula campaign, and return to the Shenandoah Valley. His troops had already boarded trains for Gordonsville. When Rufus arrived at his camp, he was greeted warmly by Jackson: "Captain, I have sent for you for a matter entirely between ourselves. You will stay with me in my tent here tonight. If General Pope does not disturb us, I am sure McClellan will not, we can have a good talk."[38]

After dinner, Jackson introduced the reason for the requested interview:

I myself see in this war, if the North triumphs, a dissolution of the bonds of all society. It is not alone the destruction of our property (which both the nation and the States are bound to protect), but it is the prelude to anarchy, infidelity, and the ultimate loss of free responsible government on this continent. With these convictions, I always thought we ought to meet the Federal invaders on the outer verge of just right and defense, and raise at once the black flag, viz., "No quarter to the violators of our homes and firesides!" It would in the end have proved true humanity and mercy. The Bible is full of such wars, and it is the only policy that would bring the North to its senses.[39]

---

37 Robert C. Carden Jr., ed., "Civil War Memories of Robert C. Carden," n.p., 1900. Carden's memories were later published in the Boone, Iowa, *Independence* newspaper, April-August 1912; P. T. Beauregard to James D. Porter, April 23, 1875, Governor James D. Porter Papers, GP 24, Tennessee State Library and Archives; *New York Times*, March 13, 1864. In an August 3, 1862, letter from Beauregard to Gen. William E. Martin, Beauregard stated: "We will yet have to come to proclaiming this war 'a war to the knife,' when no quarter will be asked or granted."

38 Jackson, *Life and Letters*, 309.

39 Ibid., 309-310.

According to Barringer, Jackson went on to say that "the people of the South were not prepared to follow such a policy." He stated that he had "cordially accepted the policy of our leaders," the implication being that President Davis and General Lee were determined to fight the war under accepted rules of conduct. Jackson now felt, however, that things were different with General Pope's threatened policies. The shift in Union policy gave Jackson the opening he needed to present his plan to Lee. According to Jackson, the Confederate commander seemed to like the idea and said he would share the proposal with Davis.[40]

Dropping the subject of war plans for the moment, Jackson complimented Barringer on the way he handled the disaster that had occurred at Willis's Church a few days earlier. He was not shy about admitting that he had questioned J. E. B. Stuart closely in regard to Barringer's overall performance thus far. Jackson now wanted to hear from the Tar Heel cavalry captain himself, on the status of his regiment. He was particularly interested in the measure of the men under Barringer's command. Jackson also wanted to know how it was possible that the men of the 1st North Carolina Cavalry had come so far in so short a time in terms of training and discipline. He listened intently as Barringer related the history of his command to date. When Barringer finished, Jackson replied with admiration: "You are fortunate to have such men to command, and the Confederacy fortunate to have such officers to lead them. With such troops I would not hesitate to risk a march even to New York or to Chicago."[41]

After repeating his growing disaffection with Richmond's insistence on maintaining a policy which Jackson deemed "a very stilted style of waging war," he got to the true point of the meeting. Barringer paid close attention as his brother-in-law laid out a daring plan to thwart General Pope and his Army of Virginia. First and foremost, Jackson readily conceded that it was impossible for the South to defend all of her borders, particularly the coastal areas where the Federals maintained a decided advantage in ships and other naval supplies. Trying to defend every piece of Southern soil would only result in stretching their lines too thin in terms of manpower and materiel. Instead, Jackson recommended "concentrating our choicest fighting men and most valuable material at a few strong interior camps, thoroughly fortified, and so located as best, at one and the same time, to protect our communications, defend our

40 Ibid., 310.

41 Ibid., 311-312.

people and territory against invasions of the enemy, and also keep up ceaseless aggressions upon them."[42]

He envisioned repeated rapid incursions into the North by a fighting force organized into "two, four, or more light movable columns, specially armed and trained and equipped for sudden moves and for long and rapid marches." These same columns would also stand ready to repel all enemy invasions as soon as they entered Confederate territory. Jackson's eyes must have fairly burned in his face as he reached his "piece de resistance." "But better, I would hurl these thunderbolts of war against the rich cities and teeming regions of our Federal friends." He would have these columns avoid all "regular battles" in favor of taking no prisoners, except noted leaders, who would be held mainly as hostages for ransom or retaliation. "All the rank and file I would parole, but only at the risk of life if the parole was violated." In other words, he would visit the evil of Pope's policy on the people of Northern Virginia, point for point. "And, so I would make it hot for our friends at their homes and firesides, all the way to Kansas—'bleeding Kansas'; and doubly so for Ohio and Pennsylvania."[43]

Jackson stated that the cavalry and horse artillery would be vital to his proposed plan. "In fact, in certain operations I would depend almost entirely on mounted troops. The one vital advantage of the South lies in the horsemanship of the Southern boy, and the personal courage of the Southern freeman."[44]

Jackson then turned to Barringer and said: "I have sent for you to say that in such a contingency I shall need your services in some high position, and I have ordered you up here to have a full conference in regard to the cavalry arm of the service, and especially your own noble regiment."

Barringer wanted to know what role he could play that would be most beneficial, should such a contingency arise. Jackson's quick reply made it obvious that the infantry commander had been considering the plan for quite some time: "In such a movement I would seek to organize my whole staff, and I should want you as quartermaster-general."[45]

---

42 Ibid., 312.

43 Ibid., 314.

44 Ibid., 315-316.

45 Ibid., 320; Rufus Barringer to Victor Barringer, January 27, 1866, Southern Historical Collection. Barringer declined Jackson's invitation to serve as his quartermaster general; Rufus

This must have come as a surprise to the Tar Heel captain, who readily admitted he had no expertise whatsoever in that area. More to the point, he was "under a pledge to my company and their friends not to leave them except by promotion in the line." Jackson's response to Barringer's apparent refusal was emphatic: "Soldiers can give no such pledge, and as to your want of military training, I know your business reputation, and on an expedition of the kind suggested a good quartermaster is of the first importance." Jackson concluded, "So, if General Lee can see his way to adopt my policy, so far as to organize a light movable column of forty thousand men, and I am put in charge to try this special mode of invasion, I will order you up for assignment."[46]

Barringer wrote, "Not another word ever passed between General Jackson and myself on the subject. In fact the only time it was even alluded to was shortly after the battle of Antietam, September 17, 1862 [after Pope's army had been absorbed by the Army of the Potomac]." The whole exercise became moot a few weeks later when Pope began moving toward Culpeper with the intention of destroying the Virginia Central Railroad, first at Gordonsville and then at Charlottesville. Time was of the essence. If Lee was to survive, he had to defeat Pope before the remainder of the Army of the Potomac joined the Army of Virginia. Pope brought an aggressiveness that McClellan had not displayed, and urgency necessitated dealing with Pope immediately. Jackson's "black flag" policy never materialized.[47]

On July 25, J. E. B. Stuart was promoted to major general and placed in command of all the cavalry in the Army of Northern Virginia. Three days later he formed a division of two brigades commanded by Generals Wade Hampton and Fitzhugh Lee (Robert E. Lee's nephew). The 1st North Carolina Cavalry, commanded by Col. Laurence S. Baker, was placed in Hampton's brigade.[48]

The regiment was ordered to remain near Richmond to observe McClellan's movements southeast of the Confederate capital. On August 5-6, Companies E, F, G, H, I, and K fought Union infantry pickets near Malvern Hill. In determining the size of the Federal force, Baker's Carolinians lost eight

---

Barringer to President Andrew Johnson, June 14, 1865, Amnesty Papers, National Archives, Washington, DC.

46 Jackson, *Life and Letters*, 317.

47 Ibid.; Hennessy, *Return to Bull Run*, 24.

48 Clark, *Histories*, vol. 1, 420; *OR* 11, pt. 3, 657.

Lieutenant General Thomas Jonathan "Stonewall" Jackson. Jackson was a brother-in-law of Rufus Barringer, and the two men shared a warm relationship. *United States Military History Institute, Carlisle Barracks, PA*

men while killing two and wounding several of the enemy. Barringer's and Capt. William J. Houston's squadrons captured 33 skirmishers.[49]

At the battle of Second Manassas, General Pope mistakenly believed that he had Jackson trapped, and that he would shortly destroy the Confederate commander's army. Pope did not know Jackson's location and was mistaken in the position of his own forces. Jackson was anything but trapped. He was right where he wanted to be, and on August 28 he attacked Pope head-on. The close quarters fighting lasted for more than two hours. More than 1,000 Federals fell, a third of the number engaged. Pope skirmished with Jackson's troops on August 29 in a series of uncoordinated attacks. Unknown to Pope, Lee and Longstreet—with 30,000 reinforcements—had marched through Thorough-fare Gap and joined Jackson on the 30th. That same day, Pope launched a massive attack against Jackson's position. Protected by a railroad cut, the Rebels slaughtered the Federals. As Union forces fell back, Lee unleashed Longstreet's troops against Pope's left flank. The retreating Yankees pieced together two brief defensive stands that gave Pope enough time to escape across Bull Run. The Union loss totaled 16,000, while Confederate casualties numbered 9,000.[50]

In this second engagement at Manassas, the 1st North Carolina Cavalry fought Pope's rear guard in a severe action at Fox's Farm. Near Fairfax Court House, the Tar Heels came close to falling into another ambush. Early on the afternoon of September 2, Capt. Thaddeus P. Siler and a scouting party from Company K reported to Wade Hampton that they had spotted a number of Federal columns moving down the road leading out of Fairfax, about one and

49 Ibid., pt. 2, 959-960.

50 Hennessy, *Return to Bull Run*, 196-201, 229-231.

one-half miles from their current position. The enemy also maintained a force on Flint Hill, overlooking the Fairfax-Alexandria Road. General Stuart directed Hampton to act. James F. Hart's battery opened fire on the defenders of the hill, while Hampton's skirmishers harassed enemy troops on the road. Unable to withstand the combined firepower, the Federals retreated toward the safety of the defenses surrounding Washington. The pursuing Confederate troopers stopped only to pick up prisoners along the way. Just before 9:00 p.m., the Confederates entered a section of the road that was heavily wooded on both sides. Flashes of small arms erupted in the dark woods near the Southern troopers.

As Hampton calmed his cavalry and ordered them to prepare to charge, they were struck by enemy artillery fire. Hampton immediately ordered the column to fall back out of range. Reaching an open field, the troopers formed for an attack on their unseen assailants, but the woods fell silent. Scouts moved into the trees, but soon returned to report that their attackers had taken the road to Alexandria. Hampton ordered his tired riders into camp for the night. Daylight revealed that, despite the vicious attack, they had suffered few casualties. The next day, they moved to within five miles of Alexandria before turning toward Georgetown to scout along the Potomac. On September 5, they passed through Dranesville on their way to Leesburg. General Lee and the Army of Northern Virginia had crossed the Potomac into Maryland the previous evening.[51]

The Invasion of Maryland

The compelling success against Pope at Manassas encouraged General Lee to strike a blow at the enemy on their home soil. He devised a plan to cross the Potomac near Leesburg and move into Maryland. For his plan to succeed, Union troops at Harpers Ferry would have to be dislodged in order to secure his rear and establish the lines of supply and communication needed to support a northern invasion. Lee expected the 14,000 Federals at Harpers Ferry, under Col. Dixon S. Miles, to withdraw in the face of a superior force of 24,000 Confederates, which included 14,000 seasoned veterans under Stonewall Jackson. Miles, however, was ordered to stand and fight before designating

---

51 U. R. Brooks, *Stories of the Confederacy* (Germantown, TN, 1994), 74-77; Robert J. Trout, *Galloping Thunder: The Stuart Horse Artillery Battalion* (Mechanicsburg, PA, 2002), 86-87.

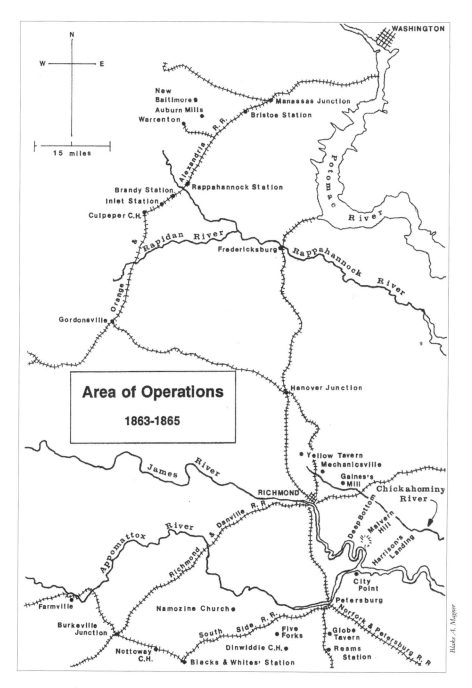

Brig. Gen. Julius White to arrange surrender terms with Jackson on September 15. Jackson captured 11,000 prisoners, 11,000 small arms, 73 pieces of artillery, and 200 wagons. The men of the 1st North Carolina Cavalry enjoyed some of the spoils from the Harpers Ferry capture. Private John M. Monie got a "much needed overcoat, a flagolet, and a fine little goat skin, which some of the ladies at home greatly appreciated."[52]

The Confederate cavalry followed behind Lee's army during the invasion of Maryland to cover any potential retreat. On September 5, J. E. B. Stuart's horsemen crossed the Potomac, moved eight miles to Poolesville, and camped for the night. The next morning, the Southern horsemen, led by the 1st North Carolina Cavalry, moved to Urbana and occupied the town until September 10. A few citizens sympathized with the invaders and openly socialized with them. It was here, on September 8, that Stuart and his officers held a ball for the young ladies of Urbana. The dance was interrupted by a skirmish at an outpost manned by troopers of the regiment. Officers left the dance to aid in the fight but soon returned to the "Sabers and Roses Ball."[53]

Next, Stuart's horsemen skirmished with Federal cavalry for several days at nearby Hyattstown. Leaving Urbana, the gray-clad troopers of Hampton's brigade followed Lee's army to Frederick, where on September 12 they were ordered to hold the access roads to the city. On September 13, at Middletown, the 1st North Carolina Cavalry skirmished all day under a heavy fire, retiring from the town as the brigade's rear guard came under severe fire. Losses included eight wounded and three missing. On the 15th, the regiment re-crossed the Potomac at Harpers Ferry.[54]

Confederate leaders had overestimated the sympathies of Marylanders toward the South in the western part of the state. The Rebels were greeted with a cool reception, rather than with cheers as liberators.[55]

Fate was with the Army of the Potomac and General McClellan on September 13 when he gained possession of the infamous "Lost Order," issued by Robert E. Lee on September 9. Special Order 191 laid out Lee's entire plan for the Maryland offensive. Though McClellan was convinced the order was

52 *OR* 19, pt. 1, 951; Monie, "Reminiscences," 19.

53 Von Borcke, *Memoirs of the Confederate War for Independence*, 2 vols. (London, 1866), vol. 1, 193-197; W. W. Blackford, *War Years With Jeb Stuart* (New York, NY, 1945), 140-141; J. H. Person to his mother, September 27, 1862, Presley Carter Person Papers, Duke University; Dedmond, "The Civil War Diary of Harvey Davis," 391; *Washington Post*, June 30, 1995.

54 *OR* 19, pt. 1, 814-815, 822-824.

55 Stehen W. Sears, *Landscape Turned Red: The Battle of Antietam* (Boston, MA, 1983), 68-69; James M. McPherson, *Crossroads of Freedom: Antietam, The Battle That Changed the Course of the Civil War* (New York, NY, 2002), 98.

genuine, he moved too slowly to keep Lee's divided forces from concentrating along the banks of Antietam Creek near Sharpsburg, Maryland.[56]

Jackson took Harpers Ferry and rejoined Lee at Antietam on September 16, 1862. On the 16th, the 1st North Carolina Cavalry marched up the south side of the Potomac and crossed the river back into Maryland. After spending the day at Harpers Ferry, the regiment marched to Shepherdstown and bivouacked for the night. Before dawn on the 17th, the Carolinians mounted and reached the north side of Antietam Creek by 9:00 a.m. They positioned themselves within a mile of General Lee's headquarters and attempted to eat breakfast. Taking artillery fire, they broke off their meal, left the woods, and took another position along the creek, where they fed without fires. The regiment then moved to the rear of Lee's headquarters. About 10:00 a.m., they headed to the extreme right flank and remained there until noon. Next, they hurried to the left to support Jackson's force, which had been pressed back into the woods beyond Dunker Church. With the line restored, the regiment deployed in support of J. E. B. Stuart's artillery.[57]

The battle on the 17th was the bloodiest single day of the war. In savage fighting, the Confederates held against poorly coordinated frontal attacks by McClellan's much larger army. Casualties were horrific, with about 10,000 Confederates and 13,000 Federals killed, wounded, or missing.[58]

Late that evening, Captain Barringer traveled about one mile from the regiment's camp to General Lee's headquarters to meet his brothers-in-law, Stonewall Jackson and D. H. Hill. Barringer recalled saying to Jackson, "General, isn't our army pretty badly worsted tonight?" Jackson answered, "Yes, but, oh! how I'd like to see the Yankee camp right now!" With a twinkle in his eye, Jackson added, "If I only had my 'movable column!'"[59]

McClellan did not renew the attack on the 18th. Lee, unable to sustain his supply line, safely retreated with his battered army toward Virginia. The cavalry covered the withdrawal. When the Army of Northern Virginia crossed the Potomac at Williamsport, the 1st North Carolina Cavalry was cut off from the

56 OR 19, pt. 2, 281-282; Sears, *Landscape Turned Red*, 123-125.

57 J. M. Monie, Letters, Antietam National Battlefield Visitor Center Archives.

58 Sears, *Landscape Turned Red*, 294-926.

59 John M. Monie to Gen. E. A. Carman, March 21, 1900, Antietam National Battlefield Visitor Center Archives; Jackson, *Life and Letters*, 319.

main crossing. The regiment sought a "blind" crossing (a fording of the river at a non-designated point), which was made at night in water more than waist deep. Rocks, brush, and other obstructions in the water made it a challenge, and Barringer later recalled that making such a crossing was "harder than fighting."[60]

On September 18, General Stuart took his two brigades of cavalry, infantry, and artillery and began a diversionary attack at Williamsport, to draw Union forces away from Lee's retreating army. Stuart's feint lasted almost two days. At sundown on September 20, his troopers re-crossed the Potomac to the northern shore above Williamsport.[61]

The next morning, Colonel Baker's hungry Carolinians killed some hogs that were feeding on corn that had been gathered for their horses. They had skinned and cooked a 150-pound hog, and had begun to enjoy their meal, when the Federals discovered their position and shelled them.[62]

The resulting skirmish continued all day on September 20. During the evening, General Hampton arrived and ordered Baker to march rapidly for the ford, as the brigade was the only Confederate force north of the Potomac. The Federals attempted to cut off the retreating cavalrymen, but they reached the ford and crossed under artillery fire. The regiment remained in the vicinity of Martinsburg, Virginia, 15 miles east of Antietam, with the rest of the brigade and cavalry corps until October 31. During this period, the cavalry protected Lee's army from any serious Federal probes. For the Army of Northern Virginia, the first great Confederate invasion of the North was over.[63]

After the Maryland campaign, complaints surfaced about the condition of the 1st North Carolina Cavalry. Sergeant William L. Barrier wrote about the issue in a letter home from Martinsburg, Virginia. "I am sorry to say that our regiment is going to sticks very fast," he complained. "We have only about three hundred horses fit for duty." Barrier also described the acrimony between Barringer and Colonel Baker, and stated that Baker had returned to his drinking habits: "Our Col. has returned to his drink. . . . Capt. Barringer in many respects is the best Capt. in the regiment, but at times there is no such thing as pleasing

---

60 Clark, *Histories*, vol. 1, 421.

61 Blackford, *War Years With Jeb Stuart*, 153-154.

62 Dedmond, "The Civil War Diary of Harvey Davis," 393.

63 Manarin, *North Carolina Troops*, vol. 2, 2.

him. He and Col. Baker are at logger heads continually, and there is doubtless something on foot among some of the officers to make changes in our regiment."[64]

Barringer also complained to North Carolina Governor Zebulon B. Vance after the Maryland campaign, writing a stinging attack on Colonel Baker. "Of over 900 men belonging to [the regiment], not over 300 have for several weeks been on duty," complained Rufus. "Of over 1,500 or 1,600 [horses] purchased, not over 650 can now be found or accounted for—& they [are] poor, many with sore backs & generally feeble. Of the large number of saddles, bridles, army & other equipment, many have been lost or thrown away. Up to six weeks ago, we had a large supply of cooking utensils, tools, &c &c. We are now without anything of the kind." He continued: "The men are nearly naked, without any adequate provision ahead against winter, as far as I can learn. They have been badly fed all summer and fall—especially on marches & picket duty. The moral character of the Regt. is going down very rapidly & it will soon be worthless—unless some very decided steps are taken to arrest the present downward course of things."[65]

Barringer blamed his commander for the regiment's shoddy condition: "Col. Baker has been warned by myself & others that the Regt. was fast going to ruin—but all to no purpose. He has relapsed into a former habit of hard drinking."[66]

Vance forwarded Barringer's letter to Secretary of War James A. Seddon, who passed the information to General Stuart. Stuart secured a written pledge from Laurence S. Baker that he would cease drinking. Based on the pledge, Stuart recommended that no further action be taken. Baker would serve valiantly at subsequent engagements, including Brandy Station and Gettysburg. He would be promoted to brigadier general after Gettysburg, but would be forced to retire from cavalry service due to a severe wound received on August 1, 1863, near Brandy Station. Vance's complaints might have helped Barringer and other North Carolinians, as Barringer would be promoted from captain to brigadier general within a year after Brandy Station. However, the promotions

---

64 William L. Barrier to his father, October 7, 1862, in Troxler and Auciello, *Dear Father*, 97.

65 Frontis W. Johnston, ed., *The Papers of Zebulon Baird Vance*, 3 vols. (Raleigh, NC, 1963-2013), vol. 1, 247-249.

66 Ibid. Barringer later recalled that he and Baker ultimately reconciled; Rufus Barringer to Victor Barringer, January 27, 1866, Southern Historical Collection.

might also have been due to the high casualty rate among officers during that period.[67]

The Chambersburg Raid, October 10-12, 1862

After the Battle of Antietam on September 17, 1862, Robert E. Lee withdrew his army to the Bunker Hill-Winchester area of Virginia. J. E. B. Stuart's cavalry screened the front of the army. General McClellan's Army of the Potomac remained in the Sharpsburg-Harpers Ferry region. With Lee positioned well west of the enemy, the Federals could move virtually unopposed directly against Richmond. Needing vital information on the disposition and intentions of the enemy, Lee directed Stuart to ride deep into Union territory on a reconnaissance mission. Lee also wanted Stuart to destroy the important railroad bridge over Conococheague Creek and gather as many horses as possible.[68]

On October 10, Stuart began his cavalry raid into Pennsylvania. It was a boldly planned maneuver. The Potomac River could only be crossed at infrequent fords, and the countryside was filled with telegraph lines to sound the alarm should Confederate forces be spotted. Fortunately, the weather was in Stuart's favor. For much of the time it was misty, preventing signal stations from spotting the Rebel troopers and relaying information on their location to Union forces.[69]

It was an all-cavalry expedition. Stuart detailed 1,800 men selected from the cavalry corps and divided them into three forces commanded by Gen. Wade Hampton, Col. W. H. F. "Rooney" Lee (Robert E. Lee's son), and Col. William E. "Grumble" Jones.[70]

Hampton's forces consisted of 175 men from the 2nd South Carolina Cavalry (Col. M. C. Butler), 175 from the 1st North Carolina Cavalry (Lt. Col. James B. Gordon), 150 from the 10th Virginia Cavalry, and 150 from the Phillips Legion. Part of the 1st North Carolina Cavalry contingent included two detailed squadrons under Rufus Barringer and W. H. H. Cowles. Lieutenant

67 J. E. B Stuart to Samuel Cooper, January 6, 1863, Virginia Historical Society; *OR* 27, pt. 2, 312.

68 Harry Hansen, *The Civil War: A History* (New York, NY, 1961), 263.

69 Blackford, *War Years With Jeb Stuart*, 164.

70 Clark, *Histories*, vol. 1, 421-422; Blackford, *War Years With Jeb Stuart*, 164; *OR* 19, pt. 2, 53.

Robert Shiver, an experienced scout, and six men from the 2nd South Carolina Cavalry (supported by the rest of the regiment) guided the crossing of the Potomac above Williamsport. Captain Cowles's detachment (Company A) covered the planned re-crossing near Poolesville.[71]

Stuart's raiders crossed the Potomac at McCoy's Ferry and proceeded to Chambersburg, which they temporarily occupied. Much of the town's potential war materiel was burned. When Stuart departed Chambersburg the next day, Colonel Butler, with the 2nd South Carolina Cavalry and a detachment from the 1st North Carolina Cavalry under Captain Cowles, was the last to leave the village. Stuart feigned a move toward Gettysburg to confuse the pursuing Federals, who were now on the alert thanks to a dispatch from Alexander K. McClure, editor of the *Philadelphia Times*. Stuart then headed south toward Leesburg with a five-mile-long string of captured horses. When he approached his old headquarters at Urbana on the midnight return march, he had a notion to revisit the "New York Reb" (a young woman of whom he had become fond since the "Sabres and Roses Ball" during the Maryland invasion). She was staying with the Cocky family. They lived several miles off the line of march and Stuart assigned Captain Barringer with an escort of 10 men from Companies C and F, 1st North Carolina Cavalry to act as his guard. The rendezvous occurred safely before daybreak. Stuart and his troopers ate breakfast at his old headquarters, despite being deep in enemy territory. With the reunion ended, Stuart and his detachment reunited with the main Confederate column.[72]

On October 12, the 1,800 cavalrymen re-crossed the Potomac at White's Ford with about 1,200 badly needed horses and vital information on Federal troop locations. The raid had been nearly a continuous march, from dawn on October 10 until 4:00 p.m. on the 12th, when the troopers reached Leesburg, Virginia, having traveled a distance of 90 miles.[73]

---

71 McClellan, *Stuart*, 159; *OR* 19, pt. 2, 58, U. R. Brooks, *Butler and His Cavalry, 1861-1865* (Columbia, SC, 1909), 80-82; *OR* 19, pt. 2, 57; Clark, *Histories*, vol. 1, 422. Barringer states that Lt. Wiley A. Barrier of Company I, 1st North Carolina Cavalry was in charge of the advance party in crossing the Potomac above Williamsport. This contradicts Butler's and Hampton's reports. Perhaps Lieutenant Barrier led the 1st North Carolina Cavalry contingent across the Potomac, but not the entire command.

72 Blackford, *War Years With Jeb Stuart*, 164-180; Clark, *Histories*, vol. 1, 422; Brooks, *Stories of the Confederacy*, 109.

73 Clark, *Histories*, vol. 1, 422; McClellan, *Stuart*, 159-160; *OR* 19, pt. 2, 58; Blackford, *War Years With Jeb Stuart*, 177-178.

Fall 1862, Battle of Fredericksburg, and Winter 1862-1863

After much prodding from President Lincoln, General McClellan began moving his troops toward Virginia. On October 26, part of his army crossed the Shenandoah River at Harpers Ferry, while the rest pushed across the Potomac at Berlin, Maryland. His objective was to force the Confederates to fight somewhere between Fredericksburg and Richmond, cut Lee's lines of communication, and drive his army back toward the Confederate capital. By November 3, the Army of Northern Virginia army was on the move, marching east from the Shenandoah Valley. On the same day, McClellan's entire army was across the Potomac, advancing toward the interior of Virginia. Alerted to McClellan's movements, Stuart, with Fitz Lee's brigade (temporarily under command of Col. Williams C. Wickham), had crossed the Blue Ridge Mountains into Loudoun County by way of Snicker's Gap.[74]

On October 30, Stuart ordered Hampton to move from Martinsburg to Upperville, 20 miles north of Warrenton. Warrenton was 27 miles northwest of Fredericksburg. Hampton completed his brigade's movement to Upperville by November 3. Hampton followed Stuart's order to skirmish with the Federals and delay them as much as possible, so that Lee could move his army across the Blue Ridge to get between McClellan and Richmond. Skirmishes occurred at many small villages in early November, including Union, Mountville, Aldie, Upperville, and Paris.[75]

During the night of November 4, Stuart moved Hampton's brigade into position against portions of Brig. Gen. Alfred Pleasonton's Union cavalry, accompanied by an artillery battery at Barbee's Cross Roads, 12 miles northwest of Warrenton. Stuart assigned Fitzhugh Lee's brigade to Hampton's right flank to await the expected Federal thrust from the north. At 9:00 a.m. on November 5, the Federals advanced against the Confederates and the battle commenced. At noon, Hampton ordered the 1st North Carolina Cavalry to send two companies to the crossroads. The remaining eight companies were soon ordered to support a battery of artillery. A large force of Union troopers, including Col. David Gregg with the 8th Pennsylvania Cavalry and the 6th U.S.

---

74 *OR* 19, pt. 2, 141; McClellan, *Stuart*, 169.

75 Blackford, *War Years With Jeb Stuart*, 182-183, *OR* 19, pt. 2, 140-142; McClellan, *Stuart*, 170-173.

Cavalry, moved east to outflank the position of the eight Rebel companies as they moved forward.[76]

Hampton directed the 1st North Carolina Cavalry to charge the enemy. With Colonel Baker still on detached service since the Chambersburg raid, Col. James B. Gordon ordered the charge and a hot fight ensued. The regiment finally drove the Federals back. However, Gordon's troopers pursued the enemy horsemen too far and received little support from Hampton's 2nd South Carolina Cavalry, which was blocked by the retreating Cobb Legion. Suddenly, a galling fire from dismounted elements Col. Benjamin F. Davis's 8th New York Cavalry, and hidden artillery, ripped into Gordon's right flank. Gordon saw no chance of getting the upper hand, and called for the regiment to break off the engagement. Gordon reported that he lost four men killed, with 17 wounded and captured.[77]

Hampton and cavalry commander Stuart continued movements to screen the Army of Northern Virginia. The Confederate troopers maintained daily contact with the Federals in an effort to discover their intentions. The 1st North Carolina Cavalry was engaged daily at many crossroads and fields, including Gaines's Cross Roads, Amissville, and Little Washington. When the Federals occupied Warrenton, the Rebels retreated south to the Rappahannock River.[78]

On November 7, 1862, Maj. Gen. Ambrose E. Burnside replaced George McClellan as commander of the Army of the Potomac. Though he had learned Lee's plans for the Maryland campaign, McClellan did not destroy Lee's army at Sharpsburg and failed to renew the attack on September 18—allowing Lee escape to Virginia. Thus President Lincoln relieved McClellan from command. Burnside reluctantly accepted the post, after questioning his own ability to perform the job. He was a large man of imposing appearance with keenly flashing eyes. He had won some important victories in February and March in North Carolina, including Roanoke Island and New Bern. Burnside was admired by his men and superiors for his courage, single-hearted honesty, natural modesty, and unselfishness. Robert E. Lee now waited to see what action the new Union commander would take.[79]

---

76 *OR* 19, pt. 2, 126, 144.

77 Ibid., 145-146.

78 Ibid.

79 Hansen, *The Civil War*, 260.

Fighting between the opposing armies greatly diminished until the battle of Fredericksburg on December 13. Between November 7 and the engagement at Fredericksburg, the 1st North Carolina Cavalry made several successful raids on Federal posts at Occoquan, 12 miles southeast of Manassas, and 10 miles farther southeast at Dumfries, capturing wagon trains and sutlers' stores. On November 27-28, 50 men from the regiment took part in a 200-man Confederate cavalry attack on a Union regiment at Hartwood Church, about eight miles from Falmouth. They captured 92 prisoners, about 100 horses, and supplies.[80]

On December 10, Hampton took cavalry detachments from the 1st South Carolina, 2nd South Carolina, 1st North Carolina, Jeff Davis Legion, and Cobb Legion toward Dumfries and Occoquan. On the 12th, Hampton's 520 troopers captured 50 prisoners and 24 sutlers' wagons at Dumfries, without suffering any losses. Hampton then proceeded to Occoquan, but retired in the face of enemy infantry and returned to camp on December 13.[81]

Meanwhile, General Burnside moved his army toward Fredericksburg, with the objective of crossing the Rappahannock River and forcing a fight between Fredericksburg and Richmond. Lee positioned his army to oppose the Federals. Burnside's plan went awry when his pontoon trains arrived late. The resulting delay in crossing the river allowed Lee to deploy Stonewall Jackson's and James Longstreet's 75,000 veterans on the opposite bank. Burnside mistakenly believed he faced only one wing of the Confederate army. Consequently, as fog lifted at mid-morning on December 13, he launched an all-out frontal assault. The Confederates were ready. Solidly established in a defensive position on high ground called Marye's Heights, located behind the town, the Confederates repulsed a succession of doomed Federal attacks. Burnside's troops were slaughtered, suffering 12,600 casualties compared to Lee's 5,300. The battered Union army withdrew to its original position on the north side of the Rappahannock.[82]

Prior to and during the battle at Fredericksburg, the Confederate cavalry guarded the rear and flanks of the army. After the battle, the cavalry made

80 *OR* 21, 15-16.

81 McClellan, *Stuart*, 188.

82 Alfred M. Scales, *The Battle of Fredericksburg: An Address by Hon. Alfred M. Scales of North Carolina, Before The Association of the Virginia Division of the Army of Virginia* (Washington, DC, 1884), 8, 12, 17-20.

numerous attacks on enemy supply routes, while the Confederate army remained in Fredericksburg. Stuart ordered detachments selected from the cavalry brigades, including 75 from the 1st North Carolina, to cross the upper Rappahannock and move against the Federal supply depots. On December 17-18, Hampton, with 465 troopers, attacked Occoquan again. This time he captured wagons and supplies belonging to Maj. Gen. Franz Siegel's corps. Union cavalry arrived and forced Hampton to retire, but not before bringing back 150 prisoners and 20 wagons.[83]

On December 26, General Stuart selected detachments from the brigades of Wade Hampton, Fitz Lee, and Rooney Lee—1,800 horsemen in all—and began a raid on Union outposts at Dumfries, Occoquan, and other depots in what became known as the "Christmas Raid." The 1st North Carolina Cavalry furnished 175 troopers under Maj. John Whitaker. Colonel Gordon did not accompany the raid but remained at the Rappahannock. The raid ended on New Year's Day and resulted in more than 200 Union prisoners, about 20 wagons, and all sorts of supplies captured. Confederate losses totaled one killed, 13 wounded, and 13 missing. Stuart safely crossed the Rappahannock on New Year's Day, leaving behind a small party of scouts commanded by John S. Mosby.[84]

The exciting raids of December were followed by picket duty until February 16, 1863, when the 1st North Carolina Cavalry was relieved by Fitzhugh Lee's cavalry. The Carolina horsemen then started the long trip back to Richmond to rest and recruit. The march to Richmond was hard on the men, due to a particularly bad spell of winter weather and the resulting deep mud on the roads, making them almost impassable. In late February, Rufus Barringer was ordered to take charge of the important Confederate stores at Hanover Junction. Barringer's Company F remained there on detached service in defense of the strategic railroad junction until after the battle of Chancellorsville, April 30-May 6, 1863. They guarded the stores against a Federal attack by several hundred of Gen. George Stoneman's raiders. Barringer's company and about 100 other detailed men were the only

83 OR 21, 695-697.

84 Ibid., 731-736; McClellan, *Stuart*, 196; Chris J. Hartley, *Stuart's Tarheels: James B. Gordon and His North Carolina Cavalry* (Baltimore, MD, 1996), 179-180. Rooney Lee had been promoted in October after the Chambersburg raid, and the 13th and 15th Virginia Cavalry were brigaded under him.

defenders. The spirited gray-clad horsemen held off Yankee forces for two days and saved the supplies. As Barringer later recalled, "I had resolved to sacrifice all rather than surrender the Junction, with its valuable stores, to the enemy."[85]

On February 13, 1863, Rufus wrote his sister Margaret concerning the possibility of getting a furlough to visit home: "Furlough & leaves of absence still dry with our Brigade. We are doing good service while thousands of others are gone home. . . . My one chance is the unit as I have had two short leaves heretofore & expect no favors at Regimental Hd. Qtrs." It appears Barringer had used up his quota of short leaves and pinned his hopes on the possibility of leave being granted for the whole unit. Unfortunately for he and his men, this was not granted.

Rufus thanked his sister for her gifts and described his living conditions: "Am much obliged for the puddings. . . . We are living very well now—drawing rice, sugar, & molasses from the Qrt Master & talk of our being relieved here by one of the Va. Brigades & are going back some 20 or 30 miles to Queens Co. to rest, recruit our horses, drill, etc. And we hope then to have good times, even if we don't all get home."[86]

Since Rufus could not go home, Mrs. Barringer made the difficult journey to Hanover Court House to visit her husband in April 1863. Rufus had been ordered there for a rest after hard service around Fredericksburg, including the defense at Hanover Junction.[87]

Stonewall Jackson wrote a letter to Barringer on February 11, 1863, containing news of all the brothers-in-law. It is probably one of the last intimate letters Jackson penned before his death on May 10, 1863:

"My dear Captain.

I regret to hear of the continued delicate health of Mrs. B. & child [Rufus Chunn Barringer]. . . . Joseph Morrison has gone home to see his mother who is seriously ill. Capt. Avery has also gone on leave of absence of 25 days. . . . Gen'l [D. H.] Hill has been assigned to duty in North Carolina. . . . Gen'l Stuart has arrived . . . and he desires

85 Rufus Barringer to Victor Barringer, January 27, 1866, Southern Historical Collection.

86 Rufus Barringer to Margaret Grier, February 13, 1863, Rufus C. Barringer Papers, University of Notre Dame.

87 Barringer, *The Natural Bent*, 69.

you [be] appointed on his Military Court of which he has the promise [from Lee]. Say nothing about this as the court is not yet secured [approved].

T. J. J."[88]

The battle of Chancellorsville is usually described as "Lee's greatest victory." It was a textbook engagement in which Lee divided his army to successfully attack the Union army's flank. Though outnumbered two to one, the Confederates achieved a stunning victory. This triumph, however, came at the expense of Stonewall Jackson's mortal wound from "friendly fire."[89]

At Hanover Junction, Barringer recalled, "it became my duty to receive and forward the dispatch from General Lee announcing at the same time the great Confederate victory and the mortal wound of Jackson." Barringer continued: "The telegraph and railroad lines were at this time all cut by [George] Stoneman's [Union] Raiders, and I only succeeded in getting the dispatch safely through by sending reliable couriers on fleet horses over different routes. But in a very few days the shout of victory was hushed and stilled in the universal wail for our fallen chieftain."[90]

During the battle of Chancellorsville, Hampton's brigade was recruiting south of the James River. Captain Barringer was again on duty at Hanover Junction when Jackson's body was taken to Richmond, and during the fallen Southern hero's funeral in Lexington. It must have been hard for Rufus to remain on duty (he probably knew Jackson had died from his wounds) while Anna Jackson, brother-in-law Lt. William W. Morrison (Jackson's aide-de-

---

88 Ibid.; Compiled Service Record of Rufus Barringer, First North Carolina Cavalry (Ninth North Carolina State Troops), from the Compiled Service Records of Confederate Soldiers Who Served in Organizations from the State of North Carolina, Record Group 109, National Archives. In a letter to Secretary of War James A. Seddon, the North Carolina members of the Confederate Congress recommended Barringer for appointment to a military court; Adele H. Mitchell, ed., *The Letters of Major General James E. B. Stuart* (Richmond, VA, 1990), 294-295. Jackson also recommended Barringer for his military court, should it be formed. Joseph Morrison and Capt. Alphonso Avery were Rufus Barringer's brothers-in-law through marriage to his first wife, Eugenia Morrison Barringer. Anna and Paul were Rufus's two children from his first marriage to Eugenia.

89 Robert K. Krick, *The Smoothbore Volley That Doomed the Confederacy* (Baton Rouge, LA, 2002), 21-22.

90 Jackson, *Life and Letters*, 318-319; Barringer, *The Natural Bent*, 92, 94-95. Jackson's favorite horse, "Little Sorrel," was taken back to the Morrison place, "Cottage Home," in Lincoln County, North Carolina.

camp), and perhaps other members of the family gathered in Richmond and Lexington. Barringer admired Jackson's military leadership and piety, and the two shared a warm relationship. Rufus must have wondered, as most others did, how the South could possibly replace General Jackson.[91]

Throughout the early years of the war, promotions were slow in coming to North Carolina Whigs, who for the most part had been against secession until President Lincoln's call for North Carolina troops to help put down the rebellion. Zebulon Vance, sworn in as Governor of North Carolina in September 1862, frequently complained to President Jefferson Davis about such a policy or "black list." A glaring example of this policy was Rufus Barringer. He had recruited a company of cavalry at the outbreak of the war and would still hold the rank of captain in June 1863, having served with distinction for 26 months in virtually all of the cavalry's engagements. Despite his family ties to Stonewall Jackson and D. H. Hill, Barringer would still have marks against him if President Davis had such a black list policy. Rufus had also studied law under North Carolina Supreme Court Chief Justice Richmond M. Pearson, who was detested in Richmond because of his court rulings. Judge Pearson considered the Conscription Act of April 16, 1862, unconstitutional, and it precipitated a long-running controversy between Governor Vance and authorities in Richmond. Another potential hindrance was the fact that Barringer had served as a Whig in both branches of the North Carolina legislature.[92]

During 1862 and early 1863, the 1st North Carolina Cavalry had matured into a dependable, reliable fighting unit. It had given a good account of itself on numerous fields and raids. On May 25, 1863, as the summer campaign began, the regiment's strength was reported at 34 effective mounted officers, 500 effective mounted men, five non-effective officers, 151 non-effective men, and seven officers and 176 men absent. Captain Rufus Barringer had fought courageously at Willis Church and other actions, and had gained the respect of his men and his superiors.

---

91 Rufus Barringer to Victor Barringer, January 27, 1866, Southern Historical Collection.

92 Glenn Tucker, *Zeb Vance: Champion of Personal Freedom* (New York, NY, 1965), 257-258.

Chapter 6

"I have recently received numerous solicitations to become a candidate for [Confederate]
Congress in the Eighth District. These solicitations I have uniformly declined. . . .
I think it better for those in service to *stand by their colors*."

— *Lt. Col. Rufus Barringer at Hanover Court House*

1863: Brandy Station, the Bristoe Campaign, and Personal Loss

After the stunning victory at Chancellorsville in early May, General Lee, Secretary of War James A. Seddon, and President Jefferson Davis decided to carry the war into Northern territory a second time. The first invasion ended in a bloody tactical stalemate at Sharpsburg, Maryland. Confederate authorities believed another push above the Mason-Dixon Line might relieve Virginia, which had been ravaged by two years of war. They also hoped it would compel the Lincoln administration to withdraw Union troops away from the coasts of Virginia and North Carolina, and out of Mississippi, where they were besieging Vicksburg. A decisive Confederate victory on Northern soil might also break the will of the Federals to continue the war, and perhaps bring recognition from abroad.[1]

On May 11, Lee ordered Jeb Stuart to move his cavalry from Orange County north to Culpeper County. By the 22nd, Stuart had nearly 7,000 troopers of Hampton's, Rooney Lee's, and Fitzhugh Lee's brigades in and

---

1   Stephen W. Sears, *Gettysburg* (Boston: MA, 2004), 7-8, 12-17; Glenn Tucker, *High Tide at Gettysburg* (New York, NY, 1958), 17, 19-20.

around Culpeper. Another 3,000 from Robertson's and Jones's brigades joined them there by June 5. Lee's plan called for Stuart to position his troopers on the right of the army to screen the infantry during the march north and protect its flank.[2]

The Army of Northern Virginia was at Fredericksburg, across the Rappahannock River from Falmouth. President Lincoln had relieved Ambrose Burnside and promoted Maj. Gen. Joseph Hooker to command of the Army of the Potomac. Hooker's cavalry and two brigades of infantry were positioned on the upper Rappahannock near Falmouth. With Lee intent on marching north into Pennsylvania, Hooker attempted to gauge whether the Confederates would move north or turn suddenly eastward toward Washington.[3]

On June 5, General Stuart reviewed his cavalry in an open field near the hamlet of Inlet Station, four miles northeast of Culpeper. More than a military parade, it was also a splendid social event of the sort the flashy Stuart loved to stage. Stuart's inspector general, Maj. Heros von Borcke, recounted events of the night before: "Invitations having been sent out to the whole circle of our acquaintances far and near, the hotels of the town (Culpeper) and as many private houses as had any accommodation to spare, were got[ten] ready for the reception of our guests, many of whom, after all, we had to put under tents. . . . Every train brought in fresh crowds of our guests, and we all assembled at the station to receive them, and forward them to their destination by the ambulances and wagons we had . . . prepared for that purpose. In the evening there was a ball at the Town Hall."[4]

The following morning, General Stuart and his staff mounted their horses and headed for the plains near Inlet Station, about two miles southwest of Brandy Station, where the huge cavalry review would be held. Von Borcke recalled:

> Our little band presented a gay and gallant appearance as we rode forth to the sound of our bugles . . . our plumes nodding, and our battle-flag waving in the breeze. . . . As our

2   *OR* 25, pt. 2, 792.

3   Sears, *Gettysburg*, 22, 43, 60-61.

4   Heros Von Borcke, *Memoirs of the Confederate War for Independence*, 2 vols. (London, 1866), vol. 2, 264-265; Stephen Z. Starr, *The Union Cavalry in the Civil War*, 3 vols. (Baton Rouge, LA, 1979), vol. 1, 374.

approach was heralded by the flourish of trumpets, many of the ladies in the village came forth to greet us . . . and showered down flowers upon our path.[5]

The review itself was a magnificent pageant. The entire division passed in review with three bands playing and a flag waving at the head of each regiment. The column then divided into brigades and regiments that performed drill. In a climactic finale, the troopers—yelling with sabers drawn—charged the artillery posted at intervals around the perimeter of the field. The gunners fired blank cartridges at the galloping horsemen in a noisy closing. The day ended with another ball "on a piece of turf near headquarters, and by the light of enormous wood fires, the ruddy glare of which upon the animated groups . . . gave the whole scene a wild and romantic effect."[6]

Not all were happy with these reviews. Some, including the irascible "Grumble" Jones, considered them a waste of resources. Jones and his brigade had just arrived on June 3-4. His men and horses were tired and needed rest, which the review of June 5 did not permit.[7]

General Lee had been invited to review the troops, but he was unable to attend. Having no trepidation over staging a review the day before offensive operations began, however, the Confederate commander gave notice that he desired to review the cavalry. On June 8, he surveyed all of his horse soldiers, about 9,500 troopers, at Inlet Station. As the 1st North Carolina Cavalry passed the reviewing officers, Stuart turned to Lee and pointed to the Carolinians: "General, there comes the First North Carolina Cavalry, which there is not a better regiment in either army." This comment, heard and recalled by Capt. William H. H. Cowles, would be proudly remembered by troopers of the regiment for the rest of their lives.[8]

The Confederate plan for the morning of June 9 called for two full infantry corps, commanded by James Longstreet and Richard S. Ewell, to move west

---

5   Ibid.

6   George M. Neese, *Three Years in the Confederate Horse Artillery* (New York, NY, 1911), 168; Starr, *The Union Cavalry in the Civil War*, vol. 1, 375; Von Borcke, *Memoirs*, vol. 2, 266-267; Starr, *The Union Cavalry in the Civil War*, vol. 1, 375.

7   Eric J. Wittenberg, *The Union Cavalry Comes of Age: Hartwood Church to Brandy Station, 1863* (Washington, DC, 2003), 253-254; Fairfax Downey, *Clash of Cavalry: The Battle of Brandy Station* (New York, NY, 1959), 85.

8   William H. H. Cowles, "The Life and Services of Gen. James B. Gordon," Address delivered in Raleigh, NC, May 10, 1887, 9; Clark, *Histories*, vol. 1, 423.

into the Shenandoah Valley and then north toward Pennsylvania. General A. P. Hill's corps would temporarily remain on the banks of the Rappahannock to cover the movement. The cavalry command, under orders to screen Lee's invading forces, included the brigades of Wade Hampton, Rooney Lee, Beverly Robertson, "Grumble" Jones, and Fitzhugh Lee (the latter under Col. Thomas Munford due to Fitzhugh's bout with inflammatory rheumatism). Also attached was Capt. James F. Hart's battery of Maj. Robert F. Beckham's horse artillery. The 1st North Carolina Cavalry was in Hampton's command. General Lee directed Stuart's cavalry to cross the Rappahannock at Beverly Ford, four miles northeast of Brandy Station.[9]

Wounding at Brandy Station: June 9, 1863

General Hooker ordered most of his cavalry and two brigades of infantry to attack the Confederates. This force of roughly 11,000 men was led by Brig. Gen. Alfred Pleasonton, the newly appointed Union cavalry commander. Pleasonton devised a plan that assumed the Rebel horsemen were still near the village of Culpeper Court House. His scheme consisted of attacks by two cavalry columns under Generals John Buford and David M. Gregg. Buford, supported by the infantry, would cross at Beverly Ford while Gregg crossed at Kelly's Ford. The two Union columns would then link up at Brandy Station. From there they intended to push on to Culpeper. However, the plan was doomed from the start because Stuart was bivouacked on Fleetwood Hill near Brandy Station, and Grumble Jones's brigade and Beckham's artillery were camped just southwest of Beverly Ford. The Federals would find themselves trying to concentrate their forces while in the midst of Confederate cavalry. On the evening of June 8, Buford's columns took position at the fords, about six miles apart, in preparation for the crossing.[10]

At 4:30 a.m. on June 9, Col. Benjamin F. "Grimes" Davis's 8th New York Cavalry led the way, splashing across Beverly Ford into a thick fog. Thus began the battle of Brandy Station, the largest single cavalry engagement of the war (including about 2,000 infantry). The immense plains at Brandy Station were perfectly suited for a cavalry fight. Major H. B. McClellan of Stuart's staff

9 John S. Salmon, *The Official Virginia Civil War Battlefield Guide* (Mechanicsburg, PA, 2001), 198-199.

10 Wittenberg, *The Union Cavalry Comes of Age*, 253-254; OR 27, pt. 1, 949-952.

recorded that the opposing forces consisted of 10,981 Federals and 9,536 Confederates.[11]

Buford did not expect the presence of a Confederate force on the other side of the river, but his attack surprised them. Many were still sleeping or cooking breakfast when the first shots were fired. Buford's attack was stalled by two guns from Hart's Battery, while Beckham's battalion escaped capture and fled to higher ground at St. James Church. The 6th and 7th Virginia Cavalry of Grumble Jones's brigade soon arrived on the scene. During the opening moments of the fight, Col. Grimes Davis fell mortally wounded on Beverly Ford Road. The 8th New York Cavalry, now leaderless, began to retreat. However, the Federals soon regrouped and again attacked the brigades of Jones and Rooney Lee. At the first sound of gunfire, Rooney had moved his troopers from Welford's Ford, just west of Beverly Ford, to a position near St. James Church.[12]

General Stuart ordered Hampton, whose troopers at Brandy Station were awakened by gunfire, to support Jones and Rooney Lee at Beverly Ford Road. Hampton left the 2nd South Carolina Cavalry, under Col. Matthew C. Butler, in reserve at Brandy Station. His three remaining units, the 1st North Carolina Cavalry (Col. Laurence S. Baker), the Cobb Legion, and Jeff Davis Legion, soon arrived and deployed on the right of Beckham's horse artillery.[13]

In the renewed attack on Jones and Rooney Lee, the Confederates took heavy losses but rallied and quickly established a strong position. Beckham's artillery deployed two miles southwest of Beverly Ford on a slight ridge near St. James Church. Hampton's brigade was just east of the guns on the ridge. Jones's brigade was west of the church and Rooney Lee's faced east along Yew Ridge. Lee deployed additional artillery one mile north of St. James Church at Dr. Daniel Green's residence. He also ordered dismounted troopers into position behind a low stone wall, 300 yards below and east of Green's house.[14]

With Maj. John H. Whitaker out of action due to illness, Capt. Rufus Barringer served as acting major of the 1st North Carolina Cavalry during the

11 McClellan, *Stuart*, 293.

12 OR 27, pt. 2, 721-722; Clark B. Hall, "The Battle of Brandy Station," in *Civil War Times Illustrated* (May-June 1990), 35; Downey, *Clash of Cavalry*, 94.

13 OR 27, pt. 2, 721-722; Brooks, *Stories of the Confederacy*, 145-146.

14 OR 27, pt. 2, 721-722; Brooks, *Stories of the Confederacy*, 146-148; Hall, "The Battle of Brandy Station," 37.

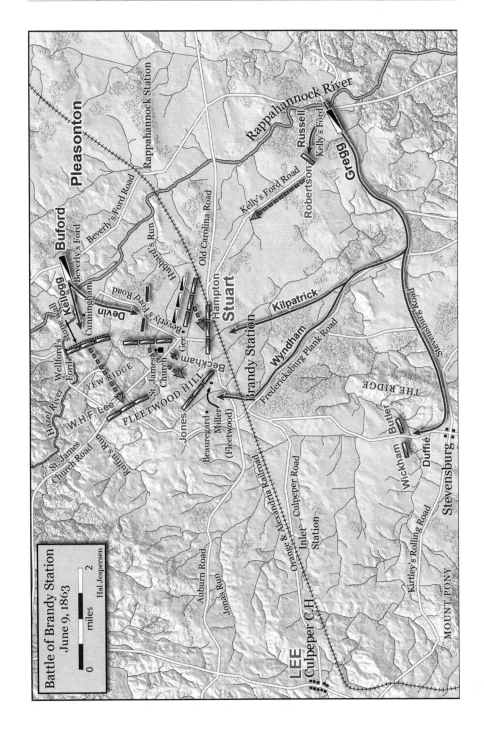

morning attacks. Hampton deployed 100 dismounted men as skirmishers and sharpshooters, including elements of the Cobb and Jeff Davis Legions and Companies G and K of the 1st North Carolina Cavalry, to dislodge enemy forces from the woods in front of them. The Confederate horse artillery remained in danger of capture. Sharpshooters from Col. John L. Black's 1st South Carolina Cavalry advanced to help dislodge the bluecoats. The dismounted Confederates made a desperate charge to save the artillery, driving the enemy back several hundred yards. Dismounted Union troopers from the brigades of Col. Thomas Devin and Grimes Davis (now led by Maj. William S. McClure) charged the Southern sharpshooters, but were driven back by the remaining mounted Confederates. An additional 100 dismounted men from Companies B, C, D, E, F, and I, 1st North Carolina Cavalry went forward as sharpshooters.

The mounted Confederates were forced back and retired farther from the woods. While dismounting a squadron into position 200 yards southeast of St. James Church, near Mary Emily Gee's house, Rufus Barringer was shot from his horse and severely wounded. Trooper William L. Barrier described the injury: "The ball struck him in the back of his upper jaw and passed out at the front part of his mouth knocking out most of his upper teeth." Chief Bugler Henry Litaker and Cpl. Walter Monroe Bell of Company F, both of whom had ridden forward with Barringer, carried their painfully wounded captain from the field.[15]

In an ongoing attempt to save their artillery, the Confederates forced the bluecoats back until they were reinforced by reserves. Buford persisted in trying to turn the Confederate left flank. He shifted most of his cavalry less than a mile northeast of Green's house to the Cunningham farm, where they stubbornly assaulted Lee's dismounted troopers behind a stone wall. However, Rooney Lee's brigade held a terrain advantage and continued to hold them off. The Jeff Davis Legion, in reserve just east of the fighting, was ordered into the battle and the Federals retreated to nearby woods. Confederate sharpshooters again advanced, regaining the ground they had lost, but Stuart soon learned that General Gregg and his 2,400-man Federal force had come in behind them.[16]

15 Clark, *Histories*, vol. 1, 424; OR 27, pt. 2, 723, 726; Rufus Barringer to Victor C. Barringer, January 27, 1866, Southern Historical Collection; *Western Democrat*, June 30, 1863; W. L. Barrier to his father, June 10, 1863, in *Dear Father*, 110.

16 *OR* 27, pt. 2, 680-687, 721-722.

Gregg came up from Kelly's Ford and slid past Beverly Robertson's force with little opposition. Robertson believed his orders were to simply hold Kelly's Ford Road. Stuart assumed Robertson would stop Gregg's advance and ignored several calls for help from the rear. The Confederate cavalry commander was surprised when Gregg's troopers attacked Fleetwood Hill— the highest ground and site of Stuart's headquarters. Hampton, pressed by Buford from the north and Gregg from the south, realized he would be entirely surrounded if the enemy gained control of Fleetwood Hill. Stuart ordered Hampton to withdraw his regiments from their positions, one at a time, and proceed to the hill.[17]

With his right flank now dangerously unsupported, Rooney Lee abandoned his defensive line along the Yew Hills northwest of St. James Church. He pulled back toward higher ground at the northern end of Fleetwood Hill. Buford's bluecoats followed, fighting Lee's rear guard all the way.[18]

Stuart, knowing that whoever held Fleetwood Hill would win the day, ordered Jones to send two regiments to hold the heights. The Union force advancing on Fleetwood Hill was larger than expected. Stuart ordered Hampton and Robertson to move up their brigades, with Jones to follow, and Rooney Lee to move on the left. Also involved in the mounted attack were Pierce Young's Cobb Legion and Colonel Black's 1st South Carolina Cavalry. Colonel A. W. Harman's 12th Virginia Cavalry and Lt. Col. Elijah V. White's 35th Virginia Cavalry Battalion of Jones's brigade led the assault. The contest for the hill was prolonged and spirited. Hampton moved the 1st North Carolina Cavalry and Jeff Davis Legion into position to turn Buford's right flank. By this time, the wounded Barringer had been carried from the battlefield. He was taken back to Culpeper, and was doing "well" late in the day. He would soon be taken to Richmond for surgery.[19]

The charging Confederate troopers swept the 2nd and 10th New York off Fleetwood Hill and recovered the ground south and east of the railroad at Brandy Station. As the Federals attempted to escape down the hill, Hampton attacked with Capt. William H. H. Cowles leading Company F and the rest of the 1st North Carolina Cavalry, supported by the Jeff Davis Legion. The fight

17 Ibid., 721-722; ibid., pt. 1, 949-952; Brooks, *Stories of the Confederacy*, 145-148.

18 *OR* 27, pt. 2, 721-722.

19 Ibid., 681, 721-722; Compiled Service Record for Rufus Barringer; W. L. Barrier to his father, June 10, 1863, in *Dear Father*, 110.

intensified on the southern flanks of the long hill. After ferocious hand-to-hand combat between two brigades of opposing horsemen, the Confederates drove the Union cavalry from the hill.[20]

Despite the loss of Barringer and many others, Colonel Baker's 1st North Carolina Cavalry remained in the thick of the afternoon fight. Lieutenant Col. William W. Blackford later recalled: "The lines met on the hill. It was like what we had read of in the days of chivalry, acres and acres of horsemen sparkling with sabres, and dotted with brilliant bits of color where their flags danced above them, hurled against each other at full speed and meeting with a shock that made the earth tremble."[21]

With the Union cavalry lingering and assembling about a mile south of Fleetwood Hill, Stuart was determined to drive them off. He ordered Rooney Lee to counterattack Gregg's forces. In the resulting charge on Buford's lines, Rooney was severely wounded in the leg. The Confederates, now including Fitz Lee's brigade under Colonel Munford, pressed Buford's horsemen back. Buford was soon ordered to pull back across Beverly Ford, and did so unmolested.[22]

Lieutenant Cadwallader J. Iredell of the 1st North Carolina Cavalry described the action: "We gave the Yankees a . . . thrashing. This only shows that it is useless for the Yankee cavalry to try to make raids when Hampton's Brigade opposes them. We were at one time entirely surrounded but General Hampton, managing his Brigade with his usual skill and good judgment, turned upon the force in his rear and soon sent them to flight. . . . All of our injured men nearly were killed or wounded in the woods while dismounted—very few in the charge. . . . Whenever we got them in the fields out of the woods, we whipped them cleverly with the Sabre."[23]

The day-long battle of Brandy Station was over. The Confederates lost 515 killed or wounded, while the Federals lost 868. The 1st North Carolina Cavalry lost five killed, 12 wounded, and 14 missing. In Hampton's brigade, the losses totaled 15 killed, 55 wounded, and 50 missing. Stuart's division also lost an

---

20 Blackford, *War Years With Jeb Stuart*, 215.

21 Ibid., 215-216.

22 Ibid., 216; OR 27, pt. 2, 683. While convalescing, Rooney Lee was captured and spent months in a Northern prison camp.

23 Letter dated June 13, 1863, C. J. Iredell Papers, Southern Historical Collection.

unusually high number of officers. Colonel Solomon Williams (2nd North Carolina Cavalry) and General Hampton's brother, Lt. Col. Frank Hampton (2nd South Carolina Cavalry) were killed. In addition to Barringer and Rooney Lee, Col. M. C. Butler, and Col. A. W. Harman were severely wounded.[24]

The prolonged battle of Brandy Station proved a tactical draw. The Confederates were surprised, but managed to rally and drive off the enemy while suffering fewer losses. Before Brandy Station and Kelly's Ford three months earlier, the Rebels thought little of the Union cavalry. At Brandy Station, however, the Federal troopers came of age by proving they could ride and fight with the South's best. The tide was changing. The Federal troopers gained confidence in themselves and their commanders, which would prove invaluable in battles to come.

In his report, Wade Hampton described Barringer's actions on June 9: "Captain Barringer, First North Carolina, who acted as field officer on that occasion, bore himself with marked coolness and good conduct." The bullet that passed through Rufus's mouth fractured the superior maxilla and dislocated the teeth of the upper jaw, resulting in permanent injury. Surgery was performed at General Hospital No. 4 in Richmond. On June 24, he left Richmond on a 30-day leave of absence. He went first to Salisbury, North Carolina, for follow-up treatment and recuperation.[25]

Rufus was examined at the hospital in Salisbury on July 8. The surgeon recommended that he be granted 30 additional days of leave. Barringer went to Concord and on to Asheville, where his wife's parents lived. Five weeks later, the chief surgeon at Asheville examined Barringer and found him still suffering from the effects of his wound. He was granted an additional 35 days of medical

---

24 Clark, *Histories*, vol. 1, 424; *OR* 27, pt. 1, 726; ibid., pt. 2, 723.

25 Jack D. Welsh, *Medical Histories of Confederate Generals*, (Kent, OH, 1995), 14. Alfred, Rufus's body servant, was probably with him at this time (his pension application indicates he served with Barringer for two years). However, it is not known if he accompanied and attended Barringer in the ambulance to Richmond. See Compiled Service Records of Confederate Soldiers Who Served in Organizations from the State of North Carolina, Record Group 109, National Archives; Compiled Service Records for Confederate Generals and Staff Officers, Record Group 109, National Archives; "Register of Officers Treated, General Hospital No. 4 1863-64," Record Group 109, National Archives. In *The Natural Bent*, Rufus's son does not mention his father returning home. However, his sister-in-law, Maria Barringer, noted in a letter that Rufus did visit Concord while recovering from wounds. While there, he almost certainly saw his children. He also spent considerable time in Asheville.

leave, and he did not return to active duty until October. As one might expect from a wound like this, it would trouble Barringer well into the future.[26]

On June 27, 1863, President Lincoln replaced General Hooker with Maj. Gen. George Gordon Meade as commander of the Army of the Potomac. On the third day of the battle of Gettysburg, the 1st North Carolina Cavalry and Jeff Davis Legion, supporting the 1st Virginia, broke through George A. Custer's 7th Michigan Cavalry two miles east of Gettysburg at Rummel's farm. Pursuing the retreating enemy, they encountered Union reserves and hand-to-hand combat ensued. After a ferocious fight, the blue-clad horsemen gained the upper hand and drove off the Tar Heel troopers.[27]

General Hampton was seriously wounded on this climatic third day at Gettysburg. As the senior colonel, Laurence S. Baker (1st North Carolina Cavalry) took command of Hampton's brigade and extricated it from the fight. Baker was slightly wounded in the withdrawal.[28]

During the 10-day retreat back into Virginia (July 4-14), J. E. B. Stuart's cavalry screened the rear, led the advance, and guarded the flanks of the Army of Northern Virginia. The pursuing Federals engaged Baker's troopers in several skirmishes during the march to safety in the Old Dominion. Sergeant James M. Pugh of the 1st North Carolina wrote, "I am completely broke down for I have been going day and night for over two weeks in Maryland and Pennsylvania and doing some of the hardest fighting that ever poor souls ever did." On August 1, Hampton's brigade, still under Baker, repulsed a Federal attack across the Rappahannock River near Brandy Station. During the fight, Baker was seriously wounded in the right arm.[29]

In August, Brig. Gen. James G. Martin, commanding the District of North Carolina, recommended Rufus Barringer for promotion to the rank of colonel to lead one of Martin's state cavalry regiments. The recommendation was never

---

26 Compiled Service Record for Rufus Barringer.

27 Edward G. Longacre, *The Cavalry at Gettysburg* (Lincoln, NE, 1993), 230-231; OR 27, pt. 1, 956; ibid., pt. 2, 724-725.

28 Ibid., 290, 298, 311-312; Eric Wittenberg, J. David Petruzzi, and Michael E. Nugent, *One Continuous Fight: The Retreat from Gettysburg and the Pursuit of Lee's Army of Northern Virginia, July 4-14, 1863* (New York, NY, 2008), 10.

29 James M. Pugh to his wife, July 12, 1863, Southern Historical Collection; Ezra J. Warner, *Generals in Gray: Lives of the Confederate Commanders* (Baton Rouge, LA, 1959), 15.

acted upon, but Barringer was destined to return to the 1st North Carolina Cavalry in October.[30]

While Barringer was on extended medical leave, the cavalry of the Army of Northern Virginia was reorganized on September 9, 1863. This reorganization created a cavalry corps of two divisions commanded by Wade Hampton and Fitzhugh Lee. The 1st, 2nd, 4th, and 5th North Carolina Cavalry were all reassigned to a single brigade under Laurence S. Baker, who had recently been promoted to brigadier general.[31]

Due to Baker's absence, his brigade was temporarily commanded by the senior brigade colonel, Dennis D. Ferebee of the 4th North Carolina Cavalry. Butler's brigade was temporarily commanded by James B. Gordon, while awaiting Bulter's return and before the appointment of Pierce M. B. Young as its commander. Gordon's and Young's commissions dated from September 28, but Gordon actually took command on October 5 and Young after October 10.[32]

On September 22, a sharp cavalry fight took place at "Jack's Shop," south of Madison Court House in Madison County, Virginia. Hampton's division fought Davies's and Custer's brigades, of Judson Kilpatrick's division, and John Buford's troopers. Major William H. Cheek temporarily commanded the 1st North Carolina Cavalry. At Jack's Shop, Buford's and Kilpatrick's Federals almost succeeded in setting a trap for Stuart's troopers, but the Confederate horsemen scattered the bluecoats and fought their way out.[33]

On September 28, due to the seriousness of Baker's wounds, Colonel Gordon of the 1st North Carolina Cavalry was promoted to brigadier general and assigned to command the brigade. James Byron Gordon was Rufus Barringer's mentor. Gordon was born on November 2, 1822, in Wilkesboro, North Carolina. He attended Emory and Henry College, and engaged in the mercantile business in Wilkesboro. He was a leader in local politics and served in the North Carolina House of Commons in 1850, the same year Rufus

---

30 Rufus Barringer to Victor Barringer, January 27, 1866. Martin wanted Barringer to command the 7th Confederate Cavalry stationed in North Carolina.

31 *OR* 29, pt. 2, 707-708; McClellan, *Stuart*, 371-372.

32 Roger H. Harrell, *The 2nd North Carolina Cavalry* (Jefferson, NC, 2004), 191-193.

33 Chris Hartley, *Stuart's Tarheels* (Baltimore, MD, 1996), 265.

Barringer served in the state Senate. Gordon, a protégé of General Stuart, would become one of the finest cavalry commanders of the war.[34]

In early September, Barringer had been notified of his promotion to major by a letter from Gordon. The letter revealed the competition between Barringer and W. H. Cheek for promotions, and stated in part: "It is with pleasure that I announce to you your appointment as Maj of the 1st N.C. Cavalry. The Regt is in very bad condition. [Captain Marcus D. L.] McLeod has been in command for some time [due to the wounding of others more qualified]; with all his goodness and amiability, he is not qualified to take command of a Regt—every one is regretting your absence. I hope you will be enabled to join us soon. I am in command of the Brigade by the casualties of war. Our animals are suffering for forage.... Cheek [still a major at this time] will be very much provoked, but I have been conscientious in the matter. Write soon. My regards to Mrs. B."[35]

Meanwhile, Barringer apparently spent the latter part of his recuperation at Hanover Court House, 18 miles north of Richmond. The courthouse was used as a hospital. During September, Rufus was visited there by his wife and young son, Paul. During his recovery, he was also approached to stand as a candidate for the Confederate Congress. However, in a letter to the public, he firmly rejected the offer: "I entered the army from a sense of duty alone, counting the cost and knowing the sacrifices. Our great object is not yet obtained, and I do not consider it consistent with my obligations here to accept any civil or political office during the war. I think it better for those in service to stand by their colors, whilst those at home should all unite in a cordial and earnest support of the authorities in feeding, clothing and otherwise sustaining the gallant men (and their families) who are fighting not only for our rights, but for the safety of our homes and firesides."[36]

34 Clark, *Histories*, vol. 4, 581.

35 James B. Gordon to Rufus Barringer, September 1, 1863, Rufus C. Barringer Papers, University of Notre Dame. This letter reveals the intense competition between Cheek and Barringer for promotions. They probably did not like each other at this point in time.

36 Barringer, *The Natural Bent*, 69; 116-117; Letter to the Public, October 17, 1863, Rufus Barringer Papers, Southern Historical Collection; *Western Democrat*, October 20, 1863; *Carolina Watchman*, October 26, 1863. The letter from Barringer from Orange Court House is dated October 17, 1863. The cavalry fight at Auburn occurred on October 14 and at Buckland on October 19. It is not clear what Barringer would have been doing at Orange Court House between the two cavalry fights. Perhaps it was due to his promotion to lieutenant colonel (dated October 17), or perhaps he was involved in receiving Col. Thomas Ruffin's body, which had been returned from behind Union lines. Ruffin was mortally wounded at Auburn on the 14th.

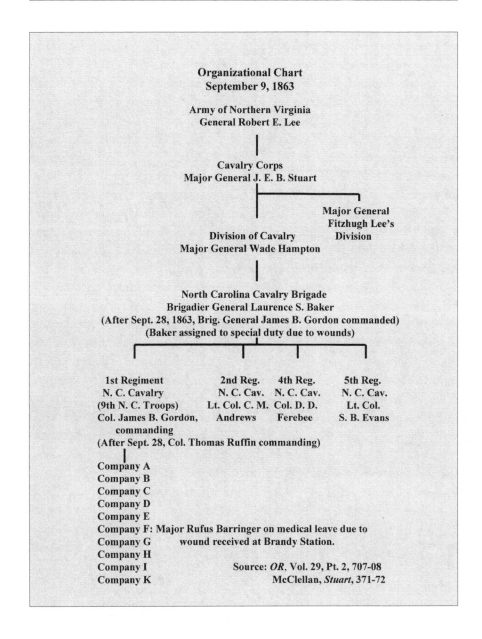

Organizational Chart
September 9, 1863

Army of Northern Virginia
General Robert E. Lee

Cavalry Corps
Major General J. E. B. Stuart

Division of Cavalry
Major General Wade Hampton

Major General
Fitzhugh Lee's
Division

North Carolina Cavalry Brigade
Brigadier General Laurence S. Baker
(After Sept. 28, 1863, Brig. General James B. Gordon commanded)
(Baker assigned to special duty due to wounds)

1st Regiment	2nd Reg.	4th Reg.	5th Reg.
N. C. Cavalry	N. C. Cav.	N. C. Cav.	N. C. Cav.
(9th N. C. Troops)	Lt. Col. C. M.	Col. D. D.	Lt. Col.
Col. James B. Gordon,	Andrews	Ferebee	S. B. Evans
commanding			

(After Sept. 28, Col. Thomas Ruffin commanding)

Company A
Company B
Company C
Company D
Company E
Company F: Major Rufus Barringer on medical leave due to
Company G   wound received at Brandy Station.
Company H
Company I   Source: *OR*, Vol. 29, Pt. 2, 707-08
Company K   McClellan, *Stuart*, 371-72

The Bristoe Campaign: October 8-November 9, 1863

On October 9, 1863, the Army of Northern Virginia was positioned 12 miles south of Culpeper, south of the Rapidan River near Rapidan Station. It began a flanking maneuver against Meade's Army of the Potomac that became known as the Bristoe campaign. Two of Meade's corps had recently been dispatched to Tennessee, making his position more vulnerable. The Union army was positioned north of the Rapidan. Lee hoped to turn Meade's flank, and get between Meade and Washington to sever Union lines of communication with the U.S. capital. However, Meade discerned Lee's trap and moved his 90,000-man army northward along the Orange & Alexandria Railroad toward Manassas. From Rappahannock Station to Warrenton, Meade cautiously looked for an opportunity to attack Lee's 60,000-man army. Lee hoped to strike a fatal blow to the enemy.[37]

The mission assigned to a large portion of the Confederate cavalry was to lead Lee's army, guiding Richard Ewell. They also harassed the Federals during Alfred Pleasonton's withdrawal across the Rappahannock. The cavalry protected the right and rear of Lee's army as it flanked Meade. Several cavalry fights occurred during the campaign, including Auburn, Buckland Mills, James City, Morton's Ford, Raccoon Ford, Stevensburg, Culpeper Court House, Brandy Station, and others. Two of the larger engagements involving the 1st North Carolina Cavalry occurred at Auburn Mills, five miles east of Warrenton, and at Buckland, five miles north of Auburn. Having returned from medical leave, Barringer and the 1st North Carolina Cavalry led charges with sabers drawn in both battles.[38]

Gordon's North Carolina Cavalry Brigade was bivouacked near Madison Court House on the evening of October 9. At daylight the next morning, the Tar Heels moved toward Culpeper Court House. One of J. E. B. Stuart's staff officers remembered an amusing incident involving Major Barringer. With his men under heavy artillery fire, Barringer received an order from General Gordon to retire to the south side of Robertson's River to escape the range of the guns. As Barringer rode out in front of his men to give the order to move, a shell from one of the Union guns "came screaming over and burst just above his head." Reacting with utmost haste, he commanded, "By shells! Right about wheel." The men later recalled with a good laugh that Barringer had meant to shout, "By fours," instead of "By shells."[39]

37 William D. Henderson, *The Road To Bristoe Station* (Lynchburg, VA, 1987), 207-208.

38 Clark, *Histories*, vol. 1, 426-427.

39 OR 29, pt. 1, 460; Theodore Stanford Garnett, *Riding With Stuart: Reminiscences of an Aide-de-Camp* (Shippensburg, PA, 1996), 13. Captain Whitney Anthony recalled that Barringer rejoined the regiment on October 13. Garnett recalled the incident at Robertson's River

General Stuart reinforced the North Carolinians with Pierce Young's brigade, and the Confederate horsemen pressed the enemy infantry. The Yankees fled to near James City, where they were reinforced by infantry and cavalry. The Rebel horseman attacked, but could not dislodge the Federals before dark. The next morning, October 11, the bluecoats retreated toward Culpeper Court House, where a spirited fight ensued. The Tar Heels pushed them out and occupied the town. Near Brandy Station, the 12th Virginia Cavalry of Grumble Jones's brigade attacked the enemy, driving Custer and Davies. Stuart added the 4th and 5th North Carolina Cavalry, in hopes of finishing the Federal horsemen, but they were counterattacked by the 18th Pennsylvania Cavalry and forced to retreat. They were supported in their withdrawal by Col. Oliver R. Funsten's regiment of Jones's brigade. On the morning of October 12, Gordon's North Carolinians moved to Warrenton, and the next day headed for Catlett's Station.[40]

During a reconnaissance mission in the late afternoon of October 13, a contingent of Stuart's troopers and Major Beckham's artillery found themselves trapped between two of General Meade's Union corps near Auburn Mills. Escape seemed impossible, but since his troops had not yet been detected, Stuart decided they would move off the road into concealing woods nearby and remain silent through the cold night. It was an extraordinary display of discipline. A correspondent reported: "All were quiet—the horses seemed to feel the necessity of it, and the very mules of the ambulances, though they had not been fed since morning, restrained from their usual demonstrative cries."[41]

However, concealment in daylight was impossible. Before sunrise on the 14th, Stuart sent Beckham's guns to a nearby hill. It was foggy at dawn, when Stuart heard musketry fire from the west. He hoped it was Robert E. Lee advancing. Stuart ordered his artillery on the hill to open fire on the nearby Federal encampment, hoping that the resulting confusion would offer him an avenue of escape. The Federals, though surprised, recovered quickly. They sent skirmishers toward Stuart's guns and threatened the capture of his entire command. He ordered General Gordon's brigade to charge the oncoming

---

involving Barringer, which probably occurred October 10. Barringer's Compiled Service Record lists his return to duty as October 13. Perhaps Barringer was with the regiment as early as October 10.

40 *OR* 29, pt. 1, 460-461.

41 Brooks, *Stories of the Confederacy*, 202.

Yankees and "cut through," led by the the 1st North Carolina Cavalry. Colonel Thomas Ruffin, commanding the Tar Heel horsemen, was mortally wounded leading a valiant charge. Gordon took over command, placed Major Barringer in charge of the regiment, and maintained control of the field himself. Captain Cowles led a charge of Company A. Barringer dashed to the front and helped rally his North Carolinians. Finally, overwhelmed by the sheer number of charging enemy cavalry, the regiment retreated.[42]

Captain Whitney H. Anthony of the 1st North Carolina later recalled that Barringer had only rejoined the command on the evening before the fight at Auburn Mills, and had not yet officially reported for duty. Anthony remembered that Barringer rushed to the front "with only a walking cane as a weapon." A second charge was led by Captain Cowles and Company A, followed by the remainder of the regiment. This time the Tar Heel charge was a complete success, and the Federals scattered in all directions. In the wild confusion and turmoil of these attacks, Stuart again limbered up his guns and escaped around the Federal rear with about 50 casualties. Barringer and about 30 of his men barreled through the Union lines and joined Stuart on the run. Rufus and General Gordon were both slightly wounded during the successful escape (Barringer in the thigh). Rufus later recalled: "The column faltered, but myself, a few officers, and about 30 men pressed forward—scattered the enemy in all directions, made our way to his rear, turned his flank, and finally got out— but with terrible loss."[43]

On October 19, Stuart and Gen. H. Judson Kilpatrick's 3rd Division fought the second cavalry battle of the Bristoe campaign at Broad Run, on the Warrenton Pike, near the village of Buckland. Led by Kilpatrick, Gen. Henry E. Davies's Federals pursued Stuart's cavalry. In accordance with a plan suggested by Fitz Lee, Stuart feigned a retreat toward Warrenton, while trying to draw Kilpatrick's troopers after him. He arranged with Fitzhugh Lee, stationed three miles south at Auburn, to attack the Federals in their flank and rear with carbines and artillery when they least expected it. The plan for a trap being followed to the letter, Stuart then pulled back, with slight skirmishing, to within three miles of Warrenton. Here, at Chestnut Hill, he paused for the expected

---

42 Ibid.; Clark, *Histories*, vol. 1: 426-427.

43 "Cavalry Fight At Buckland, Virginia, October 19, 1863," Mrs. Seth L. Smith Papers, Southern Historical Collection; Rufus Barringer to Victor Barringer, January 27, 1866; Clark, *Histories*, vol. 1, 427.

signal from Fitzhugh as Kilpatrick's troopers rapidly pursued the Confederates. Kilpatrick instructed George Custer to follow Davies, but Custer refused to move immediately. His men had been fighting all morning and had not eaten breakfast, though it was past noon. Custer also seemed to sense a possible ambush, based on the ease of the Federal advance on Stuart. Custer remained at Buckland. At the sound of Lee's artillery, Stuart's entire command remounted. With sabers drawn, they charged the oncoming Yankees. Gordon's brigade was in front and center, with Thomas Rosser's and Pierce Young's brigades on either flank and a little to the rear, in support.[44]

Stuart turned to Gordon and ordered him to advance rapidly along the pike. "Now, Gordon is your time," Stuart yelled. Gordon rode to the head of his brigade and said, "Major Barringer, charge that Yankee line and break it." The Federals were about 300 yards down the pike, "drawn in a beautiful line, with Stars and Stripes flaunting gaily in the breeze." Barringer gave the commands, "Forward, trot, march!" After a few paces he turned to the regimental bugler, Henry "Little" Litaker, to sound the charge. The call was answered with similar bugle signals and heart-stopping Rebel yells from the rest of the regiment. In a few moments, the whole command closed, with sabers drawn, on the Davies's brigade, which had been uncovered by Custer's withdrawal. Davies's troops bravely stood their ground until the column led by the 1st North Carolina Cavalry, followed closely by the remainder of Hampton's division, came within about 50 yards. Then the entire Yankee line emptied their pistols and carbines into Barringer's troopers before turning and retreating. The volley slowed the 1st North Carolina Cavalry's advance.[45]

Meanwhile, Fitz Lee's flank attack from the south struck Custer's brigade at Broad Run. Custer was ready and checked the Confederate horsemen. It was Stuart's attack, not Fitz Lee's that forced a general Union retreat, as Custer became uncovered by Davies's withdrawal. The 1st North Carolina was momentarily stopped by enemy fire, but Barringer rapidly reformed his lines and resumed the pursuit. The Yankees preserved good order, wheeling and firing at occasional intervals for more than a mile. At last Barringer ordered

---

44 *OR* 29, Pt. 1, 382, 387; Clark, *Histories*, vol. 1, 427-428.

45 Ibid., 458; ibid., 427. Barringer's promotion to lieutenant colonel was dated October 17, but had not been received as of October 19; Brooks, *Stories of the Confederacy*, 206.

Captain Cowles of Company A to break the enemy ranks. This was speedily accomplished, and the orderly Union retreat became a rout.[46]

The pursuit extended several miles and lasted late into the night. During the chase, Barringer's splendid horse, "Black Shot," became unmanageable. Breaking and disregarding his restraint, Black Shot charged out of control and ahead of the main pursuit. As horse and rider entered New Baltimore, three miles west of Buckland, a harried Barringer steered the horse against a house with great violence in an effort to stop the runaway animal. In doing so, he knocked the horse completely over, causing serious injury to his own arm and head, and disabling him from further participation in the chase. Captain Cowles took over command of the regiment for the remainder of the action.[47]

The Buckland rout was completed with the capture of General Custer's headquarters train, many prisoners, about 350 horses, and a large stack of arms and equipment. This segment of the Bristoe campaign became known as the "Buckland Races." For its service in the fight, the 1st North Carolina Cavalry was highly complimented by General Stuart and others.[48]

Captain Cadwallader Jones Iredell of the 1st North Carolina described the actions at Auburn Mills and Buckland: "You can imagine how we suffered during the night [at Auburn]. It was bitter cold, could have no fires and surrounded by the enemy. We could hear the Yankees talking as they marched on by us, but we escaped. . . . [At Buckland] In coming back down the pike towards Warrenton, the Yankee cavalry (Kilpatrick) attacked us. We led him on until we got him in a good place, when we charged and ran him back to Gainesville, a distance of 8 or 9 miles, capturing between two and three hundred prisoners. It was very exciting and afforded us about as much amusement as a fox chase."[49]

By this time, Barringer had received his promotion to lieutenant colonel. It was dated October 17, but had not been received by the October 19 Buckland fight. Barringer received a letter from General Stuart expressing his "appreciation of that ability & devotion to duty, which has enabled you to raise

46 Clark, *Histories*, vol. 1, 428; *OR* 29, pt. 1, 461.

47 Clark, *Histories*, vol. 1, 427-428, 459; "Cavalry Fight at Buckland, Virginia, October 19, 1863."

48 Ibid.

49 C. J. Iredell, letter, October 23, 1863, C. J. Iredell Papers, Southern Historical Collection.

your Regiment to such a degree of efficiency, that it should be called a pattern for others." The letter closed with the hope that Barringer might "inflict still weightier blows upon our enemy, who has so often trembled & fled before the rush of the 1st North Carolina Cavalry."[50]

Following the Bristoe campaign, the Army of Northern Virginia returned to Culpeper County and camped on both sides of the Orange & Alexandria Railroad. On November 4-5, Gordon's brigade and Fitz Lee's and Hampton's divisions were reviewed by J. E. B. Stuart, Robert E. Lee, and Virginia Governor John Letcher near Brandy Station. From near Culpeper Court House, William L. Barrier wrote: "Major Barringer is in command of the regiment . . . the supposition is that Barringer will be our Colonel."[51]

After repairing needed railroads, the Army of the Potomac crossed the Rappahannock at Kelly's Ford and Rappahannock Bridge on November 7. They inflicted heavy losses on the Confederate infantry when they captured the fortifications north of the river. Robert E. Lee withdrew his army beyond the Rapidan and prepared for winter quarters.[52]

On November 26, Meade crossed the Rapidan at Germanna and Ely's Ford, and proceeded toward Orange Court House. Hampton's cavalry division, supported by A. P Hill's Corps, stalled the Federal advance while Jubal Early's forces advanced on the left as far as Locust Grove. There, the Federals were found in strength. On November 27, Robert E. Lee decided to retire to a more defensive position on the west side of Mine Run. Believing that Meade would attack, Lee ordered his soldiers to entrench. On the morning of the 28th, Meade advanced on the Confederate position, but also ordered entrenchments. Four days later, with neither side attacking in force, Meade withdrew his forces and re-crossed the Rapidan.[53]

During the Mine Run campaign, the 1st North Carolina Cavalry fought at Parker's Store, New Hope Church, and other places. On November 29, General Stuart, with Rosser's brigade, encountered Federal cavalry on the road running from Orange Court House to Fredericksburg at Parker's Store. Stuart

---

50 Rufus Barringer to Victor Barringer, January 27, 1866; Barringer, *The Natural Bent*, 116; Compiled Service Record for Rufus Barringer; H. B. McClellan, Assistant Adjutant General, for General Stuart, to Barringer, December 7, 1863, National Archives.

51 William L. Barrier to his father, November 5, 1863, in *Dear Father*, 114.

52 McClellan, *Stuart*, 397.

53 Ibid., 397-398.

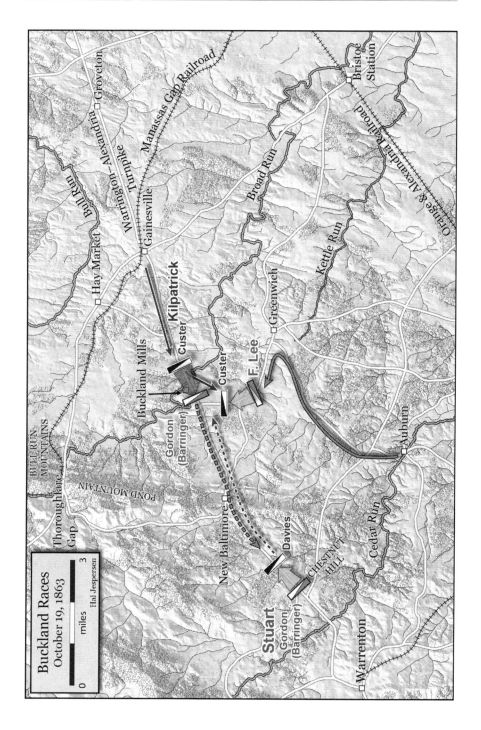

Buckland Races
October 19, 1863

0 miles 3

Hal Jespersen

ordered Rosser's horsemen to attack. Union forces pressed Rosser's cavalry back, and Stuart sent for the rest of Hampton's division, three miles to the rear. Arriving at the scene, Stuart ordered Hampton to send Gordon's troopers to attack on Rosser's right. Gordon dismounted the 2nd North Carolina Cavalry and a portion of the 5th for the attack, while Hampton sent Col. Pierce Young's brigade and Cobb's Legion to hit the Federal flank. The 1st North Carolina Cavalry was held in reserve to support the horse artillery and dismounted men. Hampton's dismounted men were thrown into the battle. After an hour's fighting following Hampton's arrival, the Federals retreated and were not pursued. Gordon's losses were minimal.[54]

Corporal Thomas O. Bunting, of the 5th North Carolina Cavalry, described some of the fighting at Parker's Store: "last night as I returned from a twelve hour hard sharp shooting with the miserable Yankees . . . it was so awful cold . . . [we] were within two hundred & fifty yards of each other shooting like the devil." Bunting recalled pursuing the enemy and the rewards of the skirmish: "We got in rear of them and ran them about three miles into the wilderness (near Chancellorsville). They had just commenced eating their dinner when we made them skedaddle out of their camp leaving almost every thing. When we got thru running them we returned to their camp & ate their dinner for them. They had nice fresh big turnips, irish potatoes, bacon, pickles & fresh beef and the best of goods, coffee, sugar & crackers, all of which we enjoyed finely."[55]

A Winter Touched by Sorrow

In December 1863, the opposing armies went into winter quarters. Gordon's brigade quartered at Milford Station on the Orange & Alexandria Railroad, 15 miles east of Warrenton. They continued to picket the Rapidan River, more than 20 miles from Milford Station. Rufus Barringer recalled an incident during this period when shortage of food was a mounting problem for the Confederate troopers. Many cavalry commands became known as foragers, rather than fighters, by people living in regions where the hungry soldiers scoured the countryside for food. Barringer recalled a visit to his camp by a Mr. Cunningham, who complained: "Colonel Barringer, my family and myself are

54 *OR* 29, pt. 1, 901-902.

55 Thomas O. Bunting, letter, December 1, 1863, Richard Henry Lee Letters, University of Notre Dame.

glad you are here; you can have all the corn we can spare; but I just tell you those last fellows out here nearly ruined me. They not only took all the corn they needed without asking, but at last they turned the animals loose in the field to trample it under foot. I am told there is no way to stop it. That regiment never knew such a thing as discipline. They say they are good fighters. I mean to try them. If they come back here again and repeat such conduct, I shall try my gun on the crowd."[56]

Barringer tried to reason against such risk and madness, but to no avail. Cunningham vowed it was his purpose to shoot any foraging troopers. Upon Barringer's return to the picket lines some weeks later, the Virginia farmer again paid Barringer a visit and confessed: "But, Colonel, I did not shoot [when the foragers returned]; and I must tell you why. Just as I got a good range on the crowd, in the dark, but with only bird shot, you know, I took aim and started to draw the trigger, when, for the first time, the idea struck me that I had two sons in another Virginia regiment, and possibly they might be in some one else's corn field at that very moment. And I tell you, Colonel, the old gun just fell from my hands, and I went right up and told the fellows the joke, and gave them leave to take all they wanted."[57]

Barringer commanded the 1st North Carolina Cavalry during November and December. In late December, Colonel Cheek returned from detached service and took over command of the regiment. Since September, he had been in charge of all dismounted men of the Cavalry corps.[58]

While Rufus had regained his health and returned to service, his wife Rosalie had not been well since her September trip to Hanover Court House. After Rosie's return to Concord, she developed tuberculosis and her health failed rapidly. Dr. John Bachman, a Lutheran minister, had known the Chunn family well during Rosalie's youth. While in the vicinity of Concord organizing his Lutheran brethren for war, he visited Rosalie several times. Having lost two daughters to tuberculosis, Bachman realized her hopeless condition before the family did. Maria (Mrs. Victor) Barringer recorded a poignant account of his

---

56 *Concord Times Weekly*, June 7, 1894.

57 Ibid.

58 *OR* 29, pt. 1, 902. On June 13, 1863, soon after the battle of Brandy Station, Stuart had assigned Major Cheek to command all the dismounted men of Stuart's Corps, encamped near Orange Court House. On September 28, Cheek was promoted to lieutenant colonel. He was promoted to full colonel on October 17.

administering the last rite of communion to his slowly dying friend on New Year's Day, 1864. Colonel Barringer had come home on a 20-day furlough, arriving on January 13. In her diary, Maria Barringer recorded: "Our dear Rosie is pretty cheered. I could scarcely contain myself when I met him [Rufus] at our gate with little Rufus in my arms, knowing his visit home was his last one to his dear wife & realizing even this, for both, the separation at the termination of his furlough. Did not go over after he came this day so as to leave them alone."[59]

On January 14, Maria wrote: "Went over to see our dear Rosalie after dinner & took my work to stay all afternoon. She seemed easier, was very quiet —had a bright pretty color in her cheek & a beaming eye—was in the sitting room in her arm chair, having opened up the parlor where her bed was to have it swept. I found so many in her room—her mother, sisters & brothers & husband writing out a regimental report—that I stayed only a few minutes, knowing much company was injurious to her. I was too sad to come home, so I went to my friend's."

At sunrise on January 15, a servant came over to alert Maria, Victor, and the children that Rosalie was dying. Maria wrote: "We rushed there to find her in her chair, propped up where she had spent the night, pulseless—the first glance told the sad reality 'that the spirit had returned to God who gave it.' Victor wept aloud as he held little Rufus in his arms to kiss the sweet lips still warm." Rosie was only 22 years old. She was buried next to Eugenia Barringer (Rufus's first wife) on the Sabbath, January 17, in the Presbyterian churchyard in Concord. The same hymns that were sung at Eugenia's funeral were sung for Rosalie's service, being favorites of Rosalie's for such occasions.[60]

Three days after Rosalie's death, Barringer wrote a letter to Gen. Samuel Cooper, the Confederate adjutant general in Richmond, requesting a 10-day extension of his leave of absence to attend to family matters.[61]

The Rufus Barringer household was broken up. The baby, Rufus Chunn, was sent to live with Rosalie's family in Asheville and Anna and Paul moved in with Victor and Maria Barringer. During the war, Anna and Paul visited the

---

59 Barringer, *The Natural Bent*, 70; *Fayetteville Observer*, January 25, 1864; Maria Barringer, diary, January 13, 1864.

60 Maria Barringer, diary, January 14 and 15, 1864.

61 Compiled Service Record for Rufus Barringer.

Chunns in Asheville during the summer and stayed with the Morrisons at Cottage Home from December to mid-January for the Christmas holidays.[62]

As 1864 dawned in sorrow for Rufus Barringer, the war was about to enter a year of combat that would see his responsibilities rise rapidly, and his military career reach its peak.

---

62 Barringer, *The Natural Bent*, 70-71.

Chapter 7

"Barringer has displayed great skill and valor, is one of the
best organizers and disciplinarians in the service."

— *Brig. Gen. James B. Gordon, recommending Barringer for promotion to brigadier general*

The 1864 Campaigns

I n February 1864, Brig. Gen. James B. Gordon assigned Lt. Col. Rufus
Barringer to command the 4th North Carolina Cavalry, stationed near the
coastal town of Woodville in Bertie County, North Carolina. Barringer relieved
Col. Dennis D. Ferebee, who had been wounded on October 13, 1863, during
the Bristoe campaign. The 4th was a small regiment, having only eight
companies until June 1864. During the winter of 1863-1864, the regiment was
in the process of refilling its ranks, and lacked a sufficient number of field
officers fit for duty. In December and January, picket duty involving a 40-mile
round trip from Milford to the Rapidan River had been especially hard on the
4th. When Gordon ordered the regiment to North Carolina to rest and recruit,
only 82 effectives were available for regimental service. By the time Ferebee
recovered from his wounds and resumed command on May 1, 1864, Barringer
had built up the regiment to more than 400 men.[1]

On May 2, a day after Colonel Ferebee returned to the 4th, Barringer
hurried back to Virginia to rejoin the 1st North Carolina Cavalry, skipping an
allowed visit home. He reached Milford, 18 miles south of Fredericksburg, as
the regiment began to scout Federal positions. On May 8, Barringer reported to
Gordon and Fitz Lee. Subsequently, Lee and Gordon became increasingly

1   Rufus Barringer to Victor C. Barringer, January 27, 1866.

concerned over the safety of Lee's wagon trains from attacks by Federal raiding parties. Gordon placed Barringer in temporary command of all dismounted men and assigned him to guard the supply trains.[2]

On May 4, the North Carolina congressional delegation and former Governor William A. Graham recommended Rufus Barringer for promotion to brigadier general, to command a new cavalry brigade that would serve in eastern North Carolina. General Gordon, who knew Barringer from their service together in the North Carolina legislature, endorsed the promotion: "Barringer has displayed great skill and valour, is one of the best organizers and disciplinarians in the service." Division commander Wade Hampton agreed in a letter to his superiors: "I cordially concur in Gen. Gordon's recommendation of Lt. Col. Barringer. The latter has been under my command for nearly two years. I know no officer better fitted to organize, to discipline or to fight troops than himself. He has borne himself with marked gallantry & he deserves promotion."[3]

However, Barringer would not lead the new cavalry brigade, which in early May was placed under the command of Brig. Gen. James Dearing. Barringer was destined to remain in Virginia with the North Carolina Cavalry Brigade.[4]

The North Carolina Cavalry Brigade

At the beginning of the spring 1864 campaign, the North Carolina Cavalry Brigade, commanded by General Gordon, included the 1st, 2nd, and 5th North Carolina Cavalry. The 3rd North Carolina Cavalry would join the brigade by the end of May. The 1st was commanded by Colonel Cheek with Barringer second in command. The 2nd was led by Col. Clinton M. Andrews, the 3rd by Col. John A. Baker, and the 5th by Col. Stephen B. Evans.[5]

William H. Cheek was from Warren County, North Carolina. Born in 1835, he was a lawyer by trade and was elected to the North Carolina legislature in 1860. Cheek and Barringer were rivals for leadership positions in the 1st North Carolina Cavalry. After the war, Cheek did not return to the bar, but engaged in

2   Ibid.

3   Compiled Service Record for Rufus Barringer.

4   *OR* 36, p .2, 959, 998.

5   Clark, *Histories*, vol. 1: 429, 465; *OR* 36, pt. 1, 1027.

business in Baltimore and Norfolk, and then returned to his plantation on Shocco Creek in Warren County. He moved to Henderson in 1884 and died there in 1901.[6]

Under General Gordon, the brigade had enjoyed fame as "The North Carolina Cavalry Brigade." It was widely known throughout the Army of Northern Virginia, and by many in the Army of the Potomac. Gordon was brilliant in battle and established the unit's reputation by his leadership in combat. An exemplary cavalry officer, he thrived on being at the head of the column and in the thick of battle. His conduct and courage were an inspiration to his men. Cavalry commander J. E. B. Stuart trusted Gordon, and often counted on him to lead in difficult situations.[7]

On May 5, Gordon's brigade was transferred from Hampton's command to a new division commanded by Maj. Gen. W. H. F. "Rooney" Lee. Rooney had been exchanged from a Union prison in March. From May 1864 through the end of the war in April 1865, the North Carolina Cavalry Brigade would serve in Rooney Lee's division.[8]

Meanwhile, on March 12, Ulysses S. Grant had been named general-in-chief of all Union armies. General George G. Meade commanded the Army of the Potomac. Grant placed two of his Western Theater protégés in top positions with the Army of the Potomac, naming Brig. Gen. James H. Wilson commander of a cavalry division, while appointing Maj. Gen. Phil Sheridan commander of the entire cavalry corps. The nature of the war changed with Grant and Sheridan in charge. Henceforth, General Lee and his Army of Northern Virginia would not be permitted to rest, even in retreat.[9]

As the spring campaign got underway, Grant sustained more than 17,500 casualties in the battle of the Wilderness on May 5-6, while Lee lost 11,000. On May 4, the 1st North Carolina Cavalry patrolled the area near Morton's Ford and as far down as Germanna Ford on the Rapidan, and detected General Wilson's Union horsemen crossing the river at Germanna Ford. Major William H. H. Cowles of the 1st notified Gen. Richard S. Ewell and J. E. B. Stuart, and promised to slow Wilson's troopers as much as possible with his detachment.

---

6 Elizabeth Wilson Montgomery, *Sketches of old Warrenton, North Carolina; traditions and reminiscences of the town and people who made it* (Raleigh, NC, 1924).

7 Manarin, *North Carolina Troops*, vol. 2, 603-604.

8 Clark, *North Carolina Regiments*, vol. 1, 429; OR 36, pt. 1, 1027; ibid., pt. 2, 954.

9 James Marshall-Cornwall, *Grant as Military Commander* (New York, NY, 1970), 132-134.

The remainder of the regiment still patrolled upriver. They shielded Ewell's left to the Rapidan, as he moved east along the Orange Turnpike. The cavalries of both sides fought on the periphery of the deadly infantry battle, which ended in a stalemate. As the Federals pulled out, they soon realized they were not heading north for the Rapidan on the old familiar path of retreat, but southward to flank the Confederates.[10]

The exhausted Army of Northern Virginia raced toward Spotsylvania Court House, a critical crossroads southeast of the Wilderness. If the Federals arrived there first, General Lee would be forced to fight through Grant's army to get into position to further defend Richmond. But Fitzhugh Lee's cavalry delayed the Federals long enough for the Rebel infantry to arrive first and stave off disaster.[11]

On May 9, General Sheridan, with Grant's approval and over Meade's objections, began a cavalry raid designed to move around the left of Grant's army near Spotsylvania. Sheridan would head south and cut Confederate rail lines, threaten Richmond itself, and lure Stuart into a fight. The brassy Sheridan was confident he could prevail in a fight with Stuart, and then safely unite with Maj. Gen. Benjamin Butler's army at Haxall's Landing on the James River, 10 miles south of Richmond. Sheridan sent 10,000 horsemen from Wesley Merritt's, David Gregg's, and James H. Wilson's divisions toward the Confederate capital.[12]

Sheridan was in no hurry, but Stuart was when he discovered a massive Union cavalry column in motion toward Richmond. Only a couple of hours after the Federals began their march, Stuart had Fitz Lee's division and Gordon's North Carolina Cavalry Brigade in pursuit from Spotsylvania Court House. Roughly 4,500 Confederate horsemen chased Sheridan's troopers, believing Sheridan intended to seize Richmond itself. Stuart, confident as always, left two brigades with the main Confederate army. Sheridan was interested in drawing Stuart into a fight, not seizing Richmond. The first battle occurred when Sheridan's rear guard held off Brig. Gen. Williams C.

10 *OR* 51, pt. 2, 888.

11 McClellan, *Stuart*, 407.

12 *OR* 36, pt. 1, 777-778.

Wickham's attacking horsemen, then turned west off Telegraph Road—the direct road into Richmond—toward Beaver Dam.[13]

Wickham's brigade attacked again, but was brutally turned back. Sheridan's troopers then moved forward to the upper bank of the North Anna River. Stuart, with Gordon's Carolinians, raced west to cut off Sheridan, and sent Brig. Gen. Lunsford L. Lomax's brigade and the remnants of Wickham's to attack the rear of Sheridan's column. The opposing horsemen skirmished above the North Anna, while Sheridan sent troopers to ransack the depot at Beaver Dam. However, Stuart arrived at Beaver Dam too late and could do little as darkness fell.[14]

The next morning, May 10, Stuart attacked with horse artillery and carbines, but the Federal troopers crossed the North Anna with minimal casualties and proceeded toward the South Anna River unmolested. Meanwhile, Stuart ordered Gordon's horsemen to harass Sheridan's rear guard, as Lomax's brigade had done the previous day.[15]

On May 11, Stuart finally succeeded in moving around Sheridan's flank, and getting between his troopers and Richmond. Stuart decided to make a stand near an old abandoned stagecoach inn called Yellow Tavern, near the intersection of Telegraph and Old Mountain Roads, six miles north of Richmond. While rallying his troopers against Gen. George Custer's Michigan brigade, Stuart was mortally wounded by a private in the dismounted 5th Michigan.[16]

The 1st North Carolina Cavalry fought the 1st Maine Cavalry, which guarded the rear of Sheridan's column at Goodall's Tavern, a country hotel about 18 miles north of Richmond. Finally, the Federals were pushed back and pursued by the North Carolinians. Colonel Cheek, the 1st North Carolina's commander, recalled that the fighting at Goodall's Tavern exemplified the reputation of the regiment among troops in the Union army. Cheek remembered: "An officer of the First Maine Cavalry, after the surrender, speaking of his regiment, made the proud boast that it was never driven from

---

13 OR 36, pt. 1, 776, 789; McClellan, *Stuart*, 410.

14 OR 36, pt. 1, 790.

15 Ibid., 789-790.

16 Ibid., 780, 791.

the field but once during the war, but, said he, we consider that no disgrace or reflection, for it was done by the First North Carolina."[17]

The day after the fight at Goodall's Tavern, Gordon's brigade pressed the rear guard of Sheridan's troopers near Brook Church, on the Brook Turnpike, five miles north of the Southern capital. Gordon's horsemen tried to keep Sheridan's raiders from reaching the Mechanicsville Pike to escape via Meadow Bridge. Gordon dismounted the 1st and 2nd North Carolina Cavalry, and placed the 5th in mounted reserve. He also dispatched Lt. Kerr Craige to Richmond to bring up artillery support. Southern fortunes brightened with the arrival of Craige and the artillery, but Federal guns soon scattered the Confederates. As Gordon's troopers fled, the Tar Heel commander was mortally wounded while trying to rally his men. A bullet struck him in the left forearm, shattering bones and exiting at the shoulder. At first the wound was not considered life threatening. However, the courageous warrior caught an infection and lived only six days. He died at the Officer's Hospital in Richmond on May 18, 1864.[18]

John Esten Cooke of Stuart's staff later recalled Gordon's passing: "And the gallant Gordon! How well I knew him, and how we all loved him! Tall, elegant in person, distinguished in address, with a charming suavity and gaiety, he was a universal favorite. Of humour, how rich! Of bearing how frank and cordial! Of courage how stern and obstinate! Under fire, Gordon was a perfect rock; nothing could move him. In camp, off duty, he was the soul of good fellowship. . . . He won his rank by hard fighting and hard work; he gave the South all he had—his time, his toil, his brain; she demanded his life, and he gave that too, without a murmur."[19]

According to Sgt. Fred C. Foard of the 1st North Carolina Cavalry, Gordon had recommended Rufus Barringer to succeed him as commander of the North Carolina Cavalry Brigade. After Gordon fell, Col. Clinton Andrews of the 5th North Carolina assumed command. He dismounted the 5th, and the battle finally ended about 4:00 p.m. when the Confederates pulled back. Meanwhile, Gen. Wesley Merritt had repaired the burned Meadow Bridge, and Phil

---

17 Clark, *Histories*, vol. 1, 466.

18 *OR* 36, pt. 1, 791; William H. H. Cowles, "The Life and Services of Gen. James B. Gordon," 9; *Richmond Dispatch*, May 13, 20, 1864.

19 John Esten Cooke, *Wearing of the Gray: Personal Portraits, Scenes and Adventures of the War* (New York, NY, 1867), 530.

Brigadier General James Byron Gordon (1822-1864) commanded the North Carolina Cavalry Brigade. He was one of the finest cavalry commanders of the war. Gordon was mortally wounded at Brook Church near Meadow Bridge, north of Richmond on May 12, 1864.
North Carolina Division of Archives and History

Sheridan decided it was time to end the raid and returned to the safety of Union lines.[20]

With Gordon dead and Colonel Cheek having been wounded at Goodall's Tavern, Colonel Barringer assumed temporary command of the 1st North Carolina Cavalry. On May 26, the 3rd North Carolina Cavalry joined the brigade, now under temporary command of John A. Baker. Four days later on May 30, Brig. Gen. Pierce Young was assigned to command the brigade.[21]

After the fight at Meadow Bridge, about 400 troopers of the 1st, 2nd, and 5th North Carolina Cavalry—along with 800 from Wickham's brigade, 750 from Lomax's, and a number of the 5th South Carolina—were engaged in an ill-fated action on May 24. Major General Braxton Bragg requested that Fitz Lee's cavalry attack Union Brig. Gen. Edward A. Wild's African American infantry at a fortified outpost called Wilson's Wharf, south of City Point on the James River. After an all-night march of 25 miles from Atlee's Station, Fitz Lee and his horsemen confronted the fort and found it to be stronger than expected. Federal gunboats fired upon Lee's cavalry, the shells bursting overhead with terrifying impact. Lee attacked the fort anyway, but lived to regret the decision. The 1,800-man Federal position was too strong to overcome. After further reconnaissance, Lee called off the mission and the

---

20 Fred C. Foard to D. H. Hill II, November 23, 1916, Fred C. Foard Papers, State Archives of North Carolina; OR 36, pt. 1, 791.

21 Clark, *North Carolina Regiments*, vol. 1, 430.

Confederate horsemen headed back to Atlee's Station. His casualties numbered about 50 men, including 20 dead.[22]

Seeking to outflank the Confederates to the east, Grant's army planned to cross the Pamunkey River near Hanovertown Ferry on May 28, screened by Sheridan's cavalry. On May 27, David Gregg's cavalry division, supported by Alfred Torbert's, crossed the Pamunkey and pushed rapidly toward the small village of Hanovertown. The Federal horsemen ran into Gordon's North Carolina brigade, commanded by Col. John A. Baker. For a time, the Carolinians held their ground, but the overwhelming numbers of Federal cavalry forced them to withdraw toward Hanover Court House. Sheridan's troopers pressed closely, and captured more than 70 prisoners before halting their pursuit.[23]

On May 31, Wilson's Union troopers ran into pickets of the North Carolina Cavalry Brigade near Hanover Court House. The Carolinians attacked the advancing Federal column and drove them back into their main force. Nearly the entire brigade was dismounted. Later in the day, the Union horsemen made a frontal assault while hitting both flanks of the Rebel troopers. The Carolinians were overwhelmed and retreated south of Hanover Court House to reform their lines. Exhausted and nearly out of ammunition, both sides halted for the night.[24]

The next day at Ashland, the 2nd North Carolina Cavalry relieved the 1st. With the 5th North Carolina, they drove Wilson's Union troopers back about one mile. Thomas L. Rosser's horsemen, with part of Rooney Lee's division, attacked the Federal rear and captured numerous prisoners and horses. However, the victory was a costly one. The North Carolina Cavalry Brigade lost another temporary commander. The dashing Brig. Gen. Pierce Young was severely wounded, and Colonel Baker again assumed temporary command of the brigade.[25]

Barringer recalled that all of these recent fights occurred in thickly wooded areas, where troopers often dismounted and fought with carbines. He

22 Longacre, *Lee's Cavalrymen*, 291; Clark, *Histories*, vol. 3, 604-605; OR 36, pt. 2, 269.

23 Robert A. Williams, "Haw's Shop: A Storm of Shot and Shell," in *Civil War Times Illustrated* (January 1971), Vol. 9, Issue 9, 12-20; Clark, *Histories*, vol. 3, 605-606.

24 Harrell, *The 2nd North Carolina Cavalry*, 280.

25 Clark, *Histories*, vol. 3, 608-609.

Brigadier General Rufus Barringer (1821-1895). This photograph was probably taken in Richmond shortly after his promotion in June 1864.
North Carolina Division of Archives and History

remembered: "[A]s the war advanced, the sabre grew into less and less favor, and . . . the revolver on horse and the rifle on foot became the preferred modes of fighting."[26]

Lt. Colonel Barringer's performance in leading the 1st North Carolina Cavalry up to this point occurred under difficult circumstances, with many officers killed or wounded in the current campaign. He continued to gain the

26 Ibid., 1: 430.

Postwar portrait of Brigadier General Rufus Barringer, circa 1880, painted by Mrs. J. E. Brown (Mrs. Laura Morrison Brown), Barringer's sister-in-law. *North Carolina Division of Archives and History.*

respect of his troopers and fought with them under trying conditions, including the ill-advised action at Wilson's Wharf. Barringer's superiors noticed not only his bravery, but his ability to organize and lead troops. With Gordon's death, these qualities would be needed in the person named to permanently command the North Carolina Cavalry Brigade.[27]

27 Gordon C. Rhea, *To The North Anna River: Grant and Lee, May 13-25, 1864* (Baton Rouge, LA, 2000), 363, 366.

Engraving of Brigadier General Rufus Barringer
by J. K. Campbell of New York. *Rowan Public Library, Salisbury, North Carolina*

Barringer Receives His Commission

On May 31, President Davis wrote
to Robert E. Lee, to recommend the
promotion of Rufus Barringer to
brigadier general. The move bypassed
colonel and elevated him to command
the North Carolina Cavalry Brigade.
The new Tar Heel brigadier was promoted over three senior colonels of the
brigade: Col. William H. Cheek (1st North Carolina Cavalry), Col. Clinton M.
Andrews (2nd North Carolina Cavalry), and Col. John A. Baker (3rd North
Carolina Cavalry). Barringer was also promoted over Col. Dennis D. Ferebee.
His 4th North Carolina Cavalry was not in the brigade, but Ferebee was still
considered for the command. Within three weeks of Barringer's promotion,
Colonel Andrews would be mortally wounded and Colonel Baker captured.[28]

28 *OR* 51, pt. 2, 973-974; *OR* 36, pt. 3, 873; Fred C. Foard to D. H. Hill II, November 23, 1916,
Fred C. Foard Papers, State Archives of North Carolina. Angered by Cheek's postwar account
of the fight at Atlee's Station during the unsuccessful Kilpatrick-Dahlgren cavalry raid against
Richmond, Foard recalled that "Cheek was deficient in soldierly qualities," and that General
Barringer was "greatly dissatisfied with him [Cheek] the last winter before [the fall of]
Petersburg, and discussed with his staff officers what best be done." According to Foard,
Barringer "decided to give Cheek one more chance and in plain terms that he would have to
brace up or give up his commission. With the sword of suspension over him, he bore himself
well in the Battle of Chamberlain Run, March 31st, '65." According to Foard, Cheek was not
shy about exaggerating his own exploits. As aide-de-camp to Barringer, Foard would have been
in a position to have firsthand knowledge that Barringer thought "Cheek was deficient in
soldierly qualities," and was dissatisfied with him. Foard claimed that Cheek took credit for
achievements that Foard's brother, Noah P. Foard, accomplished during the battle at Atlee's
Station. Barringer, in his history of the 1st North Carolina written many years later, praised
Cheek (among others) for his service during the 1864 and 1865 campaigns. A reading of the
Official Records and other first-person accounts supports the view that Cheek performed
admirably during the last half of the war. Cheek was wounded at Goodall's Tavern on May 11,
1864, and Major W. H. H. Cowles temporarily led the regiment. Barringer was promoted to
brigadier general on June 1 to command the North Carolina Cavalry Brigade. Cheek returned to
action to command the 1st North Carolina Cavalry on August 1, 1864.

Brigadier General Rufus Barringer, circa 1866, by Van Ness of Charlotte, North Carolina. *Department of Special Collections, University Libraries of Notre Dame.*

The order promoting Rufus to brigadier general was dated June 1, 1864, and he formally received his commission on June 4. The "Barringer brigade" consisted of the 1st, 2nd, 3rd and 5th North Carolina Cavalry.[29]

Matthew Person of the 1st wrote to his wife Sallie: "Barringer of our Regiment is promoted to Brigadier General and is commanding our brigade. . . . He is a slow old fellow, but a good officer." At age 43, Barringer must have seemed slow indeed to the 24-yeard-old Person. However, Barringer, would gain the respect and admiration of his men. Although a strict disciplinarian, Rufus loved the men under his command, and they would come to know it.[30]

In a letter to Confederate Congressman William A. Graham, Barringer expressed his appreciation for the politician's unsolicited help in obtaining his recent promotion: "My promotion was under peculiar and rather trying circumstances. . . . All the difficulties, too, naturally arising & expected from the promotion of a Junior over Seniors, are fast disappearing."[31]

---

29 *OR* 46, pt. 3, 873.

30 Matthew Person to his wife Sallie, June 9, 1864, Presley Carter Person Papers, Duke University.

31 Max R. Williams, ed., *The Papers of William Alexander Graham, 1864-65,* 8 vols. (Raleigh, NC, 1957-1992), vol. 6, 181. Barringer's letter to Graham was dated September 24, 1864. State senator William A. Graham was the uncle of Barringer's first wife, Eugenia Morrison Barringer. On May 4, 1864, the North Carolina Confederate Congressional Delegation wrote a letter to Jefferson Davis recommending Barringer for promotion to brigadier general. Rufus Barringer to Victor Barringer, January 27, 1866. Barringer later recalled that Ransom, Gordon, Hampton

About the time Barringer took over command of the North Carolina Cavalry Brigade, his old wound from Brandy Station began to bother him once more. According to Benjamin M. Walker, the brigade's surgeon, he had never known the general to complain about the injury. Barringer simply acknowledged it as disfiguring his face somewhat, with the loss of teeth on the corresponding side. There were no difficulties with phonation, articulation, mastication, or the senses of touch and taste. Dr. Walker remembered: "late in the summer of 1864, after a hard day's journey, we were camped at White Oak Swamp, Virginia. Shortly after repairing to my tent the General sent a messenger for me. . . . He remarked to me that since coming to his tent he had had a very singular sensation in his throat and tongue, 'a stiffness more than soreness.'" The surgeon carefully examined Rufus's throat and tongue and saw nothing unnatural about the appearance of either. Barringer stated that his tongue was badly cut by a broken tooth when he was wounded through the jaw.

Here is how his surgeon described the wound and his treatment:

I compressed the base of the tongue between my thumb and forefinger including the line of the 'wound' as designated to me, by him, but of which not the faintest scar remained. After compressing it in this way for awhile I felt some foreign substance deeply imbedded in the organ; I told him of it, and suggested something had been driven in at the time he was wounded. As he still felt very uncomfortable, and I thought more so after my discovery, he consented to have the foreign element removed, which I did by making a free incision along the lower margin of the papillae. At the depth of a quarter of an inch the bistoury [surgical knife] came in contact with the foreign substance. Introducing my forceps, I extracted a large 'goldplug' which had formerly served as a filling for a cavity in one of his molar teeth. This tooth was shattered of course, when he received the wound; and no doubt fragments of it impaled the substance of the tongue, as he told me something came out of his tongue some weeks after the injury. The gustatory, glosso- pharyngeal and hypoglosal [nerve] were left unhurt or, at least, their functions were not impaired. Neither was there any subsequent sequelae [secondary after effect]. The wound made for the extraction healed kindly. That there should have been no fistulous opening in this instance the parts being so liable to irritation from constant motion makes the case one of singular significance. Why there should have been the sensations described upon this occasion, at that particular time, is another inexplicable circumstance; his habits were the same

---

and the North Carolina delegation recommended him for command of a new brigade of cavalry that was instead placed under Brig. Gen. James Dearing.

that day that they had been many days previous, still we find him suddenly attacked with this disagreeable sensation without any assignable reason.[32]

Barringer received good treatment, but his wound, while not life-threatening, would trouble him for the rest of his days.

The Siege of Petersburg

In May, before Gen. Wade Hampton's promotion to cavalry corps commander, Ulysses S. Grant's Union army attempted to flank the Army of Northern Virginia. However, Grant failed to force Robert E. Lee out of his entrenchments at Spotsylvania, and again along the North Anna River. In June, the Union commander tried again, forcing Lee's army back toward Richmond and denying him room to maneuver. Grant then initiated a series of marches southward, attempting to flank the Confederates, but each time Lee moved successfully to block the Federals during the Overland campaign.[33]

At Cold Harbor on June 1-3, Grant believed he had discovered a weak spot, but blundered by attacking Lee's well-entrenched army. Unable to take Richmond from the north or east, the hard-driving Union commander decided to try from the south. If he could not destroy Lee's army in battle, he might wear it down by siege. Lee understood this reality, remarking to Gen. Jubal Early: "If Grant moves his army south of the James, it will become a siege, and then it will be a matter of time."[34]

By June 7, Grant's movements were fairly well developed, south and east of Richmond, and the Confederate cavalry was ordered to harass him. Barringer's brigade was detached and hastened to the lower fords of the Chickahominy River. On June 13, under the protection of Union gunboats prowling the river, Grant drove in Barringer's pickets at Long Bridge on the Chickahominy and began moving his army south of the James. The entire Tar Heel brigade hurried to support the pickets, but Grant advanced with cavalry and infantry, pushing Barringer back to White Oak Swamp. Near Riddle's Shop, Rooney Lee sent in the remainder of his division to reinforce Barringer, and held the Federals in

32 B. M. Walker, *Maryland Medical Journal* (May 2, 1878), vol. 3, 93-94.

33 Harrell, *2nd Second North Carolina Cavalry*, 267.

34 Robert Stiles, *Four Years Under Marse Robert* (New York, NY, 1904), 308; J. William Jones, *Personal Reminiscences, Anecdotes, and Letters of Gen. Robert E. Lee* (New York, NY, 1875), 40.

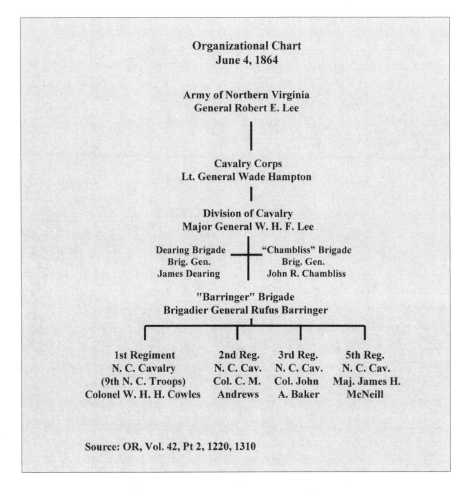

Organizational Chart
June 4, 1864

Army of Northern Virginia
General Robert E. Lee

Cavalry Corps
Lt. General Wade Hampton

Division of Cavalry
Major General W. H. F. Lee

Dearing Brigade   "Chambliss" Brigade
Brig. Gen.   Brig. Gen.
James Dearing   John R. Chambliss

"Barringer" Brigade
Brigadier General Rufus Barringer

1st Regiment   2nd Reg.   3rd Reg.   5th Reg.
N. C. Cavalry   N. C. Cav.   N. C. Cav.   N. C. Cav.
(9th N. C. Troops) Col. C. M.   Col. John   Maj. James H.
Colonel W. H. H. Cowles   Andrews   A. Baker   McNeill

Source: OR, Vol. 42, Pt 2, 1220, 1310

check until Southern infantry came up and relieved the cavalry. Barringer's brigade then followed the main Union column to Wilcox's Landing, skirmishing daily until June 18 at places like Crenshaw's, Nance's Shop (also known as Samaria Church), 13 miles southeast of Richmond, and near Harrison's Landing at Herring Creek. On June 18, Barringer's brigade crossed the James River and took position two miles south of Petersburg.[35]

Grant realized that if he could take Petersburg, with its rail networks to the south and west, Richmond would be isolated and Lee's supplies from the south would be cut off. The Army of Northern Virginia could then be defeated.

---

35 *OR* 36, pt. 1, 902, 1035; Clark, *Histories*, vol. 2, 430-431; ibid., vol. 3, 609; *The Daily Confederate*, February 22, 1865.

Meanwhile, Maj. Gen. William T. Sherman's Western army drove toward Atlanta, Georgia, pushing Joseph E. Johnston's rebel Army of Tennessee before him.

Once south of Petersburg, Grant's basic strategy (with a numerical superiority of about two to one) was to continue to push his lines ever farther to the west. He would cut the railroads that fed Lee's army and force the Confederate commander to extend his lines. Lee's 35-mile-long network of defenses eventually extended from northeast of Petersburg, around the city, to Hatcher's Run, 10 miles southwest of town.[36]

The siege of Petersburg would last nine months—the longest siege of the war. It was punctuated by a series of battles for the railroads leading to the south and west, the lifelines of Confederate resistance. These crucial railroads were the Norfolk & Petersburg; the Petersburg & Weldon (which ran south to North Carolina), the South Side (which ran southwest to Lynchburg and then to Bristol via the Virginia & Tennessee), and the Richmond & Danville (which ran from the capital city). The battles for control of these vital arteries were not major in scope, but together they wore down Lee's army by attrition. At the same time, sickness and desertion reduced Confederate ranks.[37]

Rufus Barringer and his cavalry brigade fought in many of the major engagements throughout the long siege of Petersburg. They were now a mature, respected, and hard fighting cavalry unit crucial to Lee's defenses.

Davis's Farm: June 21, 1864

Davis's Farm was located near the intersection of the Vaughan and Halifax Roads, about two and one-half miles south of Petersburg. Guarding the Petersburg & Weldon Railroad on June 21, Barringer's pickets reported the approach of a large Union infantry force with the probable mission of seizing and holding the railroad. Despite his lack of infantry support, Barringer used the thick undergrowth and other favorable terrain features to sustain a vigorous dismounted fight.[38]

---

36 John Horn, *The Petersburg Campaign* (Conshohocken, PA, 1993), 36, 77-78.; Harrell, *2nd North Carolina Cavalry*, 286-87.

37 Ibid., 292.

38 Clark, *Histories*, vol. 1, 431.

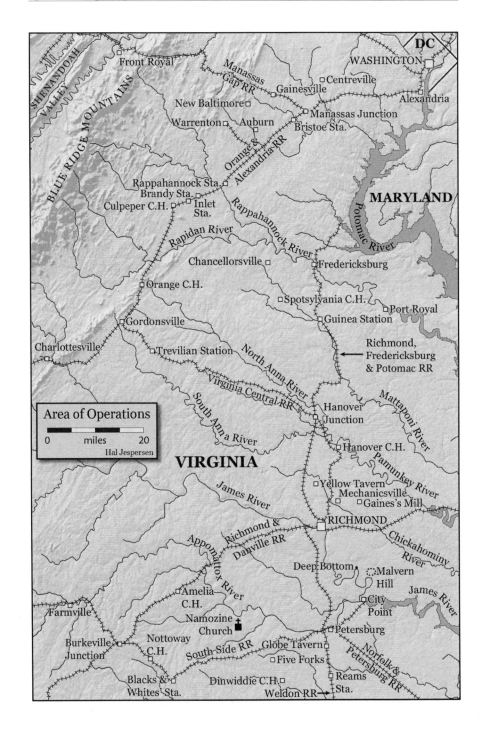

Barringer sent Capt. William M. McGregor's horse artillery to a hill at the Davis house, east of the railroad, screened from the Federals' view. He kept the 5th North Carolina Cavalry mounted in reserve to support McGregor, and to otherwise be ready for emergencies. The 1st, 2nd, and 3rd North Carolina Cavalry dismounted and formed two heavy skirmish lines, well concealed in thick undergrowth in front of the railroad. Barringer ordered the first line not to fire until the Federals were within 100 yards. This they did, and quickly withdrew as planned upon the second skirmish line. Union Maj. Gen. Francis C. Barlow's infantry mistook the flight of Barringer's first line as a rout of the entire Confederate force, and poured into the woods by the hundreds. McGregor's guns opened fire on the approaching enemy.[39]

The Yankees charging Barringer included the 111th, 125th, and 126th New York. Under heavy fire, Barlow was aghast to see his men streaming back in confusion toward their original position. They finally recovered and pushed forward, but Barringer's troopers repulsed them with repeated volleys. The Federals were finally driven back with a loss of 40 men killed and 20 captured, including a lieutenant colonel and two captains. At one point during the fight, the opposing lines were so close together that many were captured by each side within a few yards of each other. Colonel John A. Baker of the 3rd North Carolina Cavalry and Lt. Fred C. Foard (Barringer's aide-de-camp) were captured. General Rooney Lee came to Barringer's support at the close of the battle, but the Federals were ordered back by Maj. Gen. David Birney and made good their escape. Barringer's losses were 27 killed, wounded, or missing. On July 22, Foard made a daring escape by jumping from a moving train while being transported from Washington to Baltimore. He rejoined Barringer's unit in mid-September upon his return to Confederate lines.[40]

Barringer wrote to his brother-in-law, Gen. D. H. Hill, and criticized written reports and newspaper accounts of the fighting at Davis's Farm. Barringer refuted claims that Rooney Lee had driven back Barlow's infantry. Rufus protested: "W. H. F. Lee was not present until just at the close of the fight & the enemy was retreating."[41]

---

39 Ibid., 432; ibid., vol. 3, 610-611; Trout, *Galloping Thunder*, 544-545.

40 Clark, *Histories*, vol. 3, 610-611; *OR* 40, pt. 1, 348-349, 352.

41 Rufus Barringer to D. H. Hill, July 22, 1864, D. H. Hill Papers, Southern Historical Collection.

Barringer responded to Hill's strong support of a proposed policy that North Carolina troops be commanded by North Carolinians. Barringer answered: "I entirely concur with you in regard to the policy of putting N. C. officers over N. C. Troops. Do not see how we can get rid of Gen'l Dearing [a Virginian commanding North Carolina troops]. He is a good fellow & will no doubt make a fine cav'y commander. But the thing is intolerable at this stage of the war. I feel it very much in my communication with a Va. Div."[42]

Wilson-Kautz Raid: Nottoway Court House, June 23, 1864 and Staunton River Bridge, June 24-25, 1864

Grant remained intent on cutting the railroads to force the Confederates to abandon Petersburg and Richmond. He devised a plan for Union cavalry to strike and destroy the rail lines south and west of Petersburg. Grant hoped to force the Confederates to surrender or abandon the city, and to march west in search of food and supplies.[43]

The Confederates still held two of the four railroads serving Petersburg: the South Side and the Petersburg & Weldon. Fifty miles west of Petersburg, at Burkeville Junction, the South Side Railroad crossed the Richmond & Danville line. Thus, Burkeville Junction was a critical target for Grant. By capturing or destroying the junction, Grant would shut down both legs of the South Side Railroad, leaving only the Petersburg & Weldon in operation.[44]

On June 20, the Union commander formed his plan for a cavalry attack. Most of the cavalry corps had left with General Sheridan two weeks earlier on another raid. Grant assigned the 3rd Cavalry Division, under Brig. Gen. Wilson (who would later gain fame by capturing the fleeing Jefferson Davis), to make a daring raid deep into Confederate territory. Wilson was to destroy the railroad past Burkeville Junction and, if possible, rip it up as far as the Staunton River Bridge on the Richmond & Danville line. Grant assigned two brigades of cavalry from Maj. Gen. Benjamin F. Butler's Army of the James to accompany Wilson.[45]

---

42 Ibid.

43 Harrell, *2nd North Carolina Cavalry*, 296.

44 Ibid.

45 James Harrison Wilson, *Under The Old Flag*, 2 vols. (New York, NY, 1912), vol. 1, 457.

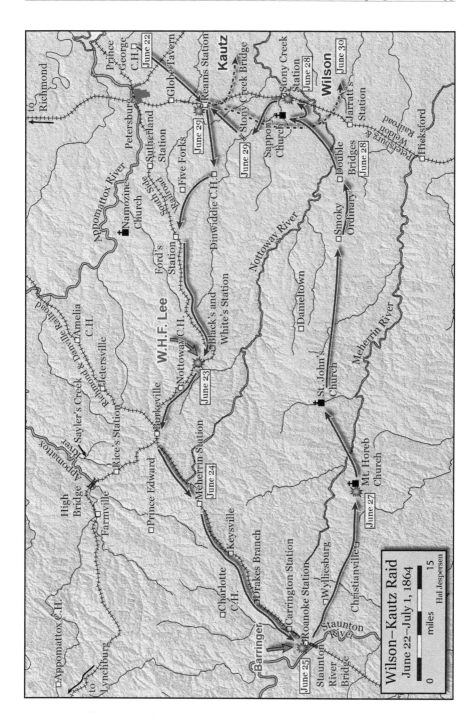

Wilson–Kautz Raid
June 22–July 1, 1864

0   miles   15

Hal Jespersen

Wilson's division (totaling 3,300) consisted of two brigades under Cols. John B. McIntosh and George H. Chapman. The cavalry from the Army of the James was led by Brig. Gen. August V. Kautz. Kautz had 2,000 troopers and a battery of horse artillery, giving Wilson more than 5,500 men and two six-gun batteries in his command.

Wilson had reservations about the raid and expressed them to Grant's chief of staff, Andrew A. Humphreys. Wilson had hoped to wait for Sheridan's return before embarking on what he believed to be a risky operation. Humphreys refused to rescind the order, but assured Wilson that Grant would make the necessary tactical moves to guarantee a safe return for the raiders. Wilson's fears were soon realized, and he would lose more than one-quarter of his command during the raid.[46]

On June 22, Wilson struck first at Ford's Depot, 10 miles northwest of Dinwiddie Court House on the South Side Railroad. The raiders captured two trains with locomotives and burned the depot, water tanks, and some wood. From Ford's Depot Wilson pushed his raiders southwest, burning every station, water tank, and bridge along the rail line. Until the afternoon of June 25, the Union horsemen relentlessly destroyed long lines of track and other crucial railroad equipment. They encountered only limited numbers of Confederate cavalry, and successfully held them off while proceeding on their mission of destruction.[47]

Meanwhile, on June 22, Rooney Lee positioned John R. Chambliss's brigade (Col. J. L. Davis) with the 3rd North Carolina Cavalry to hold off the Federals. With Barringer's other three regiments (the 1st, 2nd, and 5th North Carolina) and James Dearing's small brigade, they pursued the Union raiders. Barringer later complained: "Dearing was allowed to halt on the 2nd day [of the chase] for the want of rations." Rufus recalled that he and his troopers were ordered forward on half-rations. This did not sit well with Barringer, as it left him with "1 to 3 less companies than he would have liked to have had for the pursuit."[48]

Rooney Lee's troopers first struck the rear guard of the Federals under Col. George Chapman at Reams's Station, 10 miles south of Petersburg, on the

46 Ibid., 458, 459.

47 Ibid., 460-462; *OR* 40, pt. 1, 621.

48 Clark, *Histories*, vol. 1, 432; Rufus Barringer to D. H. Hill, July 22, 1864.

Petersburg & Weldon Railroad. The Union forces had earlier destroyed the depot and a number of platform cars. Lee's horsemen, pursuing the Federal cavalry, rode cross country via Dinwiddie Court House for the South Side Railroad and Burkeville Junction, 10 miles southeast of Farmville. During the night of June 22, the Federals continued destroying the rail line. Barringer later recalled, "For 20 miles, the entire track was taken up, cross-ties made up into great piles, and the iron laid across them so as to insure complete devastation by fire." In the same way, destruction continued the next day on the Richmond & Danville line. Barringer remembered that Federal foraging parties were sent over the countryside to "gather up horses, carry off supplies, and arrest leading citizens." In this manner the whole area "was overrun, many buildings were set on fire, and the track of the invaders became a grim scene of complete desolation."[49]

Barringer's 1,200 effective mounted troopers fought several engagements in pursuit of the raiders, without a clear victory by either side. About noon on June 23, Rooney Lee "managed, by forced march, to get his men between Wilson's and Kautz's two parallel columns." A battle with Wilson's division occurred at a small depot called Black and White's (modern Blackstone, Virginia) and at Nottoway Court House, near a railroad cut. This action was known locally as the "Battle of the Grove."[50]

General Dearing's Confederate brigade was positioned in front at Black and White's. With the 1st and 2nd North Carolina Cavalry, and McGregor's artillery, Dearing attacked Chapman's brigade of Wilson's division. The Confederates were driven back, exposing two batteries of artillery to capture. Barringer ordered the 1st, under Maj. William H. H. Cowles, to dismount and attack the advancing Federal horsemen. The guns were saved, but the Union advance continued. Barringer sent a detachment of the 2nd North Carolina Cavalry, temporarily under Maj. William P. Roberts, to maneuver across the railroad tracks to get behind the Federals. For several hours a fierce battle raged. Barringer later recalled that "whole trees and saplings were cut down by shells and minie balls until nightfall ended the conflict."[51]

---

49 Clark, *Histories*, vol. 1, 432-433; *OR* 40, pt. 1, 731; ibid., pt. 2, 687.

50 Clark, *Histories*, vol. 1, 433.

51 Ibid.; ibid., vol. 3: 613-614; Rufus Barringer to Victor Barringer, January 27, 1866; Thomas Bland Keys, *Tar Heel Cossack: W. P. Roberts, Youngest Confederate General* (Orlando, FL, 1983), 48. Major Roberts was in temporary command of the 2nd North Carolina Cavalry due to the illness

In this battle at the railroad cut, Col. Clinton M. Andrews of the 2nd North Carolina was mortally wounded, and about half a dozen other officers were killed or wounded. The exhausted troopers and animals rested the next day.[52]

A member of Dearing's brigade recalled: "[W]e had a heavy engagement, losing Major Claiborne and several men, and the brigade will always remember with pride and pleasure the timely aid of the First North Carolina Brigade in this conflict, for we had fully as much as we desired to handle." Dearing remembered that "if 'Aunt Nancy' (General Barringer) had not got there just at the time he did, that he [Dearing] would have had a much harder time, for, said he, they outnumbered us three to one."[53]

Barringer's written account of the fight stated, in part: "On the 23d ult., at Black and White's (in Nottoway county) the First Regiment, with a dash and spirit worthy of themselves, turned the tide of battle, saved the day and drove back the triumphant advance of a whole Brigade of the enemy's cavalry."[54]

Major William P. Roberts became incensed over Barringer's report of the fighting at Black and White's, and had hard feelings for his commander about it. He felt Barringer overlooked the 2nd North Carolina Cavalry's significant contributions to the fight and gave all the praise to his old unit, the 1st North Carolina. According to Roberts:

> The brigade commander [Barringer] did not witness the action of this regiment, nor did I receive an order from him during the day, but he got possessed with the idea somehow, or other, that the Ninth [1st North Carolina Cavalry] was entitled to all praise, and published an order to that effect as soon as the brigade returned to camp. I declined to have the order read to my men on dress parade, and there was friction between the brigade commander and myself, but I carried my point in the end. I did not object to his congratulating the Ninth upon its splendid behavior, but I did object to his partiality.[55]

---

of Col. Clinton M. Andrews. Before evening, Colonel Andrews returned to duty and was mortally wounded.

52 Ibid. On August 19, 1864, Maj. William P. Roberts was promoted to colonel of the regiment, skipping over the rank of lieutenant colonel.

53 Clark, *Histories*, vol. 4, 87-88.

54 Ibid., vol. 2, 102-103; Harrell, *The 2nd North Carolina Cavalry*, 299; *Daily Watchman*, July 15, 1864. Barringer's "General Orders No. 11," July 4, 1864, includes his account of the battle at Black and White's.

55 Ibid.; Keys, *Tar Heel Cossack*, 48.

Barringer later tried to address the shortcomings of his account by explicitly adding the actions of the 2nd North Carolina and Major Roberts to his subsequent written accounts of the battle. Barringer sometimes oversimplified his written accounts of combats, reporting too much from his own vantage point, and in doing so sometimes neglected the contributions of other regiments. The Tar Heel commander responded positively to criticisms from those he respected, and did his best not to repeat mistakes pointed out to him. Roberts would be promoted to colonel on August 19, 1864, to rank from June 23.[56]

On the evening of June 24, General Wilson, still quite a distance behind Kautz's leading division, struck out to catch up. Both would attack the Staunton River Bridge on the Richmond & Danville line. In response to this move, Rooney Lee ordered the two Confederate brigades to separate: Dearing would move on the Union left flank, while Barringer's 1,000 men of the 1st, 2nd, and 5th North Carolina Cavalry pursued the enemy.[57]

About 2:00 p.m. on June 25, Kautz, leading the advance Federal cavalry column, reached Roanoke Station near the Staunton River Bridge. Wilson's troopers had joined Kautz about 10:00 p.m. on the 24th at Meherrin Station, 10 miles southwest of Burkeville on the Richmond & Danville Railroad. The bridge was a strategic target, which Wilson planned to burn. More than 900 Confederates, consisting of militia from eight counties and a well drilled company from Danville, were deployed on the south side of the river. The Confederates were well positioned, and Kautz reported that he "could get no closer than 75 yards" to the bridge and lost "about 60 men killed and wounded."[58]

The Staunton River Bridge was one of the most important structures on Robert E. Lee's entire supply line. The small force defending the bridge—led by Capt. Benjamin L. Farinholt of the 53rd Virginia—successfully resisted Kautz and Wilson until Barringer's brigade came up in the rear and made a vigorous assault on Chapman's troopers. Kautz reported that "the extreme heat of the day and night were too much for the men and they were too much exhausted

56 Clark, *Histories*, vol. 1, 433; Harrell, *The 2nd North Carolina Cavalry*, 299-200.

57 Clark, *Histories*, vol. 1, 433.

58 *OR* 40, Pt. 1, 731-732, 764-765; Wilson, *Under The Old Flag*, vol. 1, 463; August V. Kautz, "Reminiscences of the Civil War," August V. Kautz Papers, U. S. Army Military History Institute, Carlisle Barracks, PA, 80.

for such desperate work." Both Wilson's and Kautz's divisions were forced to retreat and seek safety by a night march down the Staunton River through Boydton and Lawrenceville.[59]

Barringer's command had started on this expedition with about 1,200 mounted men. The exhausting march, intense heat, and incessant fighting had reduced his force to less than 300 men equal to the task of further pursuit. In this emergency, a small detail of the 1st North Carolina Cavalry, under Capt. Noah P. Foard (brother of Barringer's aide-de-camp), followed the Federal horsemen. The rest of the brigade, along with Dearing's, made a forced march east on the Union left flank. The purpose was to drive the enemy into a trap planned by Wade Hampton and Fitz Lee, south of Petersburg at Sappony Church and Monk's Neck. Hampton and Lee had just returned from their pursuit of Sheridan's cavalry and the Confederate victory at Trevilian Station. A rout ensued at Monk's Neck, and the Confederates captured 1,500 prisoners, 12 guns, and several hundred badly needed horses.[60]

The victory at Monk's Neck provided Barringer's brigade with a much needed 30-day period of rest. This respite enabled the North Carolina brigadier to turn his attention to the vital work of organization, drill, and discipline. More than half of the 1st North Carolina Cavalry was now armed and equipped with captured enemy materiel. Even Barringer's old Company F boasted that its entire outfitting had been taken from the enemy.[61]

With the brigade in desperate need of equipment, Robert E. Lee issued an order authorizing Barringer's regiments "to take possession of all cavalry arms, equipments and accouterments in the hands of civilians or other unauthorized persons in the State of North Carolina, when he is satisfied that such arms, & c., are legitimately the property of the Confederate States. All arms, & etc., dropped by our troops or the enemy on their lines of march or on the battle fields."[62]

Barringer issued a notice to all citizens of North Carolina: "Under this authority, I desire especially to gather up McClellen saddles. These saddles were captured from the enemy. There can be no private property in them. . . . This

---

59 Ibid.

60 Rufus Barringer to Victor C. Barringer, January 27, 1866; Clark, *Histories*, vol. 1, 434; ibid., vol. 3, 615; Wilson, *Under The Old Flag*, vol. 1, 456.

61 Manarin, *North Carolina Troops*, vol. 2, 6; Clark, *Histories*, vol. 1, 434.

62 *Daily Confederate*, August 6, 1864.

brigade is much in need of good saddles. Many of those we have are ruining the horses' backs. . . . Those now at home, and especially all on 'horse detail,' are required to gather up these saddles, also Sharp's, Colt's repeaters and other cavalry arms and equipment. . . . I claim no right at present either to seize or impress these arms and equipment, but I confidently expect every honest man not in the field, to give them up. They ought to be ashamed, in a time like this to be seen with them."[63]

Troopers of the brigade who were furloughed for visits home or to get new mounts were expected to enforce this authority as best they could. The brigade as a whole did not return to North Carolina to implement the order. They did, however, gather up Yankee equipment in Virginia as the opportunity presented itself, and on special detached service from time to time. Many of the 5th North Carolina Cavalry (and perhaps many in the brigade) did get furloughed during the brigade's 30-day rest period in July. Private Thomas Horne of the 5th wrote: "A large number of our men are coming home now to procure fresh horses. Mine has not been condemned yet, but can't hold out much longer unless he could get more feed and rest."[64]

On July 28, 1864, Barringer was ordered to the north bank of the James River to meet a threatened move of the enemy on Richmond. The next morning, the North Carolina Cavalry Brigade crossed the James at Chaffin's Bluff and moved toward Malvern Hill. They ran into Union infantry, and by afternoon fought as part of the Confederate line. Barringer's troopers fought in a sharp engagement 10 miles southeast of Richmond at Fussell's Mill, and skirmished well into the night as far as Riddle's Shop. They then withdrew about four miles and camped for the night. Meanwhile, the Union cavalry suddenly withdrew and reappeared in force below Petersburg. The Confederate troopers followed them south of the city.[65]

After the death of J. E. B. Stuart on May 11, Wade Hampton stood first in line of succession to corps commander. Army headquarters, however, hesitated to choose between Hampton and Maj. Gen. Fitzhugh Lee, who also commanded a division of cavalry. Between May 12 and August 11, 1864, both Hampton's and Fitzhugh Lee's divisions reported directly to Robert E. Lee.

---

63 Ibid.

64 Thomas Horne to "Mollie," July 17, 1864, Thomas Horne Papers, Wichita State University.

65 Clark, *Histories*, vol. 1, 434, 618.

Over the next three months, Hampton would prove that he was ready for corps command with impressive leadership at Trevilian Station, Samaria Church, and First Reams's Station. On August 11, 1864, Hampton received his appointment as commander of the cavalry corps.[66]

Wade Hampton was a towering, bearded 45-year-old South Carolina plantation owner and one of the South's major slaveholders. He had established himself as a man of prominence before the war, displaying leadership qualities that served him well during the conflict, and later in politics. Although he had no formal military training or experience, he quickly established himself as a hard-fighting combat leader, an able tactician, and a trustworthy reconnaissance officer. He consistently met the growing responsibilities that befell him as a brigade commander, and then as the ranking division commander in the expanding cavalry corps of the Army of Northern Virginia.[67]

The largest of the cavalry commands under Hampton was Rooney Lee's 3rd Division. Rooney, the second son of Robert E. Lee, had proved himself in battle. He relied principally on two of the three brigades in his division, Barringer's North Carolinians and John R. Chambliss's Virginians. Dearing's small brigade was the third in Rooney Lee's division. Both Barringer's and Chambliss's brigades were excellent combat units with proud traditions, led by capable hard-hitting commanders.[68]

On August 13, Grant's army began another diversion against Richmond, accompanied by a raid on the real objective—the railroads south of Petersburg. On August 14, Rooney Lee's division was again ordered north of the James to meet the Federals, this time only six miles southeast of Richmond.[69]

Private Henry M. Patrick of the 3rd North Carolina Cavalry described his picket duty during this period:

> While on picket we stand so near the Yankee pickets that we can converse with each other. Some places, the pickets are not more than fifty yards apart. They are very friendly, often offering to exchange papers, swap Sugar & coffee for tobacco. We have

---

66 Harrell, *The 2nd North Carolina Cavalry*, 310; OR 42, pt. 1, 1171, 1173.

67 Rod Andrew, *Wade Hampton: Confederate Warrior to Southern Redeemer* (Chapel Hill, NC, 2009), 70, 223, 227.

68 Richard Sommers, *Richmond Redeemed: The Siege at Petersburg* (Garden City, NY, 1981), 448.

69 Clark, *Histories*, vol. 1, 434; John Horn, *The Destruction of Weldon Railroad: Deep Bottom, Globe Tavern and Reams Station, August 14-25* (Lynchburg, VA, 1991), 9, 20-21.

very positive orders though, to have no communication with them, except by orders of our Brigade commander [General Barringer]. On our portion of the line the pickets do not fire on each other except when there is a general advance. . . . Water-melens [sic] are selling for $5 to $20 each, apples $2 per quart. We have to pay a dollar a garment for washing and profiting from past experience I now wash my own clothes. We are not allowed to carry but one jacket, 1 pr pants, which we wear, and a change only of under garments. . . . We are camped near a creek and at no hour of the day is this stream clear of soldiers washing.[70]

Private Patrick was killed two days later in fighting at White's Farm near Richmond. While Patrick was writing his letter, Grant was launching his diversion north of the James River. Majorl General Winfield S. Hancock commanded Union force consisting of his own II Corps, part of the X Corps, and Gregg's cavalry division. Grant's plan called for a simultaneous attack against the Confederate left flank and center. The II Corps marched north after landing from steamers at Tilghman's Wharf to turn the Southern left below Fussell's Mill. The X Corps departed Bermuda Hundred, crossed a pontoon bridge at Deep Bottom, and attacked the Confederate center at New Market Heights. However, the two efforts were not coordinated. After repulsing the X Corps, the Rebels shifted troops to the left and checked the II Corps.[71]

On August 15, Hancock planned to either turn Maj. Gen. Charles Field's left flank or attack a weak spot in the Confederate line. Major Gen. David B. Birney, commander of the X Corps, was ordered to lead his two divisions up a country road east of and parallel to Field's line north of Fussell's Mill. Birney's troops were in place by mid-afternoon, but events on the Charles City Road delayed his attack.[72]

Early on the 15th, Brig. Gen. David Gregg, commanding a Union cavalry division, ordered Col. John Irwin Gregg (his cousin) to send a detachment to scout White's Tavern. Colonel Gregg sent a squadron of the 13th Pennsylvania

70 Henry M. Patrick to Susan, August 14, 1864, State Archives of North Carolina; Manarin, *North Carolina Troops*, vol. 2, 259.

71 Bryce Suderow, "Second Battle of Deep Bottom, Virginia, August 14-20, 1864," in *North & South* (January 2001), vol. 4, no. 2, 12-24.

72 Ibid.

Cavalry. The squadron encountered Barringer's brigade, which had just arrived, along with the rest of Rooney Lee's division.[73]

The 5th North Carolina Cavalry met Gregg's troopers at White's Farm on the Charles City Road. A fight ensued at Fisher's Farm, and Rooney Lee ordered Barringer to chase off the Federal horsemen. Barringer sent the 5th North Carolina to attack. The Yankees were driven back across White Oak Swamp until supported by the remainder of the 13th Pennsylvania Cavalry and 8th Pennsylvania, both of which were on picket duty east of the swamp near Wilcox's house. The Pennsylvanians retired two miles south on a country road leading to Long Bridge Road. During this fight, Barringer was slightly wounded in the thigh but remained on duty.[74]

The Confederates gained Birney's rear as they pushed Gregg's detachment across the swamp. Birney delayed his movements and informed Hancock of the events. To repel the cavalry attack, Hancock sent Col. Calvin Craig's brigade from Long Bridge Road to join Gregg, and help push the gray horsemen back across Deep Run. Colonel Craig soon encountered Gregg's brigade, and the combined force pushed forward until they met Confederate cavalry.[75]

Rooney Lee ordered Barringer, after defeating Gregg's cavalry, to leave the road. Barringer left William P. Roberts's 2nd North Carolina Cavalry to guard the road. This small regiment was confronted by the superior numbers of Craig's forces and suffered heavy casualties. Roberts sent to Barringer for help and was assisted by the 5th North Carolina Cavalry. The Federals were delayed long enough for Barringer to pull back across Deep Run. Lee then placed the 13th Virginia of Chambliss's brigade on picket duty at Fisher's Farm.[76]

The next day, hard-fighting Brig. Gen. John R. Chambliss, commanding a brigade in Rooney Lee's division, was killed while rallying his troopers against a Federal advance near White's Tavern on the Charles City Road, six miles southeast of Richmond. Chambliss's brigade consisted of the 9th, 10th, and 13th Virginia Cavalry. Union Maj. Gen. David M. Gregg, a West Point classmate of Chambliss, sent the general's body and personal effects through the lines under a flag of truce. Chambliss, an outstanding cavalry officer, had

---

73 Ibid.; *OR* 42, pt. 1, 637.

74 Clark, *Histories*, vol. 3, 618-619; *OR* 42, pt. 1, 218; *Daily Richmond Enquirer*, August 23, 1864;

75 Suderow, "Second Battle of Deep Bottom," 12-24; *OR* 42, pt. 1, 637.

76 Ibid.

commanded Rooney Lee's brigade after Lee was wounded at Brandy Station, and had been in command of the brigade at Gettysburg.[77]

Rooney Lee arrived later in the day on August 16, and personally rallied the Virginians. He ordered Barringer to attack with his brigade to stop the Federal advance. In a sharp fight near White's Tavern, Barringer's troopers forced Brig. Gen. Nelson A. Miles's infantry and David M. Gregg's blue troopers to retreat all the way back to Deep Creek. This action ended the immediate threat to Richmond.[78]

Private John W. Gordon of the 2nd North Carolina Cavalry recalled the sharp fighting on August 16: "After an hour of desperate fighting, the Yankee line begins to waiver & with a yell, we charged them, at the same time pouring into their ranks the entire contents of our arms. They, in utter confusion, fly from before us, leaving their dead and wounded in the field and many of them rushing headlong into the messy bottom of the famous old White Oak Swamp, from which uncomfortable position they were extricated by our men."[79]

In all of these cavalry fights, from the time of Colonel Cheek's return to service on August 1, the 1st North Carolina Cavalry's commander performed admirably. He was brave and capable, and his leadership did not go unnoticed by either those in the ranks or his superiors.

On August 23, General Barringer recommended Cheek for promotion to brigadier general to command a brigade "when a vacancy occurs," and General Hampton concurred. Barringer stated: "I have served with Col. Cheek for more than three years & I regard him as an able, efficient & brave officer. He has commanded the Reg't for more than twelve months & has kept it in a high state of efficiency." This recommendation might indicate that whatever hard feelings Cheek may have had over Barringer's earlier promotion to brigadier general (while Cheek was wounded and absent) had abated.[80]

77 *Richmond Enquirer*, August 23, 1864; Clark, *Histories*, vol. 3, 619.

78 G. W. Beale, *A Lieutenant of Cavalry in Lee's Army* (Boston, MA, 1918), 166-170; Clark, *Histories*, vol.3, 619; OR 42, pt. 1, 242; *Daily Richmond Enquirer*, August 23, 1864.

79 John W. Gordon, diary, North Carolina Collection, Museum of the Confederacy.

80 Compiled Service Record for Col. W. H. Cheek, National Archives.

Second Battle of Reams's Station, August 25, 1864

Reams's Station was located about 10 miles south of Petersburg on the Weldon Railroad, Richmond's last link with Wilmington, North Carolina—the only major Confederate port still open to blockade runners—and the food producing coastal regions of Georgia and the Carolinas. Disruption of Robert E. Lee's supply lines would force the evacuation of Richmond.[81]

On August 18, Union forces from Maj. Gen. Gouverneur K. Warren's V Corps occupied the vital railroad near Globe Tavern, four miles south of Petersburg. The Yankees then extended their control of the Weldon line toward Petersburg, tearing up track as they went.[82]

On August 21, Barringer's brigade, having crossed the Appomattox River with Rooney Lee's division the previous day, took an active part in an unsuccessful attempt to drive the Federals away from the rail line. During this confrontation, the North Carolina Cavalry Brigade occupied the right flank of Robert E. Lee's army. The Tar Heels moved along a small road leading from Vaughan Road near Poplar Spring Church to a point on the railroad, five miles south of Petersburg.

The 3rd North Carolina Cavalry, under Maj. Roger Moore, drove the Federals from their front works back into heavy entrenchments along the tracks. The 5th North Carolina Cavalry, led by Maj. James H. McNeill, attempted to connect with the 3rd's right flank, but the forming line found itself unsupported and threatened on the right. The Confederates fell back to reform. Rooney Lee then ordered Barringer to position the 2nd North Carolina Cavalry on the left, and the 1st to the right. The new line held its ground until dark and withdrew. The brigade's losses were 68 killed, wounded, and missing (38 from the 5th North Carolina Cavalry).[83]

General Grant also planned to disrupt the railway system farther south from Globe Tavern to Hicksford (now Emporia, located 40 miles south of Petersburg). Cutting it in that region would force the Confederacy to make longer wagon runs to supply Lee's embattled army. On August 23, General Meade began the first stage of Grant's offensive. He ordered Winfield S.

---

81 Horn, *The Petersburg Campaign*, 61.

82 Ibid., 68.

83 *Daily Confederate*, February 23, 1865; Clark, *Histories*, vol. 1, 435; ibid., vol. 3, 620.

Hancock's II Corps to rip up the Weldon Railroad from Globe Tavern through Reams's Station (which had been burned by Union cavalry in late June) to Rowanty Creek, about 15 miles south of Petersburg. In all, Hancock's force consisted of about 6,000 infantry and 2,000 cavalry, supported by 16 artillery pieces.[84]

On August 23, Hancock's corps (now under Francis C. Barlow) began ripping up the railroad at the point where the V Corps had completed its demolition work at Globe's Tavern. By the evening of the 24th, the II Corps had ripped up the track to a point three miles south of Reams's Station. Once the II Corps reached Rowanty Creek, five miles farther south, Grant intended to send the VI Corps and cavalry to destroy the rest of the railway from that point to Hicksford. At the same time, General Meade's chief of staff, Maj. Gen. Andrew A. Humphreys, alerted Hancock at Reams's Station to prepare for an attack by 8,000-10,000 Confederate infantry reported moving southwest on the Vaughan Road.[85]

Meanwhile, Hampton had informed Robert E. Lee of Hancock's actions and the distance between Hancock's II Corps and the Union V Corps at Globe Tavern (approximately five miles). After a skirmish on August 22 against Col. Samuel Spear's Union cavalry brigade (which was on loan to Meade's forces from the Army of the James), Hampton sent a message to Lee asking him to dispatch enough infantry to assist the Confederate cavalry in an attack against Hancock's powerful force. In reply, Lee sent eight brigades of infantry (at this point in the war numbering about 5,000 men) under Lt. Gen. A. P. Hill to confront Hancock's 8,000 Federals.[86]

Hampton added his 5,000 cavalrymen to the battle: John Dunovant's, Rosser's, and Young's brigades (Matthew C. Butler's division), and Barringer's and Chambliss's brigades (Rooney Lee's division). Following Chambliss's death, his brigade was now commanded by Col. J. Lucius Davis. McGregor's battery accompanied the cavalry. About 3:00 a.m. on August 25, Hampton set

---

84 *Daily Confederate*, February 23, 1865; OR 42, pt. 2, 420, 436-437; Horn, *The Destruction of the Weldon Railroad*, 114-117.

85 OR 42, pt. 1, 222-223, part 2, 481; Horn, *The Destruction of the Weldon Railroad*, 119; John Horn, "Charge of the Tarheel Brigades," in *Civil War Times, Ilus.* (January-February 1991), Vol. 19, Issue 6, 46.

86 Horn, *The Destruction of the Weldon Railroad*, 119-120; OR 42, pt. 1, 222-223; ibid., pt. 2, 481; Horn, "Charge of the Tarheel Brigades," 46.

out with Barringer's brigade and the remainder of Butler's division to join Chambliss's brigade, two miles south of Reams's Station at Malone's Bridge. Hampton ordered Chambliss's brigade across Malone's Bridge toward the crossing from the southwest. Rosser's and Young's brigades were in support. Hampton ordered Barringer to take his men up the Halifax Road toward Malone's Crossing from the southeast.[87]

Early on August 25, Hancock sent Union troopers from one of David Gregg's three cavalry brigades to probe the nearest Confederate troops to determine if they had been reinforced during the night. The Confederates planned to attack Hancock's forces at Reams's Station. Fortunately for the Southerners, A. P. Hill's infantry ran behind schedule, and Gregg's troopers encountered only cavalry pickets. Based on Gregg's reports, General Humphreys concluded that no substantial Confederate infantry reinforcements had arrived in the area. Upon receiving Humphrey's assessment, Hancock sent Maj. Gen. John Gibbon's division out of its works to continue the destruction of the railroad. Barringer would command Rooney Lee's division on August 25, due to Lee's recent bout with exposure to poison oak, which resulted in his face being greatly inflamed and his eyes swollen almost closed. The Confederate troopers began the battle at 9:00 a.m. on August 25. Chambliss's brigade, supported by Rosser's and Young's brigades and two of McGregor's guns, drove Samuel P. Spear's 1st District of Columbia and 11th Pennsylvania Cavalry from Malone's Crossing. Notified by Spear of the advancing enemy cavalry, Hancock recalled Gibbon's endangered troops to their breastworks. The North Carolina Cavalry Brigade (under temporary command of Colonel Cheek) and General Barringer went on a wide swing to the east that would put them behind the Federals. While the 3rd North Carolina Cavalry protected Barringer's rear, the dismounted 1st North Carolina Cavalry attacked just east of Reams's Station at Tucker's Farm about 9:30 a.m. Supported by the 2nd and 5th North Carolina Cavalry, the 1st broke boldly through the 16th Pennsylvania, which had formed Gregg's picket line from Reams's Station east to the Jerusalem Plank Road.[88]

---

87 Horn, *The Destruction of the Weldon Railroad*, 122; OR 42, pt. 1, 942-944; Horn, "Charge of the Tarheel Brigades," 47.

88 OR 42, pt. 1, 223, 245, 251, 607; ibid., pt. 2, 487, 497; Horn, *The Destruction of the Weldon Railroad*, 123-124; Clark, *Histories*, vol. 1, 775-776.

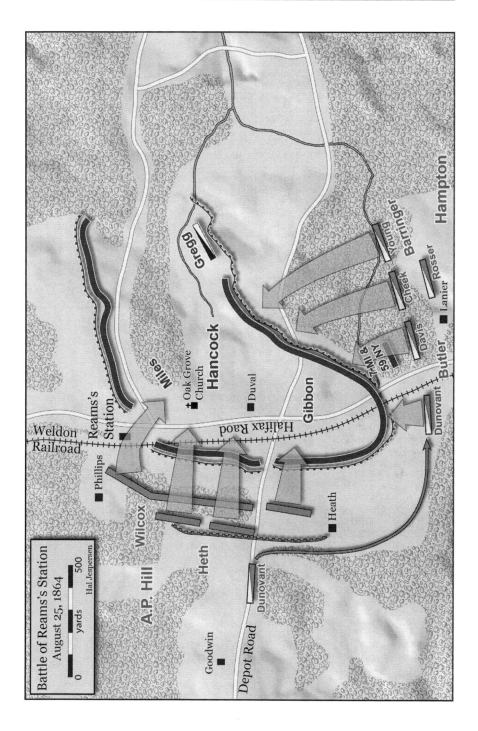

Battle of Reams's Station
August 25, 1864

0   yards   500
Hal Jespersen

Weldon Railroad

Reams's Station

Phillips

A.P. Hill

Wilcox

Heth

Goodwin

Depot Road

Dunovant

Heath

Miles

Oak Grove Church

Hancock

Duval

Halifax Road

Gibbon

Dunovant

Butler

Gregg

Young

Cheek

Barringer

TM I & 59 NY

Davis

Lanier

Rosser

Hampton

Heavy skirmishing developed near the railroad, as Spear retreated and infantry came to his aid. Hampton recalled Rooney Lee's division, commanded by Barringer, from its position to the east to rejoin the rest of the Rebel cavalry.[89]

About 5:00 p.m., Lt. Col. William J. Pegram's artillery opened the Confederate assault on the Union trenches. Within 30 minutes, in the midst of a thunderstorm, the Southern infantry charged the Federals in their breastworks at Reams's Station. Hearing the "Rebel Yell," Hampton sent forward his dismounted cavalry and McGregor's lone gun. Sighted and fired by Sgt. George W. Shreve, the gun pounded away at Gibbon's infantry. Hampton's command extended from the Confederate infantry line eastward to the railroad. Chambliss's brigade formed the left, Barringer's the center, and Young's the right of Hampton's line. Rosser's brigade remained in reserve. Hampton's troopers faced enfilading fire, but other parts of Gibbon's line began to crumble, permitting dismounted Rebel cavalry to move around his flank. From the rear, Confederate troopers delivered devastating volleys into Gibbon's line, which began to scatter. Confederate infantry of John R. Cooke's, James H. Lane's, and Dandridge MacRae's brigades, under Maj. Gen. Henry Heth, reached the breastworks almost simultaneously. Hancock's Federals, demoralized by the vehemence of the attack, "retired after a very feeble effort" in "great confusion and gave up the breastworks almost without resistance."[90]

At about the same time, on the other side of the battlefield, William P. Roberts's 2nd North Carolina Cavalry and the 9th and 10th Virginia Cavalry charged Gibbon's Union line, extending from the southern face of the breastworks. They easily drove the Federals from a line of rifle pits. Leaping the breastworks, they drove Gibbon's soldiers into the woods to the east.[91]

Hancock hoped that they could regain the lost works at Reams's Station, but Gibbon reported that his division was not equal to the task. The II Corps began a retreat north toward its original position, with Nelson A. Miles's men acting as the rear guard.[92]

---

89 OR 42, pt. 1, 942.

90 Horn, *The Destruction of the Weldon Railroad*, 154-158, 166; OR 42, pt. 1, 293-294, 943; Trout, *Galloping Thunder*, 565-566; Horn, "Charge of the Tarheel Brigades," 48.

91 Horn, *The Destruction of the Weldon Railroad*, 166; Clark, *Histories*, vol. 2, 103; OR 42, pt. 1, 943.

92 Ibid., 227, 254; Horn, *The Destruction of the Weldon Railroad*, 170.

The Confederate infantry, which had won a hard fought battle, was in no shape to pursue Hancock. Instead, Hampton's cavalry occupied the works, and the Rebel infantry returned to the Petersburg trenches, which had been greatly emptied for the fight. Union losses in the battle totaled at least 600, and the Confederates took almost 2,000 prisoners. The Rebels captured 12 battle flags, nine guns, and 3,100 stands of arms. Confederate losses totaled at least 720, most of them in the infantry. The Confederate cavalry lost 94 men, a low tally considering the ferocity of the fighting.[93]

The defeat of the Federals at Reams's Station was an impressive accomplishment. However, the Confederate infantry did not occupy the ground the enemy abandoned. Moreover, they failed to retake the Weldon Railroad. Any effort to hold the captured ground would have required more manpower than the Army of Northern Virginia could afford to expend. As a result, Robert E. Lee could not use the Weldon Railroad north of Stony Creek Depot, 16 miles south of Petersburg. His supplies had to be loaded onto wagons for the cross-country journey northwest to Dinwiddie Court House via the Flat Foot Road. From there, the wagons followed the Boydton Plank Road east into Petersburg. Accordingly, this roadway became a target of Grant's army.[94]

Rufus Barringer's daring breakthrough contributed greatly to the Confederate victory at the second battle of Reams's Station. This triumph prevented the Yankees from increasing pressure on Richmond.[95]

On August 29, General Lee wrote to Governor Zebulon B. Vance of North Carolina: "I have frequently been called upon to mention the services of the North Carolina soldiers in this army, but their gallantry and conduct were never more deserving of admiration than in the engagement at Reams Station. . . . On the same occasion the brigade of General Barringer bore a conspicuous part in

---

93 OR 42, pt. 1, 131, 608, 940; Horn, *The Destruction of the Weldon Railroad*, 171.

94 Edward G. Longacre, "The Blackest of All Days," in *Civil War Times Illustrated* (March 1986), Vol. 25, Issue 1, 19.

95 Horn, "Charge of the Tarheel Brigades," 47. Southerners rejoiced in the news of victory at Reams's Station. The mood would soon turn dark, however, when Union forces under William T. Sherman captured Atlanta, Georgia, a few days later on September 2.

the operations of the cavalry, which were no less distinguished for boldness and efficiency than those of the infantry."[96]

While the courageous fighting raged at Reams's Station, the *Raleigh Standard* published General Barringer's urgent call upon all absentees from his brigade to return promptly to their posts: "No pardon can be promised deserters. But it is believed that many have been misled by the unfortunate teachings of others. In such cases (no special aggravation appearing), they may be saved by a prompt return to duty. If arrested, they cannot but expect the death penalty, so recently inflicted on two of their command in this Brigade."[97]

Desertion became a major problem for the Army of Northern Virginia. Despite the stiff penalties deserters could face if caught, many were willing to chance it. Punishments for desertion depended upon circumstances, such as whether the soldier left as a result of imminent enemy fire, or returned voluntarily to duty. In the most severe cases, deserters faced the firing squad. Some soldiers talked about deserting, while others simply went home. Private William D. Smith of the 2nd North Carolina Cavalry wrote his father, "if I don't get a furlough or a detail before long, I shall make one of my own and come home anyhow."[98]

One less fortunate soul was Pvt. Eli Roberts of Company A, 2nd North Carolina Cavalry. Roberts had enlisted in July 1861, but deserted sometime about June 30, 1863. He later enlisted in the Union army and served in Capt. Goldman Bryson's company of Tennessee volunteers at Knoxville. On December 18, 1863, Roberts was captured by Confederates at Reem's Creek in Buncombe County, North Carolina. He was sent north as a prisoner to Petersburg, Virginia, not far from where his former brigade was quartered. On May 2, 1864, Roberts was tried by a General Court Martial. He was convicted of spying and sentenced to death. On July 22, he was executed by firing squad in the presence of Barringer's brigade at Hatcher's Run, nine miles from Petersburg.[99]

---

96 *OR* 42, pt. 2, 1,207; Clark, *Histories*, vol. 1, 471; *Raleigh Standard*, September 14, 1864; *Daily Progress*, September 5, 1864; *Richmond Daily Dispatch*, September 9, 1864.

97 *Raleigh Weekly Standard*, August 24, 1864.

98 William D. Smith to his father, September 2, 1863, Duke University.

99 Pension Application File, National Archives; Court Martial Proceedings, Henry E. Huntington Library, San Marino, CA; Manarin, *North Carolina Troops*, 112; W. A. Curtis,

Private William A. Curtis, a member of Eli Roberts's company, was one of 12 men who drew a short straw to become a member of the firing squad that executed Roberts (Company A) and James P. Brady (Company I, 2nd North Carolina Cavalry). "While it was a sad sight to witness such a scene," Curtis would remember, "it was doubly sad to have to act as one of the executioners."[100]

Wade Hampton's Cattle Raid: September 14-16, 1864

Petersburg remained under continued siege in the autumn of 1864. The Confederate army faced a mounting problem in procuring enough food for the troops. Based on intelligence from Sgt. George D. Shadburne (a renowned scout) of the Jeff Davis Legion, General Hampton developed a plan to steal a herd of 3,000 beef cattle. The animals were attended by 120 men and 30 unarmed citizens near Coggins's Point. Shadburne added that about 250 Federals from the 1st District of Columbia Cavalry were at Sycamore Church, less than three miles away. Coggins's Point was located on the James River, roughly five miles east of City Point, which was a massive supply base and headquarters of the combined Union armies. Hampton presented his idea to Robert E. Lee on September 8. Hampton received approval for the raid, which would be conducted on September 14 as Grant visited Philip Sheridan in the Shenandoah Valley.[101]

Hampton assembled and briefed his cavalry commanders for the expedition, including Thomas Rosser, Rooney Lee, David Dearing, Elijah White of Rosser's Laurel Brigade, and Matthew Butler. Barringer's brigade, with the rest of Rooney Lee's division, would guard the rear of Hampton's forces during the raid.[102]

"Reminiscences of the War," No. 19, Duke University; Thomas Horne to "Mollie," July 24, 1864.

100 W. A. Curtis, "Reminiscences of the War"; Roberts and Brady were the two soldiers mentioned in Barringer's call for absentee soldiers to return to the brigade, printed in the *Raleigh Weekly Standard*, August 24, 1864.

101 Horace Mewborn, "Herding the Yankee Cattle: The Beefstake Raid, September 14-17, 1864," in *Blue and Gray* (Summer 2005), Vol. 22, Issue 3, 10 ; OR 42, pt. 1, 26; ibid., pt. 2, 1,234-1,236; Edward Boykin, *Beefsteak Raid* (New York, NY, 1960), 177-178.

102 Mewborn, "Herding the Yankee Cattle," 12.

The cavalry had assembled seven miles southwest of Petersburg on the Boydton Plank Road, near Gravelly Run. In the early morning hours of September 14, the majority left their camps for Coggins's Point. Others, including the 2nd North Carolina Cavalry and the 9th, 10th, and 13th Virginia Cavalry, whose camps were farther south, joined later in the day.[103]

Hampton's troopers proceeded southeast down the west side of Rowanty Creek. They crossed the Weldon Railroad just north of Stony Creek Station and continued to Wilkinson's Bridge, where they bivouacked for the night.[104]

Before dawn on the 15th, the Confederate troopers crossed Rowanty Creek and headed east. They turned north on the Jerusalem Plank Road for a short distance, then veered northeast to Cabin Point. The column reached the site of the previously destroyed Cook's Bridge on the Blackwater River at midday. The Rebels were 12 miles due south of Coggins's Point and had not been detected. Lieutenant John F. Lanneau's engineers built a temporary replacement span by dusk, and it took until after midnight for all of Hampton's force to cross the river. The column continued northeast for a few miles and then split into three groups, approaching Sycamore Church from different directions.[105]

Hampton's plan called for a dawn attack by Rosser on the largest group of Federals at Sycamore Church. Rosser would quickly suppress the Yankees, and then proceed north to round up the herd. Meanwhile, Rooney Lee's division would drive away any Federals from the left and hold the roads from City Point. Dearing's brigade would remain to the right of the church. At the sound of gunfire, Dearing's men would dash to and demolish a nearby outpost at Cocke's Mill and hold the roads leading to Fort Powhatan.[106]

Rosser attacked before daybreak on September 16, and was initially thwarted by the 1st District of Columbia Cavalry. The stubborn Union troopers

---

103 Boykin, *Beefsteak Raid*, 211; Mewborn, "Herding the Yankee Cattle," 12.

104 Ibid., 13; W. A. Curtis Diary; OR 42, pt. 1, 945; Clark, *Histories*, vol. 3, 622.

105 OR 42, pt. 1, 945; Mewborn, "Herding the Yankee Cattle," 12-14; Colonel D. Cardwell, "A Brilliant Coup," in *News and Courier*, October 10, 1864; W. A. Curtis Diary; Clark, *Histories*, vol. 3, 622.

106 OR 42, pt. 1, 945; Mewborn, "Herding the Yankee Cattle," 14-15; Edward L. Wells, *Hampton and His Cavalry in '64* (Richmond, VA, 1899), 289-290; *Raleigh Daily Progress*, September 21, 1864; W. A. Curtis Diary.

were eventually overwhelmed by charges from the 7th, 11th, and 12th Virginia, along with Colonel White's 35th Virginia Cavalry Battalion.[107]

Hearing gunfire at Sycamore Church, Rooney Lee's men sprang into action. Colonel Lucius Davis's brigade took the lead and drove enemy guards and picket lines positioned on the Stage Road back toward the small village of Prince George Court House. At the intersection of Lawyer's and Stage Roads, Davis's troopers threw up breastworks to control both avenues.[108]

Following Davis's troopers, Barringer's North Carolina brigade attacked and captured about 25 of the 11th Pennsylvania Cavalry. Seeing Davis's troops retiring and throwing up breastworks, Barringer's horsemen dismounted and constructed defenses of their own to guard against the approach of any of Grant's force from the north. The North Carolinians remained here until word reached them that Hampton had bagged the cattle.[109]

Meanwhile, after driving off the Yankees at Sycamore Church, Rosser's 7th Virginia Cavalry remained to secure the camp and protect his rear while he went after the cattle. Rosser, with White's 35th Battalion and the 11th and 12th Virginia Cavalry, headed for the animals, located two miles from the church. The Rebels had little difficulty in surrounding both the herd and the guards. Rosser quickly started the herd back toward Sycamore Church.[110]

The cattle, numbering 2,468 head, were safely driven back to Hampton's camp at the church. Hearing of the successful capture, Rooney Lee's division and Dearing's brigade joined Rosser's. United again, Hampton's command began its return trip, with Rosser in the lead, followed by Dearing and then Rooney Lee. On the way, the Confederates destroyed the makeshift crossing at the site of old Cook's Bridge on the Blackwater River, delaying Federal pursuit.[111]

During the return trip, Elijah White's troopers held off an attack by Brig. Gen. Henry Davies's horsemen at Ebenezer Church for more than two hours until Rosser came to his aid. Davies then sent Col. William Stedman's brigade

---

107 OR 42, pt. 1, 28, 836; Boykin, *Beefsteak Raid*, 227-231; W. A. Curtis Diary; Clark, *Histories*, vol. 3, 623.

108 Mewborn, "Herding the Yankee Cattle," 16-17.

109 Ibid., 17, 44.

110 Mewborn, "Herding the Yankee Cattle," 44-45; OR 42, pt. 1, 821.

111 Mewborn, "Herding the Yankee Cattle," 46.

charging into the Confederate line, but they were repulsed twice, with the help of McGregor's and Edward Graham's guns.[112]

Realizing that General Kautz would not come to his aid in time, and being advised that the cattle had already passed Sycamore Church, Davies's called off his pursuit. He ordered Col. Charles H. Smith's brigade to pursue by alternate route, but that also failed.[113]

On September 16, Kautz's pursuing column was held up for some time at the Blackwater River. Due to the delay in getting his dispersed troopers started on the chase, and after a skirmish on the Jerusalem Plank Road, he decided it was fruitless to continue. The chase failed because the Federals had been surprised, were slow to gather their dispersed forces, and slow to begin the chase.[114]

The next day, the Confederate cavalrymen moved the cattle to a corral at the intersection of the White Oak and Boydton Plank roads. The following day, most of the herd was moved through Petersburg to a safer location.

Hampton's cattle raiders had covered 100 miles in three days. They captured more than 300 prisoners, 11 wagons, three flags, and a large load of supplies. They also burned three camps and rustled more than 2,400 fat steers. Hampton lost 10 killed, 47 wounded, and four missing.[115]

News of the raid shocked General Meade's headquarters. Estimates of Rebel strength had run as high as 14,000. Panic was evident, and some Federal leaders worried about the safety of City Point itself. By 10:00 a.m., when the Federals finally figured out what had happened, the panic subsided.[116]

Grant deemed the captured beef "a rich haul." Indeed those 2,468 animals were a God send to Robert E. Lee's starving army. "Hampton's steaks" furnished food to the Petersburg defenders for several weeks.[117]

Despite the success of the "Beefsteak Raid," the summer fighting had been hard on Barringer's brigade. A September 25 Inspection Report for the unit,

112 Ibid., 46-47; Cardwell, "A Brilliant Coup," *Southern Historical Society Papers*, vol. 26, 474-476.

113 Mewborn, "Herding the Yankee Cattle," 47; *OR* 42, pt. 1, 614.

114 Mewborn, "Herding the Yankee Cattle," 48-50.

115 *OR* 42, pt. 1, 946; Boykin, *Beefsteak Raid*, 284.

116 Wells, *Hampton and His Cavalry in '64*, 294-295; *OR* 42, pt. 2, 853-854, 876-878; Cardwell, "A Brilliant Coup," 474-476; *OR* 42, pt. 1, 86. Meade's lowest Rebel estimate was 6,000.

117 *OR* 42, pt. 2, 853; Wells, *Hampton and His Cavalry in '64*, 300; Boykin, *Beefsteak Raid*, 286; Cardwell, "A Brilliant Coup," 474-476.

stationed near Petersburg, counted 1,221 men "effective for the field." Many officers were listed as captured or wounded, and two absent without leave.[118]

On September 29, the 1st and 5th North Carolina Cavalry of Barringer's brigade were involved in a fight at Peebles's Farm. They drove back the enemy and re-established a picket line that had been broken earlier by Union infantry. The next day, a fight at Jones's Farm occurred, but Barringer's brigade was not actively involved. A dangerous and scary incident occurred after the fight at Jones's Farm. The Confederate cavalry had dismounted and joined with the infantry to rest. Late in the afternoon, Rooney Lee met with brigade commanders Rufus Barringer and Richard Beale. A Union sniper, perched high in a tree, took aim at the three Confederates and fired. The sniper missed several times, but then killed a nearby private. Having no sharpshooters of his own, Lee dispatched the 2nd Stuart Horse Artillery. With his first shot, Maj. William M. McGregor "blasted the sharpshooter out of the tree."[119]

During October, Barringer's cavalry was active. The brigade fought at Boisseau's Farm, Gravelly Run, and Hargrove's house with varying degrees of success. The most important battle in October was fought at Wilson's Farm on the 27th. Grant seized the Boydton Plank Road but was rebuffed by Barringer's troopers . Barringer reported his losses at 70 killed or wounded, chiefly from the 1st North Carolina Cavalry.[120]

A correspondent at the cavalry outposts reported on Wilson's Farm: "In this engagement our brigade (Barringer's) acted in a most conspicuous and most important part; it alone held in check a whole corps of the enemy's infantry for several hours, when General Barringer advanced upon them, and attacked them about night with great impetuosity, driving them in confusion from a well selected position. North Carolina may well be proud of such troops, and the gallant officer who leads them. They have established the reputation of being the backbone of the cavalry of this army."[121]

In a letter written from Stony Creek, 16 miles south of Petersburg, Barringer described some of the action at Wilson's Farm: "We had a very cold

---

118 Inspection Report, September 25, 1864, National Archives; Mary Bandy Daughtry, *Gray Cavalier: The Life and Wars of General W. H. F. "Rooney" Lee*, (Cambridge, MA, 2002), 220.

119 Fred C. Foard Papers, State Archives of North Carolina, 6-7; Sommers, *Richmond Redeemed*, 300.

120 Clark, *Histories*, vol. 1, 436.

121 *Raleigh Weekly Standard*, December 7, 1864.

weather & suffered a great deal. It both rained and snowed & we had for four nights to sleep on the cold frozen ground without any tents & without much covering. . . . We fought the Yankee forces twice & at last drove them back. We had no great losses. . . . My men captured about 100 Yankees & killed a dozen. One of the Yankees froze to death after we captured him. . . . Two shots came very near killing me. The men all thought I was hit & some of them took off & told that I was mortally wounded. We charged the Yankees & ran them a long ways & made them throw away so many things. We got so many guns, sabers, pistols, blankets, etc."[122]

In November 1864, Rooney Lee's division was stationed at Chappel's Farm in Dinwiddie County, Virginia. Barringer's brigade had three regiments consisting of five general staff officers and 2,273 enlisted men and other staff officers. They had "serviceable" horses, but only 1,659 carbines and pistols. All arms and equipment were reported to be in good condition, and the appearance and discipline of the troopers were reported to be good. Religious services were regularly held, though there was no chaplain. Still, hospital supplies and accommodations for the sick were sorely lacking, and there were no sutlers following the soldiers.[123]

Barringer's command had increased substantially since the past summer. As a result, the brigade needed weapons for 320 men who were entirely without arms. A large number of horses were without saddles, bridles, or halters. The inspector general reported: "the effectiveness of the [cavalry] command would be greatly increased by the addition of arms and saddles. There are a great many men rendered ineffective for the field for want of saddles."[124]

In a letter written from "Camp Disabled Horses [at Stony Creek]," one of Barringer's troopers expressed his view that they were liable to have to fight the enemy anytime, "but I do not think the Genl [Barringer] thinks there is much danger, or they would not send 'dead line' horses here."[125]

On December 1, two hours before daylight, 125 Federal cavalrymen attacked Barringer's 5th North Carolina Cavalry at Stony Creek Depot. Before

---

122 Rufus Barringer to Anna, December 15, 1864, Rufus C. Barringer Papers, University of Notre Dame. Rufus addressed this letter to his daughter, but it was likely intended primarily for Victor and Maria Barringer, as Anna was only nine years old at the time.

123 Confederate Inspection Report, November 30, 1864, M-935, Roll 12, National Archives.

124 Ibid.

125 W. D. Wharton to "Mollie," December 2, 3, 6, 1864, Southern Historical Collection.

the Union assault, Capt. David Waldhauer, in charge of the garrison, had ordered Lt. William Wharton of the 5th to take his 33 men to camp to eat breakfast and then bring them back. Barely into the meal, Wharton heard cannon fire and hollered for the men to "fall in." Very few of the troopers heeded Wharton's call, so he reported to Waldhauer at the double-quick without the men. Waldhauer asked, "where were the men?" In the face of an apparent mutinous situation, Wharton responded, "I could not get them together." Waldhauer ordered the bewildered Wharton to go back and get the troopers. By the time Wharton returned with just eight men, the fight was over. In 20 minutes, the Union cavalry captured 24 of Barringer's men and set fire to about 10 buildings.[126]

After the loss at Stony Creek, Will Wharton wrote: "I feel particularly safe now for I will not have to go into a fight if there is one for my men have no arms, nor ammunition & if they come, I will make tracks." On December 7-12, the Federals again attempted to seize the Petersburg & Weldon Railroad in what became known as the Hicksford Raid. On December 9, Gen. G. K. Warren struck at Belfield, a hamlet on the north side of the Meherrin River, about 38 miles south of Petersburg. Junior and senior reserves of North Carolina and Virginia (principally boys under 17 and men over 45 of the 70th and 71st North Carolina) defended the Meherrin River Bridge until the Confederate infantry and cavalry arrived, forcing the Federals to retreat. The main pursuit was made by troopers from Barringer's brigade, and led by Barringer himself. Two squadrons of the 1st North Carolina Cavalry, under Capt. George S. Dewey and Lt. Joseph W. Todd, made a mounted charge. The Federals were routed. Dewey's squadron chased the Federals into their infantry support, which was charged and dispersed. Several Yankee soldiers were wounded and a number taken prisoner. The Confederate horsemen continued to chase the Union rear guard, but were caught in an ambush after dusk and lost about a dozen men. By December 12, the Union attack had ended, but not before about 17 miles of critical Petersburg & Weldon Railroad track had been destroyed.[127]

As the time for winter quarters and Christmas approached, it became especially hard on the soldiers and their families. On Christmas Eve, however,

---

126 Ibid.

127 W. D. Wharton to "Mollie," December 7, 1864; *OR* 42, pt. 1, 444-445; Clark, *Histories*, vol. 1, 437; ibid., vol. 3, 633-635; *OR* 42, pt. 1, 516, 519; Raymond W. Watkins, *The Hicksford Raid* (Emporia, VA, 1978), 32.

General Barringer found one of his troopers in a happy mood as he rode up next to him. Will Wharton sang away with joy in his voice. The Tar Heel commander remarked, "You must feel very merry this morning." Wharton replied, "It was such beautiful weather that I could not help feeling merry & also it was Christmas." Barringer laughed heartily and proceeded toward the front of the column.[128]

In the 1864 campaigns, Barringer's brigade lost 99 killed, 378 wounded, and 127 missing or captured. Of these, the 1st North Carolina Cavalry lost a total of 138. The 2nd lost 105, the 3rd lost 153, and the 5th lost 208. Opposing Union casualties were estimated at 800 men, plus about 1,500 prisoners taken by the Confederates.[129]

By December 30, 1864, an inspection report of Barringer's brigade recorded 2,293 total men, including four general staff officers. There were 83 field and company officers and 2,205 enlisted men on duty, with 128 sick and two imprisoned. The horses were in adequate shape, and the troopers were being well fed. But there were no sutlers, and clothing was badly needed.[130]

Winter Quarters near Belfield, Virginia, 1864-1865

The winter of 1864-1865 was a difficult one for the Army of Northern Virginia, especially the cavalry. Relishing a respite from active campaigning, Barringer's brigade enjoyed some rest and recreation. Spoiling their relaxation, however, was picket duty and occasional hard fighting. The cavalry units rode 30 miles from their quarters near Belfield to their picket stations, and frequent enemy movements forced them to make long, hard journeys. The men and horses were constantly hungry. The country was virtually devoid of forage and rations were scant. If this were not bad enough, Federal raids kept Confederate communications cut for most of the winter.[131]

Reflecting doubts of Southern victory as the winter wore on, Lt. J. W. Biddle of the 1st North Carolina Cavalry wrote: "I can't see how we shall manage to raise men for the next campaign, and we must have them or we shall

---

128 W. D. Wharton to "Mollie," December 24, 1864.

129 OR 42, pt. 1, 444-445; Clark, *Histories*, vol. 1, 437.

130 Inspection Report, December 30, 1864, M-935, Roll 13, National Archives.

131 Daughtry, *Gray Cavalier*, 236.

be badly handled. Everyone seems to be in rather low spirits but still have some hope that we will yet gain our independence. Almost all agree that slavery will be abolished eventually, and enlisting Negroes will be the beginning of it."[132]

On January 30, 1865, in another reflection of Confederate military difficulties in this last winter of the war, Barringer's brigade at Belfield was down to 1,850 men. Only 1,351 of them were effective for the field, while hospital supplies and accommodations for the sick showed no improvement.[133]

Colonel W. P. Roberts was promoted to brigadier general on February 23, 1865, to rank from February 21. He took over command of a new small brigade consisting of the 4th North Carolina Cavalry, the 7th Confederate Cavalry, and part of the 8th Georgia Cavalry. Robert E. Lee, aspiring to put a North Carolinian in charge of the North Carolina brigade, had recommended Roberts for promotion, but he had left the final decision to Barringer. Rufus chose Roberts, "because he had many times proven himself a tenacious and effective fighter, and was more regular in the enforcement of camp discipline." In July, Barringer had written of Col. Dennis Ferebee: "He is truly a gallant man & I should like to see him promoted. He is (I think) a poor disciplinarian & poor judge of military men, but I have reason to believe him improving in these respects. If there is any movement in the way of a new Brig. Gen. of Cav. from our state, I will take pleasure in doing what I can for him." Barringer and Ferebee had served in the House of Commons together in 1848. Lee's recommendation, however, along with Roberts's outstanding record and the fact that Ferebee still suffered from his wounds, played a part in the final selection of Roberts. Moreover, Ferebee's organizational and disciplinary skills were not as good as Roberts's. Colonel Ferebee could not accept that he had been passed over again for promotion, and reluctantly resigned his commission "in the protection of his honor."[134]

132 J. W. Biddle to his father, January 22, 1865, Simpson and Biddle Family Papers, State Archives of North Carolina.

133 Inspection Report, January 30, 1865, Roll M-935, National Archives.

134 D. D. Ferebee to Colonel G. W. Little, March 3, 1865, Zebulon Baird Vance Papers. According to Fred Foard, Barringer chose Roberts over Lt. Col. W. H. H. Cowles of the 1st North Carolina Cavalry, indicating that Ferebee was not seriously considered. For Cowles to be promoted, Col. W. H. Cheek of the 1st would have had to be passed over; Neil Hunter Raiford, *The 4th North Carolina in the Civil War: A History and Roster* (Jefferson, NC, 2003), 84; Richard N. Current, ed., *Encyclopedia of the Confederacy*, 5 vols. (New York, NY, 1993), vol. 3, 1,341; Rufus Barringer to D. H. Hill, July 22, 1864, D. H. Hill Papers, Southern Historical Collection.

The end of February found the brigade at Stony Creek, 16 miles south of Petersburg. The condition of the division as a whole was reported as "good" except for Roberts's brigade. However, the shortage of saddles, bridles, halters, clothes, and shoes continued. Belts were also needed, as some of the men held up their pants with string. On March 1, 1865, Barringer's brigade had 78 officers and 1,298 men "effective for the field"—more than one-third of the cavalry in the Army of Northern Virginia.[135]

By 1864, the Confederate cavalry was also severely outmatched in armament by their Union counterparts. For example, Hampton's troopers generally possessed only muzzle-loaders. The regiments from the Carolinas and Georgia did not have any breech-loaders. A few in the Virginia regiments had Sharps single-shot, breech-loading carbines. These weapons were usually either captured or made in Richmond. However, the captured repeating carbines could not be widely used because of a lack of suitable ammunition. As a result, Hampton's cavalry usually carried muzzle-loaders. Most of them were Enfields, but many were less serviceable rifles. Meade's Union cavalry, on the other hand, had breech-loading carbines and Spencer repeating rifles (with seven-shot magazines). The result was clear: Confederate horsemen were woefully disadvantaged.[136]

Many of Hampton's troopers were also without revolvers (with which the Federals were amply supplied), and many were unarmed altogether. According to the "Armament Report of the Cavalry Corps, December 15, 1864," Hampton had 5,552 men in his command. Of these, 1,100 were unarmed, 925 did not have rifles, and a large number did not have revolvers. However, many men had private weapons, which would not have shown up in the armament report.[137]

The biggest weakness in the Confederate cavalry was a shortage of horses. By this point in the war, some enlisted men brought their own animals with them. If a man lost his horse in action, he was entitled to compensation that would never cover the actual cost. If a horse died of disease or became disabled, the trooper was not compensated at all. If a trooper could afford to purchase a new mount, he was granted a furlough to travel home to get it. If a man could

---

135 Inspection Report, February 28, 1865, Roll M-935, National Archives; Clark, *Histories*, vol. 2, 782; OR 46, pt. 1, 390.

136 Wells, *Hampton and His Cavalry in '64*, 91-94.

137 Ibid., 95; Inspection Report, December 15, 1864, Roll M-935, National Archives.

not get a new mount, he was often transferred to the infantry. Many troopers rode captured mounts, though by law captured animals were supposed to be turned over to the Confederate government.[138]

While the men suffered for want of food, the horses often lacked proper forage. The animals became so exhausted that some of the men asked and received permits to go home to get new ones. Such furloughs were typically 15 days. By the winter of 1864, however, many Confederate officers and enlisted men concluded that the South was beaten. Many were tempted not to return from furlough, and indeed some did not. Many, like Daniel B. Coltrane of the 5th North Carolina Cavalry, received a 15-day furlough in March 1865 to get a replacement mount. Coltrane recalled: "We Confederate privates felt that we were beaten, so by that time, we were just doggedly hanging on. I realized this and it was a great temptation to stay at home, yet I reported back on March 25, 1865."[139]

Throughout the winter, most of the cavalry commands in Virginia were reduced in numbers and efficiency. The Virginians were beset by constant temptations to seek their nearby homes. Similarly, the cavalry units from South Carolina, Georgia, and more distant states found it exceedingly difficult to maintain their numbers, when their men were allowed to travel to their far-off homes to remount. In the winter of 1864-1865, when General Sherman threatened South Carolina, Wade Hampton took Butler's division south to meet the Federal cavalry led by Brig. Gen. H. Judson Kilpatrick. Rooney Lee's division remained in Virginia.[140]

North Carolina, on the other hand, through an elaborate system of "horse details" and brigade discipline, kept most of its regiments fairly well mounted. The Tar Heel cavalry came to be relied upon not only for ordinary picket duty, but also for close quarters combat. The higher Confederate officers increasingly looked to North Carolina commands for the hard fighting.[141]

Barringer's brigade remained in winter quarters at Belfield for three months. During camp life, some civility returned to even the most worn out veterans. Social functions were rare, but were enjoyed with much enthusiasm.

138 Wells, *Hampton and His Cavalry in '64*, 97.

139 Daniel Branson Coltrane, *The Memoirs of Daniel Branson Coltrane* (Raleigh, NC, 1956), 38.

140 Andrew, *Wade Hampton*, 255.

141 Clark, *Histories*, vol. 1, 438.

For example, the brigade decided to hold an equestrian tournament, and fun-loving Lt. Fred C. Foard was put in charge of invitations and music. Each soldier was authorized and encouraged to invite his friends and relatives to Virginia for the event.[142]

The officers and others subscribed lavishly, ensuring there was plenty of money to cover expenses. Foard chartered a passenger train. Five men from each regiment, making 20 in all, accompanied Foard for the 20-mile trip to Weldon. The invited guests were to be escorted from Weldon to Belfield.

The next morning, a trainload of guests and escorts traveled to Belfield. The tournament consisted of numerous activities such as marching, exercising with sabers, and "riding at the ring" (a jousting-like practice). The champion of the jousting tournament crowned his lady love "Queen of Love and Beauty."

A "gander pulling" tournament was also held. The cavalry had scoured the countryside in search of the oldest and toughest male goose that could be found. The gander's neck was shaved clean of its feathers and lubricated with soft soap. The bird's leg was firmly attached to the end of a flexible pole with its head down so that it was just within reach of a man on horseback. The aim was to ride at full speed and jerk off the gander's head.[143]

A track about 100 yards long was laid off, with men on both sides armed with whips to lash the contestants' horses up to speed. It was no easy task to sever the gander's head, as he was alert and adverse to being decapitated. Many riders failed. One fellow, who was obviously drunk, held on to the goose's neck more firmly than he clung to his horse. The result was that the horse ran out from under the drunken rider, and he was left suspended in midair. Several hundred riders participated, but the gander came off the winner. Foard seemed somewhat ashamed to recall this tale some years later, saying that "those were war times and at times savagery prevailed."[144]

In a letter to his sweetheart, Capt. Risden B. Gaddy described the events just prior to and including another "gander pulling" tournament:

> Last night some 'Troop' gave a concert at Belfield. . . . [T]he music was splendid, the dancing graceful and the eating elegant. Some days before we had a Tournament given by Barringer's A Co. of our Brigade. The days of knights have again returned when

142 Foard Papers, State Archives of North Carolina, 14.

143 Ibid.

144 Ibid.; *Wadesboro Argus*, February 23, 1865.

man contends in open lists for the honor of crowning his 'Lady love' with flowers. . . . The Virginia ladies were present in large numbers, and so much beauty has scarcely been assembled since the days of the Crusades to view feats of arms. . . . I've wound up the day with a regular old fashioned gander pulling. His majesty having been suspended from a pole over the track where the horsemen were to run and his neck well greased with lard the sport began. . . . The fowl was the prize to the man that took the head. . . . Two hours hard riding and the head was carried amid the shouts of the crowd.[145]

Sgt. William M. Waterbury—Barringer's Scout

Irrepressible Lt. Fred C. Foard recalled some interesting stories involving Barringer's scouts. The general kept a corps of scouts (16 men) commanded by Sgt. William M. Waterbury of the 3rd North Carolina Cavalry. These scouts often operated behind enemy lines, and frequently sent in valuable information. They wore their Confederate uniforms to protect themselves against the fate of spies in case of capture. A short time before the Belfield raid, one of their number fell into the hands of Union soldiers, and it was reported that they had killed him after he surrendered. His 15 surviving comrades swore oath of vengeance, and a Federal advance on Belfield provided an opportunity. The bluecoats made heavy forced marches. It was a foot race between Union infantry and Confederate cavalry as to who would get there first. The gray-clad horsemen arrived first by a margin of less than one hour. Foard recalled: "They [the Federals] commenced their retreat, already worn down with fatigue, and we gave them scant opportunities for rest. We were pressing against their infantry throughout the entire pursuit. Many of them fell down by the roadside, collapsed from fatigue. Our scouts marched in advance of the vanguard and under their oath of vengeance, spared not one of them. One of the scouts told me afterwards, that the 15 of them killed 229 [many of whom had their throats cut] during the last day of pursuit."[146]

Foard recounted another interesting, and almost certainly exaggerated, story told by one of Barringer's scouts: "Sergeant Waterbury . . . was an expert telegrapher and, on one occasion at night, he cut the wires of the military lines

---

145 Fanny (Bennett) Gaddy Papers, Duke University. The letter is not dated, but it probably described a different tournament than the one described by Fred C. Foard. In Foard's version the gander won, but in Gaddy's version the gander lost.

146 Foard Papers, State Archives of North Carolina, 10.

that connected Grant's Headquarters with those of his corps commanders; and, concealing himself in a culvert under the road, for the greater part of the night, with the ends of the wire held against his tongue, he was able to interpret the messages interchanged between Grant and his Lieutenants without intercepting these transmissions, getting valuable information."[147]

On one occasion in November 1864, when Waterbury led a pursuit of retreating Union soldiers, his horse was tripped by wires that had been strung across the road by the fleeing enemy. Waterbury had just fired buckshot into a Union officer when he was tripped. His leg got caught under the fallen horse and he was helpless. The Union soldiers turned on him and were going to kill him when Waterbury made the Masonic signal of distress. The officer that Waterbury had just shot understood the signal and intervened on his behalf.

Waterbury had been sufficiently far ahead of his fellow scouts that they made good their escape. However, on November 19, Waterbury was taken to City Point and put into "the bull ring." It was an open-air prison consisting of a complete circle of sentinels at close intervals. Somehow, Waterbury managed to gain possession of the clothes of a Union soldier. He made a break between the sentinels, jumped over a breastwork, and ran along a ditch until he could safely emerge. He made his way through Federal camps toward Confederate lines, many miles away.

During the night, Waterbury came upon a Union cavalry camp and stole a bridle. Thereafter, when challenged by Federal soldiers, he explained that his horse had strayed off, and that he was looking for him. The ruse was successful until he reached the last Union outpost, when the commanding officer did not believe him. The officer thought Waterbury was a Union deserter and subjected him to intense questioning. The Rebel scout bore the interrogation so well that the officer told him he could pass, but a man would be sent with him to assure his return.

Thus, Waterbury resumed his escape under guard. He and his guard started out and at last came to a spring. Waterbury got down on his hands and knees to drink the water, and the unsuspecting guard did the same. Waterbury seized the opportunity, snatched the guard's carbine away from him, and took him prisoner.

Waterbury and his prisoner then headed for Confederate lines. They walked all day and night and into the second day, December 15. Waterbury was

147 Ibid., 12.

greatly fatigued, apparently more so than his prisoner. Perhaps, being a cavalryman, he was not accustomed to walking great distances. He was about five feet, six inches tall and was a good 20 pounds overweight. On January 1, he yielded to weariness and sat down on a log. The Yankee captive pretended to nod, and Waterbury lapsed into a nap. The Union soldier then seized the carbine and shot Waterbury.[148]

Ever the fortunate one, Waterbury had put on the Yankee's dress insignias. The bullet struck one of the brass eagles, which deflected the round away from his vital organs, but still went through his body, inflicting a serious lung wound. Now in control of the situation, the Yankee soldier could have shot Waterbury again or left him to die. Instead, the Union soldier went to a house in the distance on Mt. Sinai Church Road and told the occupants about the severely wounded Confederate. As fate would have it, the house was home to a Dr. Mason, an elderly physician. Waterbury was promptly moved to the house for medical care. Dr. Mason had a daughter, an attractive young lady, who became greatly interested in the critically wounded patient during his convalescence, which extended many months. The war ended long before he was back to full health. After months of imprisonment, Waterbury and Dr. Mason's daughter were eventually married. Sadly, they did not live happily ever after. Waterbury made a terrible husband, his bride was miserable in the marriage, and she died a short time later.[149]

At the urging of Rufus Barringer, Gen. Robert E. Lee wrote to Gen. Ulysses S. Grant about the Waterbury incident, when it was erroneously reported that the Confederate scout would be hanged as a spy after his capture and recovery. Lee wrote: "Waterbury was employed on outpost duty, in charge of a party, and was made prisoner in some affair of outposts in which he was engaged about two months since, and taken to City Point. Gen. Barringer has learned that subsequently, he contrived to elude the guard, and to affect his escape from your lines. . . . Brig Gen. Barringer and Maj Gen W H F Lee concur in asserting that Waterbury was simply engaged on outpost duty when captured, and was never used as a spy. The circumstances under which he was made prisoner show that he did not enter your lines voluntarily, and if he

148 Ibid., 13.

149 Ibid.

subsequently assumed a disguise it would appear to have been done to affect his escape."[150]

Subsequent correspondence between Grant and others at Point Lookout, Maryland, revealed that Waterbury was held in a general prison camp. Apparently, he was never condemned to hang for spying.[151]

During the hard winter of 1864-1865, the Confederates faced mounting problems, including shortages of food and supplies, dwindling recruits, sickness, and increasing desertions. Barringer's brigade had been reduced in numbers and effectiveness for the opening of the spring campaign. Nevertheless, Barringer's North Carolina Cavalry Brigade would chalk up one more triumph before the collapse of the rebellion at Five Forks on April 1, 1865.

---

150 John Y. Simon, ed., *The Papers of Ulysses S. Grant*, 31 vols. (Carbondale and Edwardville, IL, 1967), vol. 13, 374-375. The letter from Lee to Grant was dated February 4, 1865.

151 Ibid.

Chapter 8

"There was nothing done at Gettysburg more gallant than this charge
of the First North Carolina at Chamberlain Run."

— *Maj. Gen. Rooney Lee's report of the fighting at Chamberlain Run*

Barringer's Final Battles

The coming of the spring and the outbreak of new fighting brought
with it a small rise in the morale of North Carolina Cavalry Brigade.
Captain Cadwallader J. Iredell, of the 1st North Carolina Cavalry, expressed
optimism in a letter to wife: "Our Army is strengthening, and the men are in fine
spirits and determined." Two days later, he added, "We are going to whip every
fight hereafter. Grant is trembling in his shoes, already." Not everyone agreed.
"[A]t this time it seems that everything is quiet," wrote Sgt. James M. Pugh of
the 1st North Carolina Cavalry. "All the soldiers are waiting for peace which I
hope will come soon for I am tired of this war."[1]

Private Edward Jones of the 3rd North Carolina Cavalry, a new 15-year-old
Tar Heel recruit, wrote his father as soon as he reached Barringer's camp at
Stony Creek. He wasn't overly impressed with what he found there, at least
initially. "The Army I'm sorry to say is deserting very badly. It is by far more
general in the infantry than in the cavalry. Our regiment, I'm glad to say, has had
but two. We are drawing very good rations," he added, "& the men are well
satisfied." A week later, more comfortable with the situation in which he now
found himself, Jones wrote from near Dinwiddie Court House: "We get a third

---

1 James M. Pugh to his wife, February 6, 1865, James M. Pugh Papers, Southern Historical
Collection; C. J. Iredell to his wife, March 8 and 10, 1865, Iredell Papers, Southern Historical
Collection; J. Tracy Power, *Lee's Miserables: Life in the Army of Northern Virginia from the Wilderness
to Appomattox* (Chapel Hill, NC, 1998), 269.

of a pound of meat a day and a pound of flour & sometimes one and a half. The men, too, are well clothed. I have not seen a man barefooted since I came out. They all have good shoes. . . . I think I shall like the army first rate. The regiment is filling up rapidly now. I think in two months it will number 800."[2]

In early March, the winter respite at an end, General Barringer left Stony Creek with his 3rd and 5th regiments for picket duty near Petersburg. As the commander and his column passed by trooper Will Wharton and others not going to Petersburg, Wharton recalled, "I did not see brother nor but few of the Company this morning as they passed, for General Barringer was asking me so many questions, & giving so many orders to me, that I had not time to see anyone."[3]

On March 10, 1865, General Barringer wrote from Petersburg: "Our camp is still at Stony Creek. I am up here for two weeks with two reg'ts picketing & guarding the flank of the army. The weather is terrible & [we are] living almost without tents, cooking utensils, etc. We are having a hard time. The roads are so bad we could not bring any baggage." The Tar Heel cavalry commander still seemed optimistic about the war. He noted, "I am happy to say that since coming here I am much more hopeful than before. There's no necessity of evacuating Petersburg. The infantry is in better spirits than I expected. They are making large additions to their works. Desertions are gradually lessening & I feel sure we can stop Grant if he moves."[4]

On March 29, after arriving from the Shenandoah Valley, Philip Sheridan's Union troopers moved west on a flanking maneuver around the right of the Confederate army. General Lee's lines extended 35 miles from northeast of Richmond to Hatcher's Run, west of Petersburg. General Grant's objective was unchanged from the previous summer: force the Confederates out of their fortifications and strike them in the open with his entire army. Failing this, Grant's secondary objective was to destroy the South Side Railroad to tighten the noose around the embattled Rebels, leaving them little choice but to leave their works and fight, or be captured in place. Morale sank in the ranks of the

---

2 Edward Jones to his father, March 8 and 14, 1865, Edmund Jones Papers, Southern Historical Collection; Christopher M. Watford, ed., *The Civil War in North Carolina: Soldiers' and Civilians' Letters and Diaries, 1861-1865* (Jefferson, NC, 2003), 196-197.

3 Will Wharton to "Mollie," March 7, 1865.

4 Rufus Barringer to Margaret Grier, March 10, 1865, Rufus Barringer Papers, University of Notre Dame.

soldiers manning Lee's lines as sickness and lack of supplies and rations took their toll. The fall of Atlanta and Savannah the previous fall and William T. Sherman's rampage through that state and northward into the Carolinas only added to the gloom. The Army of Northern Virginia's desertions climbed. Between February 15 and March 18, 1865, some 3,000 left the ranks.[5]

Grant ordered Sheridan's 9,000 troopers, supported by infantry, to march to Dinwiddie Court House. Sheridan's horsemen were from three divisions: Maj. Gen. Wesley Merritt's 1st and 3rd Divisions (5,700 men) and Maj. Gen. George Crook's 2nd Division (3,300). From scout reports, Lee concluded that the route the Federals would use to attempt to turn his right flank was through Dinwiddie Court House and Five Forks. Accordingly, the Southern commander decided the best way to oppose Grant's move was to put together a mobile force of infantry and cavalry to attack Sheridan at Dinwiddie Court House, 13 miles southwest of Petersburg. Lee sent a Confederate cavalry force of about 7,400 to oppose Sheridan at this crossroads town.[6]

As the armies' moves and countermoves developed, Maj. Gen. Fitzhugh Lee commanded of all of the cavalry of the Army of Northern Virginia. General Wade Hampton, on January 20, had been ordered to South Carolina to rally defenses in the Palmetto State. With 2,500 troopers, Fitz Lee took position at Five Forks, six miles northwest of Dinwiddie Court House. About 20 miles southeast of Five Forks at Stony Creek Depot on the Weldon Railroad, Maj. Gen. Rooney Lee had Barringer's, Roberts's, and Beale's brigades, totaling about 3,000 men. Rooney Lee was also reinforced by General Rosser's division of 1,200 troopers. During the ensuing battle at Chamberlain's Bed (or Run), they would be further reinforced by 700 troopers under Col. Thomas T. Munford, commanding the remnants of Fitzhugh Lee's old division.[7]

As Sheridan moved into position at Dinwiddie Court House, his troopers got between Fitzhugh Lee's and Rooney Lee's cavalrymen. After a lengthy detour around Sheridan's command, the two Lees united on March 31 at the intersection on White Oak Road called Five Forks. Four miles to the southeast,

5   Freeman, *Lee's Lieutenants*, vol. 3, 624.

6   *OR* 46, pt. 1, 1,101.

7   Ed Bearss and Chris Calkins, *The Battle of Five Forks* (Lynchburg, VA, 1985), 10; Manly Wade Wellman, *Giant In Gray: A Biography Of Wade Hampton Of South Carolina* (New York, NY, 1949), 165. Munford, although recommended numerous times for promotion to brigadier general, never officially received the rank.

a small, swampy tributary known as Chamberlain's Bed fed into nearby Stony Creek. This inconsequential stream separated the Confederates from Sheridan's 9,000-man force at Dinwiddie Court House, and was destined to be the scene of one of the final battles of the war in Virginia.[8]

Chamberlain's Bed (Dinwiddie Court House), March 31, 1865

At this time Barringer's brigade had 1,788 officers and effective mounted troops. When the armies met during a cold rain on March 31, Barringer had only three regiments—the 1st, 2nd and 5th North Carolina Cavalry. The 3rd North Carolina Cavalry was stationed in the rear, guarding his supply train. Roberr E. Lee positioned the Confederate cavalry on the extreme right flank of his entrenched infantry. Approaching Chamberlain's Bed, northwest of Dinwiddie Court House, the Confederate horsemen discovered that Maj. Gen. George Crook's troopers had already crossed the flooded stream at Fitzgerald Ford. In response, at 10:00 a.m., Rooney Lee ordered Barringer to dismount his command to meet the onrushing Union assault.

Dismounted men from the 6th Ohio and 2nd New York had taken positions on the opposite bank. Barringer positioned the 5th North Carolina Cavalry in front, supported by the 1st and 2nd, with Beale's brigade in reserve. Capt. William M. McGregor's horse artillery supported the 5th, which would take the brunt of the attack. Barringer's troopers halted Bvt. Brig. Gen. Charles H. Smith's 1st Maine Brigade and forced them to retreat to the east bank of the rain-swollen stream. Rooney Lee ordered the 9th Virginia Cavalry from Beale's brigade to make a mounted charge in pursuit of the Union forces. However, through a mistake in the order, only one squadron of the regiment made the charge and was repulsed by Smith's brigade with terrible losses. The Federals rallied and forced the North Carolina brigade back across the ford.[9]

Mounted on his horse on the west bank of Chamberlain's Bed, General Barringer directed the movements of his men. He was never flashy like the gallant Jeb Stuart had been. Rather, Barringer was more like Wade Hampton or

---

8 Chris Calkins, "The Battle of Five Forks: Final Push for the South Side," in *Blue and Gray Magazine* (April 1992), Vol. 9, Issue 4, 17.

9 Clark, *Histories*, vol. 1, 439; ibid., vol. 3, 637; *OR* 46, pt. 1, 1,102, 1,110; Edward P. Tobie, *History of the First Maine Cavalry, 1861-1865* (Boston, MA, 1887), 397-398.

infantry leader John Brown Gordon—steady, disciplined, aggressive, and dependable.[10]

Sergeant Daniel B. Coltrane of the 5th North Carolina Cavalry described the morning's action:

> Chamberlain Run was swollen with rain and clogged with timber. It was passable only at one ford where most of the battle occurred. . . . We dismounted with cartridge box in one hand and rifle in the other, struggling to stay on our feet in the current. The 19th [2nd North Carolina Cavalry], which was mounted, went ahead of us, but they were immobilized by a Virginia squadron which broke in front of them. Somebody had made a grave mistake (resulting in the two forces getting in each other's way). Men were shot down in the ford, or swept off by the current and drowned. The Yankees were equipped with Henry rifles, which fired sixteen times without reloading, and their marksmanship was good. We were running out of ammunition, and I had only two cartridges left. Colonel [James H.] McNeill, who was beside me told me to keep them, I would have worse need of them in a moment. That was just a minute before he was killed. Some of us got across, but we couldn't stay without ammunition. We withdrew and the firing died down. Meanwhile we were hurriedly emptying the cartridge boxes of the dead in order to get enough bullets to continue the fight.[11]

Barringer's losses in the short but sharp morning battle were 20 officers and more than 100 enlisted men killed or wounded. Among those killed were Col. James H. McNeill and Lt. Col. Elias F. Shaw of the 5th North Carolina Cavalry. Among the wounded were Col. James L. Gaines, commanding the 2nd North Carolina Cavalry, and Maj. Marcus McLeod of the 1st North Carolina Cavalry.[12]

Both sides fortified their lines along Chamberlain's Bed, in preparation for the inevitable resumption of the fight. Meanwhile, Maj. Gen. George Pickett crossed Chamberlain's Bed at Danse's Ford, about one mile north of Fitzgerald's Ford. Major General Thomas L. Rosser's and Col. Thomas T. Munford's cavalry supported Pickett in afternoon fighting against Brig. Gen. Thomas Devin's cavalry division and Bvt. Brig. Gen. Henry E. Davies's 1st New Jersey, 10th New York, 24th New York, and 1st Pennsylvania Cavalry.

---

10 Clark, *Histories*, vol. 1, 438-439; ibid., vol. 3: 641-642.

11 Coltrane, *The Memoirs of Daniel Branson Coltrane*, 39-40.

12 Clark, *Histories*, vol. 1, 439; Bryce A. Suderow, "Confederate Strengths & Losses From March 25- April 9, 1865," unpublished manuscript, May 1987, revised December 13, 1992, Washington, DC.

Pickett hoped to swing south and launch a surprise attack on the Union left flank.[13]

About 3:00 p.m., with the rain having stopped, Fitzhugh Lee ordered Rooney Lee to drive the Federals from their front lines in preparation for another full attack on enemy positions across Fitzgerald's Ford. Barringer's brigade was ordered to be the vanguard of the offensive. However, the 3rd North Carolina Cavalry was still absent guarding the rear. With heavy losses in his other regiments that morning, Barringer asked Rooney Lee to withdraw the order. If that was not possible, Barringer requested that one of Lee's other brigades lead the movement. Rooney Lee sent a dispatch to Fitzhugh Lee, urging withdrawal of the possibly disastrous order, but was told by his superior that "military necessity" required that it be carried out.[14]

Overflowing and more than 150 yards wide, the run had only one crossing suitable for mounted troops, for the banks were clogged by dense foliage and obstructions. Barringer planned to position the 1st North Carolina Cavalry on the left, dismounted in line, to attack and draw enemy fire. At the proper moment, the 2nd would charge across the ford and attack the main Union defenses. The troops making this assault would be closely supported by Barringer's remaining regiment. Lee promised active support from the other brigades.[15]

To surprise the Federals, every effort was made to shield these initial movements. When everything was ready, Colonel Cheek of the 1st North Carolina Cavalry formed his line and entered the stream. The Federals concentrated a rapid fire upon Cheek and his men. When Cheek was about halfway over the stream, Barringer ordered the 2nd North Carolina Cavalry, under Maj. John P. Lockhart, to charge. The regiment moved in close column by sections of eight, with instructions to deploy to the right and left on crossing the stream as circumstances might require. The 5th was ordered to follow, partly mounted and partly dismounted, and to adopt the same line of

---

13 Clark, *Histories*, vol. 1, 439-440.

14 Ibid.; ibid., vol. 3, 642. According to Pvt. Paul B. Means of the 5th North Carolina, Maj. Gen. Fitz Lee personally came up from Danse's Ford and ordered Barringer to make the afternoon attack because Barringer was trying to have the orders withdrawn or have Beale's Virginians lead the assault, all of which ultimately delayed the offensive.

15 Ibid.

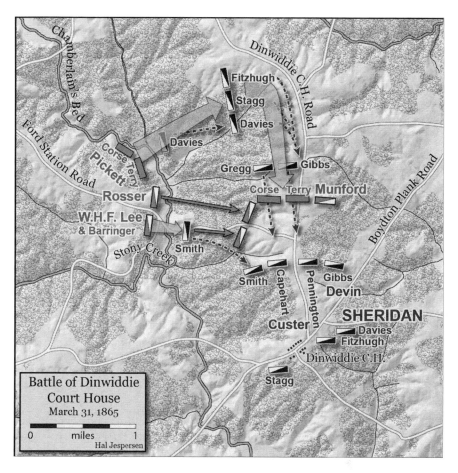

Battle of Dinwiddie
Court House
March 31, 1865

0   miles   1
Hal Jespersen

movement. General Rooney Lee ordered Beale's brigade, stationed behind and between the 1st and 2nd, to help either flank if needed.[16]

The Confederate horsemen successfully executed the plan. Lockhart drove the Federals from their works opposite the ford, while Cheek swept the lines to his left. Captain John R. Erwin and the 5th North Carolina Cavalry carried the right. The Confederate right met Charles H. Smith's brigade, while the left faced Henry E. Davies's troopers. When Davies was driven back, General Sheridan instructed Smith to "look out for his right." As the situation deteriorated, Sheridan again informed Smith, "Everything on your side is gone now—look out for yourself, and when you fall back, fall back to Dinwiddie." In 10 minutes, the entire Union line was in full retreat with the Confederates in pursuit. As he

16 Ibid., vol.1, 441.

witnessed the 1st North Carolina Cavalry advancing across the stream under deadly enemy fire, Rooney Lee exclaimed to Barringer, "Sir, the world never saw such fighting." The next day, General Lee supposedly said to a friend, "There was nothing done at Gettysburg more gallant than this charge of the First North Carolina at Chamberlain Run." The pursuit of Union forces continued for some distance with great loss to the enemy. As night fell, a halt was ordered within about two miles of Dinwiddie Court House.[17]

David Cardwell, a member of McGregor's horse artillery positioned on the south bank of Chamberlain's Bed, later revealed what happened that March day in the waning weeks of the war:

> As the brigade of General Barringer charged across the run, which was three or four feet deep, our gun was in position on a little knoll on the right of the ford by which the cavalry charged, and I had a splendid opportunity to see the whole fight. In all my experience (and I had been in over sixty fights, great and small) I never saw a more splendid charge. They simply swept everything out of their way. Every field officer of Barringer's brigade was shot, yet on pushed these soldiers. The splendid cavalry of Sheridan fled before them until they almost reached Dinwiddie Courthouse, where their infantry was in large force.[18]

Barringer's afternoon losses in the Chamberlain's Bed fight were about 100 killed or wounded, including 10 officers. The 1st North Carolina Cavalry took the brunt of the Union fire in the opening of the afternoon charge and its casualties proved significant. By the time the fighting was over, that regiment lost 17 of its 20 officers, and 80 of its 150 men engaged, most of whom were killed or wounded. The Confederate cavalry's late March triumph at Chamberlain's Bed would be its last significant tactical victory in Virginia.[19]

---

17 Clark, *Histories*, vol. 1, 439-441, 476; Tobie, *History of the First Maine Cavalry*, 397; OR 46, pt. 1, 1,110.

18 David Cardwell, "The Battle of Five Forks," in *Confederate Veteran* (March 1914), vol. 22, no. 3, 117.

19 Suderow, "Confederate Strengths & Losses," 11.; Clark, *Histories*, vol. 1, 441-442. The last Confederate tactical victory in Virginia occurred at "High Bridges" on April 6, after the Confederate debacle at Five Forks on April 1, 1865.

Sheridan's losses were 40 killed, 254 wounded, and 60 missing. Best estimates of Southern cavalry losses were 360 casualties out of 7,400 engaged, while the infantry lost 400 out of 3,400.[20]

About 3:00 a.m. on April 1, Barringer received orders to retire to his former position north of Chamberlain's Bed. He would remain there to protect the right flank of General Pickett's infantry. The exhausted Confederates, many of whom were wounded, headed back to Five Forks over roads in terrible condition from the recent rains. "I passed the regiment (the 1st North Carolina Cavalry) on the road," wrote Brig. Gen. William P. Roberts, "and its great loss both in splendid officers and gallant men made such an impression upon me that I wept like a child."[21]

After the war, Barringer penned an account of the Chamberlain's Bed fight and sent a copy to Rooney Lee. Barringer referred to Rooney Lee as being as "stern as the Iron Duke," to which Lee jokingly replied, "I must be permitted to complain of injustice done to our person in your very graphic account and that is in attributing sternness to your humble servant. I have to learn, for the first time, that there is such a trait in my character."[22]

Five Forks, April 1, 1865

On March 29, Ulysses S. Grant had begun his long awaited spring offensive against Petersburg. He ordered General Sheridan to go around the Confederate right flank to attempt to stretch Lee's defensive lines, and force Lee's troops out of their fortifications. Sheridan headed for Dinwiddie Court House and ordered Maj. Gen. G. K. Warren's 15,000-man V Corps from their winter camps south of Petersburg. They marched north up the Quaker Road to secure the strategically important Boydton Plank Road. They pushed the Confederates back into their lines along the White Oak Road, and took control of the plank road. This put Union forces in position to attack the South Side Railroad, just three miles to the north.[23]

---

20 Suderow, "Confederate Strengths & Losses," 13.

21 Clark, *Histories*, vol. 2, 107.

22 W. H. F. Lee to Rufus Barringer, October 13, 1867, R. E. Lee Family Papers, Duke University; "Cavalry Sketches," in *The Land We Love* (November 1867), vol. 4, no. 1, 6; Daughtry, *Gray Cavalier*, 284-285.

23 *OR* 46, pt. 1, 798, 1,101-1,102.

By the next day, March 30, Warren's infantry had fortified their position. Opposite them, Confederate Lt. Gen. Richard H. Anderson's Corps entrenched on White Oak Road. By the following day, when the fight at Chamberlain's Bed occurred, Rooney Lee had moved his 4,200 cavalrymen from Stony Creek to unite with Fitzhugh Lee on the White Oak Road near Five Forks, four miles northwest of Chamberlain's Bed. Five Forks was an intersection of four avenues—the White Oak, Scotts, Fords (or Church) and Dinwiddie Court House Roads. The intersection was located six miles northwest of Dinwiddie Court House, and was crucial to controlling the South Side Railroad, Lee's last supply line into Petersburg. Accordingly, Lee's cavalrymen rendezvoused at Five Forks with 5,000 infantrymen commanded by Maj. Gen. George E. Pickett.[24]

About 11:00 a.m. on March 31, a detachment of Maj. Gen. Bushrod Johnson's forces from Anderson's Corps attacked Warren's Union infantry. The Confederates pushed the Federals southwest to a branch of Gravelly Run. Warren counterattacked, reinforced by Brig. Gen. Nelson Miles's division of the II Corps. The Confederates were driven back to their works along the White Oak and Claiborne Roads. The battle of White Oak Road effectively severed most of Johnson's communication lines to Pickett's force, endangering the Confederate infantry.[25]

That same day, Warren had successfully dispatched Maj. Gen. Joseph J. Bartlett's brigade to a position behind Pickett's left flank. Realizing the precariousness of his exposed position, Pickett decided withdrew toward Five Forks as far as Hatcher's Run. Sheridan's cavalry and Warren's V Corps pressed Pickett and his infantry during their retreat toward the crossroads that would soon become famous.[26]

Once at Five Forks, Pickett had his exhausted infantry dig in and strengthen their position. The works there stretched about one-and-three-quarters of a mile, with artillery placed at strategic locations along their front. Barringer's regiments guarded the right flank. Robert E. Lee's instructions to Pickett reflected the importance of his stand: "Hold Five Forks at all hazards.

24 Bearss and Calkins, *The Battle of Five Forks*, 8; Manarin, *North Carolina Troops*, vol. 2, 278.

25 Bearss and Calkins, *The Battle of Five Forks*, 62-63, 72; *OR* 46, pt. 1, 1,287-1,288.

26 Bearss and Calkins, *The Battle of Five Forks*, 75-76.

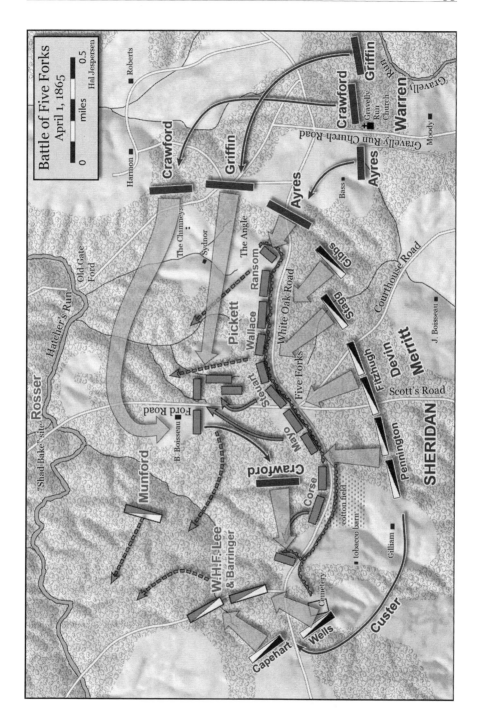

Battle of Five Forks
April 1, 1865

0   miles   0.5

Hal Jespersen

Roberts

Warren

Griffin

Gravelly Run Church

Crawford

Gravelly Run Church Road

Ayres

Moody

Griffin

Crawford

Harmon

Bass

Ayres

The Chimneys

Sydnor

The Angle

Ransom

Gibbs

Old Gate Ford

Hatcher's Run

Pickett

Wallace

White Oak Road

Gregg

Courthouse Road

Rosser

"Shad Bake" site

B. Boisseau

Ford Road

Stewart

Five Forks

Fitzhugh

Devin

Merritt

J. Boisseau

Munford

Mayo

Crawford

Scott's Road

Corse

Pennington

SHERIDAN

W.H.F. Lee & Barringer

cotton field

tobacco barn

Gilliam

Cemetery

Wells

Capehart

Custer

Protect road to Ford's Depot and prevent Union forces from striking the Southside Railroad."[27]

David Cardwell of McGregor's horse artillery, which supported the Confederate cavalry, later provided a vivid description of the aftermath of Chamberlain's Bed and the subsequent battle at Five Forks: "After the Chamberlain Run fight we lay down on the red clay of Dinwiddie County and thought we could whip anything alive. We had taken care of our wounded, buried our dead, and were ready to go to sleep. We went to sleep and slept as only soldiers can . . . when the reveille sounded at dawn on April 1, it was soon followed by 'Boots and saddles!' We were up and in the saddle after a . . . breakfast of corn pone cooked three days before and raw Nassau pork (sometimes called 'mule' by the boys, who worshipped it and got so little of it). I was hungry— 'hungry'—is not strong enough. I was so hungry that I thanked God that I had a backbone for my stomach to leap up against."[28]

Against the backdrop of the orders from Lee to Pickett to "hold Five Forks," the famous "shad-bake" incident occurred. On March 29, Maj. Gen. Thomas Rosser, who commanded a division of Virginia cavalry, had spent the day 10 miles southwest of Blackstone on the Nottoway River, catching a nice supply of shad. When Rosser moved up to Five Forks on March 30-31, he brought the shad with him. As soon as he moved his division north of Hatcher's Run, he arranged for the fish to be cleaned, split and baked over fires of dry wood. Rosser invited Pickett and Fitz Lee to the shad-bake. The relative lack of pressure from Sheridan led both men to believe they could slip away for awhile without danger. They did not want to refuse the offer of good food and drink at this point in the war. The event was a "social secret," and the two leaders slipped off to feast on the shad without telling anyone in their commands where they were going.[29]

While Pickett and Fitz Lee feasted, the Confederates waited for Sheridan's attack. Sheridan waited impatiently for G. K. Warren to come up and attack the left rear of the Confederate infantry. About 2:30 p.m., Sheridan's cavalry was spotted approaching Mary Gilliam's house, less than one mile southwest of the Five Forks intersection. The Widow Gilliam owned 2,800 acres that included

---

27 Freeman, *Lee's Lieutenants*, vol. 3, 661; La Salle Corbell, *Pickett and His Men* (Atlanta, GA, 1899), 386; Bearss and Calkins, *The Battle of Five Forks*, 76-77.

28 Cardwell, "The Battle of Five Forks," 117-118.

29 Freeman, *Lee's Lieutenants*, vol. 3, 665-666; *Philadelphia Weekly Times*, April 5, 1885.

the critical intersection. Rooney Lee's cavalry prepared for the impending attack. Lee rode up and down his line talking quietly to his officers, saying, "Brace up, [men]; it is no new thing to you. Well, why in thunder don't they come along?" Thus, Pickett and Fitz Lee were away from their troops when the Federals attacked in the late afternoon of April 1. By the time Pickett had been found, the defeat of his troops was assured.[30]

Finally, about 4:00 p.m., Sheridan drove a 9,000-man wedge of Warren's infantry between the Confederate infantry and their cavalry on the left. The Union infantry turned against the left flank of the Confederate infantry, which broke and retreated. The cavalry on the right, under Rooney Lee, battled George Custer's cavalry division all along the front at Gilliam's field. Hand-to-hand saber and pistol fighting, at close quarters, marked the engagement. The Confederates held for a time, allowing the infantry to escape. Shortly before dusk, enemy cavalry turned Barringer's right flank. At the same time, heavy Union infantry forces closed in on his left. In danger of being completely surrounded, Barringer ordered an immediate retreat. The Tar Heel commander later recalled, "We barely escaped annihilation." Remnants of his brigade headed for Namozine Church, but rallied after retreating a mile. Rooney Lee then ordered Barringer to rendezvous at Potts's Depot, midway between Ford's Depot and Sutherland's Depot on the South Side Railroad. At this point, Barringer's forces had been reduced to only about 800 men—only half of them mounted.[31]

David Cardwell of McGregor's horse artillery described the action that preceded the retreat:

After a while out in front we saw a small white puff of smoke, then another, and so on 'till it sounded like a pack of firecrackers. Then the men in the little rail pens began to come in on a run, turning and firing as they ran. As they scrambled over the works they said: "Boys, we are going to catch hell. The whole earth is covered with cavalry." Raising our eyes, we saw them coming, first at a walk, then at a trot march, and next at a gallop, and then bugles blew the charge. Did you ever hear the charge sounded? Great Caesar! It is a blare that goes to the bone, and it would make a rabbit fight a bulldog. On, on they came. We threw short fuse shells into them as fast as we could pull the

---

30 Cardwell, "The Battle of Five Forks," 117-118; *Freeman, Lee's Lieutenants*, vol. 3, 665-670; *OR* 46, pt. 1, 1,300.

31 Rufus Barringer to Victor Barringer, January 27, 1866; Clark, *Histories*, vol. 1, 442.

lanyard, and then canister. We thought that they would ride over us; but when the canister got in its work they wavered, swayed, and turned back. Oh, can you imagine yourself standing behind those light earthworks waiting for five thousand mounted men to ride over you? . . . Our men did not move. Nobody fell back but the men [the Federals] out in the rail fence. But we drew a breath when the cavalry wavered and turned. What a relief!

We looked out over that great field as the smoke cleared away and saw the bodies of the dead. The slightly wounded crawled off, afraid to raise their heads. The poor horses! Some were still in death, some struggling to get up. This charge was repeated four times, as I remember, and when they came the fourth time, we heard the spattering of bullets in our rear, to the left. In a few minutes, we saw the infantry moving towards us—at first just one or two—then three or four, and so on 'till there was a big movement through our command, and then a stampede. I had never seen our troops stampeded.[32]

Rooney Lee's division rendezvoused at Potts's Depot and prepared to battle the pursuing Federal horsemen. On Sunday morning, April 2, as Barringer's 5th North Carolina Cavalry placed a dismounted skirmish line to meet the approaching enemy cavalry, a courier rode up and said, "Petersburg has fallen, bring back this line slowly and join in the retreat." Barringer's men retired from Potts's Depot in good order. The brigade camped that night near Namozine Presbyterian Church, 10 miles northwest of Five Forks and less than seven miles from Potts's Depot.[33]

Captain Charles W. Pearson of the 5th North Carolina Cavalry described the disheartening retreat:

The brigade had been dismounted and was throwing up defenses. The road and fields soon became filled with retreating men, wagons, ambulances, and every description of army hangers-on. We were ordered to remount. The day's formation put the Sixty-third [5th Cavalry] in the rear; so that we were the last to get mounted. . . . Charging and countercharging was now going on. A general retreat now began, the enemy's cavalry making several charges, which were easily repulsed, and ceasing entirely as night came on. . . . The movement forward stopped. Company H was called for and nobly responded, promptly taking a position to cover the retreat. . . . Early next

---

32 Cardwell, "The Battle of Five Forks," 117-118.

33 Clark, *Histories*, vol. 3, 648-649.

morning [April 3] 'To Horses' was sounded and we were moved out near Namozine Church, which stood at the cross roads. We could hear the enemy's advance as our pickets were driven in.[34]

The battle of Five Forks had sealed the fate of the Army of Northern Virginia. Barringer later recalled: "At Five Forks on April 1st the last hope of the Confederacy went down in darkness and despair." Robert E. Lee's last supply line to Petersburg would be cut the next day at Sutherland's Station. He now knew that Petersburg and Richmond were lost and ordered the cities evacuated. Lee knew he could not move directly south to join Joseph E. Johnston's Army of Tennessee in North Carolina, because Grant blocked his path. Instead, he decided to try a rapid westward move in an attempt to escape his pursuers, and then move south to join Johnston.[35]

Union losses at Five Forks were about 630 killed, wounded, or missing. Confederate losses were about 545 killed and wounded with between 2,000 and 2,400 captured by the swarming Federals.[36]

Capture at Namozine Church, April 3, 1865

When news of the debacle at Five Forks reached Robert E. Lee, he ordered Lt. Gen. Richard H. Anderson to take Generals Henry A. Wise's, Eppa Hunton's, and Young M. Moody's brigades to the Ford's Church Road crossing on the South Side Railroad. Anderson gathered up Pickett's survivors and retreated to Sutherland Station. On the morning of April 2, Fitz Lee's cavalry corps united with Anderson's retreating infantry at the crossing. Anderson's corps had been reduced in the previous weeks' hard fighting to Maj. Gen. Bushrod Johnson's depleted infantry division. As Anderson's command retired to Namozine Bridge, Rooney Lee's division protected the rear, skirmishing with Col. Charles Fitzhugh's cavalry brigade, the vanguard of Union Maj. Gen. Thomas C. Devin's advancing division.[37]

34 Ibid.

35 Ibid., vol. 1, 442.

36 Bearss and Calkins, *The Battle of Five Forks,* 113; Suderow, "Confederate Strengths & Losses," 28-29

37 Keys, *Tar Heel Cossack,* 65.

That night, Robert E. Lee withdrew from Petersburg along the north bank of the Little Appomattox River. At the same time, Maj. Gen. William Mahone abandoned his lines at Bermuda Hundred, about 10 miles northeast of Petersburg, and Lt. Gen. Richard Ewell withdrew from north of the James River. Grant's Union army was soon in hot pursuit, with Sheridan's cavalry leading the chase. Lee directed his army to concentrate at Amelia Court House, where he had ordered provisions to be massed.[38]

The remnants of Pickett's and Bushrod Johnson's divisions that had escaped from the debacle at Five Forks rendezvoused during the night of April 1 near Crowder's Crossing. This point was halfway between Sutherland Station and Ford's Depot on the South Side Railroad. Early on April 2, after assembling the survivors, Pickett led them off to the northwest, followed by Bushrod Johnson's outfit. Both were now under Richard Anderson's command.

The Confederate cavalry under Fitzhugh Lee protected the rear, with Rooney Lee's cavalry division acting as the rearmost guard. The Confederate column moved northwest to Namozine Road and crossed Namozine Creek at 3:00 p.m. About one and one-half miles southeast of the creek, on high ground where Brown's Road intersected Namozine Road (Scott's Cross Roads or Corners), the men erected barricades. Fitzhugh Lee informed Bushrod Johnson that Federal cavalry was pursuing him and would be on the scene shortly. Around 5:00 p.m., the bluecoats arrived south of the intersection.[39]

Meanwhile, Sheridan's cavalry followed Bvt. Maj. Gen. Charles Griffin's V Corps up Ford's Road. Griffin had relieved Warren, who had been removed from command for not bringing up the infantry fast enough to Five Forks, and for letting his initial attack go awry. Sheridan's troopers reached the South Side Railroad at Church Road Crossing, just south of Cox Road. At this point they came in contact with Rooney Lee's cavalry, which quickly fell back. A running fight ensued, as the Federal horsemen moved north along Ford's Road past Ford's Meeting House. Eventually, they came to Brown's Road at Trinity Church and continued northward to its intersection with Namozine Road at Scott's Crossroads. As the advancing Union troopers reached this area, they

---

38 Henry Steele Commager, *The Blue and The Gray* (New York, NY, 1995), 1,132-1,133.

39 *OR* 46, pt. 1, 1,118-1,119, 1,124-1,125.

found the Confederates dug in along the ridge of Namozine Road. A halt was ordered until the division could regroup for an attack.[40]

A few miles east of Namozine Road, the Confederate infantry defending the railroad at Sutherland Station, seven miles west of Petersburg, prepared for another massive Federal attack. Nelson A. Miles of the II Corps came upon them as he moved his division up Claiborne Road. After making three attacks on the Confederate defenders, Miles forced them to scatter up Namozine Road, relinquishing their last hold on the South Side Railroad. Lee's supply line to Petersburg was irreparably cut. Since Devin's 1st Cavalry Division had led the Federal column the day before, and had seen the brunt of the action at Scott's Crossroads, Custer's more rested 3rd Division led the chase on the morning of April 3. In the vanguard were Col. William Wells's brigade, composed of the 8th and 15th New York, and the 1st Vermont Cavalry. Wells found Confederate Brig. Gen. William P. Roberts's cavalry brigade posted at Namozine Creek near the bridge the Rebels had earlier destroyed. Under heavy artillery fire, a detachment from the 1st Vermont Cavalry crossed upstream from Roberts's position. This flanking force compelled the "Tar Heel Cossack" to retire from his line. Once this was accomplished, felled trees and other obstructions were removed from the road crossing the creek, and Custer's men forded without mishap.[41]

No major defensive stands were made by the Confederates for the next five miles, until they reached Namozine Church, 10 miles northwest of Sutherland Station. To slow the progress of the advancing Federals, the Confederates placed felled trees and piles of fence rails in the road. Along this route, the Union cavalry found evidence of the Confederates' disorderly retreat. Artillery ammunition had been tossed away on the sides of the road and in the woods. The Southerners had set fire to the fences and nearby woods, causing an explosion of the shells left behind. The Federals heard the shells erupt as they rode by. The 8th New York led the advance as Namozine Road approached Cousin's Road, just east of Namozine Church.[42]

---

40 OR 46, pt. 1, 1,118-1,119, 1,124-1,125, 1,288-1,289; G. G. Benedict, *Vermont in the Civil War, A History of the Part Taken By The Vermont Soldiers in the War For The Union, 1861-65* (Burlington, VT, 1888), vol. 2, 681.

41 OR 46, pt. 1, 1,131-1,132, 1,138, 1,140, 1,288-1,289.

42 Ibid., 1,138; ibid., pt. 3, 529.

On the morning of April 3, the trailing position of the Confederate column was held by Rooney Lee's cavalry division. Rufus Barringer's North Carolina brigade was now the rear guard, having changed places with W. P. Roberts's brigade. Barringer's small 800-man force was composed of the remnants of the 1st, 2nd, and 5th North Carolina Cavalry. The 3rd guarded the wagon train. After leaving Namozine Creek, Barringer's brigade rode a few miles to the summit of a hill near Namozine Church, reaching the area about 9:00 a.m.[43]

Immediately after reaching Namozine Church, Generals Fitzhugh Lee, Rooney Lee, and Rufus Barringer met where Green Road and Cousins Road intersected. Holding a war council in the saddle, they all realized the moment was critical. Barringer, whose reddish-gray beard covered the scar from the wound received at Brandy Station, was mounted on a magnificent gray horse. At 5 feet, 6 inches tall, he stood in stark contrast to the 6-foot, 3-inch, large-framed Rooney Lee.[44]

Fitzhugh Lee, commanding all of the cavalry, said to his cousin Rooney, "General Lee, you must leave your best brigade here and hold this position to the last. The safety of our army depends upon it, and I will move on in [the] rear of the retreat with the rest of the cavalry." The three generals and their staffs knew that this order meant the destruction of the chosen brigade by overwhelming enemy forces. Rooney Lee instantly turned to his Tar Heel brigade commander and said, "General Barringer, you have heard the orders; you must do that duty here." Barringer interpreted the order ("hold this position to the last") to mean hold to the last minute, not to the last man. Facing overwhelming numbers, he intended to hold on as long as possible, but not to sacrifice his troopers to annihilation.[45]

The other generals and staffs moved off at once. As the head of the Federal column came into full view, Barringer immediately placed the 1st, 2nd and dismounted 5th North Carolina Cavalry in position for what would be the climactic battle for his brigade. The 1st held his left flank. The 2nd covered the center and the 5th held the right. The troopers were covered by a single gun of McGregor's battery. In front of the North Carolinians was an open field about 400 yards across. In the middle of the field sat the Abner Burke house. Two

43 Keys, *Tar Heel Cossack*, 65; Benedict, *Vermont in the Civil War*, vol. 2, 681.

44 John Wise, *End of An Era* (New York, NY, 1902), 333-334.

45 Clark, *Histories*, vol. 3, 650; ibid., vol. 5, 675.

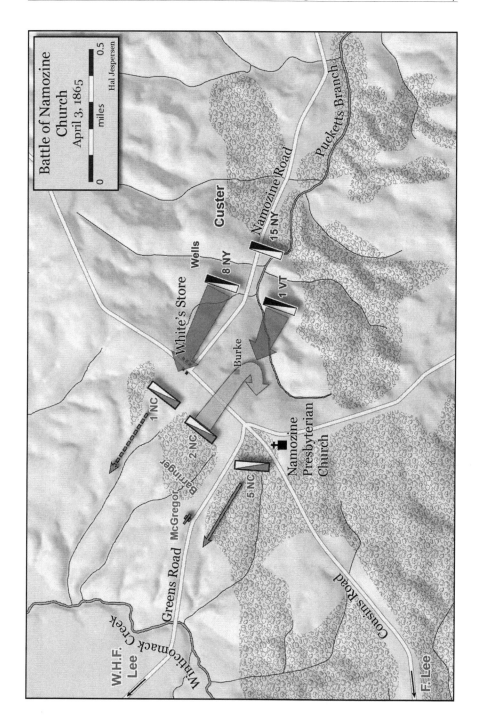

Battle of Namozine Church
April 3, 1865

Hal Jespersen

0   miles   0.5

Namozine Presbyterian Church, Amelia County, Virginia. The church, built in 1847, was headquarters for Generals Rooney Lee and Rufus Barringer in the morning of April 3, 1865. In the afternoon, it became the headquarters for General Phil Sheridan.

Bill Coughlin, North Arlington, NJ.

hundred yards east of the dwelling were woods, through which General Custer's entire division of cavalry soon emerged, as they trotted down Namozine Road.[46]

As the troopers of the 8th New York cleared the trees, they charged the Confederates at Namozine Church. They drove the Rebel pickets back before being forced to fall back themselves. The 1st Vermont joined the 8th New York and both renewed the attack on Barringer's line, with the New Yorkers attempting to turn his left flank. Seeing this, Barringer turned to his courier, Pvt. T. Frank Brown, and said, "Order that . . . [2nd] Regiment to charge and you lead it." This charge proved futile as the 1st North Carolina Cavalry, protecting Barringer's left, broke under a flank attack by the 8th New York. At this point, orders were sent to the 5th North Carolina Cavalry to retire from its position near the church and for the men to regain their horses.[47]

46 Ibid., 650-651; ibid., vol. 1, 442-443.

47 Oscar C. Palmer, "Father Rode With Sheridan, Reminiscences of Oscar C. Palmer As A Cavalryman In Company B of 8th New York Volunteers Of Cavalry From Winchester To

Barringer's withdrawal quickly became a stampede as more Federal troops, including the 15th New York, entered the fight. As the Confederates fled, artillerist McGregor fired the last shot into the blue-clad troopers while "raving like a mad man." Barringer, seeing that the 5th did not retire as ordered, dashed across the field with two staff members to guide the dismounted men through the unoccupied woods. This act saved about 100 of Barringer's troopers from capture, although their horses were lost.[48]

Oscar Palmer, a soldier in Company B, 8th New York Cavalry, later recalled the running fight at Namozine Church: "They [the Confederates] were in a piece of woods and did not fire on us until we were very close. Since there were only a few of us on advance, we could not charge until more came up, so we took shelter behind an old log building. . . . . By the time we got force enough to make an effective charge they had slipped out, leaving some [dead and wounded] laying around there that they could not very well take."[49]

As Barringer's men fell back along Green's Road, the 8th New York continued the chase. In the fight at the church, Wells's brigade captured 350 of Barringer's men, plus 100 horses and McGregor's gun. Quartermaster Sgt. Jerome B. Hatch of the 1st Vermont claimed the honor of capturing the gun. Union casualties included two killed and nine wounded in the 1st Vermont, one killed and six wounded in the 8th New York, and one killed in the 15th New York. Casualty figures for the North Carolinians were not recorded.[50]

Many years later, General Barringer remembered his role and subsequent capture in the battle:

> I was ordered by Major General Lee to hold the position as long as I safely could. . . .
> Soon the enemy appeared in force, with shouts of triumph and trumpets blowing. . . . I
> ordered the whole [force] to fall back and skirmish in retreat. The 5th Regiment, which
> was dismounted, fought with obstinacy and seemed slow to give up the contest. Before
> it retired under further orders, the enemy had gained the main road of retreat. I then
> moved this regiment by marching through forests and byways, and conducted it safely

Appomattox, 1864-1865," 6, Petersburg National Battlefield (C. M. Calkins Files); Clark, *Histories*, vol. 3, 651; Benedict, *Vermont in the Civil War*, vol. 2, 681.

48 Clark, *Histories*, vol. 3, 652-653.

49 Palmer, "Father Rode With Sheridan," 6.

50 *OR* 46, pt. 1, 1,119, 1,131-1,132, 1,139-1,140, 1,301; ibid., pt. 3, 529, 531; *New York Times*, April 7, 1865; Clark, *Histories*, vol. 3, 653; Benedict, *Vermont in the Civil War*, vol. 2, 681.

out to a point six miles above, where I hoped to find Major General [Rooney] Lee and the rest of the Brigade. Nearing this point I found it picketed. While reconnoitering to who the pickets were, I was taken prisoner, with Lt. Foard, and three couriers, by a party of Sheridan's Scouts, dressed in Confederate uniform. The Regiment, learning of my capture, made good its escape.[51]

Captured with Barringer were Lt. Fred C. Foard (aide-de-camp), Sgt. Maj. William R. Webb, Sgt. Stephen O. Terry, and Pvt. T. Frank Brown.[52]

Fitzhugh Lee reported, "Brigadier General Barringer was captured whilst in the steady discharge of his duties, and his loss was keenly felt by the command." Long after the war ended, some questioned Barringer's version of his capture, especially the part about Yankee scouts dressed in Confederate uniforms. Barringer's account, however, was verified by several contemporaries, including Sgt. Joseph E. McCabe of the 17th Pennsylvania Cavalry. McCabe had spent the entire night before the battle of Five Forks behind Pickett's lines, cutting telegraph connections to Petersburg (12 miles away) and forcing Robert E. Lee to use couriers, which greatly reduced his intelligence gathering capability.[53]

McCabe later recalled some of the details surrounding Barringer's capture:

I had gotten about six miles from the Yankee lines with my little band of six, dressed in full Confederate uniform, when in riding up the road on the way to Danville I saw a party of four or five real Southerners coming. We waited our chance to get them in proper position, and we halted them, and got the first word, and found that they belonged to the First North Carolina Brigade. They then wanted to know where we belonged. We informed them that we belonged to the Ninth Virginia Regiment. We then rode together and had some talk. While talking I saw a very fine-looking officer on a handsome horse coming. I inquired who he was, and the officer in charge of the squad said it was General Barringer. I left the party, rode and met him and shook hands with him and rode back into the party, and after getting all the information we could we took them prisoners and brought them into camp.[54]

51 Barringer, *The Natural Bent*, 119; Clark, *Histories*, vol. 1, 443.

52 Chris Calkins, *The Appomattox Campaign: March 29-April 9, 1865* (Conshohocken, PA, 1997), 82.

53 J. E. McCabe, *The Farmer and Mechanic*, September 5, 1883; *Philadelphia Weekly Times*, July 28, 1883; *OR* 46, pt. 1, 1,301.

54 Ibid.

Barringer's gray horse had been earlier taken from Col. Edwin Francis Cooke of the 2nd New York Cavalry. Cooke had been captured at Black and White's Depot on June 23, 1864, by Sgt. David F. Ratcliff of the 5th North Carolina Cavalry. Ratcliff retained Cooke's horse and superb trappings. When Barringer learned of the fine animal, he persuaded Ratcliff to exchange the horse for another. When Barringer was captured, he still rode the magnificent gray. Cooke, now a brevet brigadier general, was in the group that captured Barringer. Seeing the mounted Tar Heel brigadier, Cooke said, "I'll be damned, if yonder ain't my horse."[55]

Amelia County farmer M. A. Craddock witnessed Barringer's capture and recalled, "The severest of all trials was the sight of Gen. Lee's brave and gallant army retreating from the trenches of Petersburg. As I beheld noble Confederates go past here at Gilpin's Ford and distinctly saw the flash of the Yankee guns at them. I gave over to fears of anguish, & at that moment I could have welcomed death as a relief to my overburdened heart. . . . I witness[ed] too the capture of Gen. Barringer and Staff at my fartherest gate. They [the Yankees] were in the disguise of Confederate uniforms."[56]

Staff officer Lt. Fred Foard also left an interesting account of his commander's capture:

In a very little while I saw the dim outline of a man on horseback approaching me, who in the dim twilight seemed clothed in blue. When he came within pistol shot I fired at him and spurred my horse into a charge, cocking my pistol for another shot but by that time I was near enough to recognize General Barringer. . . . Of course suitable apologies were forthcoming. He commended me for my vigilance, although so near being a victim of it. It was so dark that I could not see the sights on my pistol else I should probably not have missed him. My pistol shot brought my men back, rushing to my assistance. We all went through the gate and before we were out of sight of the main road we saw a small body of mounted men approaching, about a dozen. I took two of our couriers, [T.] Frank Brown and [William. R.] Webb with cocked pistols in hand to see who they were. We met them at the gate. They said they belonged to the 10th Virginia Cavalry. With that, we returned our pistols to our holsters and they came through the gate. General Barringer, who kept in the background, seeing things proceeding so peacefully, rode up and introduced himself to them and told them how

55 Clark, *Histories*, vol. 3, 539.

56 M. A. Craddock to M. A. Calvin, November 15, 1865, Milas A. Calvin Papers, State Archives of North Carolina.

glad he was to see them, that he had been looking for them all day. They gave him three cheers at which he was visibly flattered. In the meantime they had silently surrounded us and at a signal each of us found the muzzles of two or three six-shooters in our faces. It was Major [Henry H.] Young, Sheridan's chief of scouts [and his troopers], disguised as Confederate soldiers, dressed in clothes taken off of prisoners. They had the drop on us and we succumbed without resistance.[57]

Sergeant Maj. William R. Webb, aide to Barringer, later recorded his version of the general's capture: "At a signal from Major Young of General Sheridan's staff, we all looked down at cocked pistols drawn from their cavalry boots, and were ordered to surrender. General Barringer tried to wheel his horse, Major Young dropped his hand on the bridle rein of the general's horse with the remark: 'General, we do not want to kill you.' Our men in just a few paces from us saw the performance and began to work their guns. Major Young said to them: 'If you can kill us and not kill your own men, fire away.' We rode rapidly with him till within the Federal lines. We were carried to Mrs. Cousins's [just west of Namozine Church], where Sheridan had his headquarters."[58]

One of Young's scouts, Archibald H. Rowland, recalled many years later that Barringer was angry at being captured by "spies." Barringer fumed, "They are spies, spies; I would hang every one of them to the highest limb if I caught them."[59]

Two days later, April 5, Major Young and his party—this time Young was dressed in the captured uniform of a Confederate colonel—met Col. W. H. Cheek, commander of the 1st North Carolina Cavalry. Also on hand were chief bugler Burke Privett and brigade color bearer Wyatt Churchill, who were out looking for Col. Roger Moore of the 3rd North Carolina Cavalry. After conversing for a few minutes, Young's men got the drop on Cheek and his staff and captured them. Cheek knew of Barringer's capture by the Yankees, as one of the staff had escaped and spread the news. Young recalled, "He, the colonel,

---

57 Narrative, Foard Papers, 20.

58 W. R. Webb, "The Capture of General Rufus Barringer," in *Daily Observer*, April 9, 1911; *Springfield Weekly Republican*, February 11, 1887.

59 Address of Arch H. Rowland of Young's Scouts at the Dedication of Young's Memorial Statue in Providence, Rhode Island, 1911, "First Hand Accounts," http://www.jessiescouts.com/JS Accounts Arch Speech.html. This speech was made in 1911, 46 years after Barringer's capture. Some memories faded, and others were sometimes embellished with the passing of that amount of time.

did not exactly bewail the fate of Barringer, for, said he, 'I am to command; I take his place.' 'Oh no!' said Harry Young. 'You do not take his place; you go to the place where he is!'" And, sure enough, Cheek joined his commander as a prisoner of war.[60]

William H. Woodall, General Sheridan's chief of scouts, received a Medal of Honor for capturing General Barringer's headquarters flag. The flag was in color bearer Wyatt Churchill's saddle bag when he and Colonel Cheek were captured on April 5.[61]

Denouement

When Robert E. Lee arrived at Amelia Courthouse on April 5, he found that the food supplies he had ordered were not there, and lost another day foraging for his starving troops. Meanwhile, Sheridan's cavalry had reached Jetersville, west of Amelia Courthouse. Lee turned north, planning to swing around Sheridan and get to Farmville. However, George Meade's infantry arrived at Sailor's Creek on April 6 and inflicted heavy losses on the shattered Confederates. By April 7, Lee's army was reduced to two infantry corps and one cavalry corps, and had lost most of its wagon trains. His diminished force reached Farmville, where it was once again forced to fight. That night, Lee resumed his retreat toward Lynchburg, but Sheridan raced ahead to Appomattox Station and blocked his advance to the west.[62]

The hopes of the Confederacy had been dashed on the field of battle. On April 9, Lee surrendered the remnants of his once powerful Army of Northern Virginia to a gracious Ulysses S. Grant in a courteous ceremony at Wilmer

---

60 William Gilmore Beymer, *On Hazardous Service: Scouts And Spies of the North and South*, (New York and London, 1912), 126-127; Manarin, *North Carolina Troops*, vol. 2, 7, 214; Clark, *Histories*, vol. 1, 778-779; D. H. Hill Jr., *North Carolina, Confederate Military History*, vol. 4, 433-434.

61 W. F. Beyer and D. F. Keydel, *Deeds of Valor: How America's Heroes Won the Medal of Honor*, (Detroit, MI, 1905), 403; OR 46, pt. 1, 1,261. In June 1916, a general review of all Medals of Honor deemed 911 unwarranted. Woodall's medal was included among them because he was a civilian scout. In June 1989, the U.S. Army Board of Correction of Records restored the medal to Woodall. The brigade flag was found in the saddle bag of the brigade color bearer, Wyatt Churchill, on April 5, 1865. Sergeant J. E. McCabe of the 17th Pennsylvania Cavalry wrote that he was awarded a Medal of Honor for capturing General Barringer, but the author has not been able to verify this claim. The *Official Records* does not list McCabe as receiving the Medal of Honor.

62 Calkins, *The Appomattox Campaign*, 85-87, 99, 114, 116.

The Headquarters Flag of General Rufus Barringer was captured on April 5, 1865, two days after Barringer's capture. The flag was in color bearer Wyatt Churchill's saddle bag, when he and Colonel William H. Cheek were captured. Colors: Field: Red; Cross: Dark Blue; Edge: White; Stars: White; Border: White. *North Carolina Division of Archives and History*

McLean's house at Appomattox Courthouse. Of those surrendered at Appomattox, only two officers and 21 enlisted men represented Barringer's brigade. For all intents and purposes, the Civil War was over.[63]

63 Clark, *Histories*, vol. 3, 582; OR 46, Pt. 1, 1,278.

Chapter 9

"President Lincoln: 'Do you think I could be of any service to you?' All laughed and
General Barringer replied with difficulty, 'If anyone can be of service to a
poor devil in my situation, I presume you are the man.'"

— *President Lincoln and captured Brig. Gen. Rufus Barringer*
at City Point, Virginia on April 5, 1865

A Prisoner of War

General Rufus Barringer had been captured in the last week of the war,
the first general officer taken to the massive Union base at City Point,
nine miles northeast of Petersburg. Barringer was also the first Confederate
general to meet President Abraham Lincoln, who visited City Point after his
tour of fallen Richmond. At the same time, President Jefferson Davis fled south
to escape capture, staying the evening of April 18, 1865, at Victor Barringer's
home in Concord, North Carolina. Rufus was transported to the Old Capitol
Prison in Washington, where he met with Secretary of War Edwin M. Stanton.
Next, Rufus was sent to the dreaded Fort Delaware prison camp, where he
remained incarcerated until the end of July. He would return home a war hero,
resume his law practice, become a republican, and urge his fellow North
Carolinians to accept Reconstruction and get on the with the business of
rejoining the Union as quickly as possible.

Phil Sheridan's Prisoner

Late in the evening of their capture on April 3, 1865, General Barringer and
his fellow prisoners were taken to Gen. Philip Sheridan's headquarters at Mrs.

Cousins's home, where they had supper with Sheridan and his staff. They slept on the floor during the night. The next morning, the Confederate officers were invited to breakfast with the Union cavalry commander.[1]

Lieutenant Fred C. Foard, Barringer's captured aide-de-camp, provided an account of the meeting with Sheridan: "His hospitality to us was in all respects graceful and well considered. His conversation [was] gracious and affable, consisting in part of warm inquiries about his friends in the old army who had fought with us. He was in a highly exuberant mood, having just won the decisive battle of the war, as Commander of a successful Army."[2]

After breakfast on April 4, the prisoners began their march to Petersburg. Rufus Barringer was allowed to retain his horse, but the remaining prisoners were dismounted. Since the narrow roads were filled with George Meade's advancing Union troops, the prisoners had to move along the side of the road, through ditches, briars, and stumps. Sergeant Maj. William R. Webb remembered: "When General Meade and his staff came into view, Major Foote hailed him loudly until noticed and, facing the guarded attention of General Meade's staff, gave him very welcome news of the safety of his [Meade's] brother-in-law, General [Henry A.] Wise, of the Confederate Army. He then introduced General Barringer. General Meade promptly rode forward to shake hands and, offering his purse, said, 'General Barringer, prison life is bad at best, and I take it you have no currency that will be of service to you on our side of the line. I will esteem it a favor if you will allow me to supply your present wants.' General Barringer thanked him, but did not accept the favor. He requested the privilege of communicating with his friends who could supply his needs. . . . [A general officer from Meade's staff] was told . . . to act as escort, and to pass the order to the Provost Marshal at City Point that General Barringer was to communicate with whomsoever he wished."[3]

Webb continued: "I have always been glad that I was present, to hear this interview between two men of great ability and culture, under circumstances so unique. Though commanders of opposing armies, they were as courteous and obliging as if they had met as personal friends. . . . I do not think I could have survived that forty-five mile walk to Petersburg, without food, and depressed in

---

1   Barringer, *The Natural Bent*, 119; Narrative, Foard Papers, 20.

2   Ibid., 21.

3   Barringer, The Natural Bent, 119; Narrative, Foard Papers, 21.

mind with the humiliation of capture, had not General Barringer, although an older man, often given me a ride, and walked himself amongst the rubbish of the roads." Webb later stated that "General Barringer commanded my admiration and my love. He was a brave soldier and a thorough Christian gentleman."[4]

When the party arrived in Petersburg about sundown on April 4, their escort left them alone while he went looking for the post headquarters to report. The commandant told the escort: "If General Sheridan paroled them, let them stay on parole, and you go with them to City Point." They slept that night on the floor of the court house in Petersburg, without any bedding for comfort.[5]

On April 5, they proceeded leisurely for nine miles and arrived at City Point a little after noon. Their escort delivered them to the post commander, Bvt. Brig. Gen. Charles H. T. Collis, who received them with civility. Lieutenant Foard was turned over to the post staff's hospitalities, while Collis entertained Barringer. Collis later recalled: "Barringer was a polished, scholarly, and urbane gentleman, scrupulously regarding his parole I had exacted from him, and deeply sensible and appreciative of my poor efforts to make him comfortable."[6]

Barringer had been courteously received and was at first assigned to one of a row of tents, apparently to await the next arrivals, Generals Richard Ewell and George Washington Custis Lee (son of Robert E. Lee). After them would come hundreds, and then thousands, of prisoners of every rank and description.[7]

General and Mrs. Collis provided comfortable quarters at their home for high ranking Confederate officers. Barringer, the only Confederate general officer then at City Point, dined with his gracious hosts on April 5. Mrs. Septima Collis later recalled: "It gave me great pleasure to have these distinguished men as my guests, rebels though they were, and I was glad to have it in my power to show them that there was a disposition to welcome the prodigals' return with the fatted calf. Being quite a 'cordon bleu' myself, it was not difficult to present

4 Barringer, *The Natural Bent*, 119-120; Laurence McMillan, *The Schoolmaker, Sawney Webb & the Bell Buckle Story* (Chapel Hill, NC, 1971), 41. W. R. Webb, "The Capture of General Rufus Barringer," in *The Daily Observer*, April 9, 1911.

5 Ibid; Narrative, Foard Papers, 22. Parole in this case was simply a promise not to try to escape before reaching their final destination. It meant they did not have to be held in chains or under close guard during the trip.

6 Septima M. Collis, *A Woman's War Record, 1861-1865* (New York, NY, 1989), 62.

7 Ibid.

an attractive menu, consisting of superb raw oysters, green-turtle soup, a delicious James-River shad, and a fillet of army beef. A bottle of whiskey and another of brandy, and a cup of good black coffee constituted the dinner which, General Barringer was good enough to say, and said it as if he meant it, was the first square meal he had eaten in two years. The General was a charming gentleman, appreciative, tolerant, and resigned."[8]

Meeting with President Lincoln

Late in the afternoon of April 5, General Collis invited Barringer to go with him to witness the dress parade of some regiments of regulars. Afterward, the two men walked over to General Grant's headquarters, where Collis excused himself to go in and receive the latest news from the front. He quickly returned, saying that Grant was not in, but that President Lincoln was present. At the mention of General Barringer's name as a prisoner, the president had exclaimed, "Can that be my old friend, [Moreau] Barringer, who had a seat next to me in Congress? Bring him in!"[9]

Meanwhile, General Barringer had requested shaving materials, which were promptly provided, and he settled down to that long deferred luxury in a nearby tent. Barringer was anxious to see what manner of man was the President of the United States. Since he was muddy, tattered, and torn, The Tar Heal Commander hardly felt presentable for such an occasion. However, brushing, shoe polish, and the completed shave restored his morale.[10]

Collis remembered the meeting:

> [General Collis] formally presented General Rufus Barringer of North Carolina to the President of the United States in the adjutant general's tent. Mr. Lincoln extended his hand, warmly welcomed the Confederate general, and bade him be seated. There was only one chair when the President arose, and this, the Southerner very politely declined to take; so the two men stood facing in the center of the tent, the tall form of Mr. Lincoln almost reaching the ridgepole. He looked at General Barringer over from head to foot and said, "Barringer from North Carolina. General, were you ever in Congress?

---

8   Ibid.

9   Charles H. T. Collis, "Lincoln's Magnanimity," in *Once A Week*, n.d., University of Virginia; Collis, *A Woman's War Record*, 63-70.

10 Ibid.

"No, Mr. Lincoln, I never was." "I thought not," said Mr. Lincoln. "I did not think my memory could be so at fault, but there was a Barringer in Congress with me, and from your state too." "That was my brother [Moreau], Sir," said the General.[11]

Until then Mr. Lincoln had worn that thoughtful, troubled expression that is known so well, but now the lines relaxed and the whole face laughed. "Well, well," he said, "Your brother was my chum in Congress. Yes sir, we sat at the same desk and ate at the same table. He was a Whig and so was I. He was my chum, and I was very fond of him. Well. Shake again." A few more chairs had been brought in and conversation drifted from Mr. Lincoln's anecdotes of the pleasant hours that he and the Honorable Daniel Moreau Barringer had spent together prior to the war and then to the merits of the military and civil leaders, both of the North and the South.[12]

Sensing that he had perhaps taken enough of the President's time, Barringer began to rise and take leave. President Lincoln spoke up and told him to keep his seat. The President remarked: "they were both prisoners, and that he hoped the General would take pity and talk with him about the times when they were both their own masters."[13]

Finally, General Barringer arose and was bowing himself out, when President Lincoln took him again by the hand and, laying the other hand on his shoulder, said with great seriousness and simplicity, "Do you think I could be of any service to you?" All laughed, and General Barringer replied with difficulty, "If anyone can be of service to a poor devil in my situation, I presume you are the man."[14]

General Collis remembered what happened next as the momentous meeting came to a close:

Mr. Lincoln drew a card from his pocket, adjusted his glasses, and turned up the wick on the lamp. Then, seating himself at the desk, he wrote with all seriousness with which he might have signed the Emancipation Proclamation. While writing, he kept up a running conversation to this effect: "I suppose they will send you to Washington and there I have no doubt, they will put you in the Old Capitol prison. I am told it isn't a

11 Ibid.

12 Ibid.

13 Ibid.

14 Ibid.

nice sort of place and I am afraid you won't find a very comfortable tavern; but I have a friend in Washington,—he's the biggest man in the country—and I believe I have some influence with him when I don't ask too much. Now I want you to send this card of introduction to him and if he takes the notion, he may put you on parole, or let up on you that way or some other way. Anyway it's worth trying." Then very deliberately drying the card with the blotter, he held it up to the light and read: "This is General Barringer, of the Southern Army. He is the brother of a very dear friend of mine. Can you do anything to make his detention in Washington as comfortable as possible under the circumstances?

A. Lincoln

To Hon. Edwin M. Stanton
Secretary of War"[15]

General Barringer could not utter a word. He made some effort to say "Thank you" or "God bless you," but was speechless. Following the commandant, he wheeled and left the tent.[16]

Outside, the commandant found him completely overcome with emotion. Collecting himself, Barringer took the commandant's arm, made his way back to the tent, and at last expressed his profound appreciation for such thoughtfulness and generosity. Barringer recalled in his diary "that his [Lincoln's] looks, dress and manners have been misrepresented [in the] South." General Collis met Barringer in Philadelphia many years after the war, and said that in discussing this meeting with Lincoln, the former Confederate general's eyes filled with tears over the "the deep damnation" of the president's tragic assassination.[17]

---

15 Collis, "Lincoln's Magnanimity"; Collis, *A Woman's War Record*, 63-70; Jerry Korn, *Pursuit to Appomattox: The Last Battles* (Chicago, IL, 1987), 113; Barringer, *The Natural Bent*, 123; Donald C. Pfanz, *The Petersburg Campaign: Abraham Lincoln at City Point, March 20-April 9, 1865* (Lynchburg, VA, 1989), 74-76. A note from Lincoln to Barringer sold at auction by R&R Enterprises (Amherst, NH), Rare Document Auctions, in April 2005 for $12,419. This note is worded differently that than reported by General Collis in his written account of the meeting between Lincoln and Barringer. The version of the note in The Natural Bent matches General Collis's wording.

16 Collis, *A Woman's War Record*, 69.

17 Rufus Barringer, *Prison Diary*, April 15, 1865, Southern Historical Collection; Collis, *A Woman's War Record*, 70.

Description of Note: One folded page, both sides, 3.25 inches by 2 inches, April 3, 1865.
Inscription: "Will the Sec. of War please see and hear General Barringer of N. C. & oblige
him if you consistently can in seeing some friends."

On April 3, 1865, nine days before his assassination, President Abraham Lincoln wrote this
note to Secretary of War, Edwin Stanton, regarding the imprisonment of Confederate
General Rufus Barringer. Lincoln, visiting the Federal Headquarters at City Point on April
5th, Virginia, gave the note to Barringer, who was being transported to the Old Capitol
Prison in Washington.

General Barringer was the first Confederate general officer captured and taken to City
Point. It happened that President Lincoln at the time and upon hearing Barringer's name,
insisted he wanted to see him. Lincoln recognized the Barringer name from Moreau
Barringer, who shared a desk with him in Congress. The two men, along with Camp
Commander, Bvt. General Charles H. T. Collis met and conversed congenially for a period
of time. Collis recorded an account of the meeting. The note sold at auction in 2005 for
$12,419. *R&R Enterprises, Amherst, NH.*

President Jefferson Davis's Stay at Victor Barringer's House during his flight from Richmond, April 18-19, 1865.

It was ironic that during the same month that General Barringer met with
President Lincoln, Rufus's brother Victor hosted Jefferson Davis as the
Confederate president fled south from Richmond. It is even more surprising
that Davis called on Victor Barringer. Victor had written a scathing letter to
Davis in January 1865, in which he castigated the president for poor leadership
and called attention to the public's loss of confidence in his administration.
Victor, clearly anguished, wrote in part:

> [N]o man can conduct us successfully through the struggle in which we are engaged,
> who has lost the public confidence. . . . I assert . . . that the loyal heart of this section is
> fast falling away from its confidence in you & your administration of affairs . . . . They
> [the complaints] may be summed up into one, which I may characterize as a total want,
> in your administration from top to bottom, of a terrible revolutionary energy &

earnestness—that high quality which, in politics, like faith in religion, can remove mountains; citizens are angry because generals are not held accountable and promptly replaced for the "defeats, surrenders, surprises, blunders, fruitless victories & lost opportunities without number"; able bodied officers and government officials are reviled for their license, wastefulness, favoritism & rank corruption. . . . It grieves me more than I can tell to witness how far, within the last 18 months, the loyal mind has been alienated from its hope & confidence in you.[18]

Nevertheless, as he fled to avoid capture, the president called upon Victor Barringer for a night's stay at his home. After the evacuation of Richmond, Davis had fled to Danville, Virginia, where he established a temporary capital. Later, he moved briefly to Greensboro, North Carolina. Finding that location untenable, Davis became a fugitive whose only hope was to escape to foreign shores.[19]

Davis followed his wife Varina and their children south. Knowing of Victor and Rufus Barringer, Davis stopped in Concord. His brief stay at Victor's home was described in a letter from Victor's wife Maria to her sister:

[T]he whole party were on horseback. My husband and I were sitting on the verandah behind the rose-shaded end of it, when we suddenly heard our front gate shut and footsteps approaching the verandah. The click of spurs announced a military guest and I went forward to receive him, Mr. [Victor] Barringer being quite lame from an inflamed knee. He asked if this was Major Victor Barringer's house and if he was at home and gave his name as William Preston Johnston, son of Albert Sidney Johnston. He then asked Mr. Barringer if he could receive and accommodate Mr. Davis for the night, stating he was too unwell to sleep in the tent set up outside the town where the rest of the party would stay. My husband acceded to his request at once and asked how many gentlemen there were in the party and on being told ten invited them all to dinner and to pass the night and remain for breakfast and suggested the body guard should pitch their tent on the vacant lot opposite. In about an hour the whole party arrived and were shown to their rooms.[20]

---

18 Victor Barringer to Jefferson Davis, January 21, 1865, in Lynda Lasswell Crist, ed., *The Papers of Jefferson Davis, Volume II, September 1864-May 1865* (Baton Rouge, LA, 2004), 345-346.

19 Barringer, *The Natural Bent*, 98-99.

20 Mrs. Victor Barringer to Maria, February 7, 1901, in *Progress* (Concord, NC, 1981), 29; *Charlotte Daily Observer*, February 3, 1901.

Davis and his entourage left the next day after lunch and headed for Charlotte. Victor soon followed in a horse drawn carriage, when he received word of Lincoln's assassination. He again met with Davis and Confederate cabinet members John C. Breckenridge and Judah P. Benjamin, as they discussed the situation.[21]

Prisoner at Fort Delaware, April-July, 1865

Lieutenant Foard of General Barringer's staff remembered what happened after Barringer's meeting with President Lincoln. Early the next morning, April 6, Barringer and Foard boarded the ship *Isaac Bell*, on parole, with instructions to report to the Old Capitol Prison in Washington. They had liberty aboard the vessel. Upon arriving in Washington early the next morning, they went out into the city as unrestrained as any of the other passengers. Foard recalled: "we reported to the Commandant of the Old Capitol Prison, Captain William P. Wood, according to our parole, to whom General Barringer presented his note of introduction from President Lincoln to Secretary Stanton. The note was at once sent up to the War Office and received a prompt reply, ordering General Barringer to be shown to Stanton's office precisely at the noon hour, which was done."[22]

In his diary, Barringer stated that Secretary of War Edwin M. Stanton was "bitter cold in manner—but changed as we talked on." Stanton told General Barringer that he would order him to be released at that hour every day, and since he now knew the way, he could come up for them to discuss what was most desirable to be done. After several interviews, Stanton told Barringer that the Old Capitol was only a receiving and distributing prison. With many more prisoners coming, it would be necessary to empty it immediately.[23]

"He [Stanton] gave General Barringer the privilege of choosing any military post in the United States for his imprisonment and of taking three friends of his own choosing as companions," Foard recalled. "In what must have been a surprise to Stanton, Barringer chose Fort Delaware (the worst choice he could have made according to the horrid reputation of the prison) and Major [R. E.]

---

21 Barringer, *The Natural Bent*, 103.

22 Narrative, Foard Papers, 21-22.

23 Narrative, Foard Papers, 22; Barringer, Prison Diary, April 7, 1865.

Foote, Bushrod Johnson's Adjutant General, Major [James D.] Ferguson, Inspector General [Fitzhugh Lee's assistant adjutant general] and myself." Barringer probably chose Fort Delaware because he had influential friends in nearby Philadelphia, Pennsylvania, who he hoped could help him.[24]

Just before dusk on April 8, Barringer, Foote, Ferguson, and Foard arrived at the prison, located on Pea Patch Island on the Delaware River about 40 miles south of Philadelphia. There they found 2,500 officers and 9,000 enlisted men in two separate stockades.

Fort Delaware occupied 90 acres with a large, granite stone fortification containing three tiers of heavy guns. It was one of the most dreaded of all Union prisons. The barracks were poorly constructed and several feet below the water level of the river at high tide. The water was held back with dikes, but the barracks were always damp and cold. High-ranking officers were held inside the walls of the fort, while the other prisoners were confined to a series of interlocking barracks around the interior yard.[25]

The post was commanded by Brig. Gen. Albin F. Schoepf, assisted by Capt. George Ahl, Sgt. Jim O'Neil, and an abusive guard nicknamed "Hackout." Conditions in the outside barracks were terrible, and many captives died in this fortress-turned-prison. Conditions were much better in the officers' quarters within the fort's walls. Barringer was assigned a room with Brig. Gen. Richard Lucien Page and several other officers.[26]

On April 9, Barringer was visited by General Schoepf and was granted parole of the island. The Tar Heel prisoner spent most of his first day in captivity talking with other captured officers. He found them still "full of hope." Barringer noted in his dairy that "the officers did their own cooking, washing, and live well."[27]

24 Ibid.

25 Narrative, Foard Papers, 22, 23-24.

26 Ibid., 22; H. L. Hart, "Prison Experience at Fort Delaware," in *Confederate Veteran* (October 1913), vol. 21, no. 10, 481; Clark, *Histories*, vol. 4, 727. Sergeant Chas. W. Rivenbark of Company C, 1st North Carolina says this man, also known as "Old Hike," was a Vermont officer named Adams. According to Rivenbark, Adams had been sent to prison after he deserted at First Manassas, but had somehow returned to service as a supervisor of guards. "[N]o meaner or utter despicable being ever cursed the earth with his presence."

27 Barringer, Prison Diary, April 9, 1865; Fort Delaware Notes, February 1997. The records of Fort Delaware indicate that Barringer was "held in Division 23, in the prison compound outside the fort."

The next day, Barringer bought some clothes and made his first visit to the "barracks," which shocked him. He described them in his diary as "horrible places—crude—crowded—close, and dirty." Upon visiting the prison hospital, Rufus described the poor captives as "sad-sad sights."[28]

On April 13, Barringer and fellow captive Richard Lucian Page were invited to General Schoepf's house, where they were introduced to Mrs. Schoepf. The commandant's wife was from the South and was sympathetic to their plight.[29]

On April 15, the prisoners awoke to find the post's flags flying at half-staff. Rumors began circulating. Barringer started for the barracks and was told by a fellow prisoner that President Lincoln had been assassinated. There was great excitement in the barracks, and some of the captives seemed buoyed by the news. However, according to Barringer, most of the men were "sad and solemn," and many became alarmed at the prospect of reprisals. Barringer and his brother-in-law, Capt. Robert Hall Morrison Jr., were hustled back to the officers' quarters. In his diary, Rufus deemed it "an awful day."[30]

Barringer remembered that he spent a lot of time during his imprisonment writing letters, reading mail, visiting fellow prisoners, listening to preaching, and attending prayer meetings.[31]

Lieutenant Foard described the barracks and living conditions:

Inside the stockade there were numerous one-story wooden structures resembling hastily and cheaply constructed hospital wards in which the prisoners were housed. The buildings had no inside finish and were very cold and damp. There were piers of bunks extending all the way around the interior, wide enough for a man to extend himself at full length across. There was only one door, no window but an occasional diamond shaped air hole, cut in the weather boards, not glazed, for light and ventilation. Each of us was provided with one blanket, so that by doubling, we could have one blanket under us and one blanket over us, when we slept. There was a large stove in the center for which a moderate allowance of coal was issued to us. A detail was made by ourselves from our own number, each 24 hours to keep the fire going. . . . There were 139 of us in the room to which I was assigned.

28 Barringer, Prison Diary, April 10, 1865.

29 Ibid, April 13, 1865.

30 Ibid, April 15, 1865.

31 Ibid.

We were fed twice a day, the allowance each time being three hard tacks with the addition of a cup of very thin soup for dinner and a microscopic morsel of meat for breakfast. . . . The scanty feeding was alleged to be in retaliation for Andersonville [the infamous prison for Union captives in Georgia].

The stockade was nearly or quite 15 feet high, with a staging around the outside, three or four feet from the top, on which the sentinels walked their beat overlooking everywhere and at all times the entire interior. . . . Our poor fellows were more than half dead when they were finally released.

The drinking water was a continual menace to health and even to life. It was contained in an immense reservoir, above ground, exposed to the sun. Warm and stagnant and putrid, it was almost sure death to drink it raw; our only resource was to boil it. Each of us had a pint tin cup and seizing upon any loose fragment of wood, we hoarded it as if it were so much gold, whittling shavings from it to feed the fire under our tin cups.[32]

While in prison at Fort Delaware, Capt. Robert E. Park of the 12th Alabama recorded events in his diary that occurred between April 30 and May 4, 1865: "Those prisoners who still refused the oath [of allegiance to the United States] held a consultation meeting in Division 22." The Amnesty Proclamation of December 8, 1863, offered pardons to those who had not held a Confederate civil office, had not mistreated Union prisoners, and would sign an oath of allegiance. "General Barringer made a long speech, urging all of us to accept the terms of the Yankees and go home, and declared that we would be banished from the country if we persisted in declining the proffered oath."[33]

Barringer's speech, recalled Captain Park, was vehemently rejected by many in attendance. Captain John W. Fellows, a former member of Gen. William N. R. Beall's staff, mounted a box and responded: "General Barringer says that if we do not tamely submit, we shall be banished from the country. What's banished but set free from daily contact with things we loathe? Banished? We thank you for it! Twould break our chains." Captain Fellows and Col. Van H. Manning, of the 1st Arkansas, urged all to remain faithful to the bitter end. All

---

32 Narrative, Foard Papers, 23-24.

33 Robert E. Park, "Diary of Captain Robert E. Park, Twelfth Alabama Regiment," in *Southern Historical Society Papers* (January-June 1877), vol. 3, 250. In his diary, Barringer recalled making a speech on May 5 that was countered by others.

of this must have frustrated General Barringer, who recognized the futility of further resistance.[34]

Rufus's son, Dr. Paul Brandon Barringer, mistakenly recalled many years later that Lincoln was assassinated while Rufus was still in the Old Capitol Prison in Washington. In fact, Barringer had been moved to Fort Delaware before the assassination occurred. Dr. Barringer also recalled (incorrectly, and with no apparent evidence) that General Barringer was questioned about the assassination: "Although delayed until August in reaching home, he was still investigated by the Federal authorities at intervals—even after the death of [John Wilkes] Booth and the execution of the unfortunate Mrs. [Mary] Surratt and all suspected accomplices." It appears that Dr. Barringer confused the capture of his father with that of Col. William H. Cheek, the commander of the 1st North Carolina Cavalry. Cheek was captured on April 5 during the Appomattox retreat, and was at the Old Capitol Prison at the time of President Lincoln's assassination. He and other Confederate prisoners were reportedly saved from an angry mob by the timely arrival of Federal soldiers sent for their protection.[35]

On May 8, 1865, Barringer wrote to Chiswell W. Dabney, who had served during the war as Barringer's adjutant general. Rufus confirmed that he had been captured "by Gen'l Sheridan's scouts in Confederate uniforms." He went on to express his concern about other matters: "I feel great anxiety to know what became of yourself, the Brigade, Ambulance, Hdqtrs. Wagon, my black horse. . . . All the privates and nearly all the officers here are agreed to taking the oath as the only alternative."[36]

On May 21, Barringer recorded in his diary his emerging beliefs on the postwar reunification of the nation. He believed the South should "accept the situation" and stated his preference "for immediate rather than gradual

---

34 Ibid.

35 D. H. Hill Jr., *Confederate Military History*, 13 vols. (Secaucus, NJ, 1899), vol. 4, 433-434; Barringer, *The Natural Bent*, 123. There is no documented evidence that Barringer was questioned by officially authorized representatives concerning Lincoln's assassination. There is no mention of any such events in Barringer's diary. The only mention of any questioning was by Paul Brandon Barringer in *The Natural Bent*. However, contrary to the younger Barringer's recollections, Rufus was already confined at Fort Delaware when Lincoln was assassinated. The Evidentiary File (M-599) for the Lincoln Assassination Trial of the Conspirators does not mention Barringer.

36 Rufus Barringer to Chiswell W. Dabney, May 8, 1865, Virginia Historical Society.

emancipation." The Tar Heel commander was "inclined to Freedman voting with restriction on all suffrage [positions of office]."[37]

In early June, Barringer began a campaign of letter writing to try to win his release from prison so he could return to his family. On May 29, 1865, President Andrew Johnson offered amnesty and the return of property to all those former Confederates who would take an oath of allegiance. However, former Confederates with the rank of colonel and above in the army, or lieutenant and above in the navy, and people owning more than $20,000 worth of property, had to apply for individual pardons. Due to his rank and prewar wealth, Barringer was excluded from the general amnesty offered by the Amnesty Proclamation. On June 3, he wrote to Union Maj. Gen. Francis Preston Blair in Washington. Blair had considerable political connections, and his brother, Montgomery Blair, served as postmaster general in the Lincoln administration. Barringer hoped Blair would intervene on his behalf. On June 8, Barringer petitioned President Johnson for executive clemency and asked Blair to use his influence to get a favorable review by the new president. Barringer knew Blair from his college days at Chapel Hill, and was in the University of North Carolina class preceding Blair.[38]

In his letter to Blair, Barringer stated: "I have never had any mere prejudices against the North, its people or institutions. On the contrary, I have ever admired its enterprise and progress & often deplored the lethargy of the South—which I half felt lay in slavery. I therefore give it up without any feeling of bitterness or sign of regret."[39]

In his June 8 petition to the president, Barringer stated that he "sought to the last to avert Secession, and greatly deplored a resort to arms." He also recalled that "I never recognized the right or policy of Secession." The captive Southern commander continued: "After the defeat of Genl. Lee on April 1st, I saw for the first time that the cause was hopeless, and I felt that further resistance was both folly and madness. Since my capture I have on all proper occasions urged my fellow prisoners to conciliation and to submission in good faith to the National authorities."[40]

---

37 Barringer, Prison Diary, May 21, 1865.

38 Ibid.

39 Amnesty Papers for General Rufus Barringer, M1003, Roll 37, National Archives.

40 Ibid.

Post commander Gen. Albin Schoepf enthusiastically supported Barringer's petition to President Johnson: "Genl. Barringer has to my knowledge given constant and clear evidence of his purpose to cheerfully submit to the National Authorities. Since his confinement he has exerted a good influence on his fellow prisoners, and I doubt not that he would do the same among his people at home." On June 14, General Barringer sent a follow-up letter to President Johnson, in which he repeated his plea and added the "oath of allegiance."[41]

Between the two letters to the president, Rufus wrote to his children: "Ah! how many sad scenes I have gone through since I last wrote you. But, while I have seen and heard of others suffering so much, Our Heavenly Father has been good to me. I have been kindly treated by the Yankees, have found many friends, and had good health, and have had plenty of plain food to eat. For all these blessings I feel very thankful."[42]

Rufus went on to explain what it was like to be a prisoner of war and described the living conditions:

I will tell you more what it is like to be a prisoner of war. They don't put us in a closed prison like a jail. They put us in a large lot, with a great high fence all around it, and one big gate. They have cheap frame houses built all around, inside, called "Barracks". . . . The Barracks are laid off in Divisions, each Division has a chief & all have to attend roll-call once a day. A Yankee srgt. calls the roll. All around the great high fence is a platform or little walk (just on top) along which the Yankee sentinels walk with their loaded guns & if we try to get out, or do anything they don't allow they holler at us & if we do not stop, they shoot us. Some officers have been in here over two years, & never been out. Some are so ragged, some so dirty (it's hard to keep clean) & some look so pale & weak. Many have almost lost their minds. When they get sick, they are taken out to the hospital, outside the big fence. There they have little beds or cots. When they get well, they make them go into the barracks. Many die. Every morning I see them carrying off 5 or 6 to be buried.[43]

On June 27, Rufus wrote a letter to his sister Margaret Grier, in which he described the despair of many in waiting for word of their release: "The place is

41 Ibid.

42 Barringer, *The Natural Bent*, 111-113; Rufus Barringer to his children, June 10, 1865, Rufus Barringer Papers, Southern Historical Collection.

43 Ibid.

getting perfectly intolerable. We can see no sense in keeping Field and General officers in Prison—merely because we chanced to be captured, while thousands of our rank are at home. However, I try to contain myself—which others do not. Some poor fellows nearly fret themselves to death. One or two, it is feared, have gone crazy."[44]

Rufus lamented the terrible conditions for the sick: "This day they, the authorities, sent off the last of the regular nurses and attendants—leaving 30 odd patients—half of them in a dying condition—to the voluntary kindness & mercy of the few officers left—most of whom are themselves unwell. Oh! It is so sad to see these noble men lying for days, weeks & months in their beds of death—slowly but surely passing away—without one word during their long affliction from families or friends at home—without once seeing a known face —& without a single comfort or consolation."[45]

On several occasions, General Barringer thought his release was imminent, only to be disappointed. He wrote a letter to Kemp P. Battle, who was active in Washington on behalf of North Carolina in trade and commerce matters after the war. The missive revealed Barringer's emerging wish to heal the country, restore peace to the Union, and bring about his release: "May I appeal to you to try & do something while in Washington to affect my release from prison? . . . I can only assure you, that, if released, I would go home fully resolved to do all in my power (in a quiet way) to restore peace, harmony, & prosperity to the country. I cherish no feelings of bitterness or hostility toward any section, class or party. My great desire now is to see the whole country again thoroughly united in . . . a lasting genuine peace; its property returned and its safety and permanency finally settled & secured."[46]

If President Johnson read Barringer's letters, he did not act upon them. There were several general release orders in June for officers at the prison, and hundreds were released. Barringer, however, was not among them.[47]

---

44 Rufus Barringer to Margaret Grier, June 27, 1865, Rufus C. Barringer Papers, University Notre Dame.

45 Ibid.

46 Rufus Barringer to Kemp P. Battle, July 18, 1865, Kemp Battle Family Papers, Southern Historical Collection.

47 Dale Fetzer and Bruce Edward Mowday, *Unlikely Allies: Fort Delaware's Prison Community in the Civil War* (Mechanicsville, PA, 2000), 140.

According to Montgomery Blair, there were extremists in Washington who "insisted that some who had engaged in the rebellion should be made to pay the penalty of their 'treason,' and as Robert E. Lee and Joe Johnston with their commands . . . had been permitted under the terms of surrender to go home, the Fort Delaware prisoners, with others, were to be held for a time to await the determination of the authorities at Washington as to final disposition." This could help explain why Barringer's release was so late in coming.[48]

Rufus's release order was dated July 24, 1865, but his diary indicates that he actually left Fort Delaware the next day. His Confederate Service Record reveals that he stopped at Dr. R. J. Powell's in Georgetown after his release, in an unsuccessful attempt to obtain a copy of his pardon. He arrived in Charlotte, North Carolina, on August 8, 1865.[49]

Barringer's four-month stay in Fort Delaware played a crucial role in forming the foundation of his beliefs on how his native North Carolina, and the South as a whole, could best put the war behind it and be restored with dignity to the Union. It was through his contact with people of the North, including President Lincoln, General and Mrs. Collis, General Meade, and General and Mrs. Schoepf, that Rufus came to appreciate their perspective and formed in his mind what actions he would take to help in the coming days of Reconstruction.

48 William J. Northen, ed., *Men of Mark in Georgia*, (Atlanta, GA, 1908), vol. 4, 296.

49 Compiled Service Record for Rufus Barringer, National Archives.

Chapter 10

The Trials of Reconstruction

Rufus Barringer—Reconstruction Politic

Rufus Barringer returned to Concord a war hero and soon found himself, as a progressive Republican, urging North Carolinians to accept Reconstruction as the fastest and least harmful way to rejoin the Union. He was in a sizeable minority, politically, and faced the wrath of Democrats and their newspapers. Nevertheless, he stood his ground against various attackers, and fought back through bold letters to the public.

Rufus lost his fortune during the war. However, he started over, built up his law practice, and regained much of his wealth. He disavowed seeking political office until nominated to serve at the 1875 state constitutional convention. He supported black suffrage as early as 1865, industrial education reform, agricultural improvements, and other progressive measures. In 1880, Rufus would be nominated as the Republican candidate for lieutenant governor in Democrat-controlled North Carolina—an office he did not win.

Reconstruction

The defeated Confederacy faced enormous problems in rebuilding the South after the war. Much of its railroad system, and most of its limited number of factories had been destroyed. Its agricultural economy, based heavily on cotton in the Deep South and grain and tobacco in the Border States, was in ruins. Many uncertainties lay ahead, including when and under what circumstances the defeated states would be readmitted to the Union.

The process by which the United States restored relations with the defeated Southern states following the Civil War was called Reconstruction, a controversial period that lasted from 1865 to 1877. Presidential Reconstruction in1865-1866 was followed by Congressional Reconstruction until 1877. When the Civil War ended, the Republican Party consisted of two main groups: "radicals" and "moderates." Upon the failure of President Andrew Johnson's approach, the Radicals in Congress demanded a new Reconstruction policy. The Radicals believed the federal government should take strong action to protect the rights of blacks and "loyal whites" in the South. They also wanted to give blacks the right to vote to help establish Southern governments loyal to the Union. This tack—not accidentally—would also assure national Republican domination.[1]

In May 1865, while Rufus Barringer was still imprisoned at Fort Delaware, President Johnson announced his plan for Reconstruction. Johnson was a North Carolina native and longtime Tennessee resident. Based on Abraham Lincoln's "let them up easy" policy and Johnson's natural sympathy toward the defeated South, the federal government offered pardons to most Southern whites. Exceptions included former Confederate officers above the rank of major, high-ranking Confederate political leaders, and their wealthy supporters. The plan called for the states to hold conventions and form new governments. These new state governments were required to abolish slavery and avow loyalty to the Union in order to qualify for readmission to the United States.[2]

In January 1865, Congress proposed the 13th Amendment to the Constitution, which abolished slavery throughout the United States. This amendment would be ratified by the required three-fourths of the states by December 1865. In March 1865, following up on this historic breakthrough toward full citizenship for all its people, Congress created the Bureau of Refugees, Freedmen, and Abandoned Lands—popularly known as the Freedman's Bureau—to exercise a benevolent guardianship over former slaves and to protect their interests.[3]

---

1   David W. Blight, *Race and Reunion* (Cambridge, MA, 2001), 51, 53.

2   Donna Lee Dickerson, *The Reconstruction Era: Primary Documents on Events from 1865 to 1877* (Westport, CT, 2003), 55.

3   Mary Beth Norton, Carol Sheriff, David W. Blight, Howard Chudacoff, and Fredrik Logevall, *A People and a Nation: A History of the United States, Brief Edition* (Boston, MA, 2012), 408.

The status of former slaves soon became the most critical issue of Reconstruction. The newly formed Southern state governments, seeking to nullify as far as possible the new status given former slaves, passed restrictive laws called "Black Codes." While many of the South's Black Codes were unduly harsh, North Carolina's 1866 laws affecting blacks were among the most tolerant. Although they did not elevate blacks to full equality with whites, they validated the marriages of former slaves, changed the laws of apprenticeship to assure more equitable terms for blacks, and declared that blacks were entitled to the same rights as whites in suits in law and equity. The statutes stipulated that criminal law applied equally to both races (except in the punishment of assault with intent to rape), provided for the admission of testimony of blacks in court, and made provisions for the protection of blacks from fraud and ignorance in making contracts with whites. Nevertheless, free blacks did not recover the right to vote, which they had lost in North Carolina during the 1835 state constitutional convention.[4]

Soon after the war ended, Southern blacks demanded recognition of their equal rights. Many Northern political organizations, such as the "Union League" and "Heroes of America," became active in the South in support of freedmen. These groups attempted to convince blacks to align themselves with the Republican Party. White Southerners, fearing such activism would lead to black insurrection, reacted with violence against the African American community. This intimidation escalated when the Ku Klux Klan was founded (largely by Confederate veterans) in Tennessee in 1866. This organization first appeared in North Carolina in 1867, with leadership that included William L. Saunders, a former Confederate colonel and future Secretary of State, and wartime Governor Zebulon Baird Vance. Vance was elected "Grand Dragon" of the Realm of North Carolina.[5]

Congress passed the Civil Rights Act in early 1866. This piece of legislation guaranteed certain rights to former slaves, but not the right to vote. President Johnson opposed federal protection of black rights as an infringement on states' rights and vetoed the bill. Congress overrode Johnson's veto, the first

---

4   J. G. DeRoulhac Hamilton, *Reconstruction in North Carolina* (New York, NY, 1914), 153-155.

5   Eric Foner, *Reconstruction: America's Unfinished Revolution, 1863-1877* (New York, NY, 1988), 110, 342; John Hope Franklin, *Reconstruction After The Civil War* (Chicago, IL, 1961), 151-152, 157-158; Hamilton, *Reconstruction in North Carolina*, 461. Saunders claimed he never took the oath of membership in the Klan.

time in United States history that a president's veto of such a major bill had been overturned.[6]

In June 1866, Congress proposed the 14th Amendment to the Constitution, which gave citizenship to the freedmen. It guaranteed that all federal and state laws would apply equally to blacks and whites. Moreover, this amendment barred all federal and state officials who had supported the Confederacy from holding high office. When Congress passed the 14th Amendment, none of the Southern states had been readmitted to the Union. Congress declared that these states must ratify the amendment before readmission. Ratification occurred in 1868, providing full citizenship to blacks.[7]

During this period, President Johnson's obstinacy and his Southern supporters helped move moderate Republicans toward the Radical wing of the party. In early 1867, Congress passed a series of bills called the Reconstruction Acts. These bills abolished the Southern states' governments established under Johnson's plan. With the exception of Tennessee, which had already been readmitted, the South was divided into five military districts and placed under military occupation. These districts were governed until readmission by a regional major general. Federal troops stationed in each district helped enforce the Reconstruction Acts.[8]

The Reconstruction Acts also defined the process for readmission for the ten remaining states that had still not rejoined the Union. Election boards would be established in each state to register all black males and all qualified white males as voters. These voters would elect a state convention, which would adopt a new state constitution. This constitution would have to give black men the right to vote. The voters would then elect a governor and state legislature. Finally, each state had to ratify the 14th Amendment, which included defining citizenship to include blacks.[9]

Johnson vetoed the Reconstruction Acts, but the Republican-controlled Congress easily overrode the veto. Congress passed two other acts challenging Johnson's authority. The Tenure of Office Act prohibited the president from

6 Paul D. Escott, *North Carolinians in the Era of the Civil War and Reconstruction* (Chapel Hill, NC, 2008), 252.

7 Eric Foner and Olivia Mahoney, *America's Reconstruction: People and Politics After the Civil War* (Baton Rouge, LA, 1997), 81.

8 Hamilton, *Reconstruction in North Carolina*, 216-218.

9 Ibid.

firing cabinet and certain other officials without the Senate's approval. The Command of the Army Act prevented the president from dismissing, without Senate approval, any general commanding any of the five new Southern military districts. In February 1868, Johnson declared these new acts unconstitutional and dismissed Secretary of War Edwin M. Stanton. Stanton supported the Radicals, who demanded that Johnson be impeached.[10]

On February 24, 1868, the House of Representatives voted to impeach President Johnson. However, on May 16, the Senate narrowly failed to pass the measure, only one vote shy of the two-thirds majority required for removal of the president. Johnson remained in office, averting a constitutional crisis.[11]

In 1869, Congress proposed the 15th Amendment to the Constitution, which made it illegal to deny males the right to vote because of their race. It was ratified the next year. New Southern state governments were established in accordance with the Reconstruction Acts. The Republicans, who had mustered little strength in the South prior to the Civil War, won control of every new Southern state government. North Carolina was readmitted to the Union on July 20, 1868, and all of the former Confederate states were readmitted by 1870.[12]

The new Republicans in the South consisted of three main groups: blacks, former Northerners known derisively as "carpetbaggers," and Southern whites called "scalawags" by their opponents (but who included many prominent Southerners in their ranks). Blacks represented the largest group of Republicans, and voted in large numbers to help form the new Reconstruction governments.[13]

Reconstruction opened the political process to African Americans in the South. Racial discrimination was banned, and black males were given the right to vote and hold political office. Moreover, for the first time, elections were held for offices that previously had been filled by political appointment.[14]

For many Southern states, Reconstruction policies established the first public, tax-supported school systems. Only North Carolina boasted a public

---

10 Foner and Mahoney, *America's Reconstruction*, 82-83.

11 Ibid., 85.

12 Richard Zuczek, *Encyclopedia of the Reconstruction Era: A-L* (Westport, CT, 2006), 131.

13 Foner, *Reconstruction: America's Unfinished Revolution*, 294.

14 Ibid., 296-977.

school system prior to the war, and it continued to operate throughout the conflict. Some North Carolina politicians had made efforts to transfer school funds for military purposes during the war, but School Superintendent Calvin H. Wiley successfully blocked those efforts. The North Carolina state constitution of 1868 required that a system of free public schools for whites and blacks be established. Blacks flocked to these schools, but whites initially refused to attend. However, as the states began segregating schools by race—in blatant disregard for the law—whites began to send their children to public academies.[15]

Most Southern whites refused to support Reconstruction governments. They objected to raising taxes to support public schools, the prohibition of many Southern leaders from holding high office, and corruption in the new governments. The primary reason for white resistance, however, was that they could not accept former slaves as voters and public office holders.[16]

Southern Democrats began regaining control of the South in 1869. Republican control ended in North Carolina in 1870, ushering in a new era of white supremacy. The use of intimidation and violence against blacks to keep them from voting played a large part in Democratic victories in the state.[17]

Reconstruction in North Carolina

After the war, President Johnson appointed William Woods Holden Provisional Governor of North Carolina, and ordered him to call a state convention for the purpose of preparing North Carolina for reentering the Union. The controversial Holden was a successful newspaper editor in Raleigh. However, as the war progressed, he had become an outspoken critic of the Confederate government and led the North Carolina peace movement. In 1864, he was the unsuccessful "peace candidate" against incumbent Governor Zebulon B. Vance. Vance won overwhelmingly, and Holden carried only three counties: Johnston, Randolph, and Wilkes.[18]

---

15 Hamilton, *Reconstruction in North Carolina*, 277.

16 Ibid., 610; William C. Harris, *William Woods Holden: Firebrand of North Carolina Politics* (Baton Rouge, LA, 1987), 261-262.

17 Ibid., 279.

18 Ibid., 163.

Holden was an important figure in North Carolina politics. In 1861, he had been sent to the state convention, to vote against secession, by the voters of predominantly Unionist Wake County. However, when President Lincoln called on North Carolina to provide troops to help put down the rebellion, Holden had joined in the unanimous vote to secede from the Union.[19]

As Provisional Governor, Holden played a central role in stabilizing the state during the early days of Reconstruction. In 1865, he was defeated by Jonathan Worth in a special election for governor. President Johnson then nominated Holden to be minister to El Salvador, but the Senate rejected his nomination. Holden returned to editing the *Raleigh Standard*, became president of the North Carolina Union League, and organized the Republican Party in the state in 1866-1867. While voters approved the new state constitution, Holden was elected governor on the Republican ticket in 1868, defeating Thomas Samuel Ashe. Upon his election, Holden gave up editorship and ownership of the *Standard*. He supported black suffrage and the Reconstruction policies adopted by the United States Congress.[20]

The new Republican Party in North Carolina, owing its existence to Congressional Reconstruction, was supported by a large number of blacks and endorsed biracial voting. Some white Unionists disagreed with this policy, but their objections were brushed aside. The Union League became effective once again, and by 1869 boasted 70,000 voters. Started in Philadelphia in 1862, the Union League was organized to publicize Southern outrages and promote Radical Republican policies.

After the Civil War, the League mobilized newly enfranchised black voters. It employed secrecy and promoted gun ownership as a means of protecting the black population. League meetings provided blacks with opportunities to debate political and societal issues, negotiate labor contracts, and plan how to care for the sick among them. Governor Holden, the first president of the Union League in North Carolina, advocated political equality between the races. The League worked primarily to ensure that blacks remained loyal to the Republican Party. It was racially integrated and became effective even in the

---

19 Ibid., 91,95, 105.

20 Gordon B. McKinney, *Southern Mountain Republicans: 1865-1900* (Chapel Hill, NC, 1978), 44-45; Hamilton, *Reconstruction in North Carolina*, 336.

western counties. During the 1867 state convention, the combination of blacks and Northern Republicans dominated the proceedings.[21]

The power of native North Carolina Unionists remained weak in most parts of the state, due to the large number of black voters. Only in the mountainous regions of North Carolina did the Republican organization remain in white Unionists hands. Unlike their counterparts in Tennessee and West Virginia, North Carolina's western Republicans were essentially a powerless minority in their state organization.[22]

The first test of voting strength for the new North Carolina Republican Party occurred in 1868. Party leaders in the mountainous counties faced the daunting task of reconciling the party's platform with the racism and conservatism of the western citizenry. The Republican State Convention, in an all-out effort to capture the western mountain vote, nominated prominent Unionist Tod R. Caldwell for lieutenant governor. Supreme Court Justice Richmond M. Pearson, also from the mountain region, announced his support for the Republican ticket, and the party found it could appeal successfully to former Unionists. The election of April 1868 brought Republican victories in the mountain region and statewide. The vote for the Republican ticket and the party-sponsored state constitution was 53 percent in the western highlands. The Republicans appealed to many white voters, garnering 73 percent of the vote in Wilkes County, whose population was only 11 percent black. Both mountain Republican candidates for Congress, however, lost their bids for office.[23]

Developing weaknesses in the Republican Party centered on racial conflicts. As in Tennessee and West Virginia, many whites in western North Carolina could not vote, while blacks could. Congressional action disfranchised these white voters, and many racially conservative western whites who could vote turned away from Republicanism. By 1869, Republicans began losing county elections, even in their strongest areas of previous support. The party split between native Unionists on one side, and "carpetbaggers" and blacks on the other.[24]

21 McKinney, *Southern Mountain Republicans*, 44-45; Horace W. Raper, *William Woods Holden: A Political Biography* (Chapel Hill, NC, 1951), 214-215.

22 McKinney, *Southern Mountain Republicans*, 46.

23 Ibid.; *Asheville Pioneer*, November 7, 1867.

24 McKinney, *Southern Mountain Republicans*, 46-47.

The Ku Klux Klan complicated the efforts of Republicans to stay in power. To combat the Klan's increasing activities, Holden hired two dozen detectives in 1869-1870. While the detective unit was not overly successful in limiting Klan activity, Holden's efforts to suppress the terrorist organization exceeded those of other Southern governors. In what became known as the Kirk-Holden War, the governor called out the militia against the Klan in 1870, imposed martial law in two counties, suspended the writ of habeas corpus for accused Klan leaders, and ordered Col. George W. Kirk (a former Union guerilla leader) to make arrests in western North Carolina. The result was a political backlash that cost Republicans the upcoming legislative election.[25]

After the Democratic Party regained majorities in both houses of the state legislature, Governor Holden was impeached by the House of Representatives on December 14, 1870. He was convicted of six charges against him by the Senate in straight party-line votes on March 22, 1871. The main charges against Holden involved the rough treatment and arrests of North Carolina citizens by state militia under Colonel Kirk, during the enforcement of Radical Reconstruction civil rights legislation. Initially, Holden had formed the state militia in response to the assassination of Senator John W. Stephenson on May 21, 1870, and the lynching of Wyatt Outlaw, a respected African American town commissioner of Graham in Alamance County. Both brutal acts were committed by the Ku Klux Klan. Holden was the first governor in American history to be impeached, convicted, and removed from office.[26]

Following Holden's impeachment, Lieutenant Governor Tod R. Caldwell took over the reins of governance. Democrats immediately called for a constitutional convention to overturn the suffrage restrictions on white voters. The Republicans focused their efforts on defeating the call for a convention, knowing removal of white voting restrictions would weaken their power, which was largely based on black voters. Republicans pressed their campaign, reminding voters that a new constitution might remove favorable advantages to the western part of the state. They were well organized and won a substantial majority in defeating the proposal for a constitutional convention, even though the mountain counties voted for it.[27]

---

25 Ibid.; Hamilton, *Reconstruction in North Carolina*, 483-487.

26 Hamilton, *Reconstruction in North Carolina*, 544-557.

27 McKinney, *Southern Mountain Republicans*, 47; *Asheville Pioneer*, July 20 and August 31, 1871.

Two Republicans vied for the 1872 nomination for governor. Incumbent Governor Caldwell, who was favored by white Unionists and the western counties, was challenged by Thomas Settle, a former state Supreme Court justice and one of President U. S. Grant's personal friends. Settle was supported by the "carpetbag" wing of the party. Caldwell swept the western counties and was popular enough in the remainder of the state to win the Republican nomination on the first ballot. Caldwell won a slim victory in the gubernatorial contest, and in November Grant won a second term as president.[28]

These Republican victories, however, were deceptive. Republican influence weakened throughout the state, particularly in the mountainous region, and the party's power declined for three primary reasons. First, it struggled to control the patronage of the Internal Revenue Service, which levied unpopular taxes on whiskey (particularly unpopular with mountain farmers). These battles divided mountain Republicans. Second, the debate over the Civil Rights Law forced the party to essentially abandon support of it, as the Democrats charged it would create black social equality with whites. Third, Governor Caldwell died in July 1874, bringing complete disorganization to the party in all of the western counties.[29]

During the 1875 campaign to elect delegates to a state constitutional convention, the Republicans remained on the defensive over the Civil Rights Bill. The Democrats made this the primary issue of the campaign. Despite the problems over race, Republicans made a strong showing, capturing a majority of the lowlands' delegates, but losing mountain delegates by a wide margin. The Democrats gained control of the convention.[30]

The Republican decline continued in 1876. Whites deeply resented Federal intervention on civil rights for black citizens, and white voters deserted the party in large numbers. Thomas Settle lost a strong race against popular Democratic wartime governor Zebulon Vance. Vance's election highlighted the Republican Party's continued decline. Just four years later, Rufus Barringer would be the Republican nominee for lieutenant governor.[31]

---

28 McKinney, *Southern Mountain Republicans*, 48; *Asheville Pioneer*, April 11 and 24, 1872.

29 McKinney, *Southern Mountain Republicans*, 49; *Asheville Citizen*, June 4, 1874; *Asheville Pioneer*, June 13, 1874.

30 McKinney, *Southern Mountain Republicans*, 49; *Asheville Citizen*, August 12, 1875.

31 McKinney, *Southern Mountain Republicans*, 50; Hamilton, *Reconstruction in North Carolina*, 644-645, 654.

"Redemption," 1870-1876

The 1876 national election led to the end of Reconstruction. Rutherford B. Hayes of Ohio won the presidency in a disputed election filled with rancor and deals favorable to the South. The Republicans allowed the former Confederate states to rejoin the Union under conditions favorable to the South, with the promise of Reconstruction unfulfilled. In 1877, President Hayes kept his cynical promise to withdraw military forces from the South, and the Radicals abandoned the freedmen out of political expediency. Thus, Reconstruction ended on an ugly note.[32]

Throughout the 1870s, the Democrats controlled North Carolina's state government. They were regarded by most whites as "the Redeemers" (bringing "redemption" from the "evils" of Reconstruction). Republicans, supported by most blacks who had the courage to vote, mounted stiff opposition but could not defeat the Democrats, who touted white supremacy to an enthusiastic white electorate. The Democratic-controlled legislature changed the election laws to keep its party's candidates in office. The legislature, fearing blacks might assume power in counties where they outnumbered whites, passed the County Government Act of 1876. This act empowered the legislature to appoint the county justices of the peace who, in turn, would name the county commissioners. Reconstruction made most Southern whites firm supporters of the Democratic Party, and for more than 40 years no Republican presidential candidate received a majority of votes from any Southern state.

Reconstruction had failed to bring about racial harmony, and after its demise, whites refused to share political power with blacks. As a result, African Americans set up their own churches and other institutions, rather than attempt to join white society. They systematically lost most of the rights they had been granted since 1865. By the early 1900s, every Southern state had enacted discriminatory "Jim Crow" laws that gave the vote only to males who could pass certain educational tests, or pay certain levies called "poll taxes." Various "Jim Crow" laws would remain in effect for most of the next century.[33]

---

32 Lloyd Robinson, *The Stolen Election: Hayes Versus Tilden—1876* (New York, NY, 1996), 182-189, 201-203.

33 William S. Powell, *North Carolina through Four Centuries* (Chapel Hill, NC, 1989), 419; Barringer, *The Natural Bent*, 114.

The most important result of Reconstruction was passage of the 14th and 15th Amendments to the Constitution. These amendments, although of limited application in the nineteenth century, would provide the basis for the Civil Rights movements of the 1960s.

Barringer's Return from the War

While Rufus Barringer was away during the war, his house in Concord, North Carolina, had been rented out. His children, Anna and Paul, had lived with Rufus's brother Victor and his wife Maria. Paul attended school during the war years, where Miss Margaret Taylor Long was his teacher. Margaret would become Rufus's third wife in 1870.[34]

In early August 1865, Victor Barringer cleaned up his law office, located on a lot between Victor's and Rufus's homes. Victor did not tell Anna and Paul why this had to be done to their "playhouse." The children's inquiries were answered with, "You wait and see." Within a few days the office had been outfitted with tables, bookshelves, and beds. The mystery was solved on August 8, when Rufus arrived home after being released as a prisoner of war. The event was recalled years later by Barringer's son, Paul:

> [I]n walked a medium-sized soldierly man in citizen's clothes, with beard all over his pale and thin face. He ran to me, picked me up, and said he was my father [Paul was about eight years old at this time]. I would not have known him from Adam. . . . He did not have a button, a shoulder strap or any insignia of rank, and I who had heard him spoken of as "General Barringer," I thought for years, was grievously disappointed. But as he was not only a man, but a man's man, we soon became fast friends. He rode well, shot well, and swam well. He knew more men in the hundred miles around him than any other two men in that section. He started to practice law in Concord and boarded at Harris's Hotel, and when he did not have strangers in his office I was with him morning, noon, and night. This year of our association is one of my most treasured memories.[35]

As a result of the war, Rufus Barringer, like countless others, had lost the considerable financial estate he had established prior to the conflict. He "staked

---

34 Ibid., 142.

35 Ibid., 114.

all and lost all," and estimated his losses at between $60,000 and $70,000. By 1870, however, he would recover and regain a substantial portion of his losses. The 1870 federal census valued his real estate at $3,000 and his personal estate at $25,000.[36]

Soon after Barringer's return to Concord, a "race riot" erupted in town on September 21, 1865, an unfortunate and ill-timed uprising. Federal military forces had left Cabarrus County in June, one of the few counties from which troops had been withdrawn. According to local newspapers, the rioters were intoxicated blacks demanding the right to vote in elections then being held. However, according to Victor Barringer, the riot was precipitated by a crowd of whites distraught over the general path of "peace with the Union." Drunk on whiskey, they ran all the blacks they could out of town. Victor was asked by the arrested blacks to represent them when they came to trial, which he did with "all the energy I could command."

Other leading citizens, including Rufus Barringer, supported the wronged African Americans. Rufus tried to maintain a low profile in his support of Victor's defense of the blacks, because he had not yet received his pardon from the federal government. Although his pardon from President Johnson was dated October 26, 1865, he did not receive it until December 1865. Victor argued that the African American citizens had not resisted being forced out of town. Nevertheless, hatred of blacks and Northerners burned in the hearts of many of Concord's white citizens. A federal military force was called in and many whites were arrested. The trial began in October at the Military Commission in Salisbury. Virtually all of the white rioters were found guilty.[37]

Barringer Moves to Charlotte

When Rufus Barringer moved to Charlotte in 1866, he was well suited to take up his chosen profession again, though he served as more of a "counselor" than "a power before a jury." He became the legal representative of many people in Concord and Charlotte, but he did not take criminal cases. For

36 Rufus Barringer to Victor Barringer, January 27, 1866; Alexander, The History of Mecklenburg County From 1740 to 1900, 204; Federal Census of 1870 for Cabarrus County, North Carolina. In modern currency, Rufus's combined estate would have been worth in excess of $700,000.

37 Victor Barringer to Daniel Moreau Barringer, November 15, 1865, Daniel Moreau Barringer Papers, Southern Historical Collection.

approximately two years, he partnered with outstanding criminal defense attorney James W. Osborne, before Osborne's death in 1868.[38]

Rufus worked as a bank and railroad lawyer, practicing largely by brief and seldom before a jury. On many occasions he represented cases before the North Carolina Supreme Court. In one case during the June 1873 term, Rufus urged the state's highest court to reverse a lower court decision against his first cousin, John Barringer, in a divorce case against his wife, Lavina Ridenhour Barringer. The issue was whether a man could serve as a competent witness if he was the only witness against his wife in a divorce action. According to John Barringer, the marriage had never been consummated. The Supreme Court agreed with Barringer, and reversed the lower court ruling. It remanded the case back to the lower court, with an order to finalize the divorce action.[39]

By 1870, Rufus had opened an additional law office in Concord, riding 15 miles from Charlotte once a week. While it is not clear why he opened this law office in Concord, his son Paul later recalled that his father had left Concord in the first place because he had not wanted to compete with his brother Victor. Victor's acquaintances at the time were more or less limited to Cabarrus County. Whatever the reason, Rufus would maintain offices in Charlotte and Concord until his retirement from the bar in 1884. Thanks to his four years of service in the Confederate army, Rufus knew practically everyone within a radius of 150 miles. He was often seen as "a conspicuous figure in his military cape with his green bag (a lawyer's 'badge' in those days) in his hand." Victor would become more widely known on the state level, and for a brief period in 1869 was appointed North Carolina's acting attorney general.[40]

Barringer's Politics during Reconstruction

While re-establishing his law practice in Concord and Charlotte, Rufus Barringer returned to politics. As a prominent citizen of Charlotte, he

---

38 Alexander, *History of Mecklenburg County*, 201-208.

39 John Barringer Papers, Raleigh: Private Collections, State Archives of North Carolina ; *Barringer v. Barringer* (1873), Chapter 69 NC, 179, 181. News of two United States Supreme Court cases involving railroads were reported in the *New York Times*, January 10 and October 18, 1884. John Barringer is the direct ancestor of the author of this book.

40 "Gen. Rufus Barringer," in *Confederate Veteran* (February 1901), vol. 9, no. 2, 70; Current, *Encyclopedia of the Confederacy*, 1,134.

Rufus Barringer (1821-1895), civilian post war photo. After the war,
Rufus Barringer declined opportunities to seek political office and
concentrated on his law practice. He was, however, active in
politics and strongly advocated acceptance of Reconstruction. He
regarded it as absolutely necessary for the welfare of the people that
the states of the South be speedily readmitted to the Union. *North
Carolina Division of Archives and History*

advocated North Carolina's acceptance of the Reconstruction Act of 1867. For
the welfare of the people, he believed the former Confederate states should be
speedily readmitted to the Union. As a liberal supporting the Radical
Republicans, Rufus held progressive positions on these political matters,
including strong support for black suffrage. He was stigmatized by some,
primarily the editors of Democratic newspapers across the state, as a traitor to
his race and section. However, as a fearless politician, he never backed down

from such charges and faced them head on. Rufus accepted the Reconstruction Act, and stood as a bold champion of the measures and principles of Republican leaders in Congress. He cooperated with the national Republican Party, whose policies and principles he believed were best suited to the country in its new and changed condition. Rufus's progressive ideas had strengthened during his tenure as a prisoner of war in the North. He conveyed his ideas clearly and convinced his influential brother Victor to change his political views to a progressive mindset.

Rufus and Victor were not the only Charlotte or Concord Republicans during the postwar era. However, with solicitor William P. Bynum and William H. Bailey of Salisbury, the Barringer brothers were among the few Republican lawyers in Charlotte and the surrounding area. Others Charlotte Republicans included Dr. H. M. Pritchard and town commissioners Dr. William Sloan and Willis Miller—all appointed mayor by Republican Governor William W. Holden. Holden also appointed laborer J. M. Hunter and J. C. Davidson as the Queen City's first black town commissioners. John T. Schenck was appointed the town's first black policeman. Richard Smith and Washington Grier were appointed justices of the peace. All of this prompted former Confederate general D. H. Hill (Barringer's brother-in-law) to question whether the ratification of the new state constitutional of May 1868, and subsequent re-admittance of North Carolina to the Union in June, was a blessing or a curse. Hill argued that rule by Federal military forces would be preferable to being governed by "the vilest of mankind, whom no gentleman would allow to enter the kitchen." Rufus Barringer saw things differently. He saw in Holden's appointments a new beginning for the South. The "new men" who now governed Charlotte and many other Southern towns "have given us the 'results of the war,' all at once, and with the plowshare of reform they struck deep into the musty institutions, habits and customs to which we clung."[41]

Through the editors of local newspapers, Rufus often wrote letters to the people of Mecklenburg County and North Carolina expressing his views on politics, education, farming, and other issues of the day. Barringer's penmanship was often nearly impossible to read, but the editors deciphered his cursive handwriting as best they could (a task which had also been difficult for

---

41 Janette Thomas Greenwood, *Bittersweet Legacy: The Black and White "Better Classes" in Charlotte,1850-1910* (Chapel Hill, NC, 1994), 54; Rufus Barringer, letter, *North Carolina Weekly Standard*, September 30, 1868.

This cartoon hung in Rufus Barringer's law office in the 1870s and 1880s. Barringer used this cartoon to encourage his clients to be willing to compromise. Note that while those involved in a dispute are pulling on opposing ends of the cow, the lawyer is seated on a stool in the middle and is getting all the milk. *Rufus Barringer (deceased), Lyme, Connecticut*

Rufus's subordinate officers during the war). Sometimes the editors printed corrections to their previous transcriptions of Barringer's letters. In a letter to the editor of the Charlotte *Daily News* (dated August 29, 1867), Barringer answered the many attacks against him, revealing a pugnacious side of his personality that simmered just below the surface of his generally amiable and genteel persona. His combativeness surfaced when anyone breached his "code of honor," which included his military service, attacks on him or his family, or the service of his fellow North Carolina soldiers. His letters to the public were effective because he was logical, scholarly, and masterful in the use of language. His bold missives of 1867 and 1868 stamped him as a man of great political sagacity and foresight—a true statesman. The August 29 letter revealed his liberal passion and values in unmistakable terms: "You will find that I am no sudden convert to what is called Radicalism. For two years I have breasted the odium of negro suffrage, as a logical result of the war; and had my views been heeded the south would be now be better off."[42]

Barringer attributed critical importance to the four months he spent in a Northern prison camp, and to his exposure to Northern people, their ideas, and

42 *Pioneer Extra*, September 12, 1867, reprinted in *Raleigh Signal*, August, 19, 1880.

perspectives: "During my stay [as a prisoner of war] I made it a special object to study the tone and temper of the Northern people, particularly the character of Yankee society, and the workings of the Yankee Institutions."[43]

Rufus supported black voting rights: "[N]egro suffrage was destined to come, in some form, no sane man could doubt. . . . It was treated as a measure of simple justice to the negro for his exemplary conduct during and since the war, his obedience to law, and his manhood on the field of battle."[44]

Some may argue that Rufus strongly supported black suffrage because he had fathered two mulatto sons. Nevertheless, he would have advocated suffrage for African Americans because Republicans and the North demanded it. He sought to persuade others that Republicans offered the best hope for reconciliation, and for North Carolina and the rest of the South in rejoining the Union.[45]

Barringer believed that the Republican Party "was the power with which the South had to deal. . . . It was the vitalizing influence of this party that had brought the war to a successful close, and thus saved their people, preserved the Union, maintained the government, and shed luster and renown on the Northern name. . . . I came to the conclusion, after full reflection, that the highest interests of the South would be promoted by her people embracing, as far as they could conscientiously do so, the progressive ideas of that party."[46]

Barringer praised the South's courageous fight, but believed it was time to lay aside the prejudices and passions of the past, and focus on rebuilding and reconciliation. "I undertook to urge the prompt and voluntary concession of qualified negro suffrage, full legal rights to that race, the education of their children, the introduction of northern immigrants, the study of the arts and sciences, attention to diverse labor, a modification of our courts, and laws to suit the altered condition of the people."[47]

Barringer blamed Southern politicians for the unfortunate circumstances that led to forced Reconstruction. He also recalled attacks against him and his family:

43 *Raleigh Signal*, August 19, 1880; *Raleigh Register*, September 6, 1867.

44 Ibid.

45 Ibid.

46 Ibid.

47 Ibid.

But the politicians clung to their old habits of pandering to sectional pride and caste.... Instead of arguments, the elegant epithets of 'dirteater,' 'negro worshipper,' 'negro-socialist,' &c., were the weapons used. This political warfare finally produced its legitimate effect [in the] North. A reaction took place. The radicals and republicans lost all faith in the controlling minds of the South. This drove them into a policy of repression. . . . At one fell swoop, we got universal suffrage, a large disfranchisement of the whites, unlimited military rule, the destruction of civil law and government, and threatened confiscation. . . . People forget 1861. . . . And yet, when a Southern man dares to rise above the passions of the hour, and tell the people the unvarnished truth, he is denounced as a traitor to his race and his section."[48]

Barringer tried to rally his fellow North Carolinians behind Republican policy: "I think I know something of the spirit and temper of the North, and if reconstruction is defeated, or if the policy of resistance is long maintained, our troubles and difficulties must increase. It is idle for the South longer to isolate herself from the outside world, or seek to repress the aspirations of the age. Governments, everywhere, are soon to rest on the broad basis of universal suffrage. . . . Let the mass of the white voters agree to unite with the colored citizens on terms of political equality—give the latter proper assurances to maintain their rights and privileges."

On January 14, 1868, North Carolina opened a constitutional convention in Raleigh and drew up a new state constitution. Democrats denounced the convention, but the Republicans prevailed. Some provisions of the new constitution included the abolition of slavery, removal of religious tests for officeholders, popular election of all state and county officials, and provisions for "a general and uniform system of public schools."[49]

The politics of the Reconstruction were extremely contentious in the South. Another letter written by Barringer further revealed the extent of the rift in North Carolina's population. On September 30, 1868, Rufus responded to the news that he had been unanimously chosen (without his consent) as a Ulysses S. Grant and Schuyler Colfax elector from Mecklenburg County for the upcoming presidential election. Barringer had hoped to stay out of politics, but this nomination and the recent Democratic National Convention in New York convinced him otherwise. In a letter addressed to members of the Republican

48 Ibid.

49 Hamilton, *Reconstruction in North Carolina*, 167-168.

committee, published in the Raleigh *North Carolina Weekly Standard*, Barringer stated: "I did not wish to take an active part in politics. I have avoided committing myself fully to any party. . . . But in view of the momentous issue, presented by the Democratic Party at New York, I go for Grant and Colfax, with all my heart, and I accept the nomination tendered."[50]

Barringer provided his political views in detail, and made clear his support for Reconstruction: "Early in the summer of 1865, I saw that reconstruction was not impossible, and I resolved to do all I could to promote it. I meant to do so, not with mere lip service, but with an honest conviction and with a heart-felt zeal. . . . I had cherished no prejudices against the North. I had learned to appreciate her wonderful energy, steadiness of purpose, enterprise, skill, and genius."[51]

Barringer continued to push for acceptance of Reconstruction, admitted his past prejudices, and argued that the course of the Republicans was the right path: "But when that overwhelming calamity came, I said promptly, and frankly, accept the results of our defeat, adopt Republican theories, and proceed in our own way and time to conform to them. I will be frank now, and admit that the progress of the war, and especially my own experience in the army, dispelled in some measure prejudices I had against the masses, and especially colored people. As a Southern born and as a Confederate officer, I never can forget the fidelity and devotion of the humbler class of whites, and of the slaves in our midst."[52]

Barringer recalled the war and its effects:

"Through four terrible years I for one never missed a tour of duty, except when wounded, on leave, or in prison. . . . My brigade entered upon the campaign of 1865, with thrice the numbers of any other in the service, and in the day of trial, thirty officers and over two hundred men sealed the last Confederate victory with their blood. Let those who enjoyed bomb-proofs and civil offices, while brave and true men battled at the front, call me what they please, I am bold to say, that the lesson of all our troubles has given me more faith in the humbler American free-man, more confidence in liberal

50 *North Carolina Weekly Standard*, September 30, 1868; *New York Times*, September 30, 1868.

51 Ibid.

52 Ibid.

institutions, and, I am not afraid to say, more respect for even Black Republican principles."[53]

Barringer called Southern leaders to task for supporting secession prior to the war, and for rejecting Reconstruction:

Go back three years: can any man doubt, it would have been better for us to have voluntarily conceded qualified negro suffrage in 1865! . . . It was all I then advised and, I feel confident, it was all the Republican leaders and masses then expected. . . . But our leaders said no! Concede nothing! And they resorted to the most desperate means to induce the people to reject everything. . . . Congress was forced to act, in order to open the way for the ideas that had triumphed in the war, for the protection of those who embraced them, and especially for the protection of unionists and four million of freedmen, still threatened with black codes and other hostile legislation. . . . Every State adopting a constitution is back to the Union; civil government is re-established; law and order again prevail. . . . These facts fully vindicate the soundness of Republican principles.[54]

Rufus voiced his concerns about what had happened at the recent Democratic Convention in New York: "That [convention] body revived in spirit, as well as in name, the Democratic party of 1860-61. The same old secession and copperhead leaders were there. . . . These desperate leaders, taking advantage of the temporary prejudices raised by the reconstruction measures, and especially negro suffrage, have not scrupled to throw down again the gauntlet of war. In their platform they solemnly declare all the reconstruction acts of Congress, though passed in strict conformity to the constitution, "unconditional, revolutionary, and void." . . . These leaders are determined that the reconstruction acts shall not succeed in pacifying the country. . . . They brought it [the war] on."[55]

Barringer praised Ulysses S. Grant: "Gen. Grant was magnanimous to us in the surrender. . . . He is neither a negro-hater nor a negro-worshipper. It can now be only his ambition to restore the Union he has saved,—to restore it in all its parts, its interests, its sympathies and its aspirations. He will not only give us

53 Ibid
54 Ibid.
55 Ibid.

peace and prosperity, but a Union we can love and a government we can honor."[56]

The Bitterness of Reconstruction Politics

As a Republican, Rufus Barringer was considered (in modern terms) a "liberal." He had supported progressive measures—including expansion of the railroads and free suffrage—as early as 1850, and black suffrage as early as 1865. He lamented, however, that "the public mind was lashed into a tempest of rage and fury against any man who advocated justice for the freedmen." His political allegiances during Reconstruction were hardly surprising, but his views were not popular and angered many who refused to embrace the new political realities in North Carolina, and in the South as a whole.[57]

He was frequently and viciously attacked by the Democratic press, and was often called "Aunt Nancy" in their editorial smears. General Barringer had been dubbed "Aunt Nancy" by a mischievous soldier in his command during the war. Tradition holds that one night in the summer of 1864 General Barringer inspected the disposition of troops for an expected fight the next day. Riding up to some sentries, Barringer called out, "Whose command is this?" A trooper answered, "Aunt Nancy's." At another post Barringer made the same inquiry and received the same answer. Father along he inquired once more, and again a soldier replied, "Aunt Nancy's." Finally recognizing that the troopers belonged to his own command, Barringer said "Oh, I'm Aunt Nancy!" Episcopal Bishop Joseph Blount Cheshire, who knew Barringer well, recalled that Rufus was "careful and prudent, attentive to details, kind and courteous, had admirable 'domestic character,' with little care for show. His soldiers good-humoredly called him 'Aunt Nancy,' in recognition of his social and domestic qualities." Moreover, Barringer was 39 years old when the war started, and thus considerably older than most of his troopers. Regardless of how the nickname "Aunt Nancy" originated, Barringer was forever saddled with it—and the epithet was used in a derogatory sense by his political enemies.[58]

---

56 Ibid.

57 *Nation*, October 26, 1865; *Christian Recorder*, October 28, 1865; John H. Haley, *Charles N. Hunter and Race Relations in North Carolina* (Chapel Hill, NC, 1987), 12.

58 *Carolina Watchman*, January 30, 1879; Cheshire, *Nonnulla*, 153.

Barringer and his brother-in-law D. H. Hill (a former Confederate general) enjoyed a cordial relationship before and during the war. However, when Barringer became a postwar Republican who supported Reconstruction, Hill disowned him. Like James Longstreet and a few other senior Southern commanders who joined the Republican Party, Barringer incurred Hill's wrath. Hill considered both men worse than "carpetbaggers" and "scalawags." Hill referred to such people as "lepers in their own community"—especially Longstreet, who accepted a government appointment as Surveyor of Customs in New Orleans.[59]

Hill and Barringer and their families worshipped at the First Presbyterian Church in Charlotte. Bishop Cheshire and Mary Alves Long remembered that the caustic and temperamental Hill refused to serve Rufus at communion. In accordance with proper procedure, Hill should have passed the elements to Barringer. Not surprisingly, church elder Hill considered Republicans "unfit to sit at the Lord's Table." He refused to serve Barringer the bread and wine, passing them instead to another person, who in turn passed them to Barringer. Angered by such treatment, Barringer resigned from the First Presbyterian Church in 1874 and began attending the new Second Presbyterian Church of Charlotte. Hill fully embraced the "Lost Cause," even in defeat, and never supported Reconstruction.[60]

In July 1872, a letter Rufus wrote to the people of Mecklenburg County, in response to charges made against him in the press, shed more light on the bitterness of postwar politics. Democrats had attacked the former general and his family: "I did not complain of personal persecution. I merely alluded to the violence shown my brother (V. C. Barringer) and myself and our families in '65 and '66, as evidence of the spirit of the Democratic leaders, long before reconstruction." These attacks had been fueled in part by the Barringer brothers' legal defense and support of blacks accused in the white-incited "race riot" of September 21, 1865.[61]

---

59 Jeffry D. Wert, *General James Longstreet: The Confederacy's Most Controversial Soldier* (New York, NY, 1993), 413.

60 Cheshire, *Nonnulla*, 155-158; Mary Alves Long, *High Time To Tell It* (Durham, NC, 1950), 74; Union Church Bulletin, "Feud resulted in Start of Church Story Says," Walla Walla, Washington, April 12, 1953), 23.

61 Ibid.

Lieutenant General Daniel Harvey Hill (1821-1889) was Rufus Barringer's brother-in-law. Hill and Barringer had cordial relations during the war, but Reconstruction politics caused them to become estranged. Hill was the president of Arkansas Industrial University (University of Arkansas) from 1877-1884.
United States Army Military History Institute, Carlisle Barracks, PA.

The letter also revealed the acrimony with D. H. Hill: "As to the account of the speaking at Long Creek, given by General Hill, everybody who heard the discussion and has read his clumsy article, sees at a glance where the 'midsummer madness' lies. And all who know the man . . . well understand that political truth and fairness are not in him. He is a chronic grumbler, has no faith in free institutions, and is the very embodiment of discouragement and discontent. . . . During the war he reviled President Davis, General Lee, General Bragg, and every prominent man above him. . . . His silly and cowardly cry of 'incendiary' against every man who dares to think for himself, cannot much longer deceive intelligent people."[62]

Regardless of his politics, Rufus Barringer remained interested in farming and agricultural improvements, and supported farmers throughout his life. In fact, he owned a tenant farm. An amusing story reveals another angle on hostile feelings during Reconstruction. Tradition holds that Rufus and a Mecklenburg farmer, who had served in Barringer's command during the war, engaged in a discussion on farming one day. When Barringer asked the farmer about his crop, the former soldier replied that a good rain was needed within the next week to ten days. Familiar with the location of the farmer's field, Barringer said, "There is no reason that the field should ever suffer from drought." The farmer asked for an explanation and Barringer replied, "[T]hat field lies below the level of the creek which flows a few hundred yards distant. At a cost of a few dollars, you could cut a shallow ditch from a certain point in the creek to the top of your

62 *Broadside*, July 24, 1872, Duke University.

field. Then a dam thrown across the creek would turn the water across into your ditch, and in half an hour your whole field and every furrow would be saturated."[63]

Rufus went on to explain the principles of irrigation that had been practiced as far back as ancient Egyptian times. The farmer listened intently to Barringer's eloquent explanation. As they finally parted, the farmer expressed his gratitude and promised he would utilize irrigation methods in the future.[64]

The following winter Barringer saw his friend again, and they discussed the results of the farmer's experiment with irrigation. He explained that the rains did not come for two weeks, but through the irrigation method explained by Barringer, his crop had flourished. However, the farmer admitted, "General, I don't think I shall ever try it again." "Why?" asked Barringer. The farmer replied, "I was bragging mightily about it and telling all of my neighbors. But they were all against me. They said they did not believe in such things; that it was flying in the face of Providence; that when the Lord did not send rain, we just had to stand it. . . . And, when I told them all that you had told me, they said they did not believe in it; that it was nothing but one of Barringer's damned radical notions, and they wouldn't have anything to do with it." Thus, for many years irrigation was not favored in Mecklenburg County. The story is humorous, but reveals the contempt that some folks had for Barringer as a result of his "radical" politics.[65]

Confrontation with Jubal Early

Rufus was passionate about his political views, but intensely proud of the service of North Carolina's soldiers during the war. He was a man of principle and was not shy about taking on anyone who questioned his loyalty and patriotism, or the character of the Tar Heel soldiers. In 1871-1872, he engaged in a bitter public feud with Jubal Early (a former Confederate general) over remarks he made about North Carolina soldiers and those who voted for the national Republicans. Early equated such people with deserters or worse: "Unfortunately, there were too many skulkers and deserters from both States

---

63 Cheshire, *Nonnulla*, 154-155.

64 Ibid.

65 Ibid.

(North Carolina and Virginia), as well as from all other States. I never had any toleration for a skulker or deserter at any time, let him come from where he might; and now, I cannot endure one who has gone over to the enemy since the war. Though he be a Virginian, I regard his crime as unpardonable, and worse than if he had deserted in the time of war."[66]

This was too much for Rufus, who considered it not only an insult to the valor of North Carolina's soldiers but a slight to himself and others who had supported the Republican ticket and President Grant in the 1868 election. The pugnacious Barringer responded:

> I am a Republican—a Radical, if you will—but I took my position on the suffrage question in 1865. . . . General Early must see, that if he intends this extract for me, he does me at least partial wrong. If he meant (as seems probable) for his Virginia comrades, Gen. [Williams C.] Wickham, Col. [John S.] Mosby, and others, who voted for Grant, then he was wholly unjustifiable in bringing it into this correspondence. . . . At last the surrender came. On the first flash of the news, this would be hero, who now talks of a "continued war" for independence, fled the country, leaving his unhappy comrades and countrymen, to meet, as best they could, the untried and untold horrors of subjugation. But no sooner does he see, that his fears of losing his neck were all imaginary—the creatures of the vain conceit of his own importance, than he returns, and returns too, with the air of "one who never surrenders." And now descending to the noise and bluster of a regular braggadocio, he turns his battery of pop-guns on his late companions in arms![67]

Jubal Early responded in kind, stating that Barringer had misinterpreted him in some respects and was totally wrong in others. Early repeated his offensive comments, and stated that he meant them for any and all to whom they applied. The *Charlotte Observer* publicly asked the two men to cease their hostilities toward each other. The message was apparently taken to heart as no further public letters were written.[68]

Politics aside, Barringer continued his lifelong service to the North Carolina Railroad. In 1870, he became a board member of the Charlotte, Columbia & Augusta line. In 1871, he was appointed one of the directors of the

66 *Raleigh Sentinel*, January 8, 1873.

67 Ibid.; *Charlotte Observer*, January 4, 1873; *Raleigh Sentinel*, December 21, 1872, January 12, 1873.

68 Ibid., December 29, 1872, January 10, 1873.

North Carolina Railroad. On April 22, 1870, as a member of the line's Committee of Finance, Barringer wrote to William A. Graham (a railroad stockholder and director) proposing divestiture of the railroad from political control by North Carolina's state government. State involvement in the railroads had been a matter of great controversy since the beginning of Reconstruction.[69]

In 1870, Barringer became involved in settling land disputes between eastern North Carolina Cherokees and the State of North Carolina. Prior to the Civil War, a number of these Indians entered into an agreement or contract with William H. Thomas, a prominent merchant and Indian philanthropist in southwestern North Carolina. As a home for the Native Americans, Thomas agreed to purchase a general boundary of land in that locality, out of the savings from proceeds of their personal labor and their annuity money. Thomas proceeded in good faith to carry out this agreement, and purchased land with the Indians' money. However, he placed the deeds in his own name, intending to execute a deed of conveyance to the Indians as a tribe, for the whole of the lands purchased. Before its consummation, however, the Civil War occurred and Thomas became financially indebted. His creditors, by due process of law, took possession of his property, including much of the land purchased for and occupied by the Indians. This action involved the title to the lands, which became the subject of constant litigation.[70]

With affairs in this condition, an act of Congress passed on July 15, 1870, empowered "The Eastern Band of the Cherokee Indians" to bring suit in the district or circuit court of the United States for a settlement of all matters connected with their funds and lands in North Carolina. A commission consisting of Rufus Barringer, John H. Oillard, and Thomas Ruttin was appointed to investigate, arbitrate, and decide upon the Indians' claim to money and land. The group reported its findings to the circuit court of the United States for the western district of North Carolina, and filed its award on October 23, 1874. The commission found "that William H. Thomas, in pursuance of the agreement and trust reposed in him, did from time to time, and from various

69 Greenwood, *Bittersweet* Legacy, 54; *Charlotte Democrat*, August 1, 1871; *Western Democrat*, April 26, 1870.

70 Henry N. Carrington, *Eastern Band of Cherokees of North Carolina*, Swain County, North Carolina Genealogy Trails History Group; Act of Congress passed in 1870, 16 *United States Statutes*, 139.

persons, purchase lands for said Indians as a tribe and community, and settled thereon, and carved up the same into towns, which purchases were definitely described in the award, and included in and made a large tract, situated on Soco Creek and Ocona Lufta River and their tributaries, known as the 'Qualla boundary.'" By this award, certain named Indians who held land within the Qualla boundary (by deed or contract from Thomas) were awarded the lands held by them as their separate property, with the quality of being inheritable, but without the power of alienation, except from one Indian to another, and then only with the assent of their council.[71]

Barringer promoted education throughout his life, and explained the principles of industrial education as he saw them: "The leading object is not to teach trades, arts or science, as such, or for the purpose of turning out from schools artisans, agriculturists, trained cooks, skilled dress makers, or skilled machinists of any sort, but to instruct children and pupils, as a part of general education, in the elementary or foundation principles of all art, science, mechanics, and other practical knowledge; and this, not by teaching theories, but by learning 'to do things.'"[72]

Rufus served on the first Board of Trustees for the North Carolina College of Agriculture and Mechanical Arts (which became North Carolina State University). He also served on the Board of Trustees of Biddle University, a black school founded by the Presbyterian Church in 1867, located on the outskirts of Charlotte. The name of the college was changed in 1923 to Johnson C. Smith University. Barringer also served on the Board of Directors of the Peace Institute, a Presbyterian school for young women located in Raleigh. Named for William Peace (its biggest contributor), the school opened in 1872 with dormitory space for 80 students.[73]

In 1874, Republican Governor Tod R. Caldwell offered Barringer the office of Solicitor of the 9th District. Rufus declined the offer, and did not run as a candidate for the 9th District Judgeship when urged to do so.[74]

---

71 United States Bureau of Indian Affairs, *Annual Report of the Commissioner to the Secretary of the Interior, Fiscal Year Ended June 30, 1902* (Washington, DC, 1902), 103-104.

72 Jerome Dowd, *Sketches of Prominent Living North Carolinians* (Raleigh, NC, 1888), 222-224.

73 Ibid.

74 *Charlotte Daily Observer,* January 3 and June 18, 1874.

While Barringer advocated black suffrage, he did not support social equality for African Americans. He abhorred governing Democrats throughout the South for their stance on race: "I frankly admit the abuse of power by the negro governments [in the] South. I go further and declare that it is a fearful blunder, not to say crime, for these people and their ignorant allies to assume to rule and govern. But this is all owing . . . to the mistaken policy and criminal blunder of Southern statesman in blindly opposing any kind of political rights to these four million people." Barringer further stated that whites were deceived in supposing that certain elements of the Democratic Party meant no hostility to blacks. "[T]heir freedom would not last a day or be worth a cent to them without the ballot." He concluded: "Let Democrats cease to question the negro his right to the ballot and all other political rights, and then learn to treat him and deal with him as any other voter, and 'negro power' is at an end."[75]

Despite the Democratic plurality in Mecklenburg County, Rufus Barringer was held in high esteem by many of the general populace. His amiable and kindly qualities had, to a considerable extent, overcome the earlier prejudices against him. A convention was held in 1875 to amend the state constitution, and Barringer was elected as a delegate from strongly Democratic Mecklenburg. There was great controversy at the convention over public schools and how to handle the race issue. Many African American Republicans seemed to accept race relations as they stood in 1875. The Republican convention delegates, black and white, feared that they might lose funding for schools entirely if they pushed too hard for integration. Many Republican delegates backed off of a proposed civil rights bill, and instead tried to find language that would unify the state and avoid prompting violence against African Americans. As a result, they proposed acceptance of a Separate Schools Ordinance.[76]

Seeking to mollify the issue of race and public schools, Barringer believed that keeping the races separate was a good way to avoid controversy. He realized white fears that African Americans would assert a right to integration necessitated enforced segregation to keep the peace: "[W]e cannot disguise the fact that society [in the] South is still greatly unsettled, and that now and then rash and revengeful parties of both races are tempted and induced to intrude upon the rights and the presence of others, and it is against all such cases, and even the chances of wrong or outrage, that this provision and similar laws are

75 *The Indiana Progress*, November 25, 1875.

76 Escott, *North Carolinians in the Era of the Civil War and Reconstruction*, 257-259.

intended to guard . . . [T]here is in the hearts of our white people, and especially the Democratic masses—an honest, long cherished, deep seated sentiment on this subject, which it is prudent in law givers to respect."[77]

Barringer continued on race relations and school segregation: "I have never doubted that the two races could dwell here on the same soil together in peace and harmony, acting and cooperating with each other in all public or political affairs, and without any disturbance in or interference with our admirable social system." Collective whites were sufficiently vague on the issue, allowing them to support enforced segregation. The separate schools ordinance passed with overwhelming support. African Americans accepted the segregation ordinance, fearing that school funding for blacks would be cut if they did not.[78]

Barringer's political career also included serving the national Republican Party. He served as an "at large" delegate from North Carolina to the 1876 and 1880 National Republican Conventions.[79]

Family Life and Civic Duty

As Rufus became immersed in Reconstruction politics, he also became interested in finding a third wife, mainly because he needed a mother for his three children. Anna and Paul Barringer walked to a county school two miles from home. Their younger brother Rufus Chunn Barringer, born in 1862, was cared for at home by a live-in housekeeper.[80]

Miss Margaret Taylor Long of Hillsborough, North Carolina, had taught as a governess in the home of Barringer's neighbor, Noah Foard. She later opened a private school. Barringer's son Paul attended this school, with Miss Long as his teacher. Rufus became acquainted with the attractive educator, and saw her frequently when he returned to Concord from Charlotte. On September 13, 1870, the couple married. Rufus was 48 years old and Margaret 32. After their

77 Ibid.; "Remarks of Gen. R. Barringer, of Mecklenburg, on 'Separate Schools,' in the Convention, Sept. 27th, 1875," in *Weekly Era*, October 7, 1875.

78 Ibid.

79 A. M. Clancy and William Nelson, *Proceedings of the Republican National Convention, held at Cincinnati, Ohio, June 14, 15, and 16, 1876* (Cincinnati, OH, 1876), A022; Eugene Davis, *Proceedings of the Republican National Convention, held at Chicago, Illinois, Wednesday, Thursday, Friday, Saturday, Monday, and Tuesday, June 2d, 3d, 4th, 5th, 7th and 8th, 1880* (Chicago, IL, 1880), 10.

80 Barringer, *The Natural Bent*, 141-142.

Margaret Taylor Long attended Burwell Female Academy in Hillsborough, North Carolina in the late 1840s. *Hillsborough Historical Commission, Hillsborough, North Carolina*

marriage, Rufus bought a new home closer to Charlotte. Two years later, Osmond Long Barringer was born.[81]

Margaret (Mag) Taylor Long was the second daughter of Dr. Osmond Fritz Long, originally of Randolph County, and Frances Helen Webb Long of Hillsborough. Margaret attended the Burwell Female Academy in Hillsborough, one of the best female Presbyterian "finishing" schools for young ladies in North Carolina. The school was operated by Robert and Margaret Anna Burwell from 1837 to 1857.[82]

Margaret Barringer attended church regularly. From the day of their marriage until 1874, the entire Rufus Barringer family worshipped at the First Presbyterian Church in Charlotte. In 1874 the Barringers transferred their membership to the new Second Presbyterian Church. Rufus was elected an elder of the church in 1875 and served until 1880, when he asked "to be relieved of the eldership upon the ground that his usefulness had been greatly impaired, if not wholly destroyed, by the scenes of political strife in which he had engaged." By 1887, the political winds had cooled and Rufus was again elected elder. He served until his death in 1895. Since his conversion in 1853, Rufus had been generous to his church, charities, and people less fortunate than he.[83]

Barringer was fond of literature, history, and political science. He often went against "the status quo" throughout the state and labored for reforms in many areas, including judicial, agricultural, and educational reforms. He was

---

81 Ibid.

82 Mary Clair Engstom, ed., *The Book of Burwell Students: Lives of Educated Women in the Antebellum South* (Hillsborough, NC, 2007), 148.

83 Robert H. Lafferty, ed., *History of the Second Presbyterian Church of Charlotte, North Carolina, 1873-1947* (Charlotte, NC, 1953), 18.

Margaret Taylor Long Barringer (1837-1918). Circa 1870. Margaret was the third wife of Rufus Barringer. She and Mrs. Thomas J. Jackson remained close throughout the rest of their lives and were active in civic affairs. *Osmond L. Barringer (deceased), Rocky Mount, North Carolina*

This photo was taken at Sugar Creek Academy in Concord, North Carolina. Shown from left to right are: Jacob Stirewalt, Thomas M. Alexander, Rufus Barringer, W. J. Harper, John R. Davidson, Mr. (-) Campbell, and Andrew Henderson. This could have been a 40-year reunion of the class of 1837, or some other reunion event. *Albert and Shirley Small Special Collections Library, University of Virginia, Charlottesville, Virginia*

also one of the founders of the Public Library of Charlotte, which became the Public Library of Charlotte and Mecklenburg County.[84]

Barringer was a strong supporter of graded public schools. Reverend J. B. Boone opened the first graded public school in North Carolina in Charlotte on October 21, 1873. The school employed six teachers and a board of directors, including Rufus. It operated for eight months, but was forced to close due to lack of funds.[85]

Barringer always supported veterans of the Civil War, and often donated money to needy former soldiers. The North Carolina General Assembly of 1891 incorporated Rufus Barringer and leaders of the state Confederate

84 Martha Watkins Flournoy, "A Short History of the Public Library of Charlotte and Mecklenburg County" (Charlotte, NC, 1952), 2.

85 LeGette Blythe and Charles Raven Brockmann, *Hornet's Nest: The Story of Charlotte and Mecklenburg County* (Charlotte, NC, 1961), 221.

Veterans Association under the name and style of "The Soldiers' Home Association." The act gave the Association a tract of land near the city of Raleigh, known as Camp Russell, to be used as the site of a soldiers' home.[86]

Prior to the war, Barringer's illegitimate mulatto sons (Thomas Clay Coleman and Warren Clay Coleman) had been slaves. During the war, Warren had worked for the Confederacy making boots and shoes. Upon emancipation, he became an apprentice to William M. Coleman, a Cabarrus planter and lawyer. William Coleman educated and trained young Warren until he was released from his apprenticeship on March 28, 1870. With the aid of Barringer or Coleman (or both), Warren set up a retail grocery business at the age of 21. The 1870 Census revealed that Warren's real property was worth $300, and his personal property $500.[87]

The same census listed Thomas Clay Coleman as single and living in a boarding house in Raleigh. Thomas married three times and had two children, Thomas and Sallie Coleman. Sallie Coleman, born in 1879, married Edward Johnson and moved to Shasta County, California. Thomas Coleman was born in 1894 and raised in East Point, Georgia.[88]

In late 1870, about the time Rufus Barringer married his third wife, Warren Clay Coleman moved to Alabama for a year seeking economic opportunity. He returned to Concord in 1871 to begin a new business career.[89]

Apparently, Rufus provided considerable assistance to Warren Coleman in his successful business ventures. However, the help was clandestine, as Barringer and Coleman continued to hide their father-son relationship. From 1873 to 1874, Warren attended Howard University where he prepared for further business opportunities.[90]

In 1873, at the age of 24, Warren married Jane E. Jones, 32. The couple had no children. In 1879, Warren combined two stores into a large general store that became one of Concord's major retail establishments. He was a proud and

---

86 R. D. W. Conner, *A Manual of North Carolina* (Raleigh, NC, 1913), 166.

87 John N. Ingham and Lynne B. Feldman, *African-American Business Leaders: A Biographical Dictionary* (Westport, CT, 1994), 152-153; 1870 Federal Census for Concord, North Carolina.

88 Marriage licenses for Wake County, North Carolina, State Archives of North Carolina; 1910 Federal Census for Fulton County, Georgia, East Point District.

89 Powell, *Dictionary of North Carolina Biography*, vol. 1, 401.

90 Ibid.

frugal man who sought wealth and fame, and extended his influence into North Carolina's black community.[91]

Moreau Barringer, Rufus's older brother, died on September 1, 1873, at White Sulphur Springs in Greenbrier, West Virginia. He was buried at Greenwood Cemetery in Baltimore. He was survived by two sons, Lewin Wethered Barringer and Daniel Moreau Barringer, Jr. After Moreau's death, his property (including 12 acres of land) was purchased by the founders of Shaw University. The school was named after its largest contributor, Elijah Shaw of Wales, Massachusetts. Part of the African American school was established on the site.[92]

Shortly after Moreau's death, two of Rufus's children, Paul and Osmond Barringer, having finished the 11th grade (the highest grade in North Carolina public schools), went on to higher education. Paul attended Kenmore University Preparatory School in Amherst, Virginia, prior to enrolling at the University of Virginia. Rufus's two younger children, Rufus Chunn and Anna Barringer, left home after high school.[93]

In the spring of 1874, Anna Barringer attended Augusta Female Seminary in Staunton, Virginia. This school was established by Miss Mary Baldwin and now is a well-known college bearing her name. During her stay there, Anna contracted typhoid fever, an infection which seemed peculiarly fatal to the Morrison family. From an exchange of letters at the time, it is clear that her illness was regarded as some sort of bilious attack, since she was nursed by her roommates. Whatever the diagnosis, she was brought home to Charlotte when the school closed in June. The rigors of travel sapped Anna's strength, and she died a few days after reaching home. Paul Barringer was deeply hurt by his sister's death, and pursued a medical career in part as a result of the experience.[94]

In 1874, thanks to his knowledge of Arabic (learned while in France with Ambassador Moreau Barringer), Victor Barringer was appointed by President Grant to represent the United States at the International Court at Alexandria, Egypt. The court's first duty was admiralty jurisdiction over the Suez Canal, and

91 Ibid.

92 Ibid., 99; Ashe, *Biographical History of North Carolina*, vol. 1, 107.

93 Barringer, *The Natural Bent*, 186.

94 Ibid.

it also held appellate jurisdiction in Cairo. Although he had never sat on the bench in his own country, Victor became an American judge in Egypt and retained the title for the rest of his life. He remained in this service for 25 years before returning to Washington, where he died on May 27, 1896. He was buried in Rock Creek Cemetery in Washington, D.C.[95]

95 Powell, *Dictionary of North Carolina Biography*, vol. 1, 103; Ashe, *Biographical History of North Carolina*, vol. 1, 129.

Chapter 11

"[A]nd for a cause dearer than life itself—the safety and independence of my people—
I went to the front, and on the tented field, and in a Federal prison,
gave the four best years of my life."

— *Rufus Barringer during the 1880 gubernatorial campaign.*

Final Public Service, Retirement, and Death

The 1880 Election Campaign

The post-Reconstruction period brought a final political battle for Rufus Barringer, followed by a precipitous retirement from politics and gradual retirement from civic activities. In his candidacy for lieutenant governor as a Republican in 1880, all of the old charges against him as a Radical Republican would be resurrected by his opponents and the predominantly Democratic press. Barringer's qualities, however, would be apparent in the service carried on by his children. Rufus would support the National Democratic Ticket in 1888, and would be accepted and praised by the same Democratic press that had castigated him throughout the postwar period.

On July 7, 1880, Rufus accepted the Republican nomination for lieutenant governor "by acclamation" at a convention in Raleigh. He campaigned strongly for the office, particularly in Mecklenburg County. The Republican ticket was led by Ralph Potts Buxton, a superior court judge from the 5th District. The Democratic ticket featured Thomas J. Jarvis (then serving as lieutenant governor) and James L. Robinson, speaker of the House of Commons.[1]

1 *Charlotte Democrat*, July 9, 1880; *New York Times*, July 8, 1880.

Rufus Barringer, 1880. Rufus was the Republican candidate for lieutenant governor in 1880, with Ralph Buxton at the top of the ticket. They were defeated even though they made a strong showing in Barringer's heavily democratic Mecklenburg County.
North Carolina Division of Archives and History

In a speech at Morganton during the campaign, Barringer discussed in detail several important issues of the day. He considered the Road Law an outrage upon the poor. The poor, he argued, were required to perform road labor for six days a year, while the wealthy and others who avoided the system did not work at all. "Who most needs and uses the public highways? Not the poor negro nor the humble white man, but the wealth, the capital, the trade, the commerce, and the agriculture of a country." Barringer had always supported working the public roads by contract, a joint system of labor and taxation. The large landowners, however, were content to put up with poor roads (which cost them nothing), rather than submit to taxation for better surfaces. Barringer pointed out that better roads meant better commerce and increased land values.[2]

Concerning county government, Barringer blamed Democrats for the disappearance of the township system, which provided for more freedom of government by localities. The township system granted people more opportunity to elect their public officials, instead of having many of them appointed. Democrats, argued Barringer, had set up a system where courthouses, legislative committees, cliques, and caucuses controlled local governments. He also cited the magistrate system as a failure. These magistrates, appointed by Democrats who had controlled state government since 1876, were corrupt according to Barringer. "Who appointed them, and how were they appointed?"

Rufus next turned to the subject of public schools. He declared that Democrats were against education of the masses. He pointed out that some big-name Democrats had deemed it dangerous to educate the laboring class. Democrats had been in power for many years, Barringer reminded his audience, and free schools had made no progress during that time. Recent legislative sessions had passed laws with funding for free schools, but the controlling Democrats had kept the money from reaching its intended purpose. He accused the Democrats of trickery, and of irregularities in handling public monies.

Concerning the railroads, Barringer spoke with authority. He had been heavily involved in railroad improvements since his legislative days in 1849. He argued that Whigs and then Republicans had been the driving force in bringing the North Carolina public railroad system into existence, but Democrats had badly mismanaged it and were now trying to sell it off.[3]

---

2 *Raleigh Signal*, August 12 and September 16, 1880; Barringer Papers, Collection 2588, University of Viirginia.

3 Ibid.

During the heated 1880 election campaign, an ugly incident occurred at Diamond Hill in Anson County. A black man named Alick Staten was attacked and seriously injured by an angry crowd for speaking out and interrupting Democrat J. A. Lockhart during a debate with Barringer. As Rufus left after the debate, he was accused of being a "Radical" and thus responsible for the altercation. After all, Barringer and the Republicans supported civil rights for blacks. Some Democrats leaders in the crowd insulted and threatened Barringer. As he rode off, part of the same crowd followed in their carriages, cursing and calling Rufus derogatory names. Some of the pursuers passed Barringer and pulled off on the side of the road, waiting for him. As Rufus rode by, he heard a voice imploring the taunting people along the road to stop their attacks on him. It was Lockhart himself, yelling, "Don't, for God's sake; don't." They soon parted company and the dangerous affair ended.[4]

Democratic newspapers in the area immediately blamed the entire ugly incident on Barringer. The *Charlotte Democrat* was particularly venomous in its attacks. Barringer fought back, and reminded the public that it was the *Charlotte Democrat* that had pushed the secessionist movement in 1860. "[W]hen the Hon. Nathaniel Boyden and I appealed for peace here in Charlotte, we were caricatured [portrayed as elderly "cry-babies"] through the streets of the city and in the columns of that paper. . . . A few short months and the widow's wail, and the orphan's cry rang throughout the land. I forgot the party, and for a cause dearer than life itself—the safety and independence of my people—I went to the front, and on the tented field, and in a Federal prison, gave the four best years of my life. The Editor of the Democrat, a younger and stouter man than I, took shelter behind a "Printing Press" and stayed at home writing me complimentary letters! 'Old Miss Nancy' does not object to just criticism, but she does protest against 'bombproofs,' 'stay-at-homes,' 'dodgers,' and political tramps, generally attempting to put her in 'strait jackets,' and then cry 'crazy,' to cover up such scenes as those at Diamond Hill."[5]

Buxton and Barringer were defeated in the election, but nearly captured the strongly Democratic Mecklenberg County. Barringer lost the election for lieutenant governor by only 6,517 votes, out of 237,718 ballots cast statewide. Barringer did not support Ulysses S. Grant for nomination as the Republican

---

4   *Charlotte Democrat*, October 15, 1880; *Raleigh News & Observer*, October 8, 1880; *Raleigh Signal*, September 30, 1880; *New York Times*, September 3, 1880.

5   *Raleigh Signal*, September 30, 1880.

candidate for a third term as president in 1880. Barringer was said to be "found with horrible feelings, too vivid and deep to be controlled, against a third term, and he readily declared himself for [Republican John] Sherman," brother of former Union general William Tecumseh Sherman. Republican James A. Garfield won the Republican nomination, and was elected President of the United States over Democratic nominee Winfield S. Hancock.[6]

Barringer remained a Republican until 1888, when he became disillusioned with the course of the national Republican Party. He switched his allegiance and joined the Democrats, favoring the tax and tariff reforms promoted by their party. *The Raleigh News* reported: "Gen. Rufus Barringer of Charlotte, who has for years been known as 'the Republican war horse,' by reason of his earnest and outspoken adherence to Republican principles, proposes to vote this time for [Grover] Cleveland, tariff reform, and tax reduction." After a Democratic victory at the polls in November 1889, speeches filled the air in Charlotte. Barringer was cheered by a festive crowd when he said he had never been a Democrat during the war. After the war, he had tried to reconcile differences in equality for blacks and whites, but failed. Concluding, he said, "But a man arose, Grover Cleveland, and I believe, so help me God, that he made the best President we have ever had since George Washington, and he had been impartial to white and colored men, and brought peace and prosperity to all our homes."[7]

Warren Clay Coleman and Black Success in the Post-Reconstruction South

While Rufus became active in state politics again, his mulatto son Warren Clay Coleman—probably under Barringer's guidance—bought land in black areas of Concord and erected rental houses. Between 1875 and 1904, he developed nearly 100 rental units. He became one of Cabarrus County's largest property owners and most influential citizens. His income by 1889, from the rental units alone, was $5,000 per year.

6   Elgiva D. Watson, "The Election Campaign of Governor Jarvis, 1880: A Study of the Issues," in *The North Carolina Historical Review* (July 1971), vol. 48, no. 3, 297; *New York Times*, February 6, 1880.

7   *Raleigh News*, October 23, 1888; *New York Times*, July 8 and October 28, 1888; *Baltimore Sun*, July 7, 1888.

Warren was a member of the North Carolina Industrial Association, a black group seeking to develop black-owned businesses. He subsequently became the association's vice president, treasurer, and president.[8]

Warren supported prohibition and called whiskey "the most malignant enemy of our race." Rufus also became involved in the prohibition movement of the 1870s and 1880s. The movement cut across denominational lines, uniting Presbyterians, Methodists, Baptists, and Episcopalians. During an 1888 election, Charlotte voters rejected prohibition by a vote of 780 to 705. Liquor interests were accused of buying votes. Barringer declared that election bribery was "not confined to immoral people, but was indulged in by some of the most respected people in town." Barringer charged that during an 1886 local option campaign, a group of prohibitionists had "almost unanimously agreed to buy votes."[9]

By 1895, Warren Clay Coleman was considered one of the South's richest black men. He helped found the National Negro Protective Association, and assisted black education at Howard University, Livingston College, and Shaw University. He supported the North Carolina Oxford Orphan's Home, and aided Professor R. M. Alexander in developing the Coleman School in Welford, South Carolina. His philanthropy also extended to the Zion Hill Church and Price Memorial Temple in Concord. He was a leader in the North Carolina Industrial Association, formed in 1888 to help black-owned businesses.[10]

In March 1895, Warren was appointed a magistrate for Cabarrus County. This appointment stirred racial resentment among those offended that a black man could now sit in judgment over white men.[11]

In September 1895, Warren attended a "colored exhibit" of black enterprise in Atlanta. His skin was so light he sometimes passed for white. A man named "Eph," a porter for the National Hotel, mistakenly took Warren into the hotel and offered him the best the house could afford. The proprietor was not present, and Eph assigned Warren a room. At this point Warren informed the surprised Eph that it was not customary for Negroes to be

---

8 Charlotte Democrat, April 26, 1889; Powell, *Dictionary of North Carolina Biography*, vol. 1, 401-402.

9 *The Concord Register*, July 29, 1881; Greenwood, *Bittersweet Legacy*, 107; *Charlotte Chronicle*, January 13 and January 15, 1889.

10 Powell, *Dictionary of North Carolina Biography*, vol. 1, 402.

11 *Concord Times Weekly*, March 21, 1895.

entertained at white hotels in the state. Warren asked to be directed to the home of church elder Settle, of the colored Methodist Church.[12]

In October 1896, local Republicans unanimously nominated Warren Clay Coleman as their party's candidate for Cabarrus County Commissioner. A week later, he withdrew from the ticket. He would almost certainly have been elected if he had not withdrawn, because the Republicans carried the county elections.[13]

Warren, though mulatto, was treated with respect by North Carolina newspapers. Apparently they could appreciate the accomplishments of an African American individual, while still condemning the black race as a whole.[14]

Warren is remembered for his organization of Coleman Manufacturing Company, one of the nation's first black-owned and operated textile factories. In mid-June 1896, he tested the climate for a such a mill. Prominent white textile leaders supported his efforts, spearheaded by Benjamin N. Duke, a wealthy tobacco manufacturer and philanthropist from Durham. Warren sought to raise stock subscriptions from black supporters, but they lacked the economic base to sustain it. Though supported by some white backers, most notably Julian S. Carr, Warren was forced to borrow from the Duke family.

The venture enjoyed some success, but basic financial difficulties and external market conditions overwhelmed the mill, which was underfinanced and opened with secondhand and worn-out machinery. The results were predictable and were accelerated by Warren's death on March 31, 1904. Duke's notes matured and the cotton mill was forced into bankruptcy. The failure ended Warren's dream for a black community to surround the manufacturing facility, generating black political power out of black capitalism. At its peak, the mill employed 300 African American workers. The mill operated for a period under white supervision, but was sold at auction in late June 1904. In March 1906, a section of the facility became part of the extensive Cannon Mills.[15]

12 Ibid., September 19, 1895.

13 *Concord Daily Standard*, October 5 and 6, 1896.

14 *Concord Times*, April 1, 1904.

15 Ibid., February 11, 1897. For additional information on Warren Clay Coleman, *see* J. K. Rouse, *The Noble Experiment of Warren C. Coleman* (Charlotte, NC, 1972). In 2002, the City Council of Concord voted to celebrate Warren C. Coleman Day each year on February 1. Previously, the city had honored Coleman by naming a portion of U.S. Highway 601 for him, and by placing several historical markers around the area. Powell, *Dictionary of North Carolina Biography*, vol. 1, 102.

Dr. Paul Brandon Barringer (1857-1941), the son of Rufus and Eugenia Barringer, served as Chairman of the Faculty at the University of Virginia (1895-1903) and the sixth president (1907-1913) of Virginia Agriculture & Mechanical College (Virginia Tech). "A name is simply a trust committed to our keeping for life, and that as time passes the obligation to keep it clean and up to standard grows stronger and stronger. This in reality is the only value there is, or that should be, attached to any old and honored family name. Henceforth you are not simply a participant in the race—you are tagged and marked participant. If there is any greater stimulus to gentle and honorable conduct and unstinted effort, I, now an old man, have not seen it." *North Carolina Division of Archive and History*

Paul Brandon Barringer and Osmond Long Barringer:
Successors in Service

From 1881 to 1884, Rufus Barringer's oldest son, Paul Brandon Barringer, studied medicine in London, Paris, and Vienna. In 1886, he became the attending physician at Davidson College in North Carolina, where he also taught anatomy, physiology, and histology. He established a medical preparatory school that became the North Carolina Medical College, the first medical school chartered in the state.

In 1889, Paul was appointed to the staff at the University of Virginia, where he subsequently taught medicine, ophthalmology, and dermatology. He served as chairman of the medical faculty from 1891 to 1895, and as chairman of the university faculty from 1895 to 1903. He also founded University Hospital. Dr. Barringer was extremely popular with the Virginia students, who affectionately called him "Oom [Uncle] Paul" after the Boer leader "Oom Paul" Krueger.

From 1907 to 1912, Dr. Barringer served as president of Virginia Agriculture & Mechanical College, later known as Virginia Polytechnic Institute. During World War I, he worked for the federal government and supervised public health measures in American coal mining areas.

Paul Barringer published a variety of scientific papers dealing with cholera, syphilis, and typhoid fever. His mother and sister had died of the dreaded typhoid. He also authored a series of controversial studies on the African American race. Among his varied intellectual interests, he was a recognized expert on venomous reptiles. Barringer was president of the Medical Society of Virginia, and served on the Virginia Board of Health and Board of Agriculture. He was a member of the North Carolina Academy of Science, and received honorary doctor of law degrees from the University of South Carolina and Davidson College. Dr. Barringer married Nannie Irene Hannah in 1892, and the couple had 10 children. He died in Charlottesville, Virginia, on January 9, 1941, and was buried at the University of Virginia Cemetery.[16]

Rufus Barringer's youngest son, Osmond Long Barringer, was quite different from his half-brother Paul. He was often described as a daredevil and maverick—independent and original. He attended Davidson College for three years. During his time at Davidson, it was reported that Osmond was involved with the discovery of the first X-ray picture in America. One night, three

16 Ibid.

Osmond Long Barringer (1878-1961) was the son of Rufus and Margaret Barringer. Osmond Barringer operated the first automobile dealership in Charlotte. He lost his fortune in the Great Depression. *Rufus Barringer (deceased), Rocky Mount, North Carolina*

students bribed a janitor to gain access to the medical laboratory on campus. After three hours of experimenting, they produced an X-ray photograph of two 0.22 caliber rifle cartridges, two rings, a pin inside a pillbox, and a human finger they had sliced from a cadaver. Osmond recalled: "We kept our picture and escapade a secret, and it was not until later that we realized we were making history for the college instead of just breaking the rules."[17]

After Rufus's death in 1895, and before getting married, Osmond continued to live in the Barringer home on North Tryon Street. He shared the residence with his mother Margaret, her two sisters Helen and Lily, her invalid mother Helen, a servant named Patsey Haynes, a butler named William Brown, two boarders, and the family dogs. Also living in the house was a short-eared owl named Minerva. The bird had been given to Mrs. Barringer by a friend when just an owlet, having fallen out of its nest. Mrs. Barringer raised the owl. She alone took care of Minerva, as no one else in the household liked the drab creature. Finally, Margaret had William set the bird free, but Minerva never left the relative safety of her mistress's back yard.[18]

Osmond owned a bulldog named "Jack," who was gentle around people but brutal to other dogs and cats. Jack was known throughout town, and had a reputation of "having no peer when it came to fighting." He killed at least 29 dogs in fights, and had "never been vanquished in any combat." Osmond and neighbor George Fitzsimons had an understanding that if Jack appeared on Fitzsimons's property, he was likely to be shot by Fitzsimons in order to protect his Scotch Collie, "Shep." Osmond warned Fitzsimons to expect the same treatment of Shep should he venture onto Osmond's property. Sure enough, one day when Osmond was out of town, Jack and Osmond's smaller dog sauntered down to the Fitzsimons house and attacked Shep. Fitzsimons, true to his warning, went out to shoot the attackers. Jack continued the attack, but the other dog fled. Shep was killed before Fitzsimons inflicted a mortal would upon Jack. Jack finally turned the collie loose, and turned and looked at Fitzsimons. "At that moment," said Fitzsimons, "he commanded my utmost admiration. I started to shoot again, but I couldn't shoot, somehow. He did not cower or seem at all afraid. He looked me in the face for a moment, and then walked

---

17 *The State*, December 12, 1936; Davidson College Archives and Special Collections; Molly Gillespie, "Physics Department," in *Davidson Encyclopedia* (1998). In 1895, German Wilhelm K. Roentgen discovered X-rays, and within eight days of his announcement on January 4, 1896, Osmond L. Barringer and two other Davidson College students duplicated the experiment.

18 Henry Edward Cowan Bryant, *Tarheel Tales* (Charlotte, NC, 1910), 58-67.

away—straight out in the front of the Lutheran church, where he fell on the sidewalk." Jacks death was reported on the front page of the *Charlotte Observer*.[19]

In 1901, Osmond Barringer married Alice Williams Cowles, his second cousin, and they had four children. Osmond owned the first automobile dealership in Charlotte. He was instrumental in establishing the first auto race track in the area, a predecessor to the modern Charlotte NASCAR track. He was a philanthropist, and often helped deserving students through college. An adventurer, he once rode a bicycle from Canada to Charlotte. He lost his fortune when the stock market crashed in 1929. Osmond Barringer died on June 29, 1961, and was buried in Elmwood Cemetery in Charlotte.[20]

Rufus's other son, Rufus Chunn Barringer, matriculated at Davidson College in 1883 and worked as a newspaper reporter in Minneapolis, Minnesota. At some time during his life, Rufus Chunn Barringer became mentally ill. His father made financial provisions for him in his will. Rufus Chunn Barringer later moved to Eureka, California, and lived there in 1918. He moved to Oregon in 1929, and celebrated his 100th birthday while living at the county home in Fairview. He attributed his long life to abstinence from alcohol. He died on August 7, 1963, at the age of 101. He was cremated and buried in Charlotte.[21]

The Death of a Remarkable Man

In his later years, though not shrinking from evident duties, Rufus Barringer formally resigned from his responsibilities as school trustee, director of the First National Bank of Charlotte, church elder, and other civic duties. During his last few years, he joined many of his generation in recording the details of significant battles in which he had participated during the Civil War. He completed a history of the Ninth Regiment of North Carolina Troops (1st

19 Isaac Erwin Avery, *Idle Comments* (Charlotte, NC, 1905), 138-141; *Charlotte Observer*, July 24, 1903.

20 Mary Norton Kratt, *Charlotte: Spirit of the New South* (Charlotte, NC, 1922), 137.

21 "Alumni of Davidson College," Davidson College Alumni Archives; Will of Rufus Barringer, February 14, 1895, Will Book M, 336, Mecklenburg County Register of Deeds Office, Charlotte, NC; *The Oregonian*, March 18, 1962.

North Carolina Cavalry), which was published in Judge Walter Clark's *Histories of the Several Regiments and Battalions from North Carolina in the Great War 1861-65.*[22]

In 1893, though retired from political activities, Rufus expressed concern over the high tariff policy of the Republican Party, and the resulting plummet in the price of cotton. He blamed the protectionist policies of President Benjamin Harrison. Rufus praised Grover Cleveland and the Democratic Party as being equal to the task of ridding the country of its over-protectionism. Barringer also admonished farmers for growing the single "King Cotton crop," resulting in high cotton production and lower prices. He encouraged farmers to raise other crops in lieu of cotton.[23]

In 1894, Rufus's health began to fail. With his usual forethought and care, Barringer "set his house in order," arranged his papers and affairs, and instructed his executor on how to handle his considerable estate to avoid confusion upon his death. Though liberal to all religious denominations, Barringer was in faith strongly Calvinistic to the end. He said, "When a young man and about to connect myself with the church, I resolved to take no man's word, and to search the Scriptures for myself. This I did and to my mind, the Presbyterian doctrine was plainly set forth in every chapter. I have never seen cause to change my belief or to be troubled by any new doctrine."[24]

Just a month before his death, Rufus wrote to his son Paul. "I am glad to say that Dr. Graham has got my case under fair control—not so much suffering and comparative freedom from nausea and vomit, and without any great drowsiness from the powder (codeine) now taking." On January 17, 1895, Rufus dictated a letter to Paul via Margaret, who added: "I regret however to have to say he has not been as comfortable the last two days—he's had to vomit twice in twenty four hours, and what alarms me is that he each time seems to throw off more & more blood clots." Dr. Graham told Margaret that the blood clots were no doubt from his examination. Graham added, "[H]is increasing giddiness is much because of want of nourishment, taking less & assimilating even less yet." Margaret noted, "[A]stonishingly, he seems not much weaker."[25]

22 Alexander, *The History of Mecklenburg County*, 205.

23 *Charlotte Observer*, September 21, 1893; *Atlanta Constitution*, March 4, 1893.

24 Alexander, *History of Mecklenburg County*, 201-208.

25 Rufus Barringer to Paul Brandon Barringer, January 7 and 17, 1895, Paul B. Barringer Papers, University of Virginia.

To the end, his mind remained clear and strong. On one of his last days, Rufus quipped to his pastor, "If you can unfold to me any new truth of that better land, do so." The minister replied, "I cannot; all I say is, we shall be satisfied when we awake in His likeness." To this Barringer calmly answered, "It is enough."[26]

He read and kept up with current events in the daily papers. On February 3, 1895, Rufus bade his family farewell, including his wife and older sister Margaret Barringer Grier. He then folded his hands, fell asleep, and died. He was 73 years old. The cause of death was stomach cancer. His wife Margaret lived until 1918.[27]

Seldom had there been an event attended by so many of Charlotte's citizens as the funeral of General Rufus Barringer. The service was conducted at the Second Presbyterian Church, where he had been an elder for 20 years. The gallery of the annex was reserved for blacks and many attended, remembering Barringer's support of causes benefiting African Americans.

The service was led by Rev. John H. Boyd. Gracious remarks were made by Rev. John A. Preston of the First Presbyterian Church, where Barringer had attended for many years, and by Dr. A. T. Graham of Davidson College. Rufus was eulogized as a forward thinker who always looked for ways to improve the lot of the common man. His Christian ideals were used as an example of the righteous life. His patriotism and public-spirited care for Charlotte were praised, as were his interest in education and his belief that the laity must take a more active role in church matters. His charity was presented as a benchmark for others. The entire service celebrated the life of a remarkable North Carolinian. He was buried in Elmwood Cemetery in Charlotte.[28]

A young woman who had spent much time either visiting or boarding at Rufus Barringer's home said, "When alone in the great crowds of New York battling poverty, it has rested and comforted me to think of his home and to know that there are such men in the world."

A contemporary said of Barringer, "He was one of the most liberal and generous citizens Charlotte had. His hand was always in his pocket to give to any good cause, and his gifts were munificent. He was imminently a just man

26 Alexander, *History of Mecklenburg County*, 201-208.

27 Ibid.; *Charlotte Observer*, February 5, 1895; *Charlotte Democrat*, February 8, 1895; *Mecklenburg Times*, February 7, 1895; Elmwood Cemetery Interment Records, Charlotte, North Carolina.

28 Charlotte *Observer*, February 5, 1895; *Charlotte Democrat*, February 8, 1895.

and business to the core. He required the last farthing promised or agreed to be paid, not for moneys' sake, but for the sake of the agreement, and yet the next moment he would give freely to some cause.

One who knew Barringer intimately noted, "The one thing about General Barringer that struck me above all others, was his love for his fellow men. He was a man of broad and true thought. We had never had any conversation, but what he spoke of the different classes and how to better their conditions. . . . He was filled with a high sense of duty. His thoughts went out beyond himself."[29]

29 Alexander, *History of Mecklenburg County*, 206, 207.

Bibliography

Manuscripts

Charles A. Cannon Memorial Library, Genealogy and Local History Room, Concord, North
    Carolina
        Eugenia Lore Papers
Duke University, Perkins Library, Durham, North Carolina
        Alfred Adams Papers
        George F. Adams and Private Barzell C. McBride Letter
        Broadside Collection
           Confederate Veterans Papers
        W. A. Curtis Diary
        Fanny (Bennett) Gaddy Papers
        R. Risden Gaddy Letter
        R. E. Lee Papers.
        W. H. F. Lee Letter
        Presley Carter Person Papers
        Jesse, Matthew, Thomas, and Samuel Person Letters
Museum of the Confederacy, Richmond, Virginia
        John W. Diary Gordon Diary
        Hiram W. Harding Diary
National Archives, Washington, DC
        Record Group 109, Compiled Service Records of Confederate Soldiers Who Served in
           Organizations from the State of North Carolina
        Record Group 109, Compiled Service Records of Confederate Generals and Staff
           Officers, and Non-Regimental Enlisted Men
        Confederate States Army Inspection Reports
        Letters Received by the Confederate Adjutant and Inspector General
North Carolina Office of Archives and History, Raleigh, North Carolina
        John Barringer Papers
        Paul Brandon Barringer Papers
        Rufus Barringer Papers
        Milas A. Calvin Papers
        Fred C. Foard Papers
        Iredell County Superior Court Minutes
        Willie P. Magnum Papers
        Minutes, Mecklenburg County, Charlotte Superior Court
        John Miller Money Reminiscences
        Civil War Collection
           James Carnie Neel Reminiscences

Henry Machen Patrick Letters
Simpson and Biddle Family Papers
Dr. James Edward Smoot Papers
Papers of the North Carolina Historical Society
      Rufus Barringer Speech
United States Population Schedules for the 1850, 1860, 1870, 1880, and 1900 Censuses of
      North Carolina, Cabarrus and Mecklenburg Counties
Zebulon Baird Vance Papers
Pamplin Historical Park, Dinwiddie County, Virginia
      Suderow, Bryce A. "Confederate Strengths & Losses from March 25-April 9, 1865," May
      1987, revised September 29, 1991
University of North Carolina at Chapel Hill, Southern Historical Collection, Louis Round Wilson
      Library
      Daniel Moreau Barringer Papers
      Rufus Barringer Papers
      Kemp Battle Family Papers
      C. J. Iredell Papers
      Edmund Jones Papers
      James M. Pugh Papers
      Mrs. Seth L. Smith Papers
      W. D. Wharton Papers
University of Notre Dame University Libraries, Department of Special Collections, Manuscripts
      of the American Civil War
            Rufus C. Barringer Papers
            Thomas Owen Bunting Papers
University of Virginia, Manuscripts and Special Collections, Alderman Library, Charlottesville,
      Virginia
      Anna Barringer Papers
      Paul Brandon Barringer Papers
      Rufus Barringer Papers
      Rufus Barringer Commonplace Book
      Victor Clay Barringer Papers
      Maria Barringer Diary
U.S. Army Military History Institute, Carlisle Barracks, Pennsylvania
      August V. Kautz Papers
Antietam National Battlefield Visitor Center Archives
      John M. Monie Papers
Tennessee State Library and Archives, Nashville, Tennessee
      Governor James D. Porter Papers
Greensboro Historical Museum, Greensboro, North Carolina
      J. D. Hodges Papers
Wichita State University, Wichita, Kansas
      Thomas Horne Papers

Newspapers

Asheville Citizen
Asheville Pioneer
Ballot (Concord, NC)
Charlotte Journal
Charlotte Democrat
Charlotte Daily Observer
Concord Daily Standard
Concord Register
Concord Times Weekly
Daily Confederate (Raleigh, NC)
Fayetteville Observer
The Indiana Progress
Mecklenburg Times (Charlotte, NC)
New York Times
Philadelphia Weekly Times
Raleigh Daily Progress
Raleigh Democratic Weekly and Semi-weekly State Journal
Raleigh News & Observer
Raleigh Register
Raleigh Sentinel
Raleigh Signal
Raleigh Standard
Richmond Dispatch
Richmond Enquirer
Carolina Watchman (Salisbury, NC)
Spectator Newspaper (Salisbury, NC)
Springfield Weekly Republican
The Adams Sentinel (Gettysburg, PA)
The Farmer and Mechanic (Raleigh, NC)
The State (Salisbury, NC)
Washington Evening Star
Western Democrat (Charlotte, NC)

Government Publications

United States War Department. *Atlas to Accompany the Official Records of the Union and Confederate Armies.* Washington, D.C.: Government Printing Office, 1891-1895.

_____. *The War of the Rebellion: A Compilation of the Official Records of the Union and Confederate Armies.* 128 volumes. Washington, D.C.: Government Printing Office, 1880-1891.

Published Primary Sources

Baker, Laurence S. "Report of Colonel L. S. Baker," *Our Living and Our Dead* (March-August 1875), vol. 2, no. 1.

Clark, Walter, ed. *Histories of the Several Regiments and Battalions from North Carolina in the Great War 1861-'65.* 5 vols. Goldsboro, N.C.: Nash Brothers, 1901.

Cunningham, S. A., ed. *Confederate Veteran.* 40 vols. Nashville, Tenn.: 1893-1932.

Dedmond, Francis, ed. "The Civil War Diary of Harvey Davis," *Appalachian Journal* (Summer 1986), vol. 13.

Foard, Noah P. "Wade Hampton's Strategy: An Attack on Richmond Foiled." *Southern Historical Society Papers* (1896), vol. 24.

Garnett, Theodore Stanford and Robert J. Trout, ed. *Riding With Stuart: Reminiscences of an Aide-de-Camp.* Shippensburg, Pa.: White Mane Publishing Company, 1994.

Hart, H. L. "Prison Experience at Fort Delaware," *Confederate Veteran* (October 1913), vol. 21, no. 10.

Hill, Daniel Harvey, ed. *The Land We Love.* 6 vols. Charlotte, N.C.: Hill and Irwin & Co., 1866-1869.

Humphreys, Andrew A. *The Virginia Campaign of '64 and '65: The Army of the Potomac and the Army of the James.* New York: Charles Scribner's Sons, 1883.

Jackson, Mary Anna. *Life and Letters of General Stonewall Jackson.* New York: Harper, 1892.

Johnston, Frontis W. and Joe A. Mobley, eds. *The Papers of Zebulon Baird Vance.* 3 vols. Raleigh, N.C.: North Carolina Office of Archives and History, 1963-2013.

Jones, J. William. *Personal Reminiscences, Anecdotes, and Letters of Gen. Robert E. Lee.* New York: D. Appleton and Company, 1875.

McClellan, Henry B. *I Rode With Jeb Stuart: The Life and Campaigns of Major General J. E. B. Stuart.* Bloomington: Indiana University Press, 1958.

Neese, George M. *Three Years in the Confederate Horse Artillery* (New York: The Neale Publishing Company, 1911.

Palmer, Oscar C. "Father Rode with Sheridan: Reminiscences of Oscar C. Palmer as a Cavalryman in Company B, 8th N.Y. Volunteer Cavalry." Petersburg, Va.: Petersburg National Battlefield, n.d.

Pool, Stephen D., ed., *Our Living and Our Dead.* 4 vols. Raleigh, N.C.: North Carolina Branch of the Southern Historical Society, September 1874-August 1876.

Rawle, William Brooke, et al. *History of the Third Pennsylvania Cavalry (Sixtieth Regiment Pennsylvania Volunteers) in the American Civil War, 1861-1865.* Philadelphia: Franklin Printing Company, 1905.

Rea, D. B. "Cavalry Incidents of the Maryland Campaign," *The Maine Bugle* (April 1895), vol. 2, no. 2.

Rhodes, Robert Hunt, ed. *All For The Union: Diary of Elisha Hunt Rhodes.* New York: Orion Books, 1991.

Jones, William, et al., eds. *Southern Historical Society Papers.* 52 vols. Richmond, Va.: Southern Historical Society, 1876-1959.

Stedman, Charles M. "Battle at Reams' Station," in R. A. Brock, ed. *Southern Historical Society Papers* (January 1891), vol. 19.

Stiles, Robert. *Four Years under Marse Robert.* New York: The Neale Publishing Company, 1904.

Tobie, Edward P. *History of the First Maine Cavalry, 1861-1865*. Boston: Press of Emery & Hughes, 1887.

Troxler, Beverly Barrier and Billy Dawn Barrier Auciello, eds. *Dear Father: Confederate Letters Never Before Published*. North Billerica, Mass.: Autumn Printing Company, 1989.

Wise, John S. *The End of an Era*. New York: Houghton, Mifflin and Company, 1901.

Published Secondary Sources

Alexander, J. B. *History of Mecklenburg County from 1740 to 1900*. Charlotte, N.C.: Observer Print House, 1902.

Ashe, Samuel A. *Biographical History of North Carolina from Colonial Times to Present*. 8 vols. Greensboro, N.C.: Charles L. Van Noppen, 1905-1917.

Ayers, Edward L. *The Promise of the New South: Life after Reconstruction*. New York: Oxford University Press, 1982.

Barrett, John G. *The Civil War in North Carolina*. Chapel Hill: The University of North Carolina Press, 1963.

Barrier, Smith. "Deutschland in Piedmont North Carolina," *The Uplift* (January16, 1937), pt. 2.

_____. "Deutschland in Piedmont North Carolina," *The Uplift* (January 23, 1937), pt. 3.

Bearss, Ed and Chris Calkins. *The Battle of Five Forks*. Lynchburg, Va.: H. E. Howard, 1985.

Boyd, William Kenneth. *North Carolina on the Eve of Secession*. Washington, D.C.: U.S. Government Printing Office, 1912.

Calkins, Chris M. *The Appomattox Campaign, March 29-April 5, 1865*. Conshohocken, Pa: Combined Books, Inc., 1997.

_____. "The Battle of Weldon Railroad (or Globe Tavern), August 18-19 & 21, 1864," *Blue and Gray Magazine* (Winter 2007), vol. 23, no. 5.

_____. *History and Tour Guide of Five Forks: Hatcher's Run and Namozine Church*. Columbus Ohio: Blue & Gray Enterprises, 2003.

Connor, R. D. W. *Ante-Bellum Builders of North Carolina*. Raleigh, N.C.: North Carolina State Normal and Industrial College History Publications, 1914.

Crawford, Mark J. *Confederate Courage on Other Fields*. Jefferson, N.C.: McFarland & Company, 1954.

Cullen, Joseph P. Cullen. *The Peninsula Campaign, 1862*. New York: Crown Publishers, Inc., 1973.

Current, Richard N., ed. *Encyclopedia of the Confederacy*. New York: Simon and Schuster, 1993

Daughtry, Mary Bandy. *Gray Cavalier: The Life and Wars of General W. H. F. "Rooney" Lee*. Cambridge, Mass.: Da Capo Press, 2002.

Davis, Burke. *The Last Cavalier: J. E. B. Stuart*. New York: Fairfax Press, 1988.

Davis, William C. *The Confederate General*. 6 vols. Harrisburg, Pa.: National Historical Society, 1991.

Dowd, Jerome. *Sketches of Prominent Living North Carolinians*. Raleigh, N.C.: Edwards and Broughton, 1888.

Downey, Fairfax. *The Clash of Cavalry: The Battle of Brandy Station*. New York: David McKay Company, Inc., 1959.

Engstom, Mary Claire, ed. *The Book of Burwell Students: Lives of Educated Women in the Antebellum South.* Hillsborough, N.C.: Historic Hillsborough Commission, 2007.

Escott, Paul D. *North Carolinians in the Era of the Civil War and Reconstruction.* Chapel Hill: The University of North Carolina Press, 2008.

Evans, Clement A., ed. *Confederate Military History.* 12 Vols. Atlanta, Ga: Confederate Publishing Company, 1899.

Faust, Patricia L. *Historical Times Illustrated Encyclopedia of the Civil War.* New York: Harper Perennial, 1991.

Foote, Shelby. *The Civil War: A Narrative.* 3 vols. New York: Random House, 1974.

Foner, Eric. *Reconstruction: America's Unfinished Revolution, 1863-1877.* New York: Harper & Row, 1993.

Ford, Lacy K. Jr. "Making the 'White Man's Country White': Race, Slavery, and State-Building in the Jacksonian South," *Journal of the Early Republic* (Winter 1999), vol. 19, no. 4.

Franklin, John Hope. *Reconstruction after The Civil War.* Chicago, Ill.: University of Chicago Press, 1961.

Freeman, Douglas Southall. *Lee's Lieutenants: A Study in Command.* 3 vols. New York: Scribner's Sons, 1942.

Geiger, Roger L. ed. *Curriculum, Accreditation, and Coming of Age in Higher Education: Perspectives on the History of Higher Education, Volume Twenty-Seven.* New Brunswick, N.J.: Transaction Publishers, 2009.

Greenwood, Janette Thomas. *Bittersweet Legacy: The Black and White "Better Classes" in Charlotte, 1850 -1910.* Chapel Hill: The University of North Carolina Press, 1994.

Hunter, Charles N. *Race Relations in North Carolina.* Chapel Hill: The University of North Carolina Press, 1987.

Hall, Clark B. "The Battle of Brandy Station," *Civil War Times Illustrated* (May-June 1990), vol. 28, no. 6.

Hamilton, J. G. de Roulhac. *Reconstruction in North Carolina.* New York: Columbia University, 1914.

_____. *Party Politics in North Carolina, 1835-1860.* Durham, N.C.: The Seeman Printery, 1916.

Harrell, Roger H. *The 2nd North Carolina Cavalry.* Jefferson, N.C.: McFarland and Company Publishers, 2004.

Hartley, Chris J. *Stuart's Tarheels: James B. Gordon and His North Carolina Cavalry.* Baltimore, Md.: Butternut and Blue, 1996.

Hattaway, Herman and Archer Jones. *How the North Won.* Chicago, Ill.: University of Illinois Press, 1991.

Heisner, Beverly. "Harriet Morrison Irwin's Hexagonal House: An Invention to Improve Domestic Dwellings." *The North Carolina Historical Review* (April 2, 1981), vol. 58, no. 2.

Heitman, Francis B. *Historical Register and Dictionary of the United States Army.* 2 vols. Washington, D.C.: Government Printing Office, 1903.

Henderson, William D. *The Road to Bristoe Station.* Lynchburg, Va.: H. E. Howard, 1987.

Hennessy, John J. *Return to Bull Run: The Campaign and Battle of Second Manassas.* Norman: University of Oklahoma Press, 1993.

Herran, Kathy Neill. *They Married Confederate Officers.* Davidson, N.C.: Warren Publishing, 1997.

Hill, Daniel Harvey. *Bethel to Sharpsburg: North Carolina in the War Between the States.* 2 vols. Raleigh, N.C.: Edwards & Broughton Company, 1926).

Horn, John. *The Petersburg Campaign: The Destruction of the Weldon Railroad, Deep Bottom, Globe Tavern and Reams Station; August 14-25, 1864.* Lynchburg, Va.: H. E. Howard, 1991.

Inscoe, John C. *Mountain Masters: Slavery and the Sectional Crisis in Western North Carolina.* Knoxville: The University of Tennessee Press, 1989.

Keys, Thomas Bland. *Tarheel Cossack: W. P. Roberts, Youngest Confederate General.* Orlando, Fla.: n.p., 1983.

Korn, Jerry. *Pursuit to Appomattox: The Last Battles.* Chicago, Ill.: Time-Life Books, Inc., 1987.

Krick, Robert K. *Lee's Colonels: A Biographical Register of the Field Officers of the Army of Northern Virginia.* Dayton, Ohio: Morningside, 1992.

Lafferty, Robert H., ed. *History of The Second Presbyterian Church, Charlotte, North Carolina, 1873-1947.* Charlotte, N.C.: The Herald Press, Inc., 1953.

Lefler, Hugh Talmage. *North Carolina History Told By Contemporaries.* Chapel Hill: The University of North Carolina Press, 1934.

Lefler, Hugh Talmage and Albert Ray Newsome. *The History of a Southern State: North Carolina.* Chapel Hill: The University of North Carolina Press, 1954.

Long, Mary Alves. *High Time to Tell It.* Durham, N.C.: Duke University Press, 1950.

Longacre, Edward G. *The Cavalry at Gettysburg.* Lincoln: The University of Nebraska Press, 1993.

_____. *Lee's Cavalrymen,* Mechanicsburg, Pa.: Stackpole Books, 2002.

_____. *Mounted Raids of the Civil War.* Lincoln: University of Nebraska Press, 1994.

_____. *The Cavalry at Appomattox: A Tactical Study of Mounted Operations during the Civil War's Climatic Campaign, March 27-April 9, 1865.* Mechanicsville, Pa.: Stackpole Books, 2003.

_____. *Lincoln's Cavalrymen: A History of the Mounted Forces of the Army of the Potomac.* Mechanicsville, Pa.: Stackpole Books, 2000.

Manarin, Louis H., et al., eds. *North Carolina Troops, 1861-1865: A Roster.* 19 vols. Raleigh: North Carolina Office of Archives and History, 1968-2013.

Mast, Greg. *State Troops and Volunteers: A Photographic Record of North Carolina's Civil War Soldiers.* Raleigh: North Carolina Office of Archives and History, 1995.

McKinney, Gordon B. *Southern Mountain Republicans, 1865-1900.* Chapel Hill: The University of North Carolina Press, 1978.

McMillan, Laurence. *The Schoolmaker: Sawney Webb & the Bell Buckle Story.* Chapel Hill: The University of North Carolina Press, 1971.

Mewborn, Horace. "Herding the Yankee Cattle: The Beefstake Raid, September 14-17, 1864," *Blue & Gray Magazine* (Summer 2005), vol. 22, no. 3.

Moore, John Wheeler. *History of North Carolina from Earliest Discoveries to the Present Time.* 2 vols. Raleigh, N.C.: Alfred Williams & Company, 1880.

Northen, William J., ed. *Men of Mark in Georgia.* Atlanta: A. B. Caldwell, 1908.

Pfanz, Donald C. *The Petersburg Campaign: Abraham Lincoln at City Point, March 20-April 9, 1865.* Lynchburg, Va: H. E. Howard, Inc., 1989.

Pickett, La Salle Corbell (Mrs. George E.). *Pickett and His Men.* Atlanta: Foote and Davies, 1899.

Powell, William S., ed. *Dictionary of North Carolina Biography.* 2 vols. Chapel Hill: The University of North Carolina Press, 1979.

_____. *North Carolina through Four Centuries.* Chapel Hill: The University of North Carolina Press, 1989.

Power, J. Tracy. *Lee's Miserables: Life in the Army of Northern Virginia from the Wilderness to Appomattox*. Chapel Hill: The University of North Carolina Press, 1998.

Rafuse, Ethan S. *McClellan's War: The Failure of Moderation in the Struggle for the Union*, Bloomington: Indiana University Press, 2005.

Raiford, Neil Hunter. *The 4th North Carolina Cavalry in the Civil War: A History and Roster*. Jefferson, N.C.: McFarland and Company, 2003.

Robertson, James I. Jr. *Stonewall Jackson: The Man, the Soldier, the Legend*. New York: MacMillan & Company, 1997.

Rouse, J. K. *The Noble Experiment of Warren C. Coleman*. Charlotte, N.C.: Crabtree Press, 1972.

_____. *Historical Shadows of Cabarrus County North Carolina*. Charlotte, N.C.: Crabtree Press, 1970.

Rupp, I. Daniel. *Thirty Thousand Names of German, Swiss and Dutch Immigrants in Pennsylvania from 1727 to 1776*. Baltimore: General Publishing Company, 1965.

Saunders, William L., ed. *North Carolina Colonial Records*, 10 vols. Raleigh, N.C.: Joseph Daniels, Printer, 1890.

Sears, Stephen W. *To The Gates of Richmond: The Peninsula Campaign*. New York: Ticknor & Fields, 1992.

_____, ed. George McClellan to Edwin Stanton, January 31, 1862, *The Civil War Papers of George B. McClellan: Selected Correspondence1860-1865*. New York: Da Capo Press, 1992.

Simon, John Y., ed. *The Papers of Ulysses S. Grant*. 32 vols.Carbondale: Southern Illinois University Press, 1967.

Simon, John Y. and Harold Holzer, eds. *The Lincoln Forum: Rediscovering Abraham Lincoln*. New York: Fordham University Press, 2002.

Sommers, Richard J. *Richmond Redeemed: The Siege at Petersburg*. Garden City, N.Y.: Doubleday & Company, Inc., 1981.

Starr, Stephen Z. *The Union Cavalry in the Civil War*. 3 vols. Baton Rouge: Louisiana State University Press, 1979-1985.

Stephenson, William. *Sallie Southall Cotten: A Woman's Life in North Carolina*. Greenville, N.C.: Pamlico Press, 1987.

Thomas, Emory M. *Bold Dragoon: Life of J.E.B. Stuart*. New York: Vintage Books, 1988.

Thompkins, D. A. *History of Mecklenburg County and City of Charlotte from 1740 to 1903*. Charlotte, N.C.: Heritage Books, 1904.

Thompson, Holland. *From the Cotton Field to the Cotton Mill*. New York: Macmillan Company, 1906.

_____. *Southern and Western Textile Excelsior*, October 2, 1897.

Trelease, Allen W. *The North Carolina Railroad, 1849-1871, and the Modernization of North Carolina*. Chapel Hill: The University of North Carolina Press, 1991.

Trout, Robert J. *Galloping Thunder: The Story of the Stuart Horse Artillery Battalion*. Mechanicsville, Pa.: Stackpole Books, 2002.

Trudeau, Noad Andre. *The Last Citadel: Petersburg, Virginia, June 1864-April 1865*. New York: Little, Brown & Company, 1991.

Tucker, Glenn. *Zeb Vance, Champion of Personal Freedom*. New York: Bobbs-Merrill Company, Inc., 1965.

Vatter, Fred J. "Whigs Restored Two Party Rule to Chatham and North Carolina," *Chatham County Line* (Fall 2004).

Venter, Bruce M. "Hancock the (Not So) Superb: The Second Battle of Reams' Station, August 25, 1864," *Blue & Gray Magazine* (Winter 2007), vol. 23, no. 5.

Warner, Ezra J. *Generals in Blue. Generals in Blue: Lives of the Union Commanders.* Baton Rouge: Louisiana State University Press, 1995.

Watkins, Raymond W. *The Hicksford Raid.* Emporia, Va.: Greensville Historical Society, 1978.

Watson, Elgiva D. "The Election Campaign of Governor Jarvis, 1880: A Study of the Issues," *The North Carolina Historical Review* (July 1971), vol. 48, no. 3.

Welsh, Jack Walsh. *Confederate Generals Medical Histories.* Kent, Ohio: Kent State University Press, 1995.

Wellman, Manly Wade. *Giant in Gray: A Biography of Wade Hampton.* New York: Charles Scribner's Sons, Inc., 1949.

Wells, Edward L. *Hampton and His Cavalry in '64.* Richmond, Va.: B. F. Johnston Publishing Company, 1899.

Wert, Jeffrey D. *General James Longstreet: The Confederacy's Most Controversial Soldier.* New York: Simon & Schuster, 1993.

Wheeler, John H. *Reminiscences and Memoirs of North Carolina and Eminent North Carolinians.* Baltimore: Genealogical Publishing Company, 1966.

Williams, Max R., et al., eds. *The Papers of William Alexander Graham.* 8 vols. Raleigh, N.C.: North Carolina Office of Archives and History, 1958-1992.

Wilson, James Harrison. *Under The Old Flag.* 2 vols. New York: D. Appleton and Company, 1912.

Wittenberg, Eric J. *The Union Cavalry Comes of Age: Hartwood Church to Brandy Station, 1863.* Washington, D.C.: Potomac Books, 2003.

Thesis

Krieger, Marvin. "Warren Clay Coleman, Promoter of the Black Cotton Mill: An Analysis of An Early Effort to Develop Black Economic Power." Master's Thesis, Wake Forest University, 1969.

Index

Sheridan R. "Butch" Barringer lives with his wife Pam in Newport News, Virginia. Butch graduated from Virginia Tech and worked as a mechanical engineer and project manager for nearly four decades with NASA.

Butch's interests include studying the Civil War, with an emphasis on Confederate cavalry, and physics and cosmology. Butch has two other books under contract with Savas Beatie: a biography of General Thomas L. Rosser, and an edited memoir written by Rosser. Butch is currently at work on a biography of Colonel Thomas T. Munford.